Philip L. Rhodes and his yacht designs

Philip L. Rhodes
and his yacht designs

RICHARD HENDERSON

INTERNATIONAL MARINE
Camden, Maine

OTHER BOOKS BY RICHARD HENDERSON

First Sail for Skipper
Hand, Reef and Steer
Dangerous Voyages of Captain William Andrews (ed.)
Sail and Power (with B.S. Dunbar)
The Racing-Cruiser
The Cruiser's Compendium
Sea Sense
Singlehanded Sailing
Better Sailing
East to the Azores
Choice Yacht Designs

First McGraw-Hill paperback edition, 1993.

Published by International Marine
10 9 8 7 6 5 4 3 2 1

Copyright © 1981, 1993 International Marine, an imprint of TAB Books. TAB Books is a division of McGraw-Hill, Inc.

Library of Congress Cataloging-In-Publication Data
   Henderson, Richard, 1924-
   Philip L. Rhodes and His Yacht Designs.
   Includes index.
   1. Yacht building. 2. Rhodes, Philip L. (Leonard), 1895-1974. I. Title. VM331.H364
623.8'1223'0924   81-81416
   ISBN 0-87742-415-2 AACR2

Questions regarding the content of this book should be addressed to:
International Marine
P.O. Box 220
Camden, ME 04843

Questions regarding the ordering of this book should be addressed to:
TAB Books
A Division of McGraw-Hill, Inc.
Blue Ridge Summit, PA 17294
1-800-233-1128

This book is printed on acid-free paper.

This book is dedicated to Philip H. Rhodes, Roger C. Taylor, and Bruce W. White, without whose help this book could not have been written.

Contents

Foreword

by Philip H. Rhodes

I am confident that my father would have been just as delighted as I am with this broad overview of his life and professional career. It could not have been an easy task for Richard Henderson, for while there was almost too much material to work from in one sense, there was little documentation relating to other important aspects. The long time — almost three years — required for the researching and writing of this book is an indication of the author's devotion to his task.

My father's career could in a sense be said to have spanned the heyday of custom sailing yacht design. The day of the custom boat has not disappeared, but it is nothing like it was in my father's most active years. Increasingly, yachts today are conceived by in-house design teams to be built on molds that must be amortized over dozens or even hundreds of boats, and there is little or no designer-owner contact. And while my father did become involved in a significant way with the stock-boat market, there is no doubt in my mind that his fondest memories were those of the one-on-one relationships that developed in the course of his custom designs. Most of these encounters led to lifelong friendships.

Richard Henderson's anecdotes and the recollections of clients make most pleasant reading — the more so to me, since many stories were totally new. This book is a significant addition to the literature of a glorious era.

Preface

A book about Philip L. Rhodes is long overdue, for he is universally accepted as one of the all-time greats in the field of yacht design. The examples of his work presented in this book were chosen for one or a combination of the following reasons: the selections are among the most beautiful and functional of the Rhodes designs; I personally know or know about these boats; they are either representative types most often associated with Rhodes, or else they are in some way unusual; and, finally, they are "important" boats, those that have been influential or have had exceptional racing or cruising records.

One of the difficulties in writing about the oeuvre of a prolific and versatile designer such as Rhodes is that it is necessary to omit some very good boats. Almost every owner of a Rhodes boat feels that he has something very special, and that is entirely understandable, but there is a limit to the number of craft I can discuss at length — there are just too many. Therefore, I have concentrated on about 90 yachts, and the Appendix includes more than 300 additional boats with some abbreviated information about them.

The selection of yachts featured in this book should be of interest to the aesthete and the pragmatist alike, for most of the boats are feasts for the eyes, yet they are also marvelously practical cruisers with speed, seakindliness, and comfort. Many Rhodes yachts are very much sought after today, which is not surprising, since so many of today's stock boats are either racing machines, unsuitable for shorthanded cruising, or else clumsy cruisers that can't get out of their own way under sail. On the other hand, the sailing yachts of P.L. Rhodes are very often multipurpose boats, which are commodious yet smart, well-mannered sailers. In addition, they have the kind of traditional beauty that instills pride of ownership and holds up long after the fads have faded.

This book could not have been written without the considerable help of Philip H. (Bodie) Rhodes, a fine naval architect himself, who spent many hours and days locating the plans of his father's boats. Bodie did a number of the inked tracings of the plans years ago when he worked for his father, and he did a new drawing of the famous sloop *Caper* especially for this book.

Another designer and former employee of Phil Rhodes who has been very generous in supplying me with information is my friend Robert E. Wallstrom. Bob greatly admired Phil and regarded him almost as a second father.

Other sailors — friends, fans, associates of Phil, and/or owners of Rhodes boats — who have been most helpful are: James McCurdy, Robert M. Steward, Donald H. Sherwood, Dr. Roger P. Batchelor, John T. Snite, Carleton Mitchell, William R. Adams, Jerry E. Cox, Edward L. Doheny III, Paul Hoffmann, Horace W. Fuller, Pierre de Saix, A.E. Luders Jr., Harry C. Primrose, John L. Chapman Jr., Henry Strong, Richard C. Kenney, William Passano III, David Baker, A.E. Thurber Jr., Weston Farmer, Thomas M. Meers, Dr. Roy O. Scholz, Robert G. Howard, E.L. Goodwin, Joseph J. Reinhardt, Oivind Lorentzen Jr., Richard S. Nye, Kenneth Gates, Christopher Gates, Charles W. Wittholz, John Rousmaniere, David J. Bohaska, Julie Holz, Arnold R. Holt, Kathleen M. Brandes.

At the Mystic Seaport, assistance was given by Virginia Allen, Carole Bowker, Philip L. Budlong, Benjamin Fuller, and Gerald Morris.

Special mention should be made of research contributions by my wife, Sally, and most particularly by International Marine's Editor, Bruce White. And, finally, I want to thank my daughter, Sarah, for her splendid job of typing the manuscript.

It has been a privilege to put together this book, and I hope that it will help perpetuate the legend of a great designer.

Richard Henderson
Gibson Island, Maryland

Philip L. Rhodes and his yacht designs

Part One
A Brief Biography

Philip L. Rhodes, Naval Architect 1895-1974

Philip Leonard Rhodes was fond of saying: "If it doesn't look right, it is not right," and anyone who has ever seen a boat created by this gifted naval architect should know that he practiced what he preached. In addition to being a first-class marine engineer, he was also a true artist with an exceptional "eye for a boat." Widely acclaimed as a remarkably versatile designer, Phil Rhodes created every kind of craft from the smallest dinghy to huge cargo ships. Whatever kind of vessel he produced, it invariably had the look of rightness about it. His sailing yachts in particular, with their beautifully proportioned hulls and graceful sheerlines, are works of true design harmony. Not only are Rhodes yachts handsome; they somehow appear to be uniquely suited to their purpose.

Rhodes had no great seafaring tradition in his background, and he grew up far from salt water. His forebears were hearty pioneering folk, and he himself was a pioneering naval architect. Some of the areas he helped explore and develop were: hydrofoils for speedboats, centerboards for ocean racers, light displacement for small cruising sailboats, butt welding for steel vessels, advanced construction in aluminum and noncorrosive steel,

fiberglass construction for large cruisers, and fast sailing cruisers with unusual capabilities under power.

Born on January 15, 1895, near Thurman in southern Ohio, Phil was the sixth and last child of Orin K. Rhodes, a manufacturer of wooden wheels, wagons, and carriages. Phil's mother's maiden name was Orpha P. Scott, and one of her ancestors, James Scott, was a scout for General George Washington.

The birth certificate of Philip L. Rhodes indicates he was born in a township with the rustic name of Raccoon in Gallia County, but his family soon moved to nearby Gallipolis on the Ohio River, where young Phil received his first exposure to watercraft. He became enchanted by the river traffic, especially the steamboats with their huge, thrashing paddle wheels. These craft must have had a particular appeal for him, because when he was a teenager, he reportedly acquired summer work in a minstrel show aboard a riverboat.

At a very early age Phil began to make sketches of boats. From his father, perhaps, he inherited great manual dexterity, and he was undoubtedly shown how to handle tools. A footstool that he made as a

Phil Rhodes' father, Orin K. Rhodes (with mustache), standing in the doorway of his wagon and carriage shop.

young boy is solidly put together with beautifully fitted dovetail joints. It has been said that he learned a lot about wood from his father, but this may be an overstatement, since his father died when Phil was only 12. Probably, though, he learned a thing or two from his stepfather, for his mother married Albert J. Berry, a master carpenter.

Around 1905 the Rhodes family moved to the central Ohio town of Newark, where Phil's mother ran a rooming house. A short distance from the house was an abandoned canal, probably part of the old Ohio-Erie Barge Canal System, and Phil soon began carving model boats, which he would ''tank test'' in the canal.

In the summertime the Rhodes family often went to nearby Buckeye Lake, where Phil received further exposure to the water and had his first real experience with small boats. For a summer or so he worked in a lakeside amusement park and serviced small ''drive-it-yourself'' launches. Although much of his time was spent fending off the boats to prevent crash landings, he learned something about engines by tending to the one-lungers that powered the launches.

It was at Buckeye Lake that Phil became acquainted with Mary Helen Jones, a Newark High School classmate who eventually became his wife.

In high school, the versatility of Phil Rhodes became manifest, for not only did he show ability as a student, but he also did well in athletics, excelling in track and basketball, and he even tried a bit of dramatics. At the same time he continued developing his drafting skills, and decorative drawings from his high school yearbook show that he could draw a variety of subjects. His main interest, however, was boats, and during the summer of 1913, Phil designed and built a single-step hydroplane speedboat. He called it *Dusty*, his high school nickname.

Dusty Rhodes graduated from Newark High in 1914. The quotation under his name in the yearbook is certainly prophetic, for it says:

Some time he will surely win fame
For ambition is his middle name.

It is also interesting that the yearbook reported: ''Philip Rhodes won two prizes for articles published in *Motor Boating* magazine.''

Upon graduation, Phil attended Denison University in Granville, Ohio, but after the first year, he

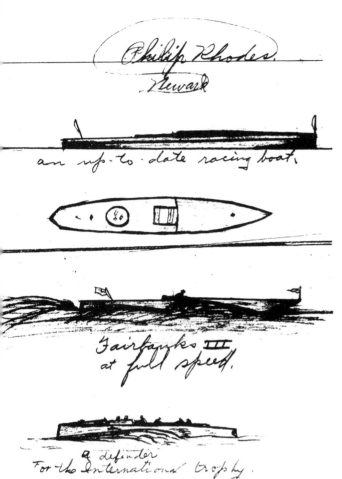

Far left: *Early sketches by Rhodes as a schoolboy give a hint of things to come.* **Above:** Dusty, *the backyard hydroplane Phil built with his own hands when he was 18 years old.* **Left:** *"Dusty" Rhodes in his Newark (Ohio) High School yearbook.*

became less than satisfied with the curriculum. Also, he told a friend that he regarded the college as being a bit "starchy."

The accompanying lines drawing of a hydroplane, another *Dusty,* which was drawn by Phil while he was at Denison, shows where his principal interest lay. He had wanted to become a naval architect, but Denison did not offer the courses he needed. In 1916 he transferred to the Massachusetts Institute of Technology, which was well known even then for its fine courses in naval architecture and marine engineering. The transfer was encouraged by one of Phil's teachers, Carrie M. Kirby, who loaned him $100 to help with his education. The loan was paid back three years later, plus four percent interest.

At MIT, Phil studied under Professor C.H. Peabody, who wrote a standard text on naval architecture, and the eminent designer George Owen. The young student thrived in this atmosphere, and in 1917 he became a paid half-time assistant to Professor Owen.

Until this time Phil had mainly been interested in powerboats, and he continued to enter and win design contests in *Motor Boating* magazine. A 1917 design that attracted considerable attention was *Jerry,* a motorboat with a centerboard and a small sloop rig, which was done for *Motor Boating's* Ideal series. Number eight in the series, *Jerry* was Phil's ideal cruiser, and she forecast his direction in the design of cruising centerboarders and motorsailers. She also gives us a definite hint of the budding designer's growing interest in sail. Indeed, in the article on *Jerry,* Phil espoused a belief that "a man becomes a better seaman and navigator who has a little knowledge of the handling of sails." This design led to one of Phil's first commissions, a shorter yawl-rigged version of *Jerry* named *Tern.*

The earliest Rhodes design using sail as the primary means of propulsion seems to be the 30-foot auxiliary yawl *Volante,* which was an Ideal series prizewinner in 1919. Compared with most of Phil's later designs of this type, *Volante's* sheer is rather flat due to her raised deck, her keel is longer and has more drag, and her hull shape is less symmetrical.

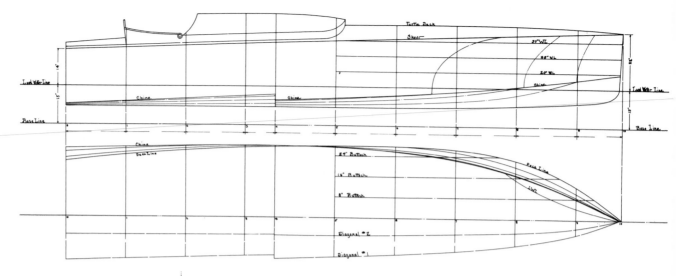

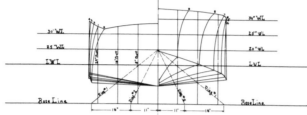

Lines of an 18½-foot hydroplane designed by Phil in 1916 when he was attending Denison University in Ohio.

Massachusetts Institute of Technology

Notification of Appointment

Boston, October 15, 1917.

DEAR SIR:

I take pleasure in informing you that at the last meeting of the Executive Committee of the Corporation, you were appointed

Half-time Assistant in Naval Architecture

for 1 year, from the beginning of the academic

year 19 17, at a salary of $250.00 per annum.

This salary will be paid in 8 monthly instalments, the first payment being due November 1, 1917.

Very truly yours,

Richard C. Maclaurin

President.

Instructors and Assistants, in addition to departmental duties, are responsible to the Faculty for service in connection with the Fall, Midyear, and Spring examinations.

Mr. P. L. Rhodes.

Phil's notification of appointment to his job as a half-time assistant in naval architecture at MIT.

No one seems to know exactly when Phil first became interested in sailboats, but it has been reported that his first assignment at MIT was to design a catboat. Undoubtedly he was influenced strongly by George Owen. Although Owen had designed a number of motorboats, he was mainly associated at that time with sailboat designs, especially Universal Rule P, Q, and R boats. In addition, he was a skilled builder of sailboat models, which Rhodes greatly admired. While under Owen's tutelage, Phil made a few sailboat models, including a beautiful half-model finished bright and held together with tapered dovetails. It is now owned by his daughter.

It seems likely that Phil's interest in sailboats was also stimulated by F.W. (Casey) Baldwin, that colorful jack-of-all-trades and master of many. While he was still at MIT, Phil met Casey, and in his spare time he would go to Baddeck, Nova Scotia, and assist him on hydrofoil projects. (At this time Casey was working on hydrofoils with Alexander Graham Bell — a story told in the book *Bell and Baldwin,* by J.H. Parkin.) This was the beginning of an off-and-on association that lasted until after World War II. Phil may have assisted in development work on the famous HD-4 hydrofoil, which established a world speed record of 70.86 m.p.h. in 1919.

Rhodes maintained his interest in hydrofoil craft

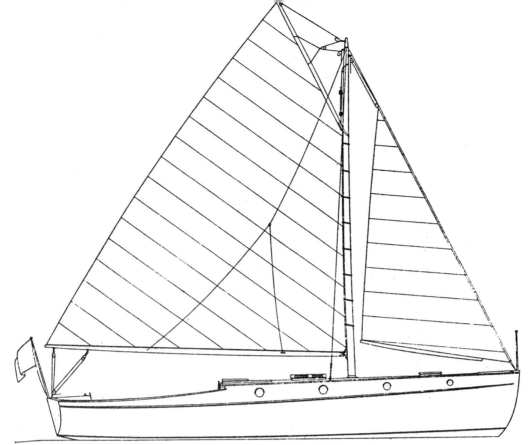

The 1917 design of the 40-foot motorsailer named Jerry *was a prizewinner in* Motor Boating's *Ideal Series.*
(Motor Boating, *September 1917*)

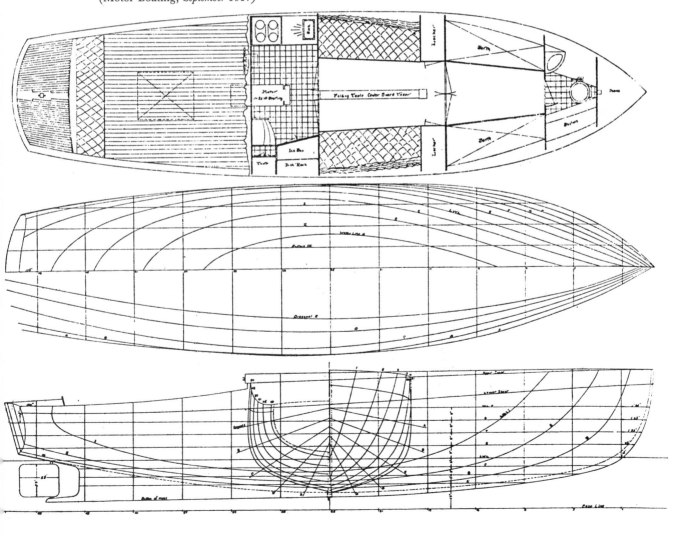

Volante, *the first known Rhodes sailboat design,*
was also a prizewinner in Motor Boating's *Ideal Series.*
(Motor Boating, *July 1919*)

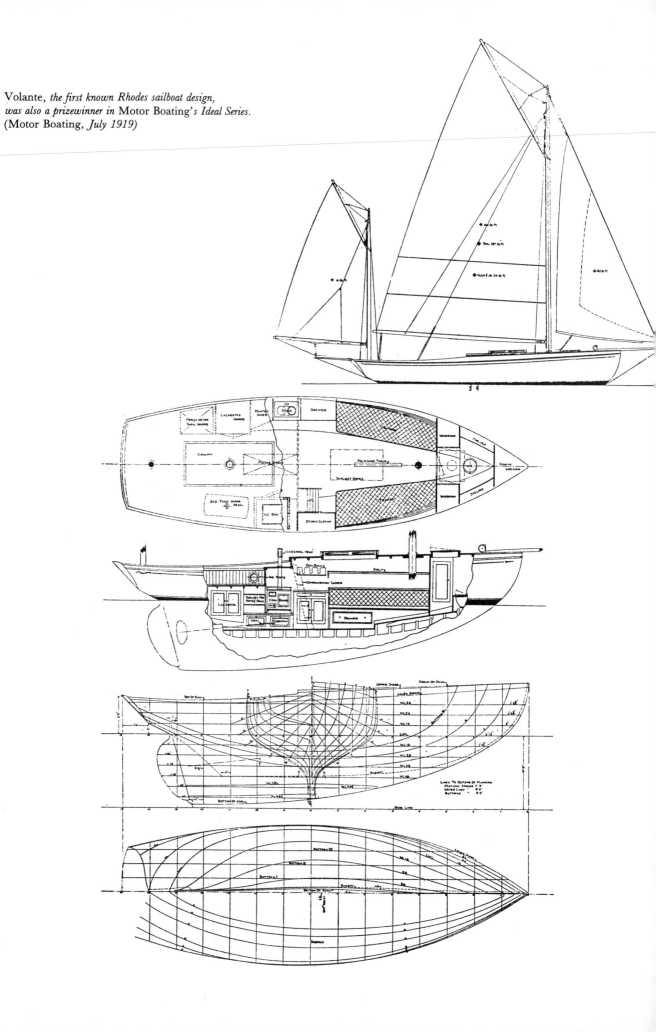

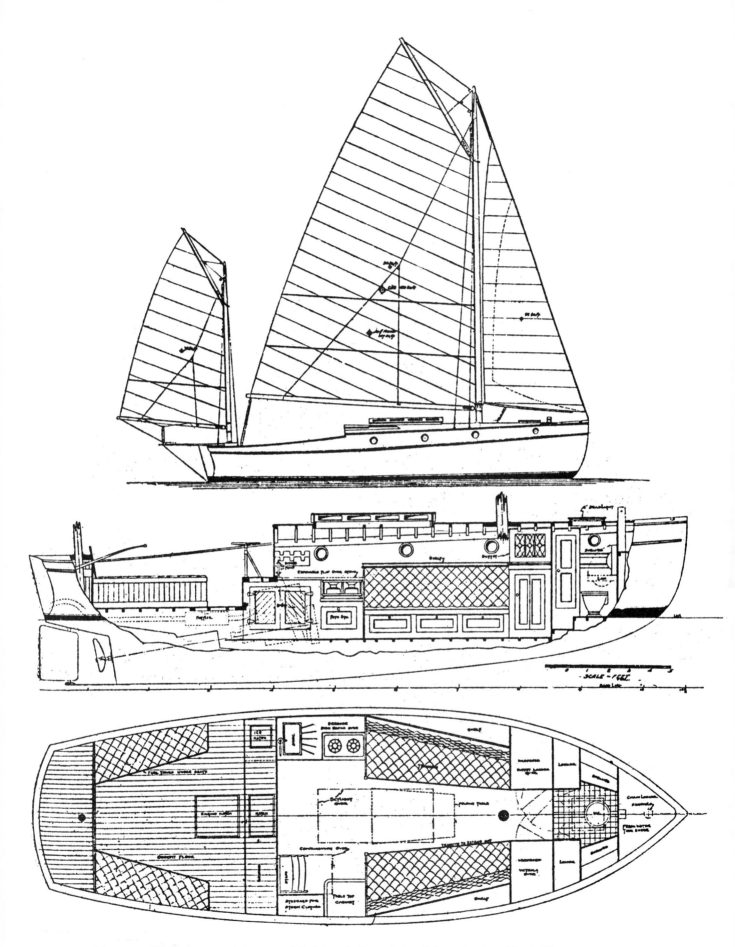

Tern, *one of Phil's first commissions, was derived from the* Jerry *design.* (Motor Boating, *May 1920*)

for many years. His design index shows 13 of these boats designed between 1928 and 1930, and most of these were done in collaboration with Casey Baldwin, including the well-publicized HD-12 runabout and the outboard motor hydrofoil boat HD-13, which was very successful as a racer. Later he designed the hydrofoil *Miss United States* for speed-boat enthusiast Bob Evans of Detroit. During World War II he helped Casey Baldwin design a smoke-producing hydrofoil that was to be used to screen slow-moving amphibious craft. These smoke layers were to be expendable, unmanned, and without external controls or guidance. The project was deemed unnecessary and eventually abandoned. The last of the hydrofoil designs recorded in his index is a 45-foot craft designed in 1948 for the "Government of Canada."

Baldwin may have influenced Phil's interest in sailboat design because Casey had an infectious enthusiasm for sailing. Only a few years after his earliest association with Phil, Casey sailed across the Atlantic in the ketch *Typhoon,* and he became a charter member of the Cruising Club of America. Casey was also a boatbuilder, and when Rhodes was first exposed to the Bell-Baldwin operation at Baddeck, Casey was completing for Gilbert Grosvenor the 54-foot yawl *Elsie,* which, incidentally, was designed by Phil's mentor, Professor Owen.

In September 1918, Rhodes received his degree in naval architecture and marine engineering from MIT. He had been in an ROTC program in high school, and after the United States entered World War I, Phil enlisted in the Army Engineers. Upon graduation from MIT, he was assigned to the scientific division of the Boston Navy Yard for training in naval construction. When the Armistice was signed in November 1918, Phil left the service and soon moved back to Ohio, where he found employment with the American Shipbuilding Company at Lorain on Lake Erie. At this yard, which specialized in building ore carriers, Phil started with menial work, such as "bucking rivets," but he received three promotions within seven months and became a practical shipfitter. He was always proud of his experience at American and appreciated the value of learning about shipbuilding from the ground up.

One of the reasons Phil decided to work in Lorain was that Mary Jones, his high school sweetheart,

Phil Rhodes as a student at MIT in Boston.

was teaching school in nearby Cleveland. They soon became engaged and were married in June 1920.

Several months before the marriage, Phil left Lorain and went to work for the Union Shipbuilding Company in Baltimore, Maryland. Just after the honeymoon, the couple moved to New York City, because Phil was assigned to the company's office there. His job with Union, which included work in the Hull Design Section, ended when the yard closed down as a result of postwar cutbacks in shipbuilding. Phil was forced into non-marine mechanical engineering, and for a time he sold conveyor belts for the Bartlett and Snow Company.

During this period Phil lost none of his enthusiasm for boat design, and he was drawing numerous plans in his spare time. He even received some commissions. The earliest commission shown

West Wind, *a 24-foot auxiliary designed in 1921 for Julian Cendoya, was the first commission listed in Phil's personal records.*

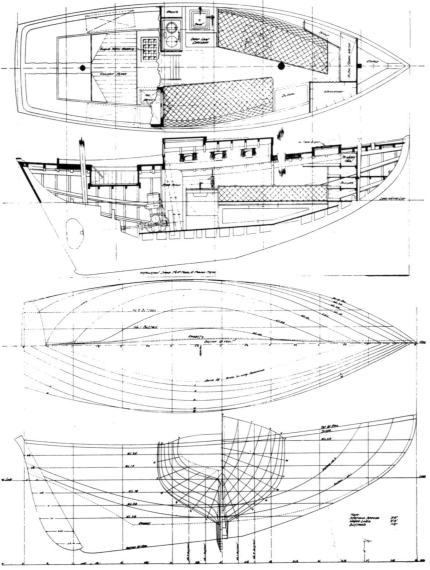

in his personal design index is for a 24-foot auxiliary sloop named *West Wind* designed for Julian Cendoya, Jr., in 1921. (About a year later, Phil designed another boat for Cendoya. This vessel was the 36-foot schooner *Mary Jeanne II,* whose plans were published in the August 1922 issue of *Motor Boat.)* Around this time Phil met Herbert Stone, the editor of *Yachting* magazine, and later the two became good friends. In 1924 Phil was commissioned by *Yachting* to work up plans for a 32-foot schooner. This vessel appeared in the magazine's April issue, and it was described as ''an exceptionally wholesome and able little boat.'' Encouraged by the positive reactions of

The knickered designer with his first-born child, Philip H. (Bodie) Rhodes.

more than a few yachtsmen, Phil decided to set up his own small design office in New York City.

Although it has been reported that Rhodes opened his first office in 1924, the late naval architect Weston Farmer said that he helped Phil set up this office (at 103 Park Avenue) more than a year later, and this agrees with information from another old friend of Phil's, Donald H. Sherwood. The earliest Rhodes advertisement with the 103 Park Avenue address seems to have been in the December 1925 issue of *Yachting*.

That first design office was so small, according to some reports, that visitors often had to stand in the doorway. Nevertheless, a lot of first-class designs emanated from this ''hole-in-the-wall,'' and the room was large enough for Phil to have an assistant from time to time. One assistant who worked there for a very brief period to pick up a few tricks of the trade was a young aspirant named Olin Stephens, who went on to become a world-famous designer and perhaps Phil's greatest rival in the creation of ocean-racing yachts. An early face-off occurred when a Rhodes-designed, gaff-rigged cutter named *Skal* finished second to Olin Stephens' *Dorade* in the 1931 transatlantic race.

In the early days at 103 Park Avenue, Phil frequently lunched with a group of sailors that included such stimulating conversationalists as ''Porthole Pete'' Chamberlain (Shakespearean scholar, designer of marine fittings, and inventor of a galley stove) and Henry Howard of *Alice* fame. Howard's boat *Alice* was a 52-foot centerboard yawl designed by Commodore Ralph M. Munroe, known for the *Presto* and other shoal-draft cruisers. *Alice* attracted a great deal of attention, especially after Howard wrote a number of articles and a book about her. It could well be that some of Howard's enthusiasm for offshore centerboarders rubbed off on Phil, because Rhodes became quite interested in this type of boat, and eventually he developed a real identity with the oceangoing centerboarder, although his boats were usually considerably deeper than *Alice*.

The first Rhodes boat of this type to gain wide recognition was a yawl designed for John R. Hogan named *Ayesha*, which finished third in her class in the 1932 Bermuda Race. Phil was aboard during that race, and, while it seems highly improbable, Cruising Club historian John Parkinson, Jr., wrote that

Phil at the drafting table in his first ''hole-in-the-wall'' office at 103 Park Avenue, New York City.

Rhodes even skippered the boat. *Ayesha* might be considered the beginning of a series of fairly shallow centerboard ocean racers, which, considering the type, had moderate proportions, easy, flowing lines, and rather symmetrically shaped hulls. They also had distinctive, sweeping sheerlines, which became a Rhodes trademark.

Another type of boat that appealed to Phil was the double-ender. Some of this interest may go back to George Owen, because the professor was an admirer of cruisers with pointed sterns. But undoubtedly Phil developed a special feeling for the type, after he was commissioned by Samuel Wetherill, an editor of *Yachting* magazine, to design what turned out to be a highly modified keel version of a well-known centerboard double-ender named *West Island*. This assignment resulted in some publicity for Phil, because the boat, which was eventually built by Wetherill and named *Tidal Wave*, was discussed extensively in *Yachting*. More than a dozen Rhodes double-enders followed in the wake of *Tidal Wave* during the late 1920s and early 1930s. Most were variations on Wetherill's boat — which had a Norwegian type of stern with outboard rudder — but Phil also turned out some very successful canoe-sterned boats.

Early in his design career, Phil was introduced by Donald Sherwood to Clarence Davis of M.M. Davis & Son, boatbuilders in Solomons, Maryland. This was the beginning of a worthwhile relationship, for Phil designed a number of fine boats that were built by the Davis yard. This included some lovely small- to medium-sized sailing cruisers, several bugeye yachts, and stock motor cruisers. Davis also built a

Phil (with pipe) on board his Bermuda Race-winning design Kirawan *during her triumphant passage to the "Onion Patch" in 1936. Despite conditions shown in the photo, taken near the end of the race, the race was, for the most part, rough and windy. (Courtesy of Robert M. Steward)*

smart little sloop named *Nixie,* which Phil had designed for his own use. Other early relationships with builders leading to some repeat business were with the Ollendorff Boat Company, the Minneford Yacht Yard, and The Anchorage, run by William Dyer.

Despite his considerable success, the depression created some lean periods in Phil's business, so as early as 1932 he began to associate himself with the old and well-established naval architectural firm of Cox & Stevens, which was noted for producing large, expensive yachts. Phil's presence allowed the firm to expand its business in the area of smaller racing and cruising sailboats (under 60 feet on the waterline). A formal contract was drawn up in 1934 that officially linked Rhodes with Cox & Stevens. It gave Phil greater security yet allowed him to keep his

identity and to receive full credit for the craft he designed. This proved to be a happy arrangement for both parties.

Phil had already shown his ability to design some exceptionally slippery cruising boats when he had his own firm. Aside from the aforementioned *Ayesha* and *Skal* he designed the speedy 43-foot cutter *Bangalore,* which had an outstanding record on the Great Lakes for 24 years. Under the ownership of E.B. Lumbard, she won the Chicago-Mackinac races in 1939 and 1940.

Phil's talent for producing truly outstanding ocean racers came into full flower soon after he joined Cox & Stevens. In 1935 he designed the lovely and successful 46-foot cutter *Narada* for L. Corrin Strong and the 53-foot cutter *Kirawan* for Robert P. Baruch. A year later he turned out such distinguished craft as the 57-foot yawl *Alondra* for Robert B. Noyes, the 41-foot yawl *Golden Eye* for H.P. Wells, and the 46-foot ketch *Arabella* for Elihu Root, Jr. Not much later came the Great Lakes winners *Escapade,* a 72-foot yawl for Henry Fownes, and *Copperhead,* a sleek 48-foot sloop for John T. Snite. All these boats had successful racing records, but the most outstanding were *Escapade,* which won five Port Huron-Mackinac races; *Arabella,* which excelled abroad; *Alondra* (later Carleton Mitchell's *Caribbee),* which twice won the Southern Ocean Racing Conference; and *Kirawan,* which, with Phil on board, won fleet first in the 1936 Bermuda Race.

In 1937, Phil designed for Ralph Friedmann the auxiliary ketch *Tamaris,* the first of a series of large cruising sailboats with exceptional performance under power. This unique vessel combines the advantages of a sailboat with those of a motor cruiser, yet it can outperform the average motorsailer under sail and even under power. Said to be the first yacht of butt-welded steel construction, *Tamaris* was made practically unsinkable, with five watertight compartments and a double bottom. Her accommodations are unusually luxurious, and her shallow but seaworthy double-ended hull, powered by twin screws, enables her to go almost anywhere.

During the post-depression years, increasing effort by a number of builders and designers was put into producing stock boats, which could be built at minimal cost and, in the case of sailboats, could be used for class racing. One of the most successful stock auxiliaries was the Rhodes 27, which was designed in 1938. The following year the concept of an ultra-economical, semi-mass-produced cruiser was introduced with the Bounty design. This 39-foot wood sloop designed by Rhodes and built by the Coleman Boat Company was produced on an assembly line. Her preassembled parts were shaped using molds and jigs. Good waterproof plywood had recently been developed, and a lot of this was used in the boat's construction, so Bountys could be sold for much less than conventionally built boats.

Prior to the mid 1930s, Phil had done most of the drawings for his own designs. He was a highly skilled draftsman with such a degree of fine-line precision that his office nickname was "Hairline Phil." (A great admirer of his draftsmanship was none other than L. Francis Herreshoff.) But in the mid-1930s, after the death of Bruno Tornroth, Cox & Stevens' chief designer, Phil was given total design and engineering responsibilities, and his administrative duties curtailed his work at the drawing

Graceful sheerlines, exemplified by this group of early profile drawings, became a Rhodes trademark.

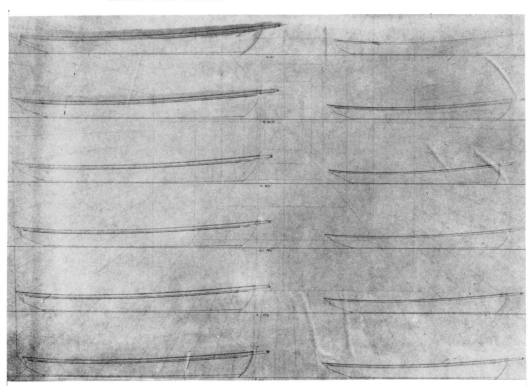

board, especially since the firm was taking on an increasing volume of commercial and government work. Nevertheless, during the period leading up to World War II, he usually worked on preliminary drawings in the evenings at home. During the day at his office he was in close communication with his draftsmen and carefully watched over the designs as they developed. Phil's longtime employee Joseph Reinhardt recalls an incident in which his boss gently but firmly chastised a draftsman for taking too much liberty with a Rhodes preliminary sketch. The sheerline had been altered on the finished drawing, so Phil went back to his own sketch, showed it to the draftsman, and stated in no uncertain terms, ''This is the way it should be.''

In small yacht work during this period, the firm received quite a few repeat commissions from yacht promoter Harry P. MacDonald and also from South Coast Boat Building head Walton Hubbard, to whom Phil was introduced by Weston Farmer. Later, during the war, a number of jobs came from promoter Donald B. Abbott. Although relatively few ocean racers were turned out at this time, at least one exceptional boat should be mentioned. This was the 46-foot yawl *Carina,* designed in 1941 for James Rider and later campaigned by Richard S. Nye. She had an outstanding record on the Great Lakes and one year in England, but her greatest achievement was a fleet first in the 1952 Bermuda Race.

At the outbreak of World War II, Cox & Stevens concentrated on military contracts, and the tremendous workload required a drastic increase in the design staff. For a while, Phil had 498 men working under his direction, and their offices occupied 6½ floors of a building at 11 Broadway in New York. His responsibilities during the period were the designs of Navy auxiliaries, patrol craft, minelayers, minesweepers, school ships, salvage vessels, tugs for the Army and Navy, barges and sub chasers. He also supervised a great deal of conversion work on large liners, such as the *America, Manhattan, Kent, Republic, Colombie, Carnavon Castle,* and *Normandie.* Rhodes maintained an office on board the *Normandie* during her conversion to a troopship, and his scientific service staff later assisted in calculations for the liner's salvage after her fire and sinking in New York harbor in 1942.

A major effort was devoted to hospital ships, for

Philip L. Rhodes during his middle years posed in front of a picture of his famous design Tamaris.

under Phil's direction 14 of these vessels, including the *Hope, Mercy,* and *Comfort,* were designed for the U.S. Navy; a staff of 25 men was maintained in Montreal to convert the liner *Letitia* into one of the world's largest hospital ships. Rhodes also had a 50-man staff in New Orleans for nine months preparing plans for the rehabilitation of the French aircraft carrier *Bearn.*

At the close of World War II, there was a fairly good market for yachts, but Rhodes could not afford to cut back to any great extent on his commercial work. Early postwar activities included the design of 410-foot cargo vessels for the Canadian government; 180-foot motor coasters for the Dutch East Indies; 240-foot motorships for service between Portugal and the African east coast; 3,000-ton motor cargo ships for the Royal Netherlands Steamship Company; 10,700-ton steamers for the Holland-America Line; large tugs; sludge vessels; fire boats; dredges; fast personnel boats for oil companies; and steam turbo-propelled vessels for the Yangtze River, which were said to have the "first ever" hulls built of high-tensile, noncorrosive steel. It would be difficult to name a type of vessel that Rhodes did not design at some time during his career.

Phil's first love, however, was always for yachts, especially sailboats, and somehow he found time to design some exceptional sailers that ranged in size from small dinghies to the magnificent Rhodes 77s.

Cox & Stevens was dissolved when Daniel H. Cox retired in 1947, and the firm's name was changed to Philip L. Rhodes, Naval Architects and Marine Engineers. Phil continued doing a lot of commercial work, but he gradually became more active in the design of yachts. In the early 1950s he designed a number of large motorsailer types, such as the 77-foot *Criterion,* 79-foot *Dolphin,* and 84-foot *Sea Prince.* Somewhat later he did a good many smart racing-cruising sailboats, including an outstanding class of boats measuring 29 feet on the waterline (*Altair* and *Erewhon* and their sisters), as well as the second *Carina,* which probably was Phil's most successful ocean racer.

In yacht work, at least, 1957 was an especially fruitful year for Phil. This was the year he designed the magnificent 98-foot ketch *Curlew III* (later *Fandango)* and the smaller ketch *Kamalii,* which followed in the tradition of the Rhodes 77s. It was also the year he designed the highly successful sloop *Caper* and the 12-meter boat *Weatherly.* As every sailor knows, *Weatherly* won the right to defend the America's Cup in 1962, and she defended successfully.

Rhodes boats have been built all over the world: In Germany, England, Scotland, Canada, Uruguay, Holland, Italy, Spain, Japan, Hong Kong, and, of course, in nearly all the major American yards. Rhodes yachts were built at such top yards as Abeking & Rasmussen, DeVries Lentsch, Nevins, Burger, Kretzer, Luders, and Palmer Johnson. Phil was only interested in top-quality construction; he even withdrew his name from one of his designs because he did not approve of the way the boat was being built.

Illustrative of his appreciation for sound construction is the fact that Phil sometimes used the adjective "delicious" to describe a well-built boat. Plans and specifications sent to the builder of a Rhodes boat were always extremely thorough, and Phil had a reputation among builders for great accuracy. In one case, the preliminary plans were so complete that the builder did not ask for further plans to construct the boat. Needless to say, Phil was not pleased. In the postwar years, many Rhodes boats were built abroad because of cheap labor and the high quality of workmanship, but Phil was always concerned about communicating the fine points of construction. On at least one occasion, to make the details perfectly clear, he sent a foreign yard plans that were seven feet long.

In the early days, his favorite building material was wood, but with the decline of high-quality wood and skilled woodworkers, he turned to other materials, such as steel, aluminum, and fiberglass.

Phil was one of the first yacht designers to recognize the advantages of fiberglass construction for fairly large craft. His 40-foot Bounty II was the first large stock sailboat built of the material. Some other well-known Rhodes designs in fiberglass are the Swiftsure, Ranger, Vanguard, Meridian, Reliant, Rhodes 41, Chesapeake 32, Tempest, and Outlaw classes. In addition, many of his popular small boats that were originally designed for wood construction, such as the Penguin dinghy and the Rhodes 19, were later produced in fiberglass.

During the 1960s, when Rhodes was turning out so many molded sailboat designs, he was also designing a number of large motor yachts for steel construction (but often with aluminum deckhouses) with overall lengths in excess of 100 feet. These included the *Chambel III, Pilgrim, A and Eagle,* and *Manu Kai.* A well-known large motorsailer launched in 1970 is the 123-foot, three-masted schooner *Sea Star,* which Phil designed for Laurance Rockefeller. One of the last and largest Rhodes yachts was a 170-foot diesel cruiser designed for the Cannes Investment Company.

Never one to rest on his laurels, Phil kept working at his beloved profession until his death in 1974. He died from a cardiovascular condition at the age of 79, and his passing was mourned not only by his family and friends but also by yachtsmen everywhere who knew how to appreciate lovely boats.

Philip Rhodes had a warm and friendly personality, and it seems that all who knew him liked him. He

The designer during his later years in his office at 369 Lexington Avenue, New York City.

was never too busy to correspond with the owner of a boat that he had previously designed, and he became close to many clients. As his son put it, "Almost every client was a friend forever." Designer Bob Wallstrom, who was a Rhodes employee for a number of years, wrote me: "I can well understand why owners felt a close friendship to PLR, for he would really take them to his heart as their design progressed, and I don't think he abandoned them later, either."

Rhodes employees included a lot of naval architects who are now well known. Besides Bob Wallstrom, Olin Stephens, and Joseph Reinhardt, there were such respected designers as James Mc-Curdy, Charles Wittholz, Al Mason, Robert Steward, William Tripp, Frederick Bates, Ralph Jackson, Francis Kinney, Richard Davis, Henry Devereaux, and Winthrop Warner. These men not only regarded Phil as a friend but also learned from him and greatly admired his work. Another admiring associate (but not an employee) was Weston Farmer, who told me that he considered Rhodes to be one of the greatest artists who ever lived.

Phil was active in several important boating organizations, including the Motor Boat and Yacht Advisory Panel of the U.S. Coast Guard Merchant Marine Council and the American Boat and Yacht Council. He was also a member of the New York Yacht Club, the American Yacht Club, and the Cruising Club of America. A longtime member of the latter's Measurement Rule Committee, he helped develop the CCA Rating Rule, which governed the handicapping of U.S. ocean racers for about 35 years.

As a sailor, Phil was perhaps not as experienced as some of his confreres, but he went offshore whenever he had the time and opportunity, and he had enough experience to understand thoroughly what the sea demands of a vessel and the need for attention to details in every design. He sailed in three Bermuda Races, on board his own creations *(Ayesha, Kirawan, and Escapade)* and, of course, he raced in many lesser events. Several people who sailed with Phil told me that he was a valuable crew member. He was not at his best at work on the foredeck but was a competent tactician, sail trimmer, and helmsman — as well as a delightful shipmate. Also, he gave owners the confidence to drive their Rhodes-designed boats to the fullest extent.

A devoted husband, who would jokingly say that his ambition was to outlive his wife, Phil was brokenhearted when Mary died in 1973. He was also a good father who managed to find time to spend with his children despite the pressures of business. An inkling of Phil's interest in his children can be gleaned from the fact that after the birth of his first child he made an elaborate graph that recorded the baby's day-by-day change in weight. Phil had three children: Philip H. (nicknamed Bodie), Daniel D., and Sylvia, who is now Mrs. Carl Harrison, Jr. Of course, Phil was delighted when his eldest son decided to follow in his footsteps and become a naval architect. Bodie worked as a yacht designer for his father for about 14 years before he struck out on his own to form with James McCurdy the successful design firm of McCurdy & Rhodes. Daniel has for many years been a prominent yacht broker.

The basic design philosophy of Philip Rhodes was to give a client the best possible boat for his particular needs. Phil did not try to impose any pet ideas on clients, but he gave them ample guidance. He was most anxious to give his clients what they wanted, but he seldom let their demands adversely affect the looks of their boats.

Furthermore, Phil would not let any special requirements, including the ability to rate exceptionally well under a handicap rule, ruin the soundness and safety of his designs. Despite the fact that he was an innovator who was not afraid to try something new, Phil was basically conservative in that he favored wholesome, seamanlike yachts. Bodie Rhodes wrote me, "Under no circumstances would he permit anything that wasn't safe or first class in every way to come out of his office."

There is no question that Philip L. Rhodes was among the most versatile of naval architects, one who could produce, as his advertisements claimed, "correct designs" of "any size — any type — any service," but Phil will be remembered best for his distinguished thoroughbred yachts. They are not only superbly functional, but they also have an elegance and ageless beauty that is all too rare in yacht design today.

Part Two
Yacht Designs
of Philip L. Rhodes

1

Mary Jeanne II
An Early Seagoer

One of Philip Rhodes' first clients was Julian Cendoya Jr. of Santiago, Cuba, and in the early 1920s he gave the budding young designer no fewer than five yacht commissions. As mentioned previously, it was Cendoya who commissioned the earliest recorded cruising boat in the Rhodes design index, the 24-foot sloop *West Wind*. The attractive schooner *Mary Jeanne II* was designed a year later, in 1922, and the work was done in Phil's spare time, before he hung up his shingle as a full-time naval architect.

In writing about *Mary Jeanne II* in the August 25, 1922, issue of *Motor Boat* magazine, Phil Rhodes confessed that Cendoya had rejected his first preliminary sketches of the schooner because they were too yachty. "He wanted a ship," Phil wrote. "He is a man with a complex for sturdiness in a boat and a strong dislike of polished brass and brightwork, except below." Phil then produced this design for a strong, rugged boat, yet one with graceful lines. Her strength can readily be seen in the construction plans, which show closely spaced frames, massive partners, continuous deck beams in way of the masts, and double bilge stringers. The long iron keel gives the hull extra longitudinal strength and also affords protection during a grounding.

Mary Jeanne II is a heavy boat, displacing over 24,000 pounds on a 29-foot 3-inch waterline. However, with 800 square feet of canvas in her lowers plus a topsail, she has plenty of sail to drive her. One might expect her to be a bit tender, having a ballast-to-displacement ratio of about 27 percent, but this is not so. The gaff rig keeps the center of effort low, and it was intended that she carry 3,000 pounds of concrete blocks as bilge ballast. Furthermore, this schooner has a beam of 11 feet 1 inch, which is generous for a keelboat with a deck length of 36 feet 1 inch, and her lines show good form stability.

Rhodes calculated that under her lower sails *Mary Jeanne II* has a wind-pressure coefficient of 1.56, which indicates that she is, in fact, exceedingly stiff. As Rhodes wrote, "This means that in order to heel this boat 20 degrees, her rail still out of the water, the pressure of the wind on the sails will have to be 1.56 pounds per square foot of canvas. This is a real breeze [20 m.p.h.], a regular spar-cracker." Although the classic text, *Skene's Elements of Yacht Design*, shows the norm for keel sailboats of *Mary Jeanne II*'s waterline length (29 feet 3 inches) to be less than 1.20, Rhodes felt that a vessel must have a coefficient of at least 1.50 if she were to be con-

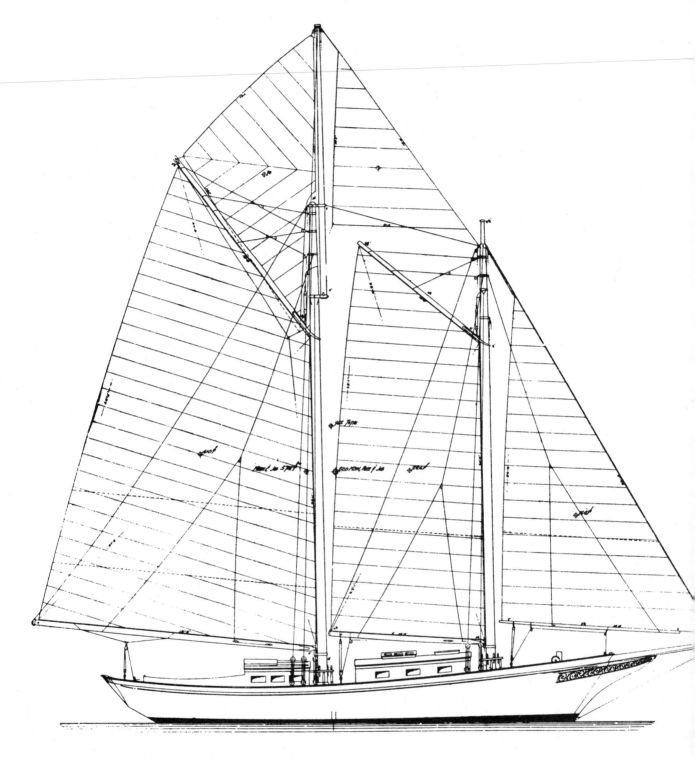

Although Mary Jeanne II *is one of the few schooners that Phil Rhodes designed, he once proclaimed, ''The gaff-headed schooner offers the greatest possibilities in crowding on sail.'' She is 36 feet.* (Motor Boat, *August 25, 1922*)

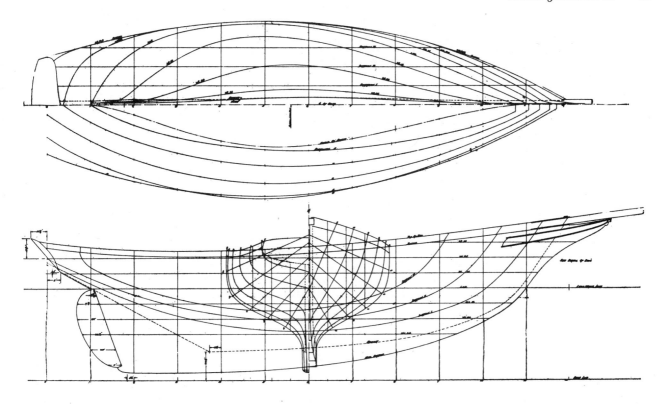

Above: *The lines of* Mary Jeanne II *show her firm after body and a hull shape that is less symmetrical than many later Rhodes yachts.* **Below:** *Exceptional longitudinal strength is afforded by the full-length iron keel and heavy double bilge stringers. Note the massive partners and deck knees.* (Motor Boat, *August 25, 1922*)

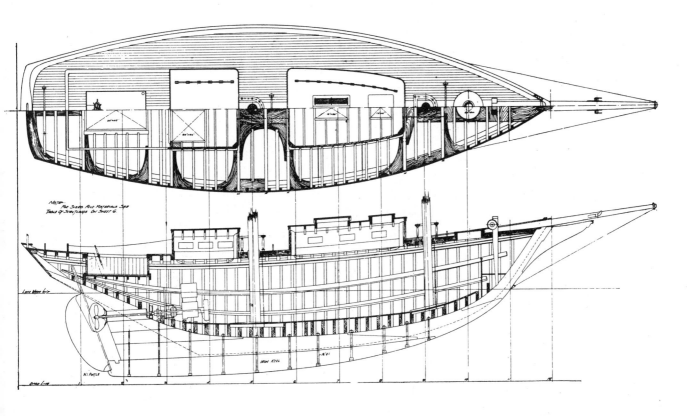

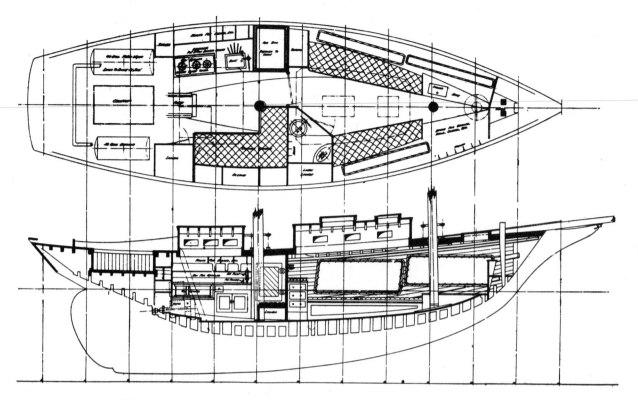

Owner Julian Cendoya instructed Rhodes to make Mary Jeanne II's galley ''part and parcel'' of the after cabin. The sectional drawings show certain details of the accommodations that cannot be shown on the interior arrangement plans. (Motor Boat, August 25, 1922)

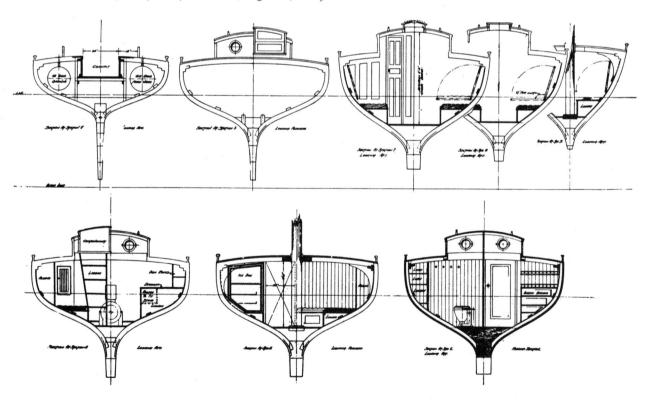

sidered a "real sea-boat." This should leave little doubt that Phil had a strong belief in stiffness as a necessary requirement for offshore yachts.

The schooner rig is often maligned because it creates so much work for the crew, but *Mary Jeanne II*'s rig is quite manageable, despite her topmast. Both her foresail and jib are self-tending, so that when the lower sails alone are set, not a sheet need be touched when coming about. Furthermore, the after main shrouds, set well abaft the mast, obviate any real need for running backstays. The little "queen" staysail needs tending when coming about, but it is only necessary to shift sheets; the sail doesn't have to be taken in, because the foresail gaff clears its foot. At any rate, the rig is sufficiently easy to handle that Phil suggested the boat might be allowed into the singlehander class of the Cruising Club (presumably the Cruising Club of America, founded the same year in which the schooner was designed).

There are two independent deckhouses, which causes a separation of the after and forward cabins. Although one can move from one cabin to the other below decks, it is necessary to duck low when passing under the main deck between the houses. The cabin arrangement was Cendoya's idea, and the after cabin is somewhat similar to the arrangement found on many modern small cruisers, where there is a dinette on one side of the boat and a galley stretched along the other side. This is not the best plan for offshore work, but it is a cozy arrangement for harbor use. Phil described the dinette as follows: "I'll venture to say that the corner transom borrowed from Ralph Stock's *Dream Ship* with its alcove for books, tobacco and other good things, will be a favorite spot around meal time." It would probably also be popular during the "happy hour" on a cold or rainy evening while waiting for a meal to be cooked.

With such features as a topmast, deadeyes, pinrails, and a clipper bow with decorative trailboards, Cendoya's schooner might now be considered a character boat. Such boats are picturesque, but they are sometimes "dogs" under sail. However, there's no reason to worry too much about *Mary Jeanne II* in this regard. She might not go to windward like a modern boat, but given a little breeze, she should definitely perform respectably.

2

Seawitch
Designed on the Dining Room Table

After he went into business for himself full time, one of Phil Rhodes' first commissions was the trim little yawl *Seawitch*. Although her plans (dated December 15, 1926) show the office address as 103 Park Avenue in New York City, the yawl's original owner, Donald H. Sherwood, says that most of her plans were drawn on the dining room table in Rhodes' home.

Don Sherwood first became aware of Phil when he came upon a small Rhodes-designed daysailer, which he described as having "a graceful sheer and an air of competence." Don was so taken with the little boat that he inquired about her designer, and before long, he made contact with him. After an exchange of letters and a number of meetings, Don asked Phil to draw up finished plans for *Seawitch*. This commission marked the beginning of a long-time friendship. *Seawitch* was built in 1927, and Phil had the pleasure of cruising and racing on her a number of times in the late Twenties and early Thirties.

M.M. Davis of Solomons, Maryland, built the yawl, which measures 34 feet by 26 feet by 10 feet by 4 feet 10 inches. He agreed to do so only after considerable persuasion by Don Sherwood. At that

time, the Davis yard primarily built workboats and had never bid on a yacht to be built to rigid designer's specifications. Clarence Davis was afraid that if he were held to a fixed price and written specs he would not make a profit. Sherwood won out, and the Davis yard subsequently went on to make a reputation as builders of high-quality yachts. Sherwood introduced Rhodes to Davis, and a considerable number of Rhodes' early designs were built at the Solomons yard.

Clarence Davis' initial unfamiliarity with deep-keel yachts is shown by an amusing anecdote related by Sherwood in the privately published collection of his logs, entitled *The Sailing Years*. The story concerns the stability of a Rhodes-designed deep-keel cutter named *West Wind*, which was launched shortly after *Seawitch*. Don was then vice-president of a company that manufactured railroad wheels, and he had supplied the iron ballast keel for *West Wind* as well as for *Seawitch*.

To appreciate the point of this story, one must remember that the Davis yard knew only Chesapeake Bay boats, which are broad of beam, shoal draft with centerboards, and heel very little. Keel boats heel quickly, but stiffen as the leverage of the

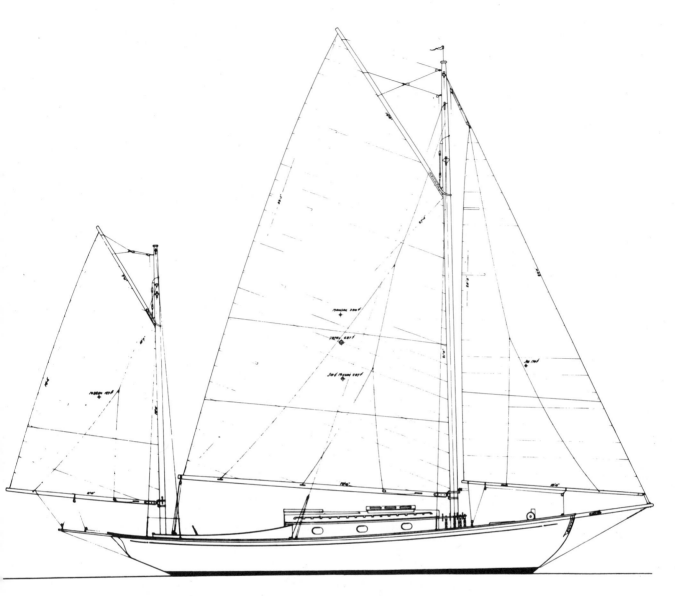

The 34-foot Seawitch *with her original gaff rig. (This boat's name was originally one word on the plans, but later it became two words, and still later it was changed back to one word.)*

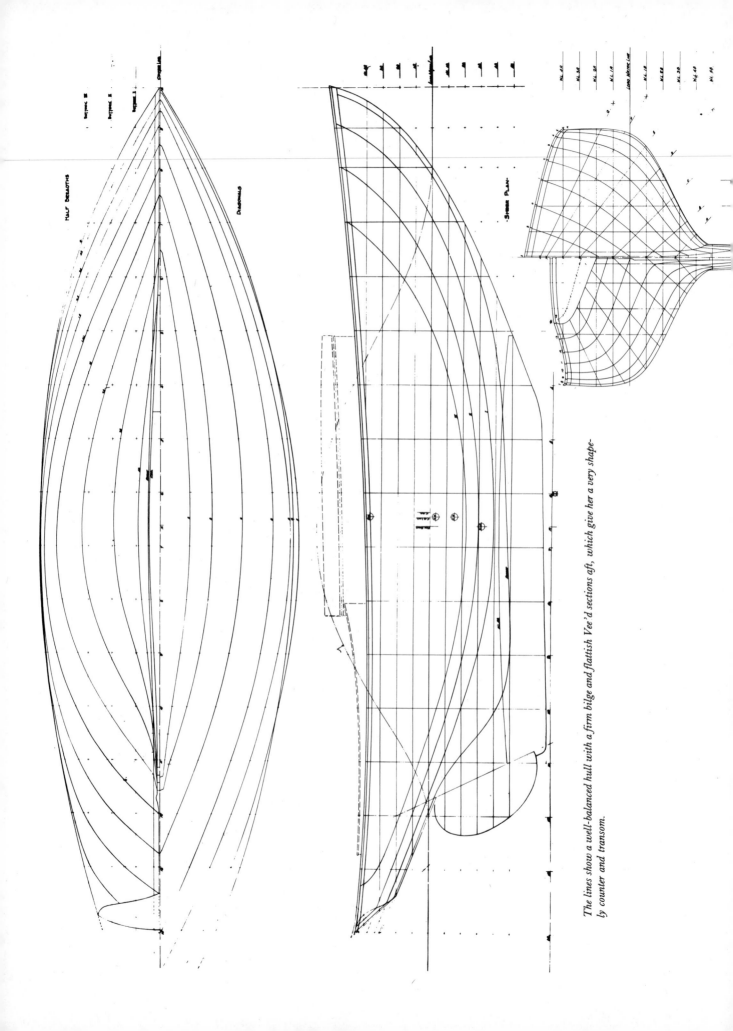

The lines show a well-balanced hull with a firm bilge and flattish Vee'd sections aft, which give her a very shapely counter and transom.

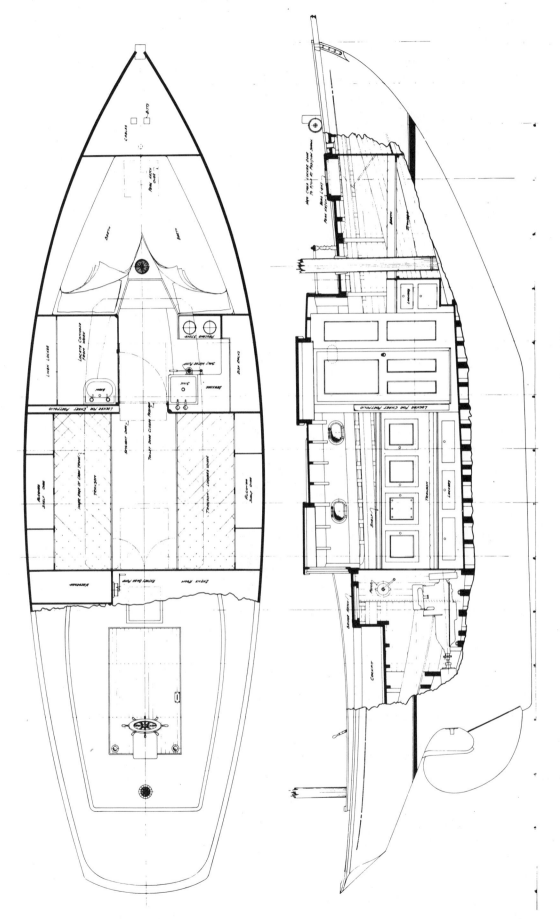

For a small boat, Seawitch has an unusual layout below with her galley amidships. Notice the galley sink's saltwater pump. Rhodes specified a low seat and shelves for tools in the engine room.

Seawitch *with her modern rig sailing off Vinalhaven, Maine, in the early 1960s. (Courtesy of Arnold R. Holt)*

keel comes into force and practically cannot be capsized. In due course the *West Wind* was launched, and shortly after, I had a long distance telephone call from Phil Rhodes, who started off without preliminaries and in a distressed voice asked me to lend him $5,000. When I inquired what the emergency was, he told me that he had to buy the *West Wind* and scrap it because it was a failure. Now the *Seawitch* had been sailing for a year, most successfully, and I was at a loss to know what had gone wrong. It then came out that Clarence Davis, who had walked on the decks of hundreds of stable Bay boats, went down to look at the *West Wind,* lying without mast alongside the dock. When he stepped

aboard she gave a nice little roll, which so frightened Clarence that he jumped back onto the dock in a panic and went to his office to call Phil over long distance. He told him that the *West Wind* was so tender he was afraid to step the mast. He thought she would capsize. Now, I could not conceive that such a stiff hull with 3,000 pounds of my carwheel iron on the keel was so tender, so I persuaded Phil to have the yard step the mast. She proved overly stiff, and I don't believe she ever got her decks wet, even in a gale of wind. Only the hurricane of 1938 in Gardiner's Bay, Long Island, could kill her, as I am sure with sea room she would have always been on top.

Despite Davis' discomfort with building yachts to a rigid contract, *Seawitch* was well built. Her keel, frames, and deadwood were of clear white oak, and her skin was of longleaf yellow pine, with planks long enough to reach from stem to horn timber to avoid butt joints. She was still going strong when I last saw her, in Maine in the mid-1960s.

Her accommodations are a bit unusual in that the galley is amidships. This is customary on a boat that is large enough to have a paid hand on board, but *Seawitch* is a bit small to have a professional. Nevertheless, this makes for an uncluttered companionway, and it leaves room aft for a large wardrobe and a good-sized engine room. There are four fixed berths, which is an ample number for a boat of this size. Some of the details shown in the arrangement plan are interesting, notably the large rotary bilge pump, the locker for chart storage, and the fife rail at the base of the mainmast.

Seawitch was originally rigged with a gaff main and mizzen. Although she was given a marconi rig in 1932, she had sailed reasonably well with her gaff rig against marconi-rigged boats of her size. This statement may raise a few eyebrows, but present-day sailors often do not realize how effective the gaff rig can be. It spreads a lot of canvas and nicely fills the space between masts. Of course, gaff-headed sails without vangs twist off a lot and lose efficiency, especially when close-hauled, but even jib-headed sails twisted excessively in those days, because cruising sailors seldom carried boom vangs. The gaffs on *Seawitch* were relatively short, and they were peaked up quite high.

From firsthand experience I know that *Seawitch* was able and fast in comparison with the boats of her day; my father raced his 34-foot Alden yawl against her for many years. Although Sherwood was gracious enough to say that my father "consistently" beat him, I remember the racing as being very close, and *Seawitch* won her share of silver. In those days, there were two important local races, one approximately 50 miles and the other about 100 miles. The latter, known as the Cedar Point Race, was more often won by my father's yawl, *Kelpie,* but I think the 50-mile affair, called the Poplar Island Race, was more often won by *Seawitch*. At least Don retired the large silver pitcher, which was awarded only when a yacht had won fleet first a number of times.

Racing in those days was quite informal. In fact, there were virtually no restrictions on sails in the first Cedar Point Race in 1929. Don described how one crew set a squaresail and on another boat the cabin carpet was hung from the main boom to increase sail area. On board *Seawitch*, a well-known crew member, yacht broker Gordon Raymond, climbed aloft and lashed to the masthead a boathook, which supported a jury topsail fashioned from a Fishers Island boat's spinnaker. Phil Rhodes was aboard *Seawitch* for that race.

In 1984, the current owner of *Seawitch*, Jack Strickland, wrote me from the Virgin Islands that he had been racing his boat in all the Classic Yacht Regattas in the area, and she had been first, second, or third in all. After 57 years, she remained "a fine sailer and still [was] doing her stuff."

3

Tidal Wave and Her Descendants
"A Distinctly Novel Boat"

Phil Rhodes was always fond of the double-ended hull form. He probably didn't feel that the pointed stern was necessarily more seaworthy than any other kind of well-designed stern, but he admired the character and symmetry of double-enders. In fact, he called the symmetrical Viking ships "gorgeous creations," and he occasionally made sketches of those ancient craft. Rhodes didn't necessarily try to sell his clients on double-enders, but he was seldom displeased when clients asked for them, as many did. Phil turned-to enthusiastically on such commissions and produced some lovely creations.

Perhaps the first Rhodes double-ender resulting from a firm commission was a strikingly handsome copy of a Colin Archer Redningsskoite. She was designed in 1926 for Julian Cendoya, the same man who commissioned *Mary Jeanne II* (see Chapter 1). The sail plan for this boat is charmingly decorated with sketches, which include a Viking ship and a Redningsskoite.

Undoubtedly the most famous early double-ender designed by Rhodes, and one that set a pattern for future designs, was the 32-foot 4-inch ketch *Tidal Wave*. (Her other dimensions were a 31-foot waterline, an 11-foot beam, and a 5-foot draft.) This

boat came into being after Samuel Wetherill, an associate editor of *Yachting* magazine, commissioned Phil to design a keel version of a centerboard double-ender named *West Island,* which had been inspired by the Block Island cowhorn. *Tidal Wave* turned out to be more of an original Rhodes design than a modification of *West Island,* but there is a close resemblance in the above-water profiles of the two boats.

Designed in 1927 and built at the Minneford Yacht Yard at City Island, New York, during the winter of 1929-30, *Tidal Wave* was a great success. Although there had been gloomy predictions from the "experts" that her considerable beam and her 21,000 pounds of displacement would make her slow, she proved to be fast, close-winded, and a good performer in light airs as well as fresh winds. Furthermore, she was stiff, able, and comfortable, although these qualities were not as much of a surprise. Writing about *Tidal Wave* in his book *Good Boats*, Roger Taylor speculated that she would sail rings around a Colin Archer Redningsskoite or a Hanna-designed Tahiti ketch. Whether or not she ever brushed with these well-known traditional double-enders, the Rhodes ketch certainly has

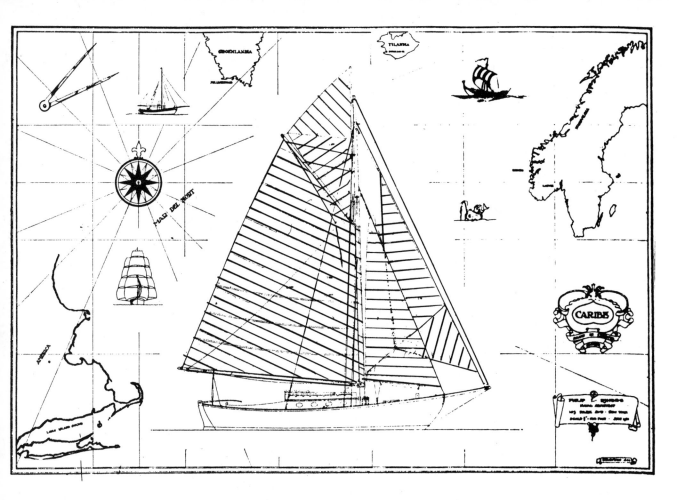

Caribe, *a 26-foot Redningsskoite that Rhodes designed for Julian Cendoya in 1926. The plan's decorative sketches even include a Viking ship.* (Yachting, *December 1926*)

shown her heels to faster boats. Racing in Long Island Sound and farther east, she won such events as the Bayside-Block Island Auxiliary race, the Huntington-Cornfield Auxiliary race, and the Riverside-Middle Ground race. It must have given Sam Wetherill great satisfaction to demonstrate *Tidal Wave*'s ability — especially to show a skeptical friend, who, during the boat's construction, had asked when the animals would be brought on board.

Even by today's standards, the Rhodes double-ender is a smart performer, for her present owner, Jerry Cox, comments that *Tidal Wave*'s '' . . . light air speed is eerie, especially reaching, and nobody believes her footing ability. Averaging tacks in ideal air, she gets 30 degrees actual and 27½ degrees with good momentum.'' The angles Jerry refers to are presumably those at which his boat sails to the apparent wind when close-hauled. If so, this is remarkably close-winded for a ketch-rigged seagoing cruiser, especially considering her moderate draft.

Despite having a keel ballast-to-displacement ratio of only 28 percent and a fairly tall rig, which supports 659 square feet of sail, *Tidal Wave* has good stability at normal sailing angles due to an ample waterline beam of 10 feet and flaring topsides that add another foot of beam at the deck. Sam Wetherill wrote that he carried 1,500 pounds of bilge ballast, but Jerry Cox wrote me: ''Carrying only two-thirds of her recommended inside ballast, she's as stiff as any high ballast-ratio plastic.''

One feature Cox likes about the rig is the forward position of the mainmast, which he says ''gives me all kinds of boat control in varying conditions.'' He sometimes sets a half-wishbone backstaysail, or ''mule,'' and he even carries it when singlehanding. In earlier times, *Tidal Wave* carried a sprit topsail, also called a mule. Both of these unusual sails fill the space between the main and mizzen and trim to the head of the mizzenmast, but the backstaysail is more handy because, unlike the sprit topsail, it need not be taken in when changing tacks.

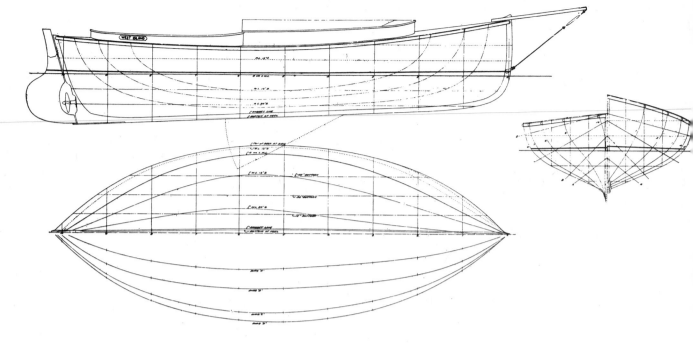

The lines of West Island, *a 30-foot 10-inch highly modified version of a Block Island cowhorn, which inspired the design of* Tidal Wave. (Yachting, *May 1927*)

About the only fault anyone could find in *Tidal Wave*'s sailing performance is that she carried a strong weather helm in a breeze. Phil Rhodes admitted this and wrote that his interpretation of a keel version of a Block Island boat had been a bit too literal, which resulted in *Tidal Wave*'s having a very deep and effective forefoot. "It was much the same as having a centerboard in the bow," said Rhodes. Another reason for the center of lateral resistance being fairly far forward is that Phil cut away the keel aft for fear that the boat would be slow in stays.

Most of *Tidal Wave*'s owners complained about her heavy helm, but Jerry Cox solved the problem to his satisfaction. He cropped the main boom by 18 inches and the mizzen boom by 12, while he lengthened the mainsail's luff by 21 inches. These changes move the center of effort farther forward, but the real helm-tamer is a trim tab 3½ inches wide and 4 feet 10 inches deep, installed on the trailing edge of the rudder. The tab is a simple solution; it is turned to leeward and with a light helm, the rudder can remain amidships, with the tab tuning out the weather helm. The rudder itself is narrower and deeper than the original, and it may be a little more vulnerable to damage from grounding, since it extends below the aft end of the keel. However, the keel is deeper amidships, and this configuration gives the rudder reasonable protection. At any rate, after these changes Jerry noted, "Her arm-breaking weather helm was gone at last."

Wetherill planned *Tidal Wave*'s interior and incorporated some uncommon features. For instance, she has an unusually wide cabin sole for her size, and her galley is forward, which is not customary on a boat that carries no paid hand. Wetherill wrote that he liked the forward galley because it was out of the way, where the cook would not be jostled by people using the companionway. Furthermore, he claimed that the arrangement allows a good forepeak for stowing gear. He also noted that ventilation is better in getting rid of cooking odors because the natural flow of air below decks is from aft to forward. Although there are many who advocate an after galley, Wetherill loved his arrangement and he sometimes praised it in his *Yachting* articles. About the lack of berths in the forepeak, Wetherill wrote: "*Tidal Wave* was to be a man's boat, so none of this forward stateroom business for me."

Tidal Wave attracted a great deal of attention after she made her debut. This was partly because of her character and performance and partly because of Wetherill's articles about her in *Yachting* magazine. As a result, there were a number of requests of Rhodes for similar double-enders. The next yacht design after *Tidal Wave* was a 30-foot LWL double-ender for noted architect William E. Baker. And a

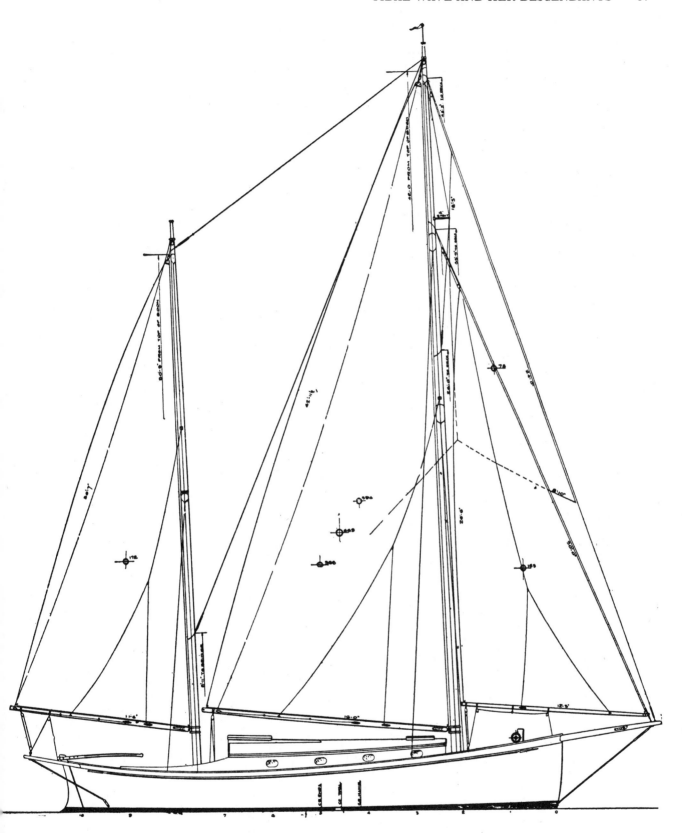

Tidal Wave, *which is 32 feet 4 inches, has a big rig, but she can carry it well, primarily because of her 11-foot beam.* (Yachting, *November 1930*)

little later, in 1927, Phil drew a seven-meter version of Wetherill's boat for Julian Wright, an American lawyer living in Paris. In 1930, Phil designed for Baker a slightly smaller version of *Tidal Wave*, which was the well-known *Dog Star* (at one time named *Tide Rip*).

Dog Star measures 30 feet 8 inches long overall and 27 feet 1 inch on the waterline, while her beam is 10 feet 2 inches and her draft is 5 feet. Compared with *Tidal Wave, Dog Star* has more overhang forward, less forefoot, and more depth to the keel aft. This underwater configuration makes the boat balance and track exceptionally well, eliminating *Tidal Wave*'s helm problems.

Her steering characteristics were described in Phil Rhodes' write-up of a sail he made on her from Greenwich, Connecticut, to Providence, Rhode Island.

"I remember particularly one thing that I always like to mention to anybody interested in this design. We were paralleling the Connecticut shoreline with a steady following breeze of about 12 miles velocity,

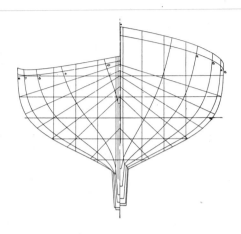

The lines of Tidal Wave *show a hull that looks as if it could sail equally well forward or backward. She sails ahead with remarkable ability, although Phil Rhodes admitted that her lateral plane should have been concentrated a bit farther aft for more perfect helm balance. The flam and flare of* Tidal Wave's *topsides help keep the decks dry and provide a reserve of stability until the rail is submerged.*

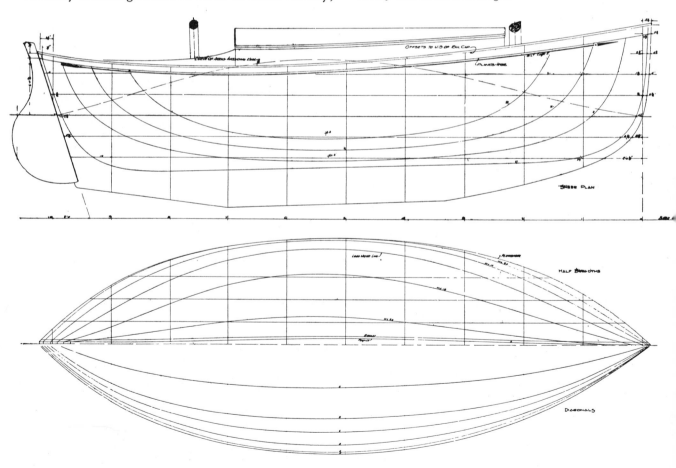

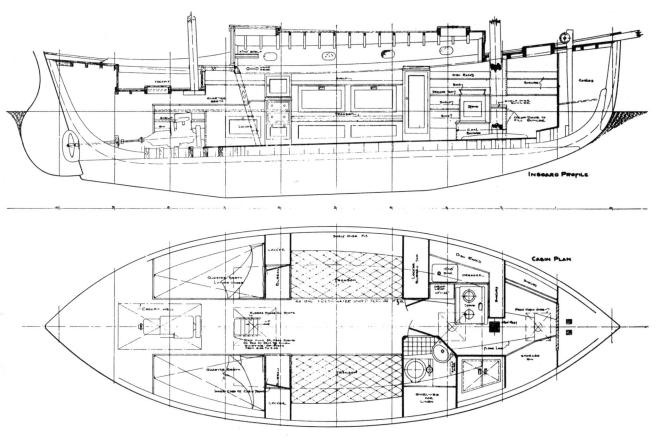

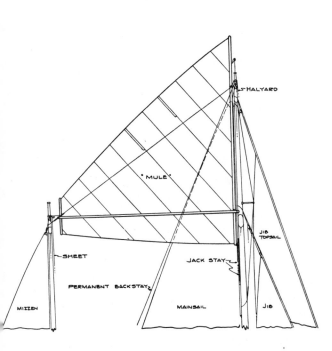

Top: *The somewhat offbeat accommodations of* Tidal Wave *reflect Sam Wetherill's thinking. He wanted "a man's boat" and an unjostled cook.* (Yachting, *November 1930*) **Above:** Tidal Wave's *early "mule" or sprit topsail, which had to be reset when changing tacks.* (Yachting, *March 1931*)

and with the sails wing and wing, she sailed for 12 miles with the tiller swinging free. Not a person touched it during that period. We then ran into a sharp 90-degree change in the wind, putting us on a reach, and we lashed the helm and she sailed herself down to Point Judith. In other words, this boat is very nicely balanced."

There is a similarity in the accommodations of *Dog Star* and *Tidal Wave* in the positioning of their galleys and in their number of berths. Both have four fixed bunks; however, the larger boat has two quarter berths, while the smaller has two bunks forward instead of quarter berths.

A measure of *Dog Star*'s appeal is that, some 40 years after she was designed, she served as the basis of a fiberglass auxiliary designed by Rhodes. The fiberglass version is known as the Traveller 32, and it was marketed in the 1970s by Seacomber Inc. of Alameda, California. This boat's forefoot is cut away more than that of *Dog Star,* the profile line being decidedly concave just forward of the keel. While somewhat less attractive in appearance, this configuration makes the boat a bit more nimble than *Dog Star* without markedly sacrificing her self-steering ability. Another change is that the Traveller

A fairly recent photo of Tidal Wave *showing her modern ''mule'' or half-wishbone backstaysail, which need not be lowered when tacking. (Photo by Tim Gleason)*

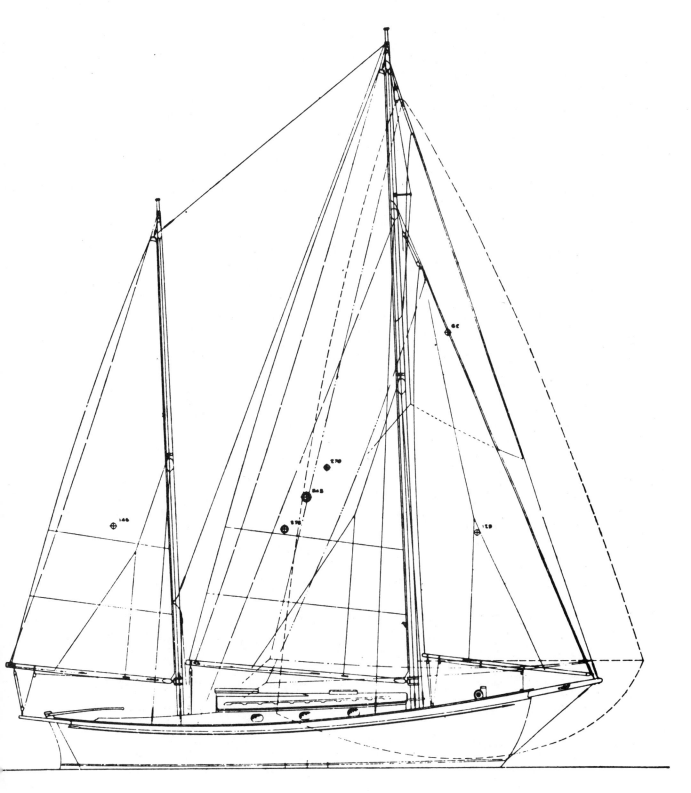

Dog Star, *a smaller modification of* Tidal Wave, *carries 545 square feet of sail, which is ample for an off-shore cruiser of under 31 feet overall.* (Yachting, *February 1932*)

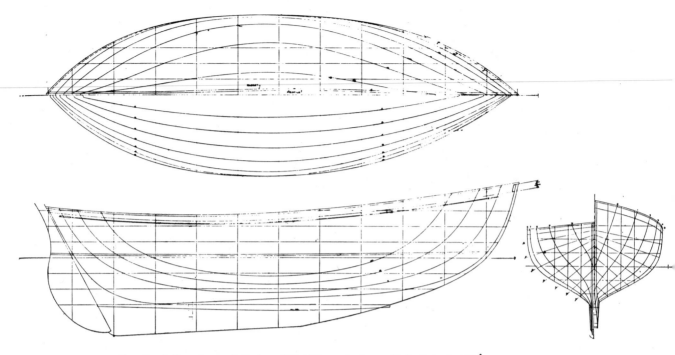

Dog Star's *lines show a similarity to* Tidal Wave, *but her profile is distinctly different with the raking stem, deeper keel drag, and more cutaway forefoot.* (Yachting, *February 1932*)

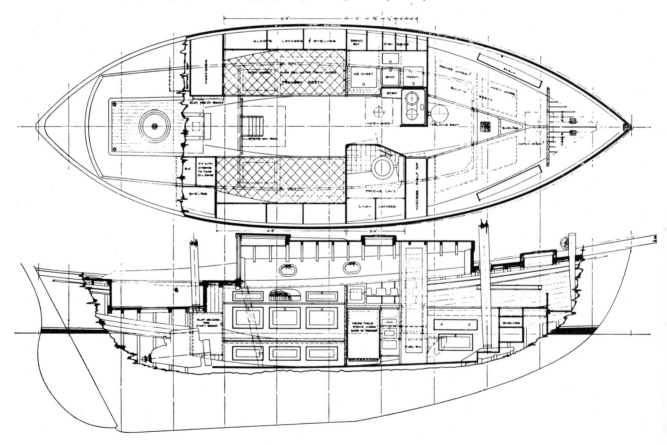

Dog Star's *arrangement below eliminates* Tidal Wave's *quarter berths and adds a stateroom forward.* (Yachting, *February 1932*)

This photo of Paunette, *a sister of* Dog Star, *is enough to quicken the heartbeat of many a small-boat voyager. (Courtesy of Mystic Seaport)*

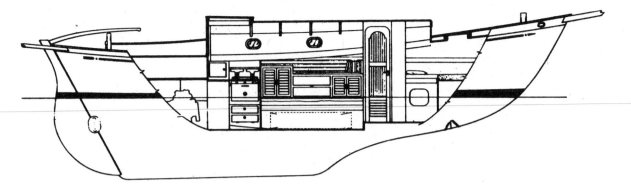

The Traveller 32, a fiberglass version of Dog Star *with a more cutaway forefoot and a moderate toe to the keel.*

was given hollow garboards, whereas the wooden design had been given a "hard rabbet" in the interest of simplifying construction.

Compared with *Dog Star,* the Traveller's accommodations are perhaps more practical. The galley has been moved aft, where it is more convenient to the cockpit and where there is less motion, and there is a chart table near the companionway. She also has different sleeping arrangements in the main cabin, with a berth and sliding transom on one side and an extension double berth on the other side. The enclosed head is small, but it has a wash basin, which is near the boat's centerline so it won't overflow during a knockdown.

There are two rig options, ketch or cutter. The latter undoubtedly gives better performance on most points of sailing, but the ketch rig has some advantages in ease of handling. Still, the cutter should not be at all difficult for a small crew to handle, especially if she were fitted with a roller-furling jib. One minor advantage of the cutter is that having the mainmast nearly amidships permits the forward hatch to be located in the forward end of the cabin trunk rather than in the foredeck. The cabin top location is drier and it facilitates passing up sails stowed below in the forward cabin. It also leaves the foredeck clear for handling headsails and ground tackle.

About five months after Phil designed *Dog Star,* he drew up the plans for *Yojo,* a double-ended ketch that was intended to be an improved *Tidal Wave.* The interior arrangements of both boats are about the same, as are the basic dimensions (31 feet LWL, 11 feet beam, and 5 feet draft), but *Yojo* is 2 feet 7 inches longer on deck, and her underwater profile is almost identical to that of *Dog Star.* In addition, she has 689 square feet of sail as opposed to *Tidal Wave's*

659. A near sistership named *Queequeg,* designed for Professor Burton Varney of UCLA, was used extensively for oceanographic research. She proved to be both seaworthy and fast. Professor Varney entered her in the 1934 Honolulu race and she won her class, beating several larger competitors boat-for-boat.

A newer version of *Yojo,* designated as an "S" or supplement design, was drawn in 1960. A well-known boat of this class is *Skaimsen,* which is said to self-steer remarkably well. Her bow has been extended so that her overall length is 36 feet 5 inches and her forefoot is cut away just a wee bit more than *Yojo's.* Below decks the two boats are almost identical, except that the newer version has a chart table near the companionway. This boat has 25 square feet more sail area than *Yojo* has. Both boats displace 19,850 pounds and their lead keels weigh 7,425 pounds; this gives them a respectable ballast ratio of a little more than 37 percent.

Tidal Wave and her descendants aroused such interest and their concept proved so popular that Phil received requests for plans and information up until the time he died, and as a matter of fact, his son still gets occasional inquiries about these double-enders. As late as 1966 Phil wrote, "I hear about her *[Tidal Wave]* and her near sisters all the time and seemingly from everywhere."

Phil Rhodes was fully aware that he had not made a major breakthrough in yacht design — he wrote, "I know perfectly well that there is nothing new in boats" — but he did recognize that *Tidal Wave* had rare qualities and he gave Wetherill complete credit for his part in the conception. In a letter to Wetherill, Phil said, "With her speed, stability, seaability, easiness, dryness, easy handling, short draft, accommodations, and good looks (to most), it is my

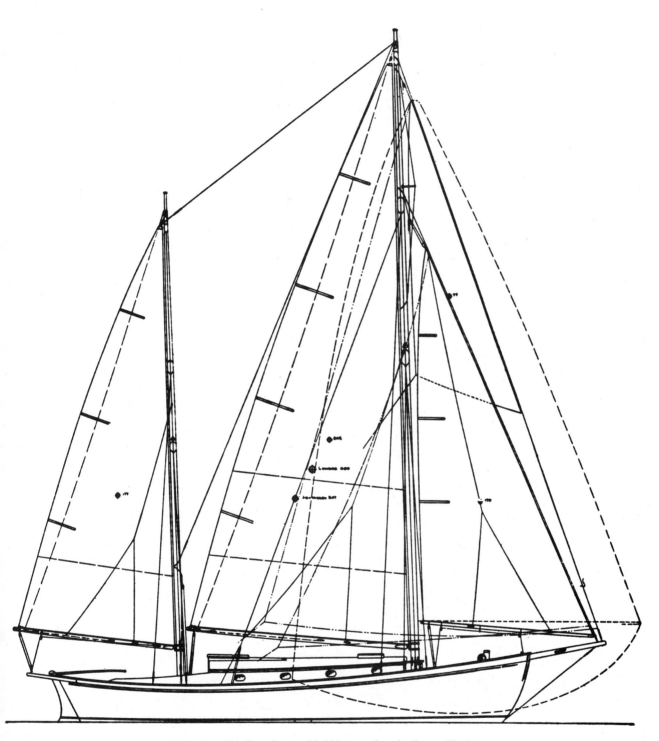

Yojo *is 2 feet 7 inches larger than* Dog Star, *with 689 square feet of sail area.* (Yachting, *August 1931*)

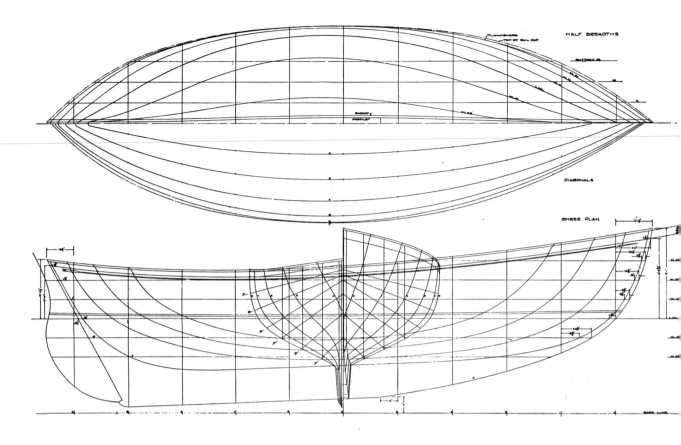

The lines of Yojo *show an almost scaled-up version of* Dog Star. *A nice feature for long-distance cruising is the keel configuration, which allows easy handling on a marine railway.* (Yachting, *August 1931*)

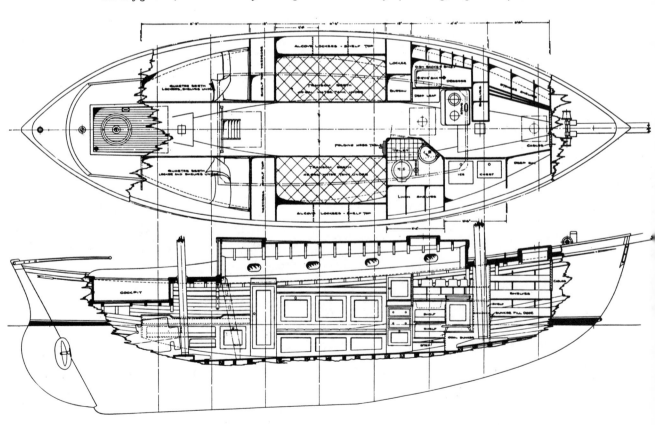

Yojo's *arrangement is very much like that of* Tidal Wave. (Yachting, *August 1931*)

opinion that weighing good and bad points together, the *Tidal Wave* type has more desirable features than any other type of small cruiser. I am not wedded to any one type, and I say this knowing that any one particular feature may spoil her for this or that yachtsman. She is a distinctly novel boat in many respects, and I feel that, thanks to your courage, I have developed a new type of cruiser.''

4

Windward
A Graceful Cutter

The lovely 36-foot cutter *Windward* was almost the next yacht to follow *Seawitch* and *West Wind* down the launching ways at the M.M. Davis yard. Her registration certificate shows that she was built in 1929, but according to a letter written by Don Sherwood in 1927, the cutter was actually under construction that year. In addition, there were two other boats later built to the lines of *Windward*. I understand that one near sister is somewhere on the Great Lakes, and the other, named *Windlass,* is now on Long Island Sound. *Windward,* originally built for Aubrey King of Baltimore, Maryland, has always been on the Chesapeake, and she has spent the vast majority of her years at Gibson Island, Maryland. My good friend Harry C. Primrose, and his father before him, owned the cutter for a great many years.

I never sailed on *Windward,* but I have seen her sailing many times and have even raced against her a few times. Back in the summer of 1952, my wife and I were the proud owners of a new 30-foot hard-chine plywood sloop, and we had a real tussle with *Windward* during a week of racing on the Gibson Island Yacht Squadron Cruise Week. Our boat was a light-displacement fin-keeler, and we could often sneak past *Windward* downwind, but she could take

our measure on almost any other point of sailing in a decent breeze. *Windward* was the eventual winner in our class, and we had plenty of opportunity to view her lovely stern.

Windward's lines show a quite symmetrical hull with balanced overhangs, but her waterlines above the LWL are rather full aft, which gives the boat some bearing when she heels. She has a sweeping sheer and a cocked-up stern, which is so characteristic of many Rhodes designs. The body plan shows a flat-bottomed keel, with the flat area carried up on the keel's leading edge. One might think that this would cause some head resistance, but the well-sloped forward edge must minimize this. Dimensions of the hull are: length overall, 36 feet; length on the waterline, 25 feet; beam, 9 feet 6 inches; and draft, 5 feet.

One rather unique feature of *Windward* is her small cabin trunk, which enhances her looks and also gives her tremendous deck space. The teak deck is understandably tired (actually exhausted) looking now, since it is over 50 years old, but at one time it was extremely handsome. Unlike the deck of *Mary Jeanne II* (Chapter 1), which is made up of straight planks running fore and aft, *Windward*'s deck has

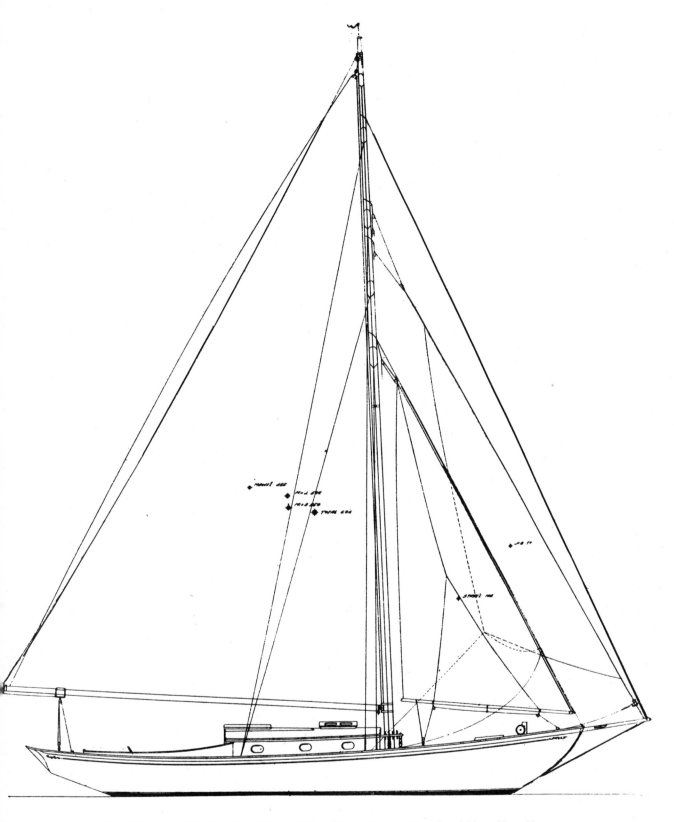

The 36-foot cutter Windward's *original sail plan. The small staysail proved useful in sudden midsummer squalls, which are common on the Chesapeake. The jib was fitted with a Wykeham-Martin roller-furling gear.* (Yachting, *March 1928*)

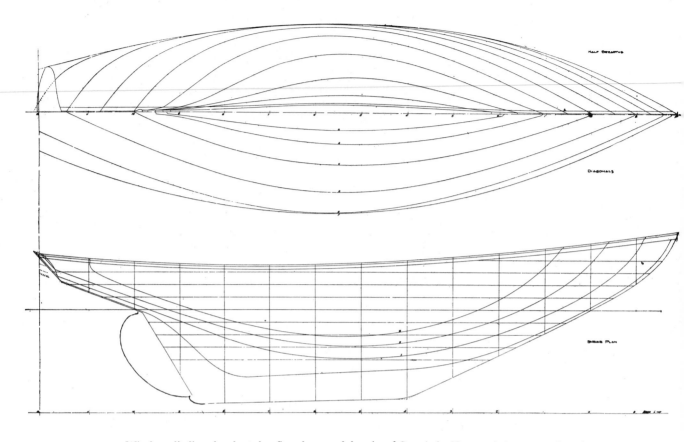

Windward's lines show her to be a finer, longer-ended version of Seawitch. *Not every designer can make such a pronounced sheer look just right.* (Yachting, *March 1928*)

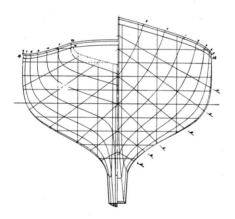

planks that are curved and notched into a king plank.

The small cabin trunk somewhat influenced the arrangement below, because there is not enough headroom to have a separate stateroom forward. The accommodations consist of one continuous cabin without dividing bulkheads, although the head, aft near the companionway, is completely enclosed. Such an arrangement trades off two-cabin privacy for superior ventilation and a feeling of spaciousness.

The original cutter rig, with 630 square feet of sail area, had a low-aspect-ratio mainsail and its forestay did not reach the masthead. In 1950 the Rhodes office drew up a more modern rig for her. The boom was shortened so that it could clear a permanent backstay, and she was given a masthead foretriangle, making it possible for her to carry a good-sized jib. The new rig moves the center of effort a bit farther forward, but Harry Primrose and the boat's most recent owner, John Chapman, say that her

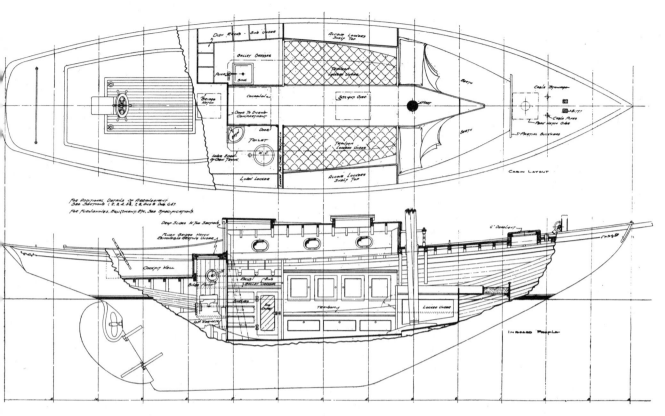

Above: *She has good accommodations for two for lengthy cruises, or four on shorter trips.* Below: *The sectional drawings show some interesting details of her construction and joinerwork. Note the big access door to the engine compartment.* (Yachting, *March 1928*)

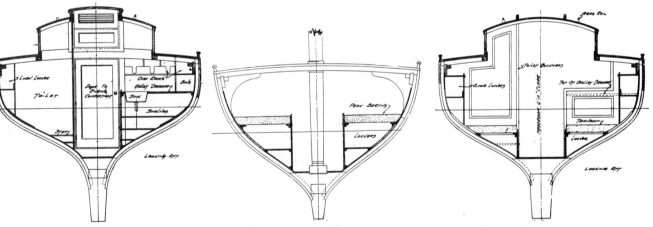
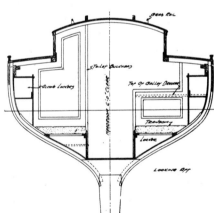

good balance was not adversely affected. In fact, John can leave the wheel for considerable periods and *Windward* will sail herself perfectly.

As of this writing, *Windward's* hull is reasonably sound, but her decks need replacing. For this reason primarily, John Chapman reluctantly decided to sell his beloved cutter, which he has owned for 22 years. His remorse in giving her up is understandable, for her exceptional beauty makes her a keeper boat, the kind one wants to keep for a lifetime.

Left: *A fairly recent photo of* Windward *with her masthead rig. The lovely cutter is still going strong. (Courtesy of John Chapman)*

5

Loretta
A Bugeye Yacht

With its sharply raking masts, clipper bow, and pronounced sheer, the Chesapeake working bugeye is a distinctive and picturesque craft. Therefore, it is not surprising that, in the 1920s and 1930s, when there were still a number of bugeyes "drudging" for oysters, there was some interest in bugeye yachts. About the prettiest boats of this type were those designed by Philip Rhodes, and his design index lists three such vessels. Details on the first, a 30-foot-waterline version, are sketchy, but more is known about the two that followed. Both were designed in 1929 and built at the M.M. Davis yard. The larger of the two, named *Orithia*, measures 61 feet 7 inches by 46 feet 10 inches by 16 feet by 4 feet 6 inches (board up). Built for Haliburton Fales, of New York City, she was intended for cruising on Long Island Sound. The other Rhodes bugeye (the boat featured here) is *Loretta*, and she was designed for Frank H. Reagan of Baltimore.

The typical Rhodes-type bugeye yacht, such as *Loretta*, is actually a far cry from a working bugeye, although their rigs and general appearance above the waterline are not too dissimilar. The workboats were normally double-enders (although a few had round sterns) with low freeboard and very shallow

draft. In contrast, *Loretta* has a counter stern, a less symmetrical hull, more freeboard, and greater draft, even though she is a shallow centerboarder. She is 55 feet overall, 45 feet on the waterline, and has a 16-foot beam and a draft of 4 feet with the board up.

The Rhodes boat is undoubtedly the smarter sailer, and she is certainly more seaworthy than the typical workboat model. Oyster-dredging bugeyes have tremendous initial stability due to their broad beam and flattish bilge, but with little or no deep ballast and very low freeboard, they have a poor range of stability. *Loretta* does not have the range of a typical deep-keeled yacht, either, but it would be far better to go offshore in her than in a Chesapeake working bugeye (if there were any chance of encountering a real storm).

A comparison of *Loretta*'s rig with that of an authentic bugeye shows that the yacht more closely resembles a ketch, with a slightly larger foretriangle and a smaller mizzen. Incidentally, the latter sail is referred to as the mainsail on a real bugeye, but on this yacht it might be appropriate to call the after sail a mizzen. On both boats the masts have considerable rake, but they are stepped in different locations, with *Loretta*'s mizzen being farther forward to allow a

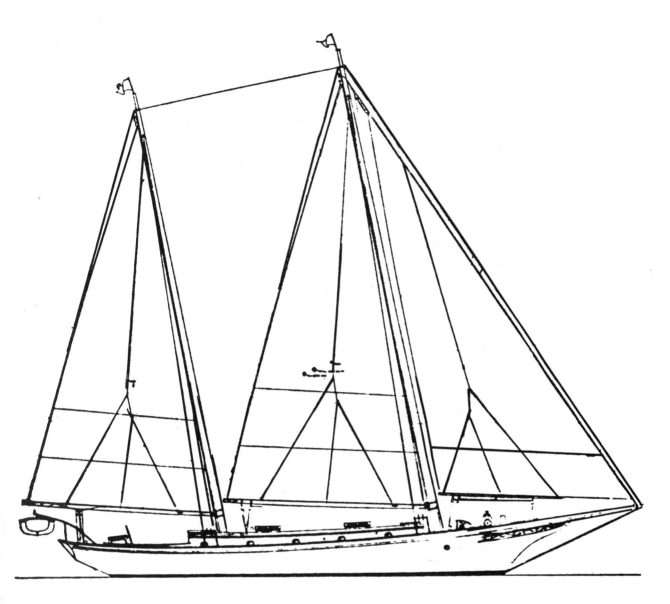

Orithia, *one of the two best-known Rhodes bugeye yachts built by M.M. Davis. She is 61 feet 7 inches long.* (Yachting, *September 1930*)

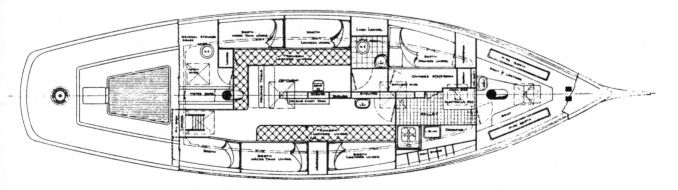

Orithia's *accommodations plan shows an exceptionally roomy main cabin with five pilot berths and transoms that could seat about a dozen people.* (Yachting, *September 1930*)

Orithia *under sail. She and*
Loretta *did not contrast very much
except in hull color, one being white
and the other black.*

large, uninterrupted cockpit well, and the work-boat's foremast being farther forward to provide a large deck space for oysters or cargo.

It has often been asked why the bugeye carries so much rake in her masts. The reasons for this seem to be partly that it avoids the need for backstays, and the halyards can be used to lift cargo. There used to be a theory that mast rake allowed a boat to sail closer to the wind, but bugeyes are certainly not close-winded, nor is there any real need for them to be. Rake does affect a boat's balance, and the forward position of *Loretta*'s masts might induce a lee helm in light airs if her masts weren't raked. A disadvantage of extreme rake is that it can cause the sails to swing inboard in very light going, but the flip side of the coin is that it causes the booms to cock up in the air when they are broad off, and this helps avoid tripping them when the boat is rolling. No

matter what the pluses and minuses are, the rake gives the boat character and even a look of speed.

Obviously, there is a big difference in the arrangement plans of *Loretta* and a working bugeye, since the craft are conceived for entirely different purposes. The workboat has only a small cabin aft but a large deck space amidships over a cargo hold, while the yacht has a comfortable cockpit aft, large enough to hold deck chairs, and a long cabinhouse just forward of the mizzen. With such a shallow keel, *Loretta*'s centerboard trunk protrudes into her cabin, but on a boat of her size, this causes no serious problem. The trunk's after end is used for a table in the main saloon, and the forward part of the trunk divides the middle cabin area into two private staterooms. The boat is nicely arranged for a live-aboard paid hand, with the fo'c's'le containing a pipe berth and head. The galley is also located forward. About the only

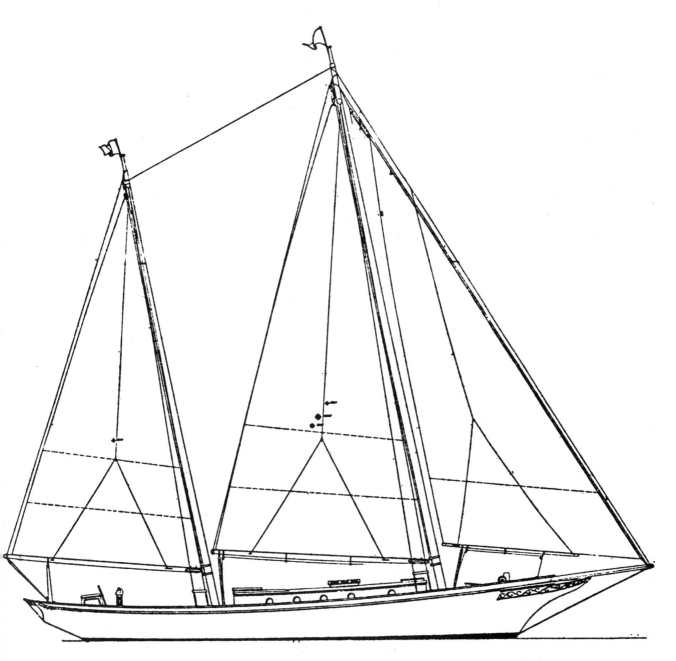

Loretta *has a smaller mizzen than* Orithia *has.* Loretta, *at 55 feet, is shorter. A workman at M.M. Davis said one of these bugeyes sailed well and the other did not. (He didn't say which.)* (The Rudder, *1929*)

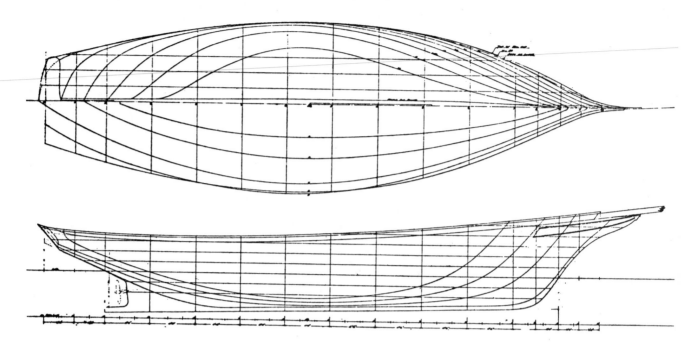

Loretta's *lines show her long, shallow keel, hollow waterlines forward, and straight buttocks aft. Her sections are well rounded.* (The Rudder, *1929*)

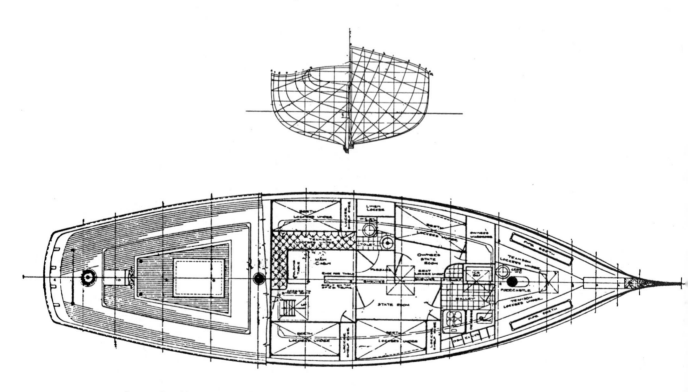

Loretta's *cabin trunk is shorter than* Orithia's, *but she also has plenty of room below and greater privacy with her two staterooms.* (The Rudder, *1929*)

Loretta *at anchor. Her black hull with gleaming varnished rail highlighting her sheerline makes an exceedingly handsome silhouette.*

problem with this plan is that meals served in the saloon must be carried from the galley through the starboard stateroom. This is probably one reason why the owner has staked his claim to the smaller port stateroom, the other reason being that the head is on the port side.

Loretta is not only comfortable, she is also striking in appearance. Her topsides were originally black, and this accented the gold cove-stripe and trailboard decorations, while the long, low cabin trunk, finished bright, emphasized the low, sleek profile of the hull. The bugeye pedigree is plain to see, but *Loretta* also has a bit of the look of the more dashing and rakish Baltimore clipper.

6

Skal
The Runner-Up

When the Olin Stephens-designed *Dorade* won the 1931 Transatlantic Race by a huge margin, she rightfully received considerable publicity. The runner-up in the race received little attention and was soon forgotten. However, she, too, had done well, especially considering that she was the second smallest boat in the fleet of 10, that she did not have a good handicap rating, and that her rig was relatively old-fashioned. She was the Rhodes-designed gaff-rigged cutter *Skal.*

Skal was designed in early 1930 for George V. Smith and Hobart Ford, both of whom were well-known yachtsmen on Long Island Sound. The latter was one of Rhodes' many repeat clients. The cutter was built by the Casey Boatbuilding Company of Fairhaven, Massachusetts, and her measurements are 48 feet by 37 feet 6 inches by 12 feet 6 inches by 7 feet. She was completed in time to sail the 1930 Bermuda Race and did fairly well, finishing 11th out of 42 boats.

Although *Skal* had a very respectable racing record, she was primarily intended as a seagoing cruiser. In a profile on co-owner Ford that appeared in *Yachting,* it was stated that, "Able cruising boats

are his vice . . . ." *Skal* proved able indeed. On her return passage from the 1930 Bermuda Race, for instance, she successfully weathered an 80-mile-an-hour blow.

Her 1931 Transatlantic Race, under new owner Richard F. Lawrence, also proved her mettle. Nearing the English coast, she ran into a storm and was forced to shorten down to trysail and jumbo. Then, running up the English Channel toward Plymouth, she encountered rain squalls with wind strengths approaching gale force. While local fishing boats reefed down, *Skal* pressed on under her three lowers and topsail, overhauling a steamer and a steam trawler in the process. Through it all, *Skal* performed well, and her crew had nothing but praise for her.

Alan Gray, one of her crew members on that Transatlantic Race, wrote an account of the race for *The Rudder* magazine. He waxed enthusiastic about the vessel: "*Skal* is an admirable sea boat, and it is not too much to say that all aboard her were fully as comfortable as those on some of the larger craft. Her motion, even in our worst weather, was remarkably easy, and she was very dry. No water was taken into the cockpit, except on the day that we went to the

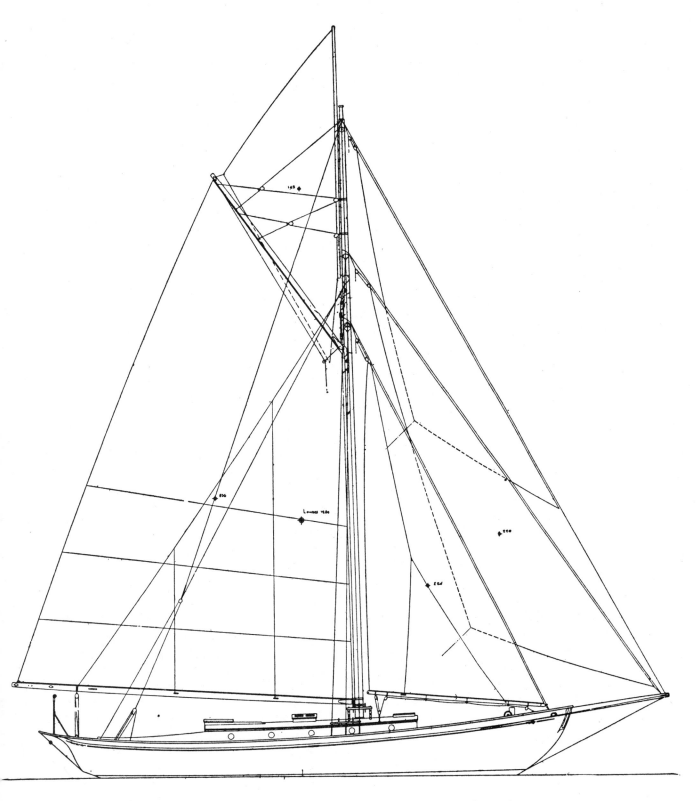

Skal, *with her triple-headsail gaff rig. Her sail area can be extended quite far aloft with her jackyard topsail,*
which might more properly be called a ''jacky topsail,'' since its yard is parallel to the mast. She is 48 feet long.
(The Rudder, *December 1930*)

Right: Skal's *body plan helps explain her power and affinity with the sea. The curvaceous sections also give the hull great strength.* **Below:** Skal *has a fairly long keel, but the hull profile is cut away forward partly for balance and helm response, as well as to reduce the wetted surface. The easy buttocks probably account for the crew's remark that "she throws no quarter wave."* **Bottom:** Skal's *layout with the galley and plenty of bunks aft is a sensible arrangement for a seagoer.* (The Rudder, *December 1930*)

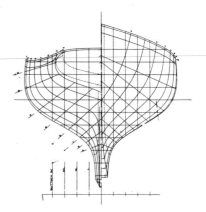

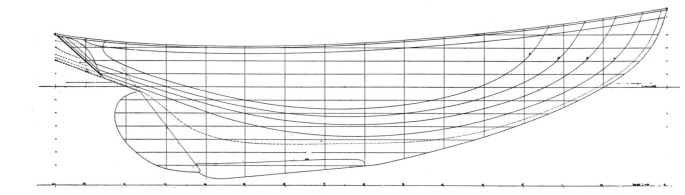

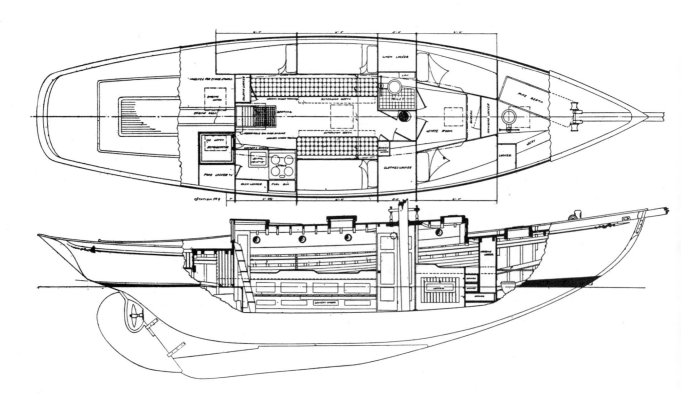

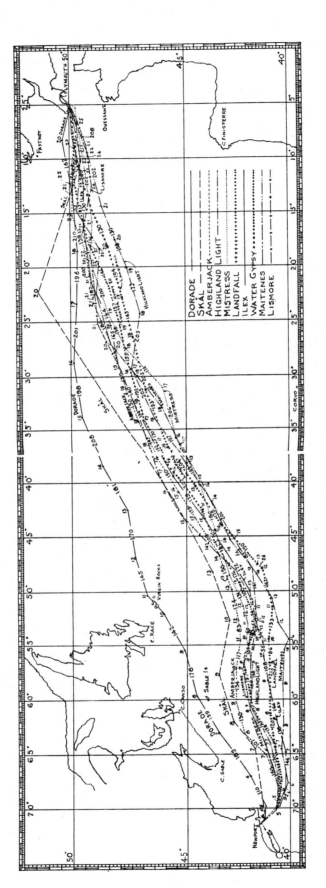

Skal's track in the 1931 transatlantic race shows that she stayed fairly far south in the early stages but went unnecessarily far north near the end of the race. (You Are First by Francis S. Kinney. Dodd, Mead)

Skal *under sail carrying a huge, vertically cut reaching jib and a small, yardless topsail.* (Yachting, *September 1931)*

storm trysail. Probably her best point of sailing is running, for she made remarkable runs during the days when the wind was well aft, and she handles very well in following seas. As far as we could determine, she throws no quarter wave.''

Even a cursory examination of *Skal's* plan shows why she is such a splendid sea boat. Her fairly long keel helps keep her on course, while the ample draft allows a deep, well-protected rudder for good steering control and permits deep external ballast for reserve stability. Moderately short ends, together with her almost-champagne-glass sections and considerable displacement, make for exceptional seakindliness. In addition, she has sufficient beam for sail-carrying ability, comfort, and the alleviation of the rhythmic rolling that often occurs on narrow boats. It seems safe to say that *Skal* has a more comfortable motion than the much narrower *Dorade* when running in a seaway. The Rhodes sheerline is not only handsome, but it helps keep water from coming over the bow and stern. Of course, the low

cabin trunk with small ports are good features for the heaviest weather at sea.

In those times many seamen still felt that the gaff rig was the proper one for offshore work. They argued that there is less tophamper with this rig, especially when the gaff is lowered in a gale, and that there is less chance of being temporarily becalmed in the troughs of ocean waves because of the quadrilateral shape of gaff-headed sails. *Skal's* rig is not the handiest one, with its running backstays, topsail, triple headsails, and long bowsprit. Nevertheless, the individual sails are fairly compact, and they are inboard when *Skal* is snugged down in heavy weather under staysail and main alone. In light weather she can spread a lot of canvas, 1,280 square feet of it, not counting her large balloon jib and spinnaker.

Down below, *Skal* sleeps eight, with three pilot berths and two extension transom berths in the main cabin, two bunks in a forward cabin, plus a pipe berth in the fo'c's'le. In addition to the enclosed head amidships, there is a W.C. in the fo'c's'le for a paid hand. Unlike many boats having crew's quarters forward, the galley is aft, where there is less motion. The engine room under the bridgedeck originally housed a Gray 4-50 gasoline engine.

What is particularly appealing about *Skal* is her good looks. In contrast with many modern cruisers, she has moderate freeboard, an exquisite sheerline, handsome balanced ends, and an unobtrusive cabin trunk. This is the kind of hull that can always be considered up to date, for it has character and integrity.

7

Narwhal and Saona
Early Canoe-Sterned Sailers

Philip Rhodes designed a number of successful canoe-stern sailboats, and perhaps the earliest of these is the well-known 40-foot cutter *Narwhal,* which was designed for H.S. Sayres in November 1930. She is a development of *Tidal Wave* (indeed, on her plans she is labeled "cutter of the *Tidal Wave* type"), and Phil simply used *Tidal Wave*'s midships sections as a basis and lengthened her ends. It is interesting that the Rhodes index (see Appendix) shows that Phil designed a 40-foot cutter like *Tidal Wave* for Sayres in April 1930. Presumably this boat was never built, the design being superseded by the canoe-stern version.

Just why the canoe stern was chosen for this particular boat is not certain. It does have some advantages over a Norwegian-type stern with an outboard rudder, affording better protection for the rudder, reducing wetted surface, and allowing less rudder ventilation. It is quite possible that Sayres simply preferred the looks of a canoe stern.

Narwhal was built by the Minneford Yacht Yard at City Island, New York, in 1931. Except for her overall length of 39 feet 11 inches, she has the same dimensions as *Tidal Wave:* 31 feet on the waterline, 11 feet of beam, and a 5-foot draft. The accommoda-

tions are also quite similar to those of *Tidal Wave,* except that in *Narwhal* there is only one quarter berth aft, and there are two bunks forward of the galley.

Narwhal is known to be a fast boat, which is not surprising, for she has a generous cutter rig that supports 864 square feet of sail. The foretriangle is tremendous, having a base almost as long as the distance between the mast and the stern. Her standard headsails are staysail, jib, and jib topsail, but she could probably carry a huge masthead reacher in light airs that would give her awesome power.

Under various owners, *Narwhal* has had a respectable racing record. In her first season, she made quite a splash on Long Island Sound, winning Riverside Yacht Club's Commodore Pierce day race, winning the Huntington-Cornfield Auxiliary Race (by 4 hours over Alf Loomis' cutter *Hotspur*), taking the *Yachting* Trophy for the best corrected time of any boat under 40 feet in Bayside Yacht Club's auxiliary handicap race, and placing first in the Harlem-Cornfield Light Race. In the latter race, sailed in a heavy summer easterly, she was the only boat to finish, the others having either broken down or dropped out voluntarily.

She was the smallest boat in the 1938 Bermuda

When Narwhal was designed, the "slot theory" of sailing aerodynamics was in vogue, and her sail plan provides plenty of slots in addition to considerable area. She is 39 feet 11 inches long. (Yachting, May 1931)

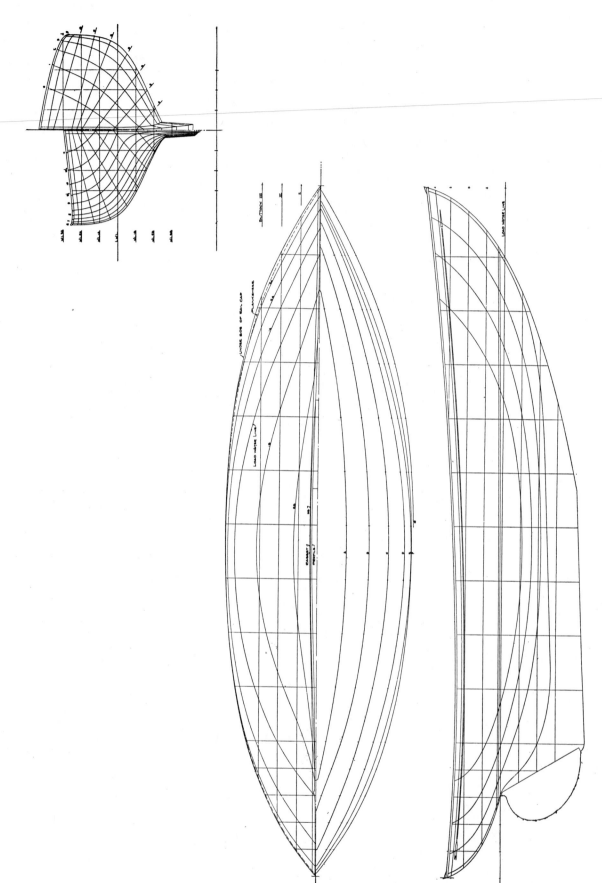

Narwhal's lines show her close kinship with Tidal Wave, despite the fact that her ends are drawn out and she has an entirely different stern. (Yachting, May 1931)

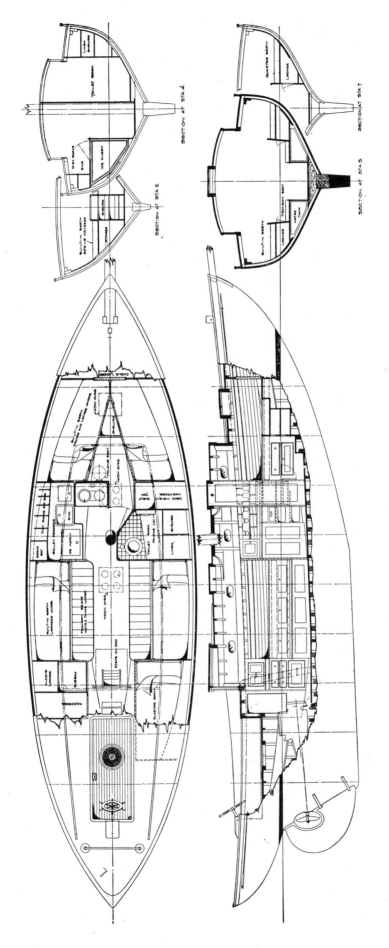

Narwhal's *interior arrangement is yet another variation on the Tidal Wave theme.* (Yachting, May 1931)

Narwhal *makes a lovely sight as she sails along close-hauled, showing off her triple-head rig.* (The Rudder, *November 1931*)

Race fleet, and she finished a creditable 16th in fleet and 5th (out of 19) in her class in what was a big-boat race. (Incidentally, on the homeward voyage after that race, a Bermudian stowed away, and this caused some problems with the U.S. Immigration Service.)

Narwhal was wrecked in the 1938 hurricane, and her owner at that time, Robert Leeson, sold her to insurance underwriters. The cutter was eventually repaired; Leeson and two other men bought her

back a number of years later. This certainly illustrates the high regard he had for the boat. In 1952 Leeson and the other owners raced to Bermuda and won the Finley Trophy for the top-placing boat over 15 years old. As late as 1958, under a new owner, Richard Warren (but with Leeson on board), *Narwhal* sailed in the Bermuda Race and finished eighth out of 28 in class.

Following in *Narwhal*'s wake was another well-known small cruiser having a canoe stern, the ketch

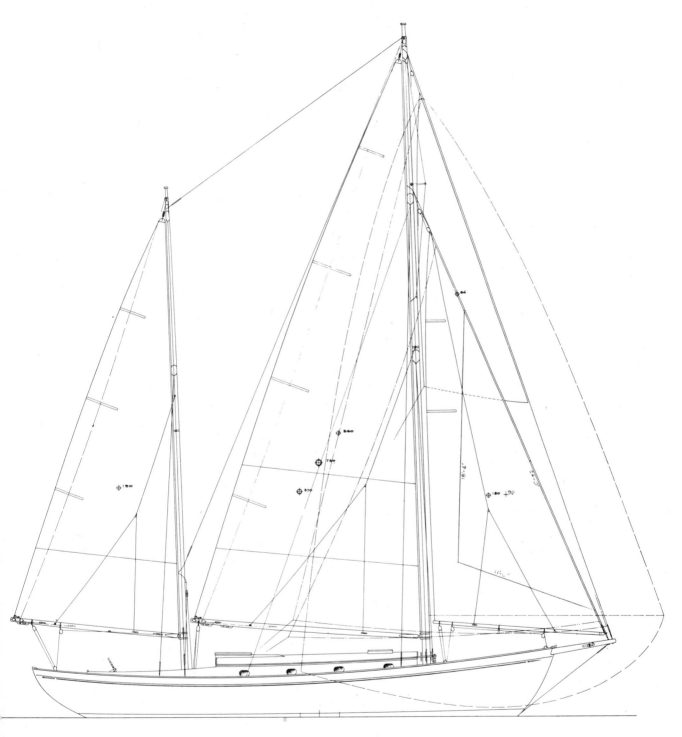

Although it appears that some rig efficiency has been traded for handiness on the 39-foot centerboard ketch Saona (Lady Patty), *she nevertheless had a surprisingly good racing record.*

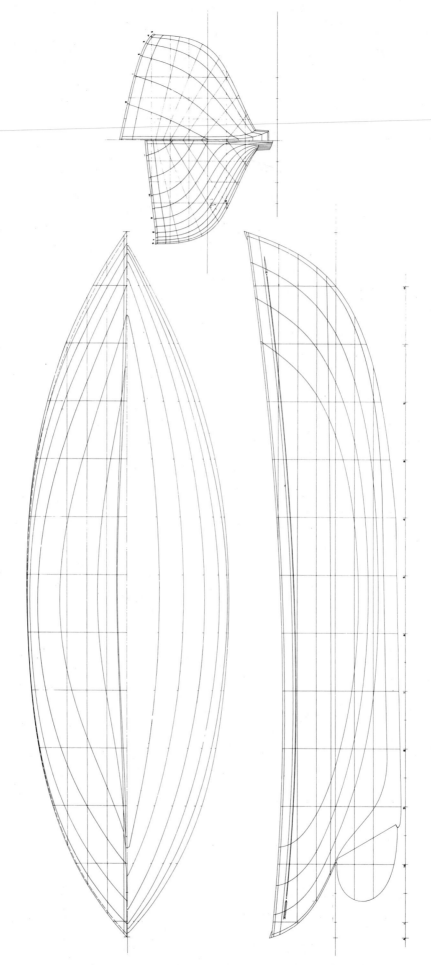

Saona's lines show that her hull is similar to Narwhal's, except that she has a deeper forefoot, a shallower keel, more beam, and shorter overhangs.

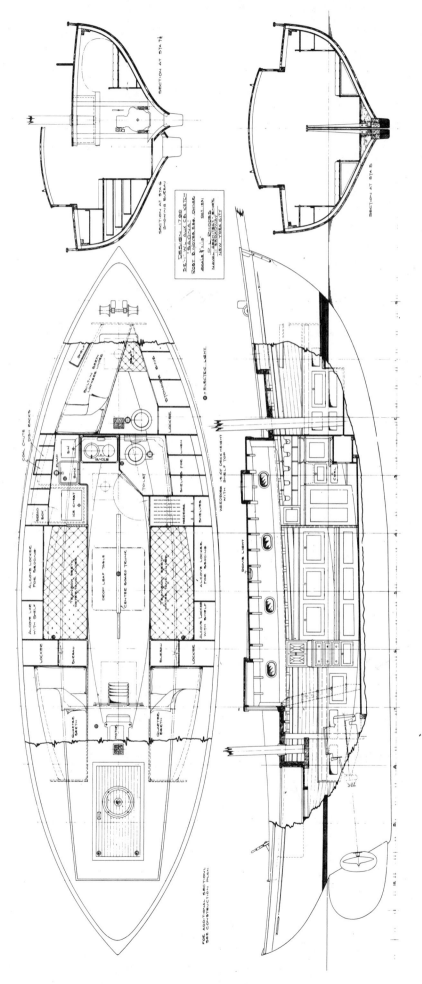

'Saona's accommodations are also a variation of those of 'Tidal Wave, but she has separate quarters for a paid hand.

Saona, later named *Lady Patty.* She might be considered a centerboard version of *Narwhal.* With a length of 39 feet overall and 32 feet on the waterline, *Saona* is similar in size to *Narwhal,* but she naturally draws less (her draft being 3 feet 9 inches with the board up), and her beam is 6 inches greater to provide similar sail-carrying power. Rhodes designed *Saona* for Robert B. Noyes in 1931, and she was built several years later by M.M. Davis & Son at Solomons, Maryland.

Her arrangement plan is quite similar to *Tidal Wave*'s, except that the fo'c's'le is planned for a paid hand. It is partitioned off from the main cabin and has its own head, bunk, and access hatch.

Saona looks like more of a cruiser than a racer, with her prominent forefoot, long keel, pointed stern, and ketch rig. Under the name *Lady Patty,* when owned by James W. Crawford, she raced for several years in the Southern Ocean Racing Circuit and was surprisingly successful, winning the 1951 Havana Race. Someone who knows her record related to me that "she beat boats she had no business beating." Her owner, later a recipient of the coveted Blue Water Medal, also sailed her to Hawaii in the 1953 Transpac Race and returned to the East Coast by way of San Francisco, the Galapagos Islands, and Panama.

During a homeward passage after the 1948 Havana Race, she was struck by an unusually strong squall at night. Carrying her jib and mizzen, she was knocked flat by the powerful blast. Unfortunately, a porthole had been left open, and the boat nearly sank. Crawford described the experience in *Yachting* in August 1961. He estimated that, if the ketch had not righted herself for two more minutes, she would have foundered. Little damage was done except to the sails, and Crawford called her an "exceptionally able" boat.

8

Ayesha and Alondra
Distinctive Centerboarders

Of all the different types of vessels Philip Rhodes designed, he is probably best known for his comfortable, fast oceangoing centerboarders. The first design of this kind to bring him notoriety was the yawl *Ayesha*, which finished third in her class in the 1932 Bermuda Race. Up until that time, it was rare for a centerboarder to compete, let alone finish in the money, in a distance offshore race. Her crew were lavish in their praise of her behavior in rugged conditions. As one report put it: "She had proved not only to handle perfectly at all times, but to be dry and comfortable, with a soft, easy motion in the toughest kind of going. Seasickness among the crew in the race was noticeable by its absence." Phil Rhodes was aboard *Ayesha* during the race, and naturally he was delighted with the boat's performance. The experience undoubtedly encouraged him to pursue the development of this type.

There was nothing new about offshore centerboarders, even at the time of *Ayesha*. One champion of the type was Ralph M. Munroe, a predecessor of Rhodes, and Phil knew his work well. As mentioned in Part One of this book, Phil had in the early days occasionally lunched with Henry Howard, owner of the famous Munroe-designed *Alice*, and it is certain-ly possible that some of Howard's enthusiasm for seagoing centerboard yachts could have rubbed off on him. At that time, however, Phil was a struggling young designer, so his earliest shoal-water boats really resulted from the particular needs of his clients. In the case of *Ayesha*, John Hogan, her original owner, wanted a boat that would be safe and comfortable at sea yet could be kept in a shallow harbor.

Although Phil had designed a number of centerboard cruisers prior to *Ayesha*, Hogan's yawl is usually considered the archetype of the shoal-draft ocean racer normally identified with Rhodes. In referring to a write-up of *Ayesha* in *Yachting* magazine (August 1932), William W. Robinson, *Yachting* editor and author of a series of articles entitled "Great Yacht Designers," wrote: "The analysis of her could almost be used as the text for describing a 'typical' Rhodes boat over the years." The 1932 article described *Ayesha*'s hull as follows: "Her lines and sections show clearly what a sweet craft she is, with firm yet easy sections, moderate deadrise, sweeping sheer, nicely proportioned ends and good freeboard. The buttocks and diagonals are unusually easy for a shoal, rather wide hull."

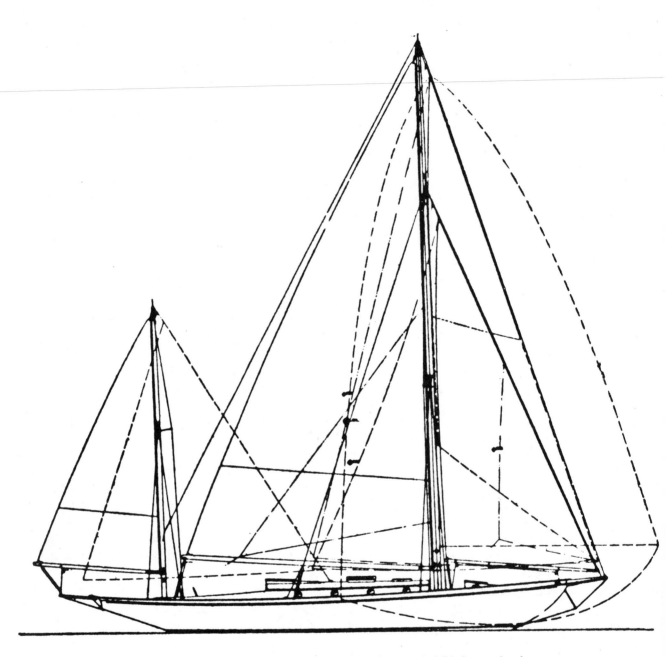

The sail plan of the 46-foot yawl Ayesha, *famous prototype of the typical Rhodes centerboard ocean racer.*
(Little Ships and Shoal Waters *by Maurice Griffiths)*

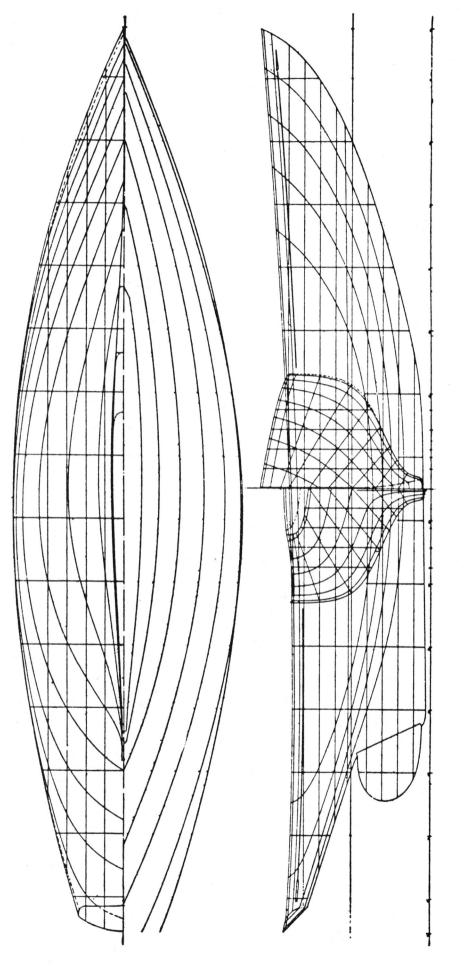

Ayesha's lines show an easy, seakindly hull with a good turn of speed. She has an angle of deadrise at the mid-section of about 26 degrees and straight buttocks aft that give her a long run. Her keel is a bit shallower than most subsequent Rhodes boats of this type.

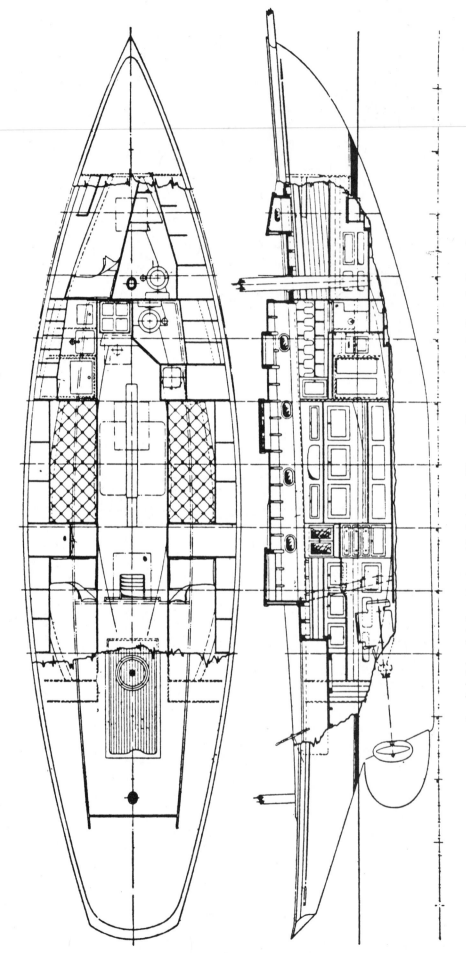

Ayesha's below-decks layout is almost identical to that of Saona, with two quarter berths, forward galley, and isolated fo'c's'le for a paid hand.

Ayesha *showing her stiffness in a 35-mile-per-hour breeze.* (Little Ships and Shoal Waters *by Maurice Griffiths*)

Unlike Munroe's extremely shallow boats, which were intended for real gunkholing and banks crawling, the ocean-racing centerboarders of Phil Rhodes have relatively prominent keels with reasonably deep outside ballast. The Rhodes boats are most likely abler ocean sailers, even though the Munroe craft made a number of successful offshore and coastal passages, for a boat like *Ayesha* is bound to have greater ultimate stability for a given weight of ballast. It is interesting to note that most of the Rhodes centerboarders of the ocean-racing type that followed *Ayesha* had keels of even greater depth. The famous yawl *Carina* (Chapter 28), which might be considered the culmination of Rhodes centerboarders, has a keel deep enough to provide positive stability up to 128 degrees of heel, with only 34 percent of her displacement in ballast.

Ayesha was built by the Henry Nevins yard at City Island, New York, in 1932. Her dimensions are 46 feet LOA, 33 feet 2½ inches LWL, 11 feet 8½ inches beam, and 4 feet 2½ inches draft. She carries 925 square feet of sail area in a yawl rig that is fairly well spread out fore and aft by generous overhangs that are extended with a short bowsprit and boomkin. *Ayesha* is a stiff boat, and this is verified by a photograph of her shown in Maurice Griffiths' book *Little Ships and Shoal Waters* that shows her under unreefed working sails in a 35-knot wind. Yet she was also noted for her light-weather performance.

The layout below is arranged for privacy. The forward cabin, intended for a paid hand, is completely separated from the main cabin, with its only entrance through a booby hatch on the foredeck. Abaft

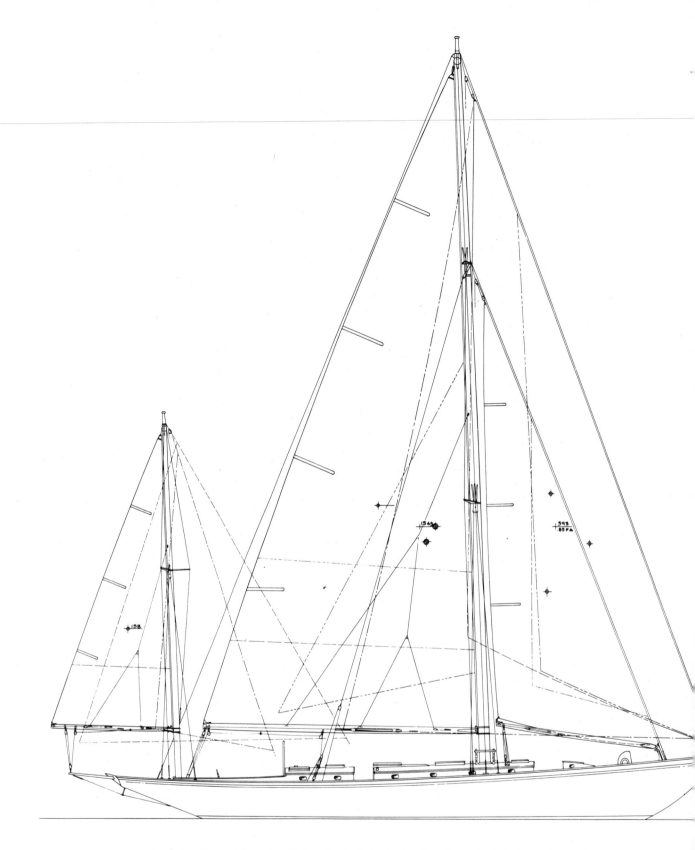

Alondra's sail plan differs primarily from Ayesha's in that there is no bowsprit, the mainmast is stepped farther aft, and the booms are shorter. There is also more space between the staysail stay and headstay for tacking a genoa jib. Alondra is 57 feet 6 inches long.

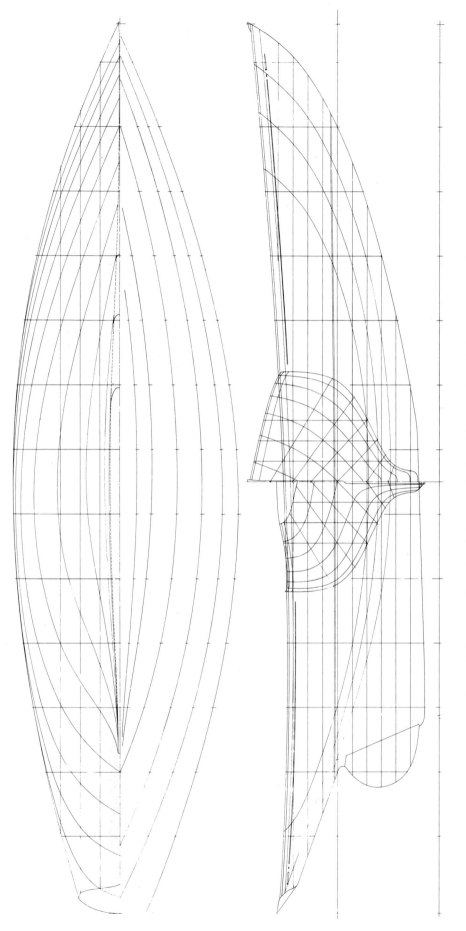

Alondra's lines are similar to Ayesha's, except that her keel is more salient, which may account partly for her superior windward ability. Her bow is a bit more snubbed, and this appearance is accentuated by her lack of a bowsprit.

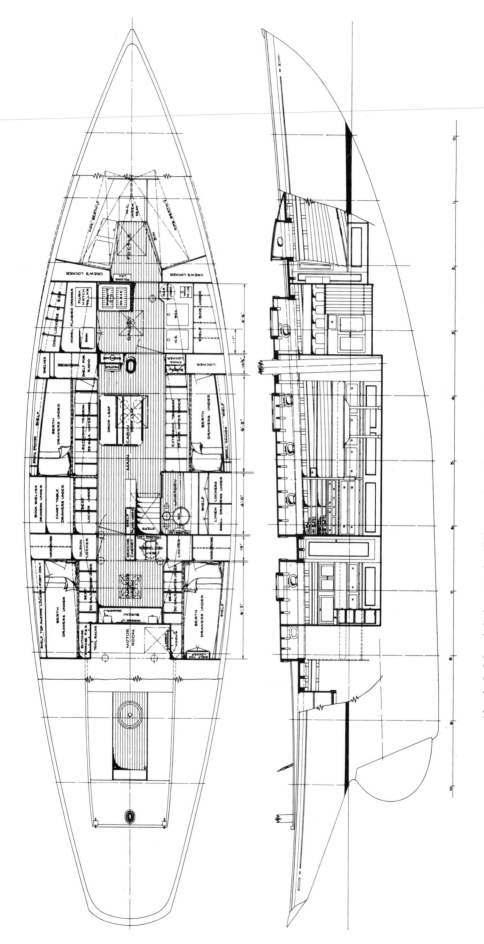

Alondra's below-decks layout trades off the convenience of an after companionway for privacy in the owner's stateroom aft. A curious specification is the storage areas for suitcases.

Alondra, *as Caribbee,* beating under her well-stretched genoa, which helped her win many important races. *(Courtesy of Mystic Seaport)*

the fo'c's'le is the galley and enclosed head, and still farther aft is the saloon, with two transom berths and two quarter berths. About the only thing lacking is a chart table near the companionway; for some reason this was seldom an important consideration in those days, even on moderately large boats.

The lines for the yawl *Alondra* were drawn in 1936, and she was labeled "*Ayesha* type" in the Cox & Stevens design index. She was ordered by Robert B. Noyes, *Ayesha*'s owner at that time, who very much liked Rhodes' concept of centerboard ocean racers, but wanted a larger, more comfortable boat. Both hulls are very similar in form, except that *Alondra*'s keel is deeper. The newer boat also has a deeper rudder, which better assures that it will work well at high angles of heel. Like her predecessor, *Alondra* was built by Henry Nevins, and her measurements are 57 feet 6 inches by 42 feet 7 inches by 14 feet by 6 feet 3½ inches.

A comparison of her accommodations with those of *Ayesha* shows many improvements, most of which were possible because of *Alondra*'s greater size. The larger boat has a private owner's cabin aft with its own head; there is room for a good-sized chart table; ample beam allows berths and sliding transoms in the main saloon; the forward galley is much larger; and the fo'c's'le can be entered from below as well as from a booby hatch on deck. An interesting feature is her separate cabin trunks. This allows one to enter her companionway, located amidships, without having to climb up on the cabin top, and it allows a shorter companionway ladder. Another advantage is that it permits full-width deck beams nearly amidships, which strengthens the hull.

Alondra became most famous under the name *Caribbee*, when she was owned by Carleton Mitchell. In 1947, Phil designed a 58-foot clipper-bowed centerboard ketch for Mitchell, but cost estimates for building the boat proved exorbitant; so at the suggestion of Henry Nevins, Mitchell bought *Alondra*, which was available at a much lower price and came very close to the kind of boat he wanted at that time.

Alondra's original rig was more modern than that of *Ayesha*, with a large foretriangle, a stemhead rig, and no bowsprit, but Carleton Mitchell has indicated that when he bought the boat, the rig had become out of date and was inefficient for racing. He said: "The main problem was lack of stiffness of the

rig, and very unhandy leads of sheets, etc. The headstay sagged badly, the floating spreaders caused the mast to snake when [the boat was] driven in a seaway, and the backstay arrangement made it impossible to carry a mizzen staysail until almost dead off the wind, when it was ineffective." Mitchell intended to do some serious racing in this boat, so he took his problems to Rod Stephens, the acknowledged expert on yacht rigging. Stephens specified changes, including the addition of some hull strapping, which enabled the rigging to be set up very taut. Some other changes were: new sheet leads, a redesigned headstay, and a quick-release fitting on the forestaysail stay. While never slow previously, *Caribbee* was decidedly faster after the expert tuning by Stephens, especially when beating to windward in a breeze.

During the five years that Mitchell owned *Caribbee*, he raced her frequently and very successfully. She was the top boat in the Southern Ocean Racing Conference in 1952 and 1953. She raced across the North Atlantic in 1952 and took fleet second (first to finish and first in class). At Cowes Week that same year, she won 3 races out of 4 starts. In addition, she was cruised extensively in American waters and abroad. Of *Caribbee*, Mitchell has written: "I believe I may objectively say no boat of her size and type during a similar period has given more service or pleasure to her owner. . . .."

Caribbee was a large part of the inspiration for her owner's next boat, the Sparkman & Stephens-designed centerboarder *Finisterre*, which won the Bermuda Race three times in a row, and Mitchell has often been asked why he did not have Rhodes design her. Mitchell explains that, although he greatly admired the hull designs of Rhodes, he had developed a lot of faith in the rigging expertise and racing know-how of Rod Stephens, and primarily for that reason he decided on the design firm of Sparkman & Stephens. Mitchell says, "I am sure Phil Rhodes understood my reasoning, and I am happy to say our friendship never flagged. It was Phil who chose me to be navigator of *Weatherly* for the America's Cup trials of 1958. I think Phil was the best designer of strictly cruising, live-aboard, sailing craft of this century, and certainly the wide range of successful vessels he produced are a monument to his genius."

9

Nixie and Some Descendants
Phil's Own Boat

In 1932 Phil Rhodes designed the little 22-foot-waterline sloop *Nixie* for his own use. Her designed displacement was 4,025 pounds, considerably less than that of typical small American cruisers of her day, and it might be said that she was ahead of her time in this regard. In fact, Phil wrote in 1958 that *Nixie* had the same characteristics of the light-displacement boats of the 1950s. Being a modest man, however, he was quick to add that "there was nothing new about it even then [in the 1930s]."

In writing on the subject of light displacement for a chapter of *The Expert's Book of Boating* (published in 1959), Rhodes opined that light displacement for large cruisers would not catch on in the United States, for American owners insisted on heavy accommodations, engines, and tankage. He wrote: "These things [luxurious accommodations and heavy gear] and light displacement do not go hand in hand." Of course, as one looks at today's IOR ocean-racing fleet, it might seem that Rhodes' prophecy about the popularity of light-displacement designs has been proven wrong, but these modern boats are not real cruisers, and the emphasis seems to be primarily on speed, with considerable expense to comfort, handiness, and seakindliness. At any

rate, Rhodes seemed to feel that light displacement was most suitable for small cruisers, since they seldom were heavily loaded and were not taken on distant cruises.

Rhodes wrote about his thinking behind *Nixie* in the January 1933 issue of *Yachting*.

In analyzing my own present requirements, I decided that a small boat, smart and handy for day sailing and offering sufficient accommodations for semi-serious cruising, would be the answer. Chief among the conditions governing this decision was the mandatory assertion of my three youngsters, the oldest being seven, that they constitute a permanent fixture in the crew. Hence the small boat, one which I can at all times manage with one hand while I chastise, or defend myself, with the other. It should have a small rig and properly a light displacement. A centerboarder, with its ability to explore the inlets, was a temptation, but the centerboard trunk would interfere with the interior, and a fin keel with all ballast outside would give a longer range of stability and consequently greater safety for the above-mentioned crew. Finally, I wanted a boat that could be built economically, in keeping with the spirit of the times; not a cheaply built boat, for there is a difference. Out of this emerged the *Nixie*. She is

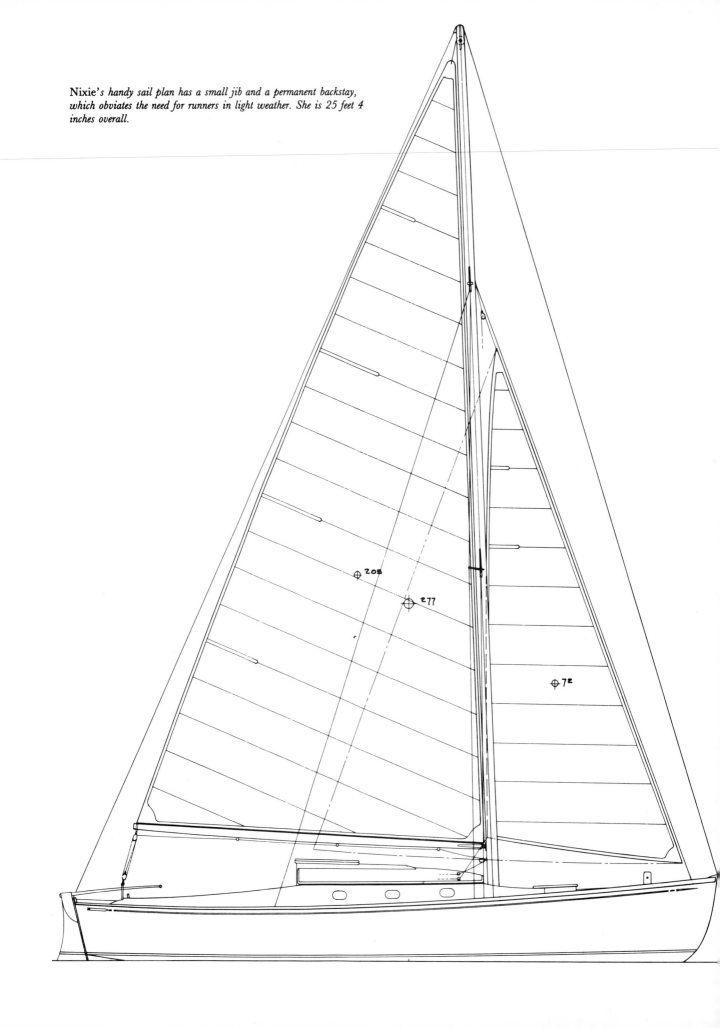

*Nixie's handy sail plan has a small jib and a permanent backstay,
which obviates the need for runners in light weather. She is 25 feet 4
inches overall.*

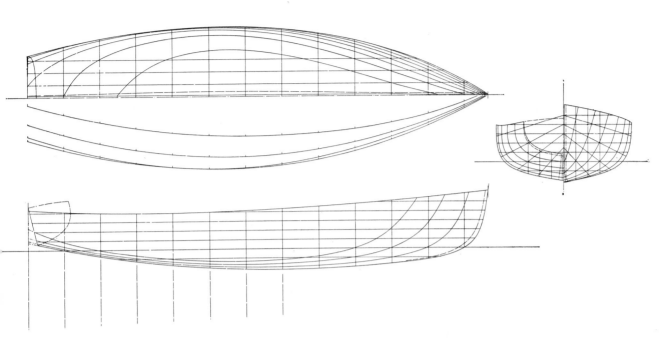

Above: Nixie *has little of her hull under water. The full stern and fine bow, uncharacteristic of the typical Rhodes heavy ocean racer, is appropriate for this boat with her small size, light displacement, and lack of stern overhang.* (Yachting, *January 1933*) **Below:** Nixie's *accommodation plans. The inboard profile plan also shows the keel, a trapezoidal fin that, coincidentally, is identical in profile to that of the later Lapworth-designed Cal 40. The rectangular drop slides shown in the section drawing are the sensible type that will not easily fall out during a knockdown.*

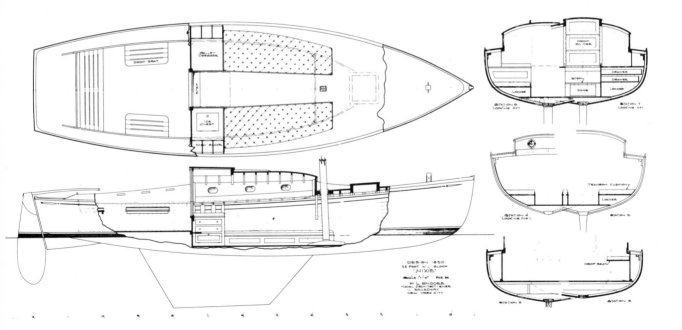

Nixie *slipping along under sail. As Phil Rhodes put it, she is ''making no fuss and leaving none.'' (Courtesy of Mystic Seaport)*

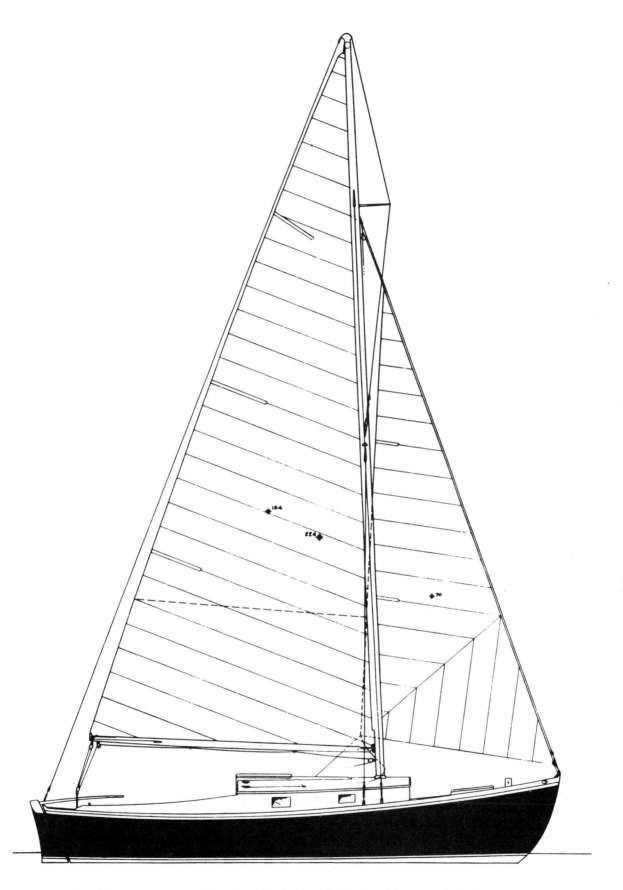

The 20-foot 6-inch Dater's sail plan is even handier than Nixie's, *since it has no running backstays.* (Your New Boat *by the Editors of* Yachting)

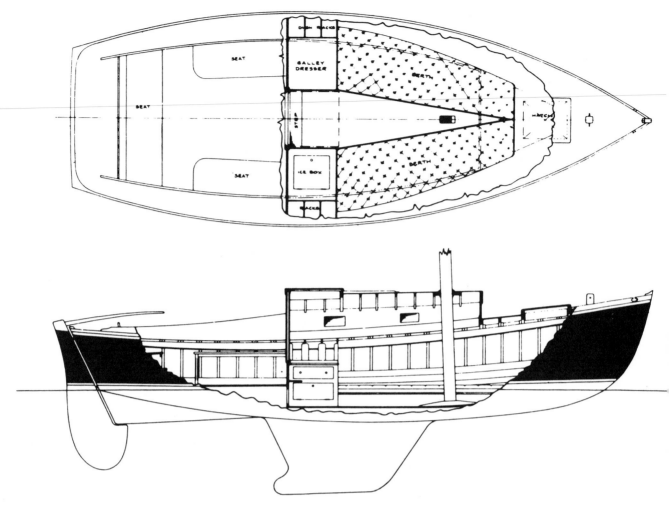

The Dater's accommodation profile shows certain construction details and a Star-boat-like keel. An interesting feature is that the keel is easily removable for shipping or inspection. (Your New Boat *by the Editors of* Yachting)

25 feet 4 inches overall, 22 feet on the waterline, with a molded beam of 7 feet 6 inches and a draft of 4 feet. The sail area amounts to 277 square feet.

Nixie's lines drawings show a very shallow hull with little deadrise and a fairly large radius at the turn of the bilge. Her stern is rather full, but the entrance is sharp, with a slight hollow in the lower waterlines forward. The bow is snubbed, but it seems to balance the stern, and the lack of overhang provides a long waterline for speed. There is no keel shown on the lines drawing, but the accommodation plan shows a trapezoidal type of fin. The boat proved extremely fast and maneuverable. She is the only sailboat he ever owned, with the exception of a Dyer Dink (hull #1).

The cabin is small, but there are two comfortable berths and an adequate galley. It appears that a

head might be placed under the forward hatch. Although the cockpit is too large for maximum safety at sea, it is roomy and comfortable for daysailing, and *Nixie* was not intended for offshore work. Furthermore, Phil felt that the deep cockpit offered more security for his young children. The plans show hand-grip holes in the coamings to help the children hang on during a knockdown or in rough waters. The wide sole is not far above the waterline, and this allowed water to enter the cockpit through the scuppers, but Phil solved this problem, when it arose, by plugging the scuppers with soft-pine stoppers. A somewhat distinctive feature is the coamings forward between the cabin trunk and forward hatch. The coamings are really extensions of the cabin trunk, and Phil wrote that they make the house appear lower than it really is. They also protect the forward portholes from water on deck, and the space

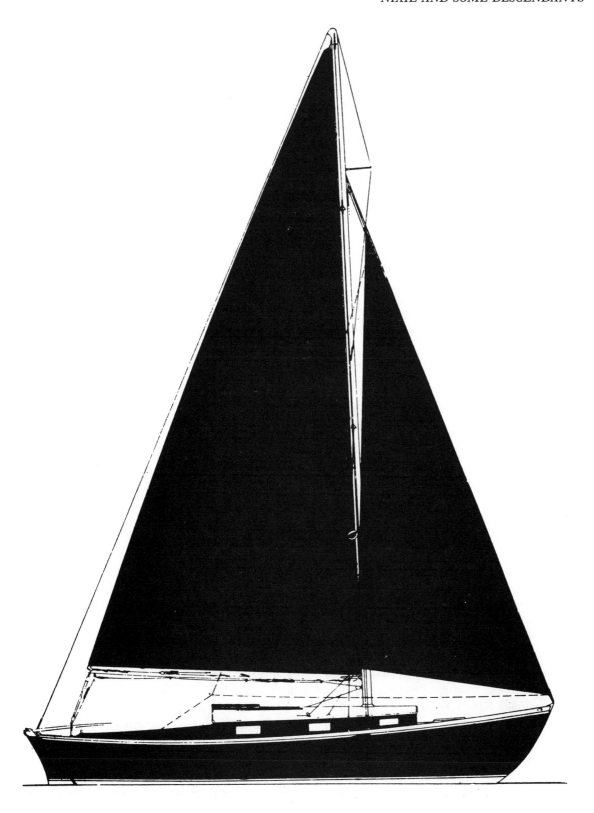

The Caller, at 27 feet 6 inches overall, is a larger version of the Dater with a small inboard auxiliary. (Your New Boat *by the Editors of* Yachting)

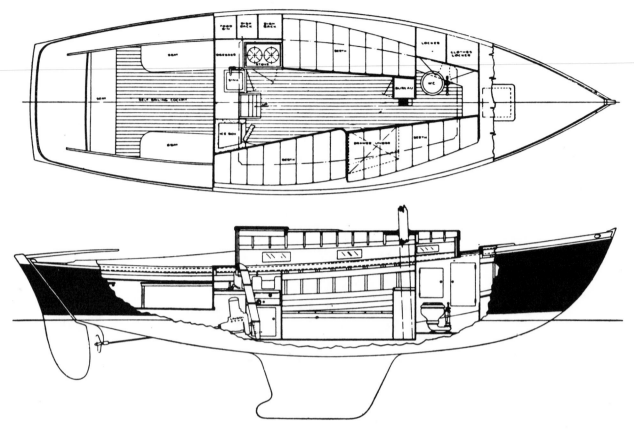

The Caller is nicely arranged below, with a real galley, three bunks, and a semiprivate head. (Your New Boat *by the Editors of* Yachting)

between the coamings makes a handy stowage area for coiled halyards.

Nixie paid a visit to Gibson Island, Maryland, in the fall of 1932, and she made a great impression on the local yachtsmen. Phil wrote in *Yachting* (January 1933): "I tried her out as did almost everyone else frequenting that yachting center. I am told that several of my friends shamefully neglected their own boats to sail *Nixie*. During the month she was there they had ample opportunity to test her under almost all conditions up to and including a 57-mile (by the anemometer) squall. She is not intended for such stuff and the only interesting feature of this latter episode is that nothing happened except that after dousing the mainsail she clawed off the lee shore under her jib. All who have sailed her liked her immensely and I trust I do no violence to proper restraint when I say that I believe she fulfills exactly the express conditions governing her design . . . ."

Some years later, two well-known stock boats were developed from the *Nixie* design. They were the

Dater and the Caller classes, both designed for and marketed by the Donald B. Abbott Company of Mamaroneck, New York. The Dater is only 20 feet 6 inches long overall and 18 feet on the waterline, but she has the same beam as *Nixie* (7 feet 6 inches). A bolted-on iron fin keel, which is quite similar in shape to a Star boat's keel, gives her a draft of 3 feet 8 inches. The outboard rudder is somewhat unconventional in that the lower part, extending below a shallow skeg, is semi-balanced so that the water flow offers some assistance in turning the helm. Accommodations are similar to those of *Nixie*, and a three-quarter sloop rig carries 222 square feet of sail area. The Dater is said to be lively, maneuverable, and fast.

The larger Caller measures 27 feet 6 inches LOA and 22 feet 6 inches on the waterline. She has a beam of 8 feet 6 inches, draws 4 feet 6 inches, and carries 365 square feet of sail on a three-quarter rig. Her bow has a bit more overhang, which enhances her looks, and the larger size allows three bunks, a semiprivate arrangement for the head, and a full built-in galley. There is a doghouse version of the Caller, which provides 6-foot headroom, but the standard low cabin trunk is more pleasing aesthetically.

The Dater is a little small for an inboard engine, and when she was first built during World War II, gasoline was far more scarce than it is now, but the postwar Callers were fitted with small auxiliaries, such as 5 horsepower Lauson motors. Except for the propeller and shaft, the underwater configuration of the Caller is almost identical to that of the Dater.

The Caller and Dater classes were outgrowths of the 1932 creation that Phil Rhodes best summed up himself: ''A smart, safe little hooker for afternoon sailing and old enough to stay out at night. She is a sweet sailing little outfit, making no fuss and leaving none.''

10

Mimi II
Big Boat in Miniature

The most appealing characteristic of the 24-foot sloop *Mimi II* is that she is a very handsome big boat in miniature form. She has the big boat look of grace, power, and seakindliness combined with small boat handiness and daintiness. Perhaps she could be considered to represent the direct opposite of a prevalent trend in today's design philosophy. A great many modern racing-cruisers might be thought of as scaled-up dinghies, but *Mimi* is more like a traditional ocean racer scaled down.

When I was a youngster living on my family's boat in the harbor at Gibson Island, Maryland, I would gaze longingly at this lovely little sloop, which was moored nearby. She was my ideal boat at the time, and I dreamed of owning her or a sister boat. Her original owner, Dr. Roger P. Batchelor, has since become a valued friend. He is extremely well informed on subjects relating to naval architecture and the history of yachting, and at one time he wanted to become a naval architect. Dr. Batchelor was a Rhodes admirer and they became good friends after he asked Rhodes to design *Mimi II*. She was designed in 1932 and, according to Dr. Batchelor, the commission was most welcome, for Phil was going through a lean period at that time.

Mimi was inspired by a 23-foot centerboard sloop that Phil had designed for H.H. Larkin back in 1928. Dr. Batchelor was very much taken with her looks when he saw her plans in *The Rudder* magazine. The doctor and Phil decided to make *Mimi* just a little larger and to give her a slightly deeper keel without a centerboard. In comparison to the Larkin boat, *Mimi II* appears to be more able and seakindly, with her well-ballasted full keel drawing 4 feet, deeper bilge with more deadrise, and slightly greater freeboard. She is a bit roomier below and has a larger, deeper rudder for better steering control.

As was customary when Rhodes took on a new commission, every detail was thoroughly discussed, and numerous preliminary drawings were made. Phil wanted to be absolutely certain that the boat was right before building was begun. Evidently Dr. Batchelor was well satisfied, for he enjoyed her for more than 40 years, and he had the confidence to handle her when he was well into his eighties.

Dr. Batchelor usually sailed her singlehanded. I was fortunate enough to accompany him once and had a most enjoyable sail, which left me greatly impressed with the little sloop's performance. She seemed fairly fast and powerful for a small boat, car-

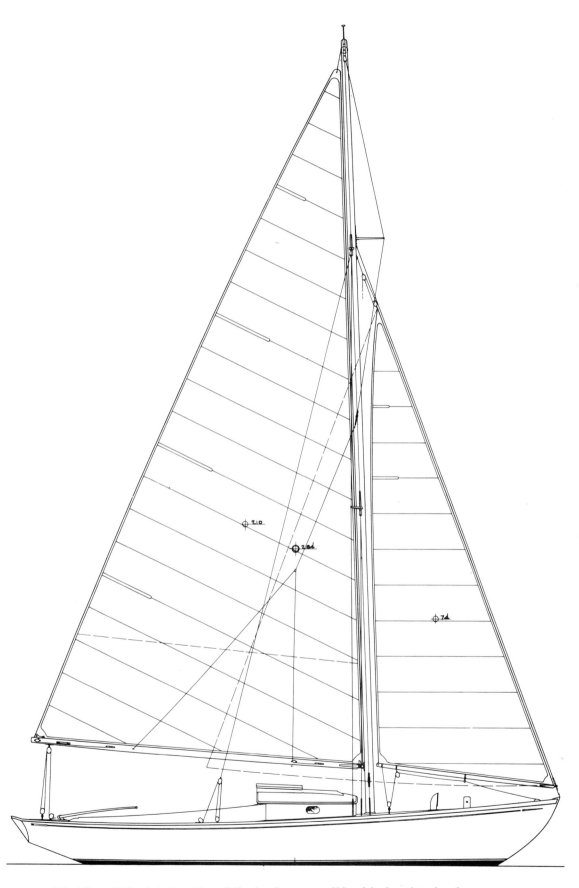

Mimi II, *at 24 feet, is petite, yet her sail plan is quite generous. Although her boom is too long for a permanent backstay and runners are needed, she is easy to handle with her self-tending jib on a bar traveler, which doesn't become fouled as often as a track with a slide.*

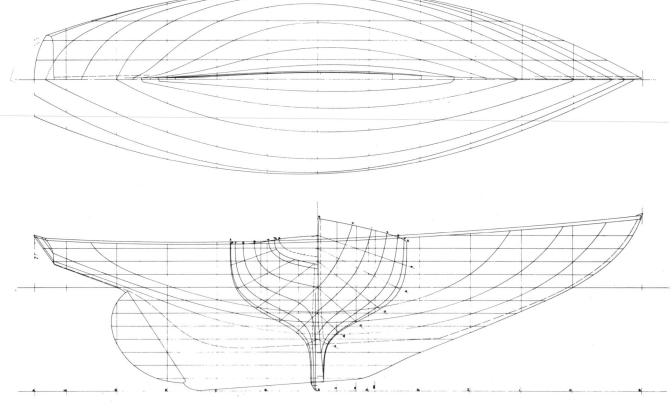

The curvaceous lines of Mimi II *show a boat that seems considerably larger than she is.*

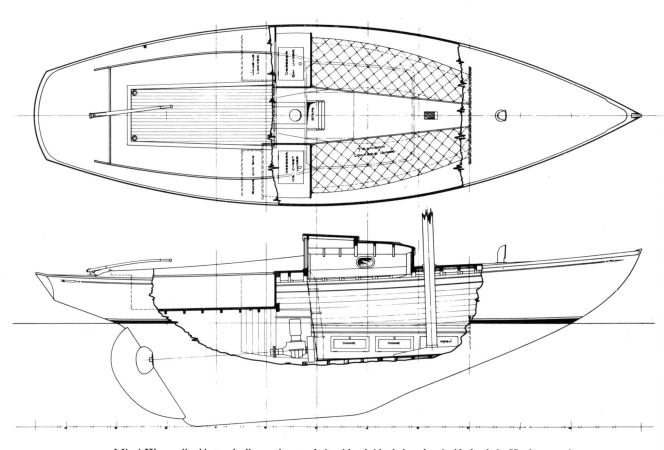

Mimi II's *small cabin trunk allows a large cockpit with a bridgedeck and a sizable foredeck. Headroom under the trunk is 4 feet 4 inches.*

Left: Mimi II *working to windward in light air. (Courtesy of Dr. Roger P. Batchelor)* **Below:** *Dr. Batchelor singlehanding his beloved* Mimi II. *(Courtesy of Mystic Seaport)*

ried way through a chop, and held a steady course. She was not as responsive nor as quick in stays as a more modern boat of her size, but she was gentle, consistent, and had an easy motion.

In many respects, *Mimi II* is very suitable for singlehanding. She is a handy size, the sail area is only 284 square feet, the helm can be left briefly without the need of securing it, and the boat's motion is not so quick as to throw the singlehander off balance. Although the rig has running backstays, they need not be set up in moderate weather. The jib is self-tending, while the 210-square-foot mainsail allows ample boat speed and reasonable balance under main alone. An indication of her easy handling (and, I might add, her owner's considerable skill) is that Dr. Batchelor nearly always picked up his mooring under full sail, despite having an auxiliary motor.

With an overall length of 24 feet, a waterline length of only 18 feet, and a modest 7-foot beam, *Mimi II* could not be expected to have much in the way of accommodations. Her cabin trunk has been kept small to allow for a large cockpit. Nevertheless, the cabin has room for two comfortable bunks and a small galley with icebox. The deep hull allows ample sitting headroom without the need of a high cabin trunk.

Although Dr. Batchelor's advanced age influenced him to sell his boat, it can certainly be said that few sailors have stayed afloat for such a long period of time. (Indeed, he often remarked that he would keep sailing until the Coast Guard declared him a "menace to navigation.") Had it not been for the steadiness and predictability of *Mimi II*, Dr. Batchelor might have retired from sailing much earlier than he did.

In 1982, *Chantey,* the boat that inspired the creation of *Mimi II*, was still going strong. Her owner, Stephan R. Allmon, wrote me that he sailed her 40 days during the summer and that she was in perfect shape.

11

Maruffa
A Classic Yawl

Henry B. Babson of Chicago was one of many Rhodes repeat clients. Phil had designed some small rowing dinghies for him, and then in 1934, the well-known yachtsman came to Rhodes for a large cruising yawl. There were a number of requirements for this boat, foremost among them that she be a comfortable, seaworthy cruiser, but with enough speed to enter ocean races with a reasonable expectation of doing well. His other requirements were: comfortable accommodations for six, a deckhouse, a saloon unencumbered with berths, and a draft of no more than 8½ feet.

Babson approached a handful of other designers with the same requirements, but in the end, he chose the Rhodes design. Named *Maruffa,* she evidently served Babson well, for after a year of ownership, he indicated that if he were to do it again, he would make the same choice. (His later Rhodes commissions included the Great Lakes 30, the racing yawl *Tahuna* (Chapter 20), and the first of the famous Rhodes 77s, which he named *Maaroufa* (Chapter 24).)

Regrettably, *Maruffa* met her end not long ago on a round-the-world cruise.

This fine yawl was 67½ feet long overall and 49 feet 7 inches on the waterline. Her beam was 15 feet 3 inches, while she had a draft of 8½ feet. She was sturdily constructed by the F.F. Pendleton yard in Wiscasset, Maine. Her planking was of 1¾-inch Philippine mahogany over white oak frames, 14 inches on centers. Her hull was strengthened by diagonal strapping and bronze floors in way of the mast step.

Although not designed primarily as a racing boat, she was quite similar to a few boats Phil designed around that time for ocean racing. A case in point is a 47-foot-waterline yawl that Phil designed in 1933 for a contest under the newly proposed Cruising Club of America Rule. This yawl has more draft than *Maruffa,* but she is strikingly similar in hull form and rig. Both boats have moderate, seakindly hulls with particularly easy, smooth-flowing lines, and fairly symmetrical forms. Phil was never known for creating rule-beaters, for he was primarily interested in producing wholesome and attractive designs, but *Maruffa* and the contest yawl rated reasonably well by virtue of their fairly short load waterlines, ample beam and freeboard, and generous displacement. One minor feature that seems preferable in *Maruffa* is that her counter was less flat

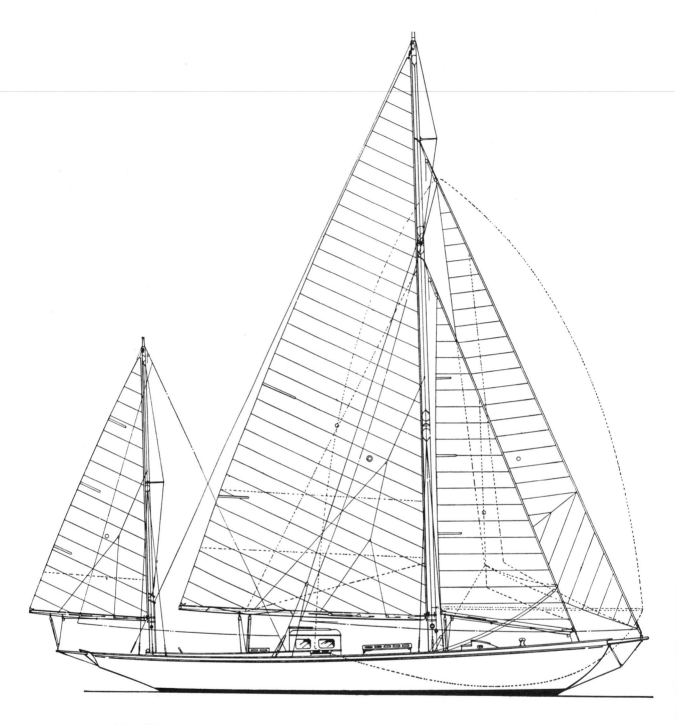

Maruffa's *original rig. Later she was given a masthead rig for greater speed in light airs. She is 67½ feet* overall. (Sail and Power *by Uffa Fox*)

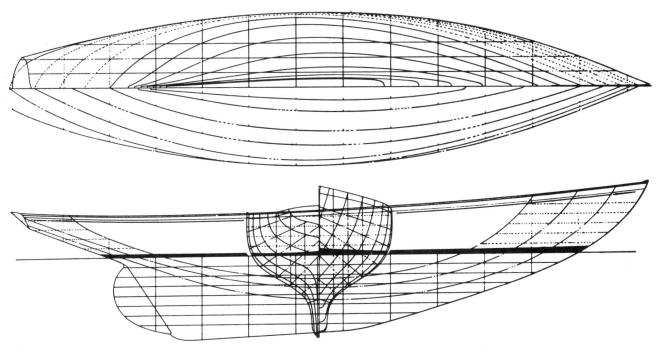

By today's standards Maruffa *was a rather narrow boat with a moderately long keel and fairly straight* waterlines amidships. *Her behavior in rugged conditions was relatively docile.*

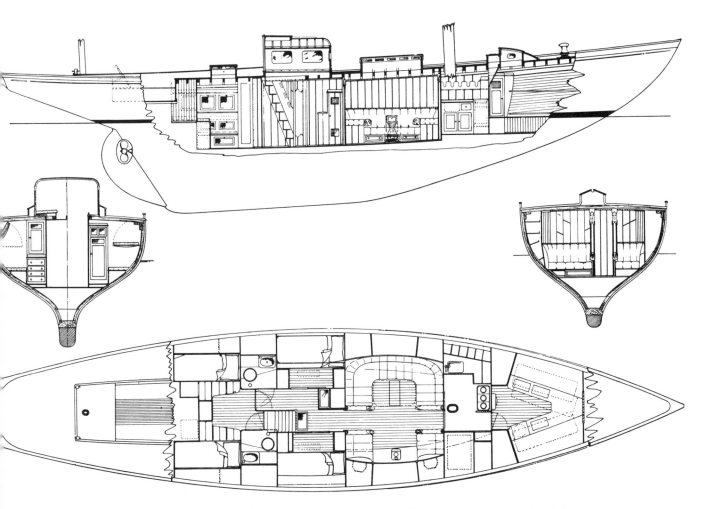

Maruffa's *arrangement offers an unusual amount of privacy and is homelike, in that the saloon is not intended for sleeping. The high deckhouse serves not only as a sitting and navigation area, but also as a shelter for the companionway, which is subject to spray in its farther-forward-than-normal location.* (Sail and Power *by Uffa Fox)*

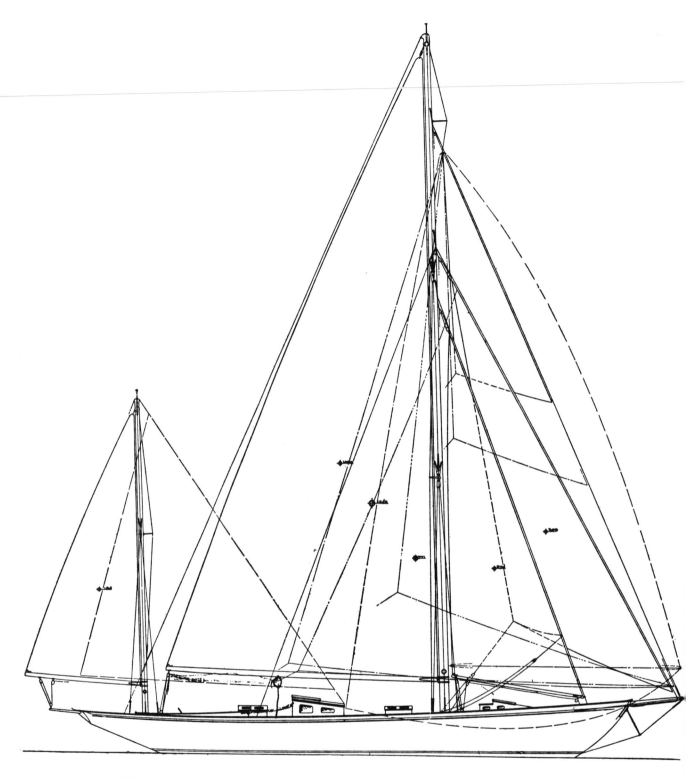

This 63-foot 4-inch yawl is a forerunner to Maruffa *and designed to the then newly devised CCA rule. There is little difference in the rigs of the two yawls, except that the CCA boat can carry three headsails at a time.* (Yachting)

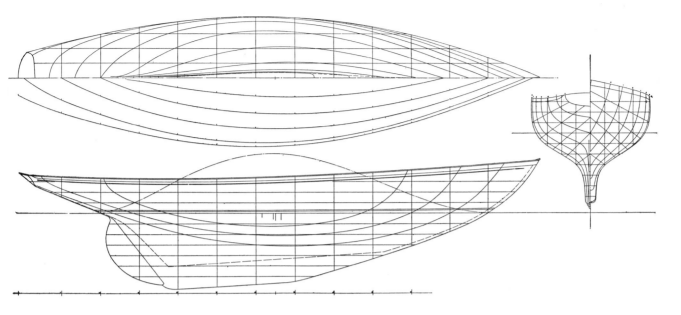

The CCA yawl's hull is similar to Maruffa's, *except that she has a deeper keel and flatter sections under the counter.* (Yachting)

than the other yawl's, and this minimized slamming in a seaway.

Maruffa's layout below was unusual in that she had more staterooms than had most boats of this size, and the saloon was strictly a sitting area without sleeping arrangements. One side of the saloon had a U-shaped settee around a table, and there was a particularly cozy arrangement on the opposite side, where there were two facing upholstered seats around a heating stove. The plans show some elaborate carvings in the saloon. Abaft this area were the owner's stateroom, two enclosed heads, and two guest staterooms, while the galley and crew's quarters were forward. A less obtrusive deckhouse/cockpit shelter might be desirable for aesthetic reasons and to improve the helmsman's visibility, but as it was, the shelter was fairly narrow and quite far forward of the wheel, which minimized obstruction of the helmsman's vision.

The original sail plan shows that much of *Maruffa*'s 2,078 square feet of canvas was carried in the mainsail, while the headsails were relatively small. Later, however, she was given a more powerful masthead rig. The short bowsprit extended the base of the foretriangle, opened up the slot between the two forward stays, and provided a means of catting an anchor. With the jib downhaul, shown in the detailed drawings of the running rigging, it was not

absolutely necessary for a crew member to venture onto the bowsprit when the jib was lowered. These detailed drawings also show how many jobs can be done with simple tackles rather than with powerful, expensive winches. (Nowadays, we are becoming so dependent on winches that, as one wag put it, "We'll soon need a two-speed self-tailer to pick up our sandwich.")

Maruffa had a rather unusual (for her time) engine installation in that her 4-cylinder DM-186 Buda diesel was above her propeller shaft and connected to it with V-belts. As noted designer/author Uffa Fox

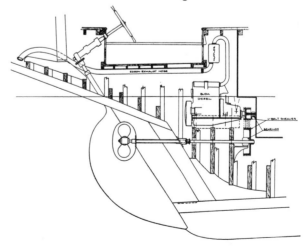

Maruffa's *auxiliary engine installation showing the V-belt reduction drive and high, looped exhaust.* (The Yachtsman, *December 1935*)

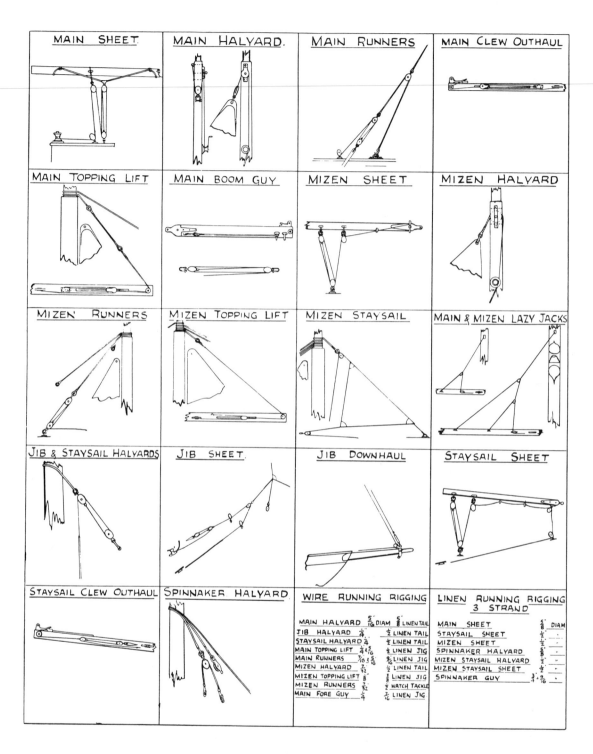

Some details of Maruffa's *running rigging. Have we forgotten today that tackles are often a satisfactory and in-expensive substitute for winches?* (Sail and Power *by Uffa Fox*)

Maruffa *sailing close-hauled. She has a fine ''bone in her teeth'' but is not pushing too much water. (Photo by James McVie)*

pointed out (and also Rhodes office literature), there are a number of advantages to this arrangement:

"(1) This type [of drive] suffers less from misalignment than any other. (2) It is noiseless. (3) Should the propeller strike anything, there is enough flexibility to absorb the shock and not transmit it through the crank shaft to the engine, and (4) No arrangement so far designed gives less overall length." Another point is that the arrangement allows a horizontal shaft without the need to bury the engine deep within the bilge. The exhaust shows a high loop under the bridgedeck. Unlike some modern boats, *Maruffa* probably never took water into her engine through the exhaust outlet.

Maruffa was owned and sailed extensively for many years by John Graham of Seattle, Washington. He raced her quite successfully, and her good showings include a class second in the 1959 Transpac. She did particularly well in the Swiftsure Race over a number of years, setting a course record, winning overall, and being first boat to finish several times. In 1964 and 1965, Graham sailed *Maruffa* to the Mediterranean and back, a cruise that covered some 29,000 miles. On her return passage she sailed the more than 2,000 miles from the Cape Verde Islands to Antigua in 10 days and six hours. Not bad for a heavy seagoer designed in 1934.

In the early 1970s she was used for sail training and for oceanographic research. One of her missions for the Woods Hole Oceanographic Institution was the recording of whale sounds in the North Atlantic near Sable Island. She also took part in the Bermuda to Newport, Rhode Island, Tall Ships Race, which was held to commemorate the United States Bicentennial in 1976.

The last word on *Maruffa* is that she was wrecked in 1979 at South Island, New Zealand, during a world cruise. At the beginning of a passage from New Zealand to Australia, she ran into heavy weather off the Foveaux Straits. When running for shelter, *Maruffa* grounded on a rocky shore and was soon battered beyond repair. Although the crew was able to save itself, one man's leg was severed when it became caught between the pounding hull and a rock. It was a tragic end to the long, successful career of a classic yawl.

12

The Minneford Cutter and Little Sister
Two Transom-Sterners

In the depression-struck early Thirties, Cox & Stevens and other design firms producing huge yachts experienced very difficult going. It became necessary to concentrate on commercial work and to produce smaller yachts, which were affordable to more people. Also, there was a gradual increase in the number of standardized stock designs partly because they could be produced more inexpensively. Phil Rhodes was taken on by Cox & Stevens to extend the firm's business into the small boat field, and one of his earliest designs after officially joining the company was a small stock auxiliary cutter for the Minneford Yacht Yard of City Island, New York.

Designed in 1935, the Minneford cutter is a husky cruiser measuring 32 feet 9 inches by 27 feet by 10 feet by 4 feet 10 inches. Rhodes and Minneford made every effort to keep the construction as inexpensive as possible, but at no sacrifice to strength or hull shapeliness. The boat has a seakindly form with her short ends, moderately slack bilges, long keel, and ample freeboard with sprightly sheer.

Phil Rhodes was not really partial to any one type of stern, and he claimed that any type could be efficient and seaworthy if properly designed, yet on smart sailing cruisers he seems to have used relative-

ly few transom sterns with outboard keel-attached rudders. The Minneford cutter, however, certainly shows his skill in handling this type. Her profile shows a nicely raked transom handsomely bowed and with a generous crown. It appears to have a wineglass shape that will cause little drag when the quarter wave is elevated. The outboard rudder is beautifully shaped, and even if it doesn't conform to the most modern ideas in rudder shapes, it is deep for effective steering and has generous area abaft the propeller for good control under power.

The deep bilges, ample freeboard, and considerable cabin-top crown allow six feet of headroom below without the need for a high cabin trunk, and this greatly enhances the boat's appearance. She sleeps four, and the two forward bunks seem to be pipe berths that lift up so that sails or other gear can be stowed in lockers beneath. The enclosed head is aft, where it is handy from the cockpit, but the trouble with this arrangement is that it takes away space that could be used for the galley or a chart table. The galley opposite the head is quite complete, however, and counter space is gained with a flush cover that fits over the sink.

The cutter has plenty of sail area, 738 square feet,

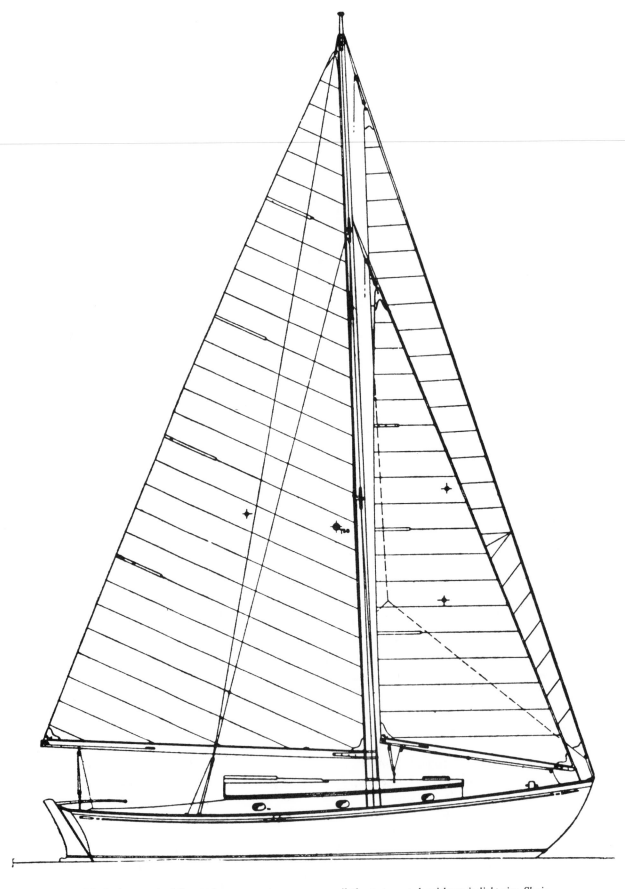

The husky, seagoing Minneford cutter was given a generous sail plan to prevent sluggishness in light airs. She is 32 feet 9 inches overall. (The Rudder)

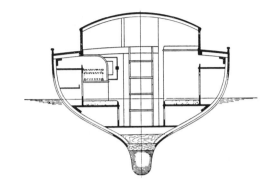

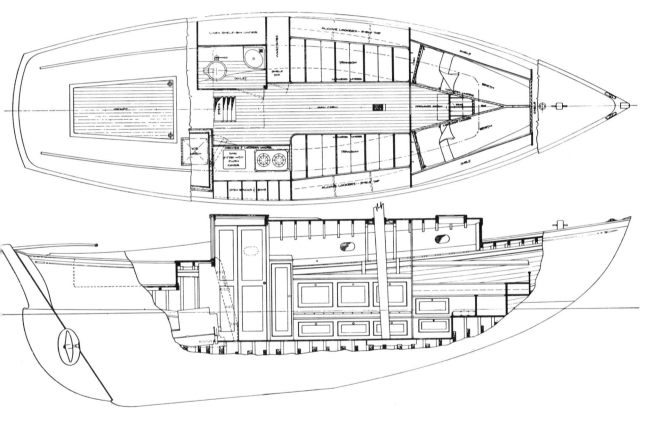

The Minneford cutter has an aft-galley–aft-head layout, which accentuates cockpit convenience. The cockpit seems higher than it need be, but this provides plenty of room for servicing the engine. (The Rudder)

but it is not the easiest rig to handle because of the running backstays and the narrow slot between the two forward stays, which necessitates threading jibs through the slot when coming about or jibing. On the other hand, the forestaysail is quite large, and it is fitted with a boom and traveler so that the sail is self-tending. If the main boom were shorter, a permanent backstay could be fitted, and a short bowsprit would widen the slot between forward stays, but this might upset the boat's balance. The keel has considerable drag, which puts the center of

lateral resistance quite far aft, so the total center of effort must also be reasonably far aft for good balance. One solution to the slot problem might be a single-head rig with a fairly high-aspect-ratio working jib having a boom on a pedestal.

A very similar but smaller version of the Minneford cruiser was designed by Rhodes in 1938. This later development has a sloop rig and a doghouse at the after end of her cabin trunk, but she is very much like her Minneford forerunner in hull form, with her

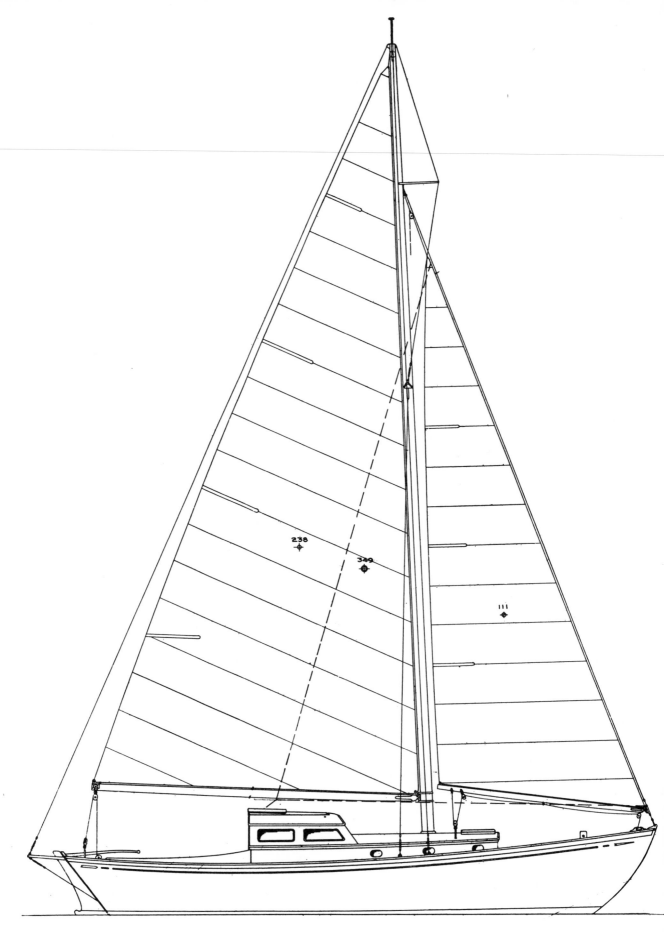

Compared with the rig of the Minneford cutter, the Little Sister's *rig is much easier to handle.* Little Sister *is 27 feet 2 inches long.* (Yachting, *December 1938*)

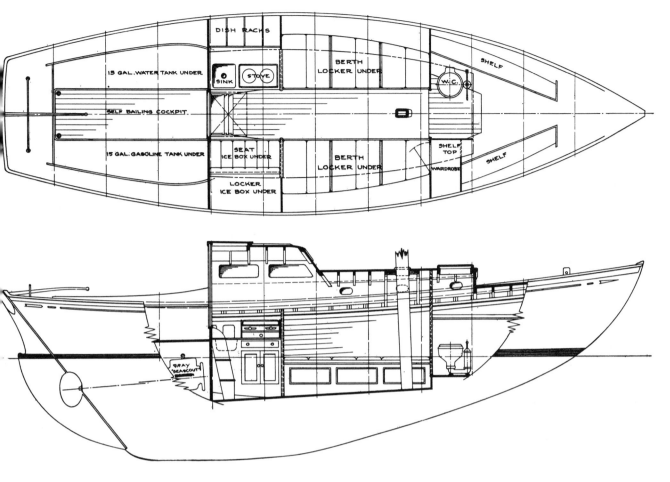

There is plenty of stowage space forward in the Little Sister. *An unusual feature is the seat with cushioned back just inside the companionway.* (Yachting, *December 1938*)

pronounced sheer, spoon bow, transom stern, and shapely outboard rudder. Minor differences in the two hull configurations are that the newer boat has a little more rake in her transom and a slightly different keel profile with less drag or depth aft. The net effect is a bit less wetted surface and the repositioning somewhat farther forward of the center of lateral resistance.

This boat, named *Little Sister,* was produced for Harry P. MacDonald, an early and active promoter of stock cruising boats. He marketed this design as a stock boat, which became known as the Little Sister class. The first boat was built by Gray Boats in Thomaston, Maine. Her measurements are 27 feet 2 inches by 22 feet 1 inch by 8 feet 3 inches by 4 feet 2 inches.

Little Sister's doghouse is distinctive, and perhaps a mite too high, but it provides 6 feet 2 inches of headroom below, and the windows admit a lot of light into the cabin. There are only two good-sized berths, but this allows plenty of room for the huge forepeak for stowing the sails and other gear. The head is also in the forepeak, an arrangement that allows good privacy for such a small boat. The galley is aft, and an unusual feature is the seat over the icebox. Unfortunately, the sink seems to be blocked slightly by the companionway steps. For this size of boat, the cockpit is comfortably large.

The fractional sloop rig is easy to handle because of the small foretriangle and absence of running backstays. Mast support aft is provided by a permanent backstay attached to a "V" boomkin, which encloses the rudder head. This arrangement necessitates a relatively short main boom as compared with the Minneford boat, but balance is preserved with the farther-forward center of lateral resistance and a fairly small jib. The working sail area is listed as 349 square feet, which doesn't seem like a great deal, but

HARRY P. MACDONALD

Presents

The outstanding boat of the year

The Little Sister

☆

Designed by

PHILIP L. RHODES

of Cox & Stevens, inc.

☆

Sails by

HATHAWAY & REISER

☆

$3600

Despite her high doghouse, the Little Sister *is a handsome boat with a springy sheer and attractive transom with shapely outboard rudder.*

MacDonald said the boat is a splendid sailer. This was confirmed by a write-up of the boat in *Yachting* in 1938, which described her light-air performance as being like that of a racing sloop and her moderate-wind ability as being comparable to a Rhodes ocean racer. Promotional literature even claimed that in a chop she "goes to windward like a 60-footer," a statement that might raise a few eyebrows. If she could sail upwind like a smart 30-footer, she would be more than satisfactory.

The two boats presented in this chapter are fine examples of Rhodes auxiliary cruisers with transom sterns. MacDonald didn't give the name of *Little Sister's* big sister, but she could very well have been the Minneford cutter.

13

Narada and Her Sisters
Too Good to Change

During her short life, the cutter *Narada* certainly made her mark, and her legacy continues today. In the late 1930s and early 1940s, she attracted a lot of attention on the Chesapeake Bay because of her stellar racing record and her eye-catching beauty. Then, during World War II, while serving with the "Corsair Fleet" on anti-submarine duty, she again gained notoriety when she sank following a collision with a Navy ship at the entrance to the Chesapeake. Today, her memory is perpetuated by the coveted Narada Memorial Trophy awarded annually by the Gibson Island Yacht Squadron, under whose burgee she sailed, and by her near-sisterships, built after she was sunk.

Narada was designed for L. Corrin Strong of Washington, D.C., and she was built by M.M. Davis at Solomons, Maryland. Phil Rhodes was at her launching in June 1936, but according to Corrin Strong, he refused to get up on the viewing platform, from which a group of friends was watching the christening. Whether this was from modesty or concern about how *Narada* would be launched and how she would float is not known, but Phil told Corrin that "he was worried enough as it was, without tak-

ing on anything additional." Apparently there was some cause for concern, for it was a very hot day, and the tallow lubricating the ways was melting and running off. Several hundred pounds of crushed ice was used to keep the tallow cool, and finally, after a bit of coaxing, the cutter slid into her element. To no one's surprise, she floated on her lines perfectly.

Narada seldom had any problems moving through the water. She proved unusually fast against the cruising boats of her day and won more than her share of silver. A newspaper account (in the *Baltimore Sun*, June 3, 1940) described one of her more successful races as follows: "*Narada* outsailed everything in sight, including the Naval Academy's big *Vamarie* and William H. Labrot's *Stormy Weather*, both among the finest in the ocean racing game. *Narada*'s performance was probably as fine a one as bay racing has seen in many a day. It was by no means her kind of weather. No racing freak, but a substantial, able cruising boat that could take her afterguard across the Atlantic in perfect safety, she nevertheless ghosted along on the slick bay like a Star boat . . . ."

Before she was built, *Narada* was tank tested at the

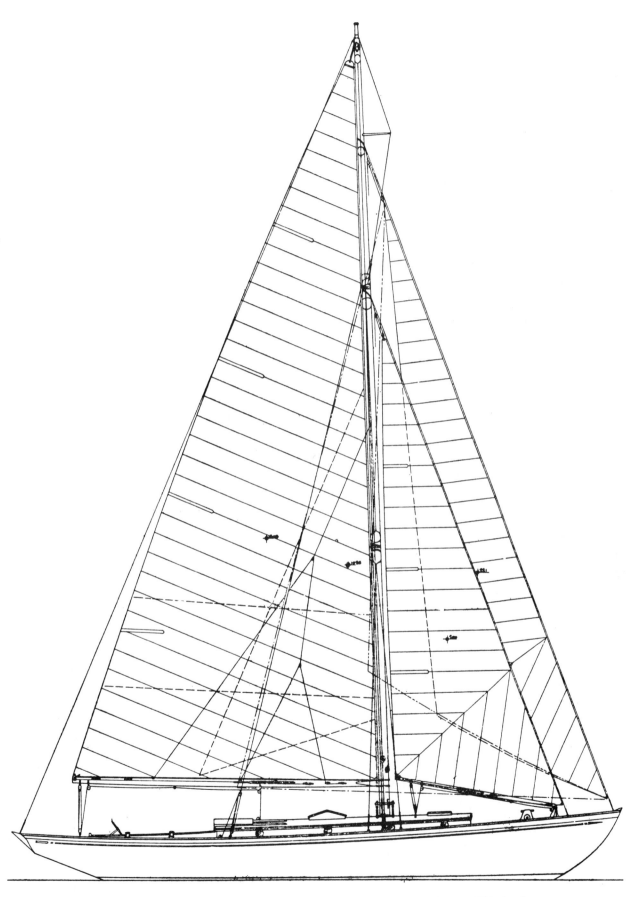

Narada, *Chesapeake champion of the late 1930s and early 1940s, was 45 feet 10 inches long. This plan shows her original ⅞ rig.*

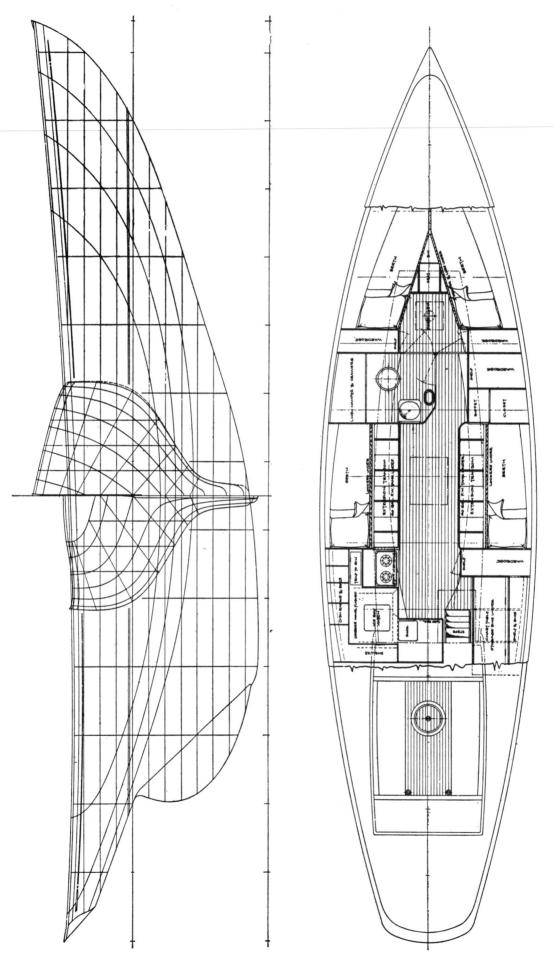

Top: *The balanced, smooth-flowing lines of Narada influenced the design of such winners as Kirawan, Copperhead, and Carina (I).* **Above:** *Narada's layout below is hard to beat for practicality. (The Rudder, January 1937)*

Narada *at sea, as seen from the*
Alden schooner Tradition.
(Courtesy of L. Corrin Strong)

Stevens Institute of Technology in Hoboken, New Jersey, and apparently her model was used for many years as a standard of comparison for models of other boats of her type. She must have been considered a highly successful boat, and her lines tell the story, for they are exceptionally smooth and easy flowing. The hull was quite symmetrical, with well-balanced ends, although her upper stem appeared to be slightly snubbed.

Narada originally had a seven-eighths rig, with 1,026 square feet of sail area, but in 1939 she was given a masthead rig, allowing her to carry larger headsails to catch the light airs of the Chesapeake. She had two sets of spreaders on her mast, which provided excellent shroud angles, but her lower spreaders were low enough to create a problem that Rhodes probably never anticipated. Young boys, including Corrin Strong's children and myself, considered it great sport to climb the mast and jump into the water from the spreaders.

Narada's dimensions were: 45 feet 10 inches LOA, 34 feet LWL, 11 feet 3 inches beam, and 6 feet 6 inches draft. Her size allowed spaciousness above and below decks and uncramped accommodations for a full crew. There was also plenty of stowage space. The forward stateroom had ample floor space and its own door into the head. There was a pilot berth and an extension transom on each side of the main cabin, and she had a skylight over the table to provide plenty of light and air. Aft, near the com-

Narada *on a close reach in a fresh breeze carrying her full main and forestaysail.*

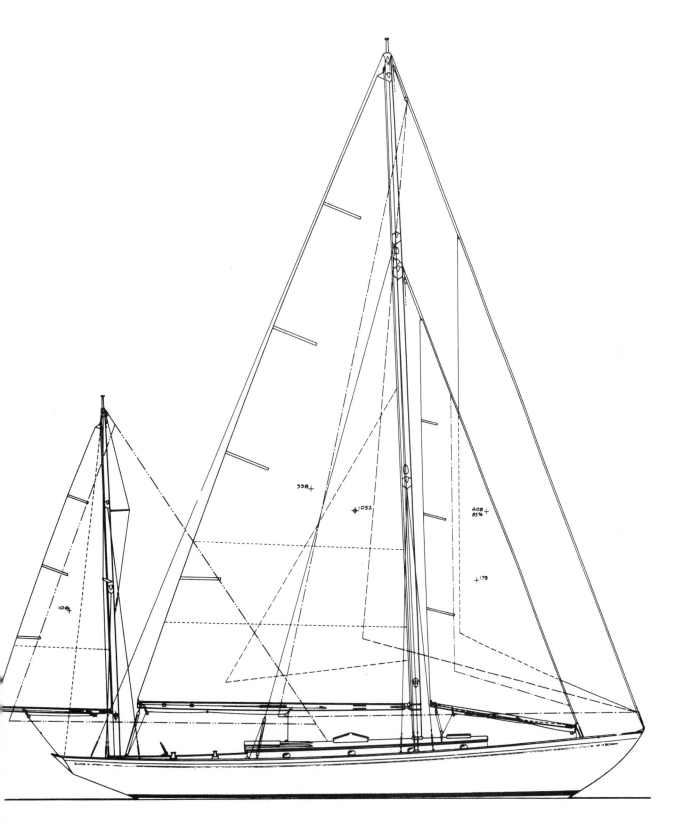

Pavana, *Corrin Strong's postwar version of* Narada, *with a slightly longer bow (she is 46 feet 8 inches overall) and masthead yawl rig.*

Pavana close-hauled. *The genoa should be tacked closer to the deck for racing efficiency, but the gap under the foot provides a fine view of the handsome deck and cabin trunk. Then, too, the helmsman can see where he is going.*

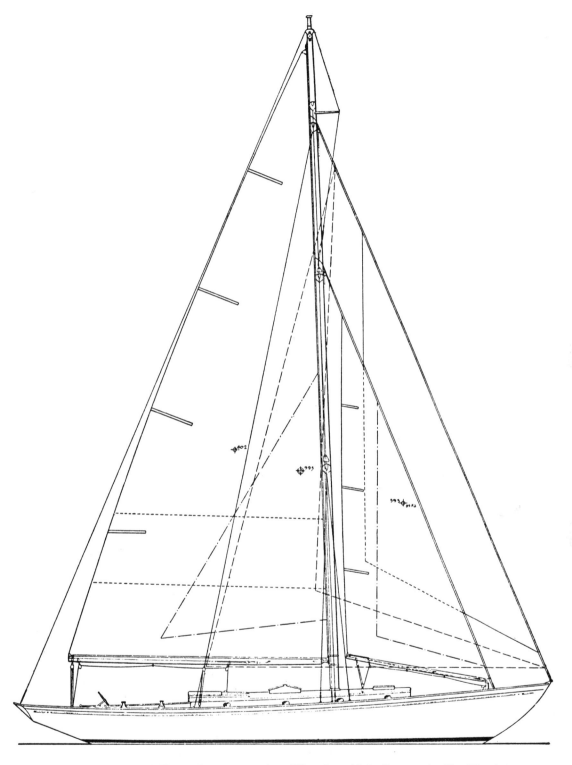

White Squall, *Donald Sherwood's postwar version of* Narada, *with her ⅞ cutter rig. She differs from* Pavana *only in her rig*. (Yachting)

White Squall *prior to her launching at the Balco Yacht Company in April 1950. A nice feature is the open rail at the stern. (Photo by W.G. Schepleng)*

panionway, there was a good-sized galley on the port side and a chart table and foul-weather-gear locker to starboard.

Of course, it was a great loss to Corrin Strong when *Narada* was sunk, and he made several attempts to salvage her. Corrin knew almost exactly the location of the accident, and his boat sank in water that was not too deep for salvage, but she never could be found.

After the war, *Narada* received the greatest possible endorsement: Corrin Strong and Donald Sherwood (who had owned *Seawitch,* described in Chapter 2) went to Phil Rhodes and asked for new boats almost identical to *Narada.* The new Strong vessel was named *Pavana* and the Sherwood boat *White Squall.* These boats were so much like *Narada,* even down to their accommodations, that they were assigned *Narada's* design number and were designated as supplemental designs. About the only

difference was that their bows were drawn out, increasing their overall lengths by 10 inches. The original boat was just too good to change.

There were other boats referred to as *Narada's* sisters, such as the yawl *Cherry Blossom* and the cutter *Elda,* which was eventually lost on a Bermuda reef, but these boats were different enough to be given their own design numbers.

The only major difference between *Pavana* and *White Squall* is in their rigs; the former is a masthead yawl, while the latter is a seven-eighths-rigged cutter. With their drawn-out bows, both boats have longer foretriangle bases than *Narada* had. Although *Pavana* has a taller foretriangle and carries 57 square feet more sail area than *White Squall,* the latter's J measurement is greater, and this allows a better-shaped spinnaker. Another minor drawback of *Pavana's* rig is that the total center of effort is farther aft, which adds a little more weather helm, but this can be alleviated in a fresh breeze by dropping the mizzen. The boomed, self-tending staysails on both boats allow easy handling in heavy weather.

Both of the supplemental designs were built by the Balco Yacht Company in Dundalk, Maryland, in 1949-50. I attended the christening of *White Squall* in April 1950 and had the pleasure of meeting Phil Rhodes for the first time.

Later that year I raced to Bermuda and sailed back on *Pavana*. Although we finished only in the middle of our class, the boat proved comfortable, able, and easy to steer. Despite a crew of eight men, the cabins never seemed terribly crowded. Some privacy was lost, however, when co-skippers Pete and Hank Strong, sons of Corrin, removed one of the head doors to reduce weight, and this may have enabled us to complete the 635-mile course about three seconds sooner than if the door had remained. On the other hand, perhaps it was a psychological ploy to make the crew try its hardest to reach Bermuda in the quickest possible time.

Neither *Pavana* nor *White Squall* had particularly good racing records on the Chesapeake, primarily because they were too heavy for the light winds of the area, but both boats excelled in a decent breeze. When *White Squall* was moved to the Great Lakes, she made quite a name for herself. One year, in heavy weather, she won the 377-mile Rochester Race by seven hours. In 1956, she also won the overall prize in the 130-mile Freeman Cup Race against a fleet of 60 boats in exceptionally rugged weather that caused over 20 boats to seek shelter.

Pavana proved her speed as well as her seaworthiness when she crossed the North Atlantic in 1953. Corrin Strong was then the United States ambassador to Norway, and he wanted to have *Pavana* over there for daysailing and cruising the fjords with Norwegian friends and American guests (including my wife, Sally, and myself). She was sailed across by Peter Strong with a small crew in remarkably fast time. They covered the 3,300 miles in 24½ days and did so without setting light sails.

The *Narada* sisters gave (and presumably are still giving) a great deal of pleasure to their owners. These boats are seaworthy, lovely to look at, and extremely versatile. Indeed, Rhodes remarked that the *Narada* design was one of his favorites.

14

Kirawan
Bermuda Race Winner

The first ocean racer to bring Phil Rhodes considerable international fame was the cutter *Kirawan,* which won the 1936 Bermuda Race. This was a rugged, heavy-weather contest, with winds sometimes on the nose and gusting up to 45 m.p.h. *Kirawan* reveled in the conditions and was the third boat in a fleet of 44 to finish. She finished only one hour and 18 minutes after the 72-foot *Vamarie,* the elapsed-time winner, and she beat the famous, higher-rated *Stormy Weather* boat-for-boat. *Kirawan* was by no means among the largest boats in the fleet. In fact, at 53 feet overall, she was given time by 27 yachts. Her success was due to her being pushed harder than the rest of the fleet and to her weatherliness, which allowed her to hold high and not be driven off to leeward in the blustery conditions, as was much of the fleet. Also, Phil Rhodes was aboard for the race, and it was suggested that his presence was a decisive factor in keeping her going, for he knew how hard she could be driven.

Kirawan was designed for Robert P. Baruch of the Manhasset Bay Yacht Club on Long Island Sound. She was built by Jakobson and Peterson in Brooklyn, New York (later Jakobson Shipyard of Oyster Bay), and launched only a month before the

124

start of the Bermuda Race. Although she was designed with the Bermuda Race in mind (her owner had specified that she have a favorable rating and that she rate at the top of Class B), she was also meant to be suitable for weekend cruising on Long Island Sound. For this reason, she was given a generous sail plan to push her along in the Sound's gentle breezes.

Baruch's boat might be considered a larger version of *Narada,* for the two designs are quite similar in hull shape and rig; the main difference is in size. *Kirawan* is 7 feet longer and measures 38 feet 9 inches on the waterline, having a beam of 12 feet 6 inches and a draft of 7 feet 6 inches. She carries 1,342 square feet of sail area and displaces 20 tons.

Minor differences between the hulls of *Narada* and *Kirawan* are that the latter has a straighter profile at the bottom of the keel, a slightly greater rudder stock angle, a bit more overhang aft, and a smaller transom. *Kirawan* has less relative beam, as would be expected on a larger boat, for the larger the boat, the less proportional beam is needed for a given amount of stability. Her crew found that initially *Kirawan* heeled readily, but became very stiff well before her rail dipped. This characteristic is fitting for an off-

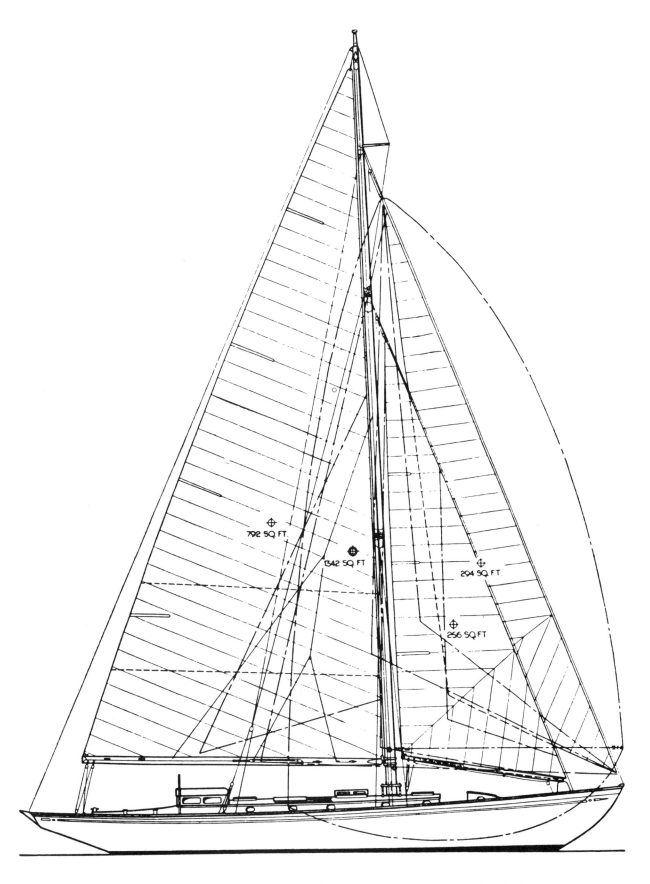

The ⅞ cutter rig of Kirawan. *When she first appeared, her rig was considered by some to be light, but it proved amply strong for the heavy-weather Bermuda Race. It is a significant tribute that very few Rhodes boats have lost their rigs.* (Sail and Power *by Uffa Fox*)

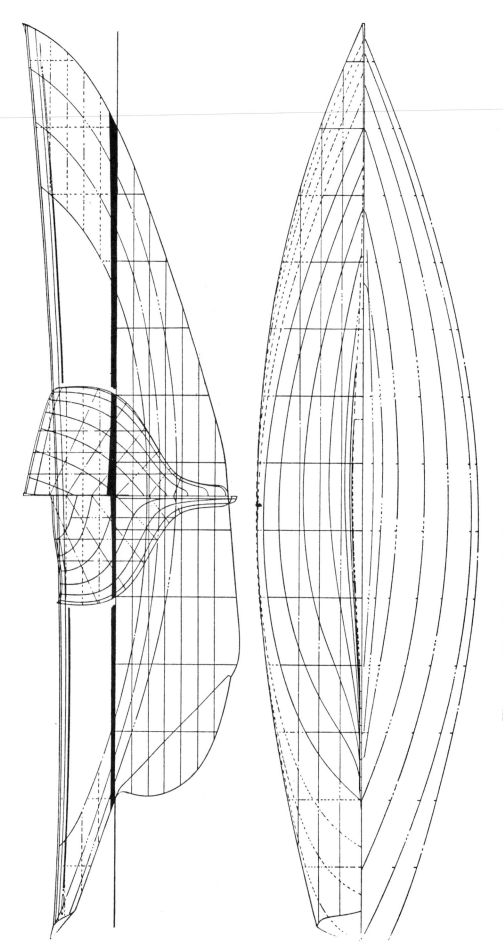

Kirawan, at 53 feet, is almost an enlarged version of Narada, although there are some minor differences at the stern. She has an exceptionally well-balanced hull. (Sail and Power by Uffa Fox)

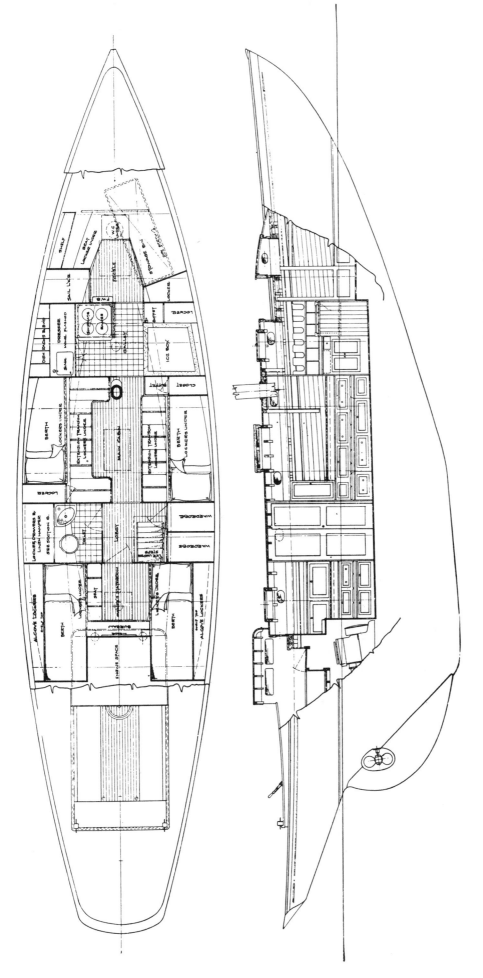

Kirawan's accommodations lack a chart desk, but a chart cupboard was undoubtedly kept in the more convenient location under her cockpit shelter. Her shelter attracted much attention and was often imitated. (The Rudder)

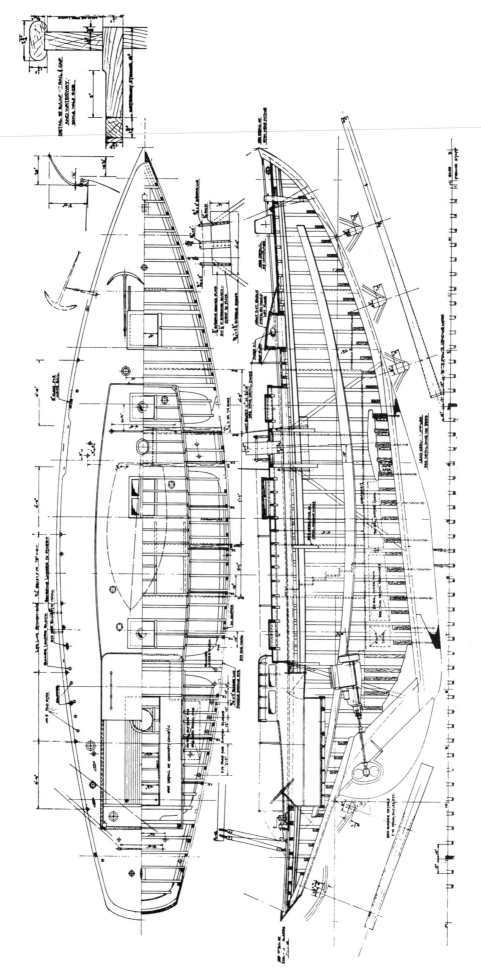

Kirawan's sturdy construction, including extra floors in way of the mast step, hanging knees, and diagonal strapping of bronze, gave Rhodes and Robert Baruch the confidence to drive her during the race. (The Rudder)

Kirawan *on a reach. In those times, many skippers believed in a lot of sail twist so that the jib and main could work together, but current theory would have the main vanged down and the jib led forward. (Photo by Harry Merrick. Courtesy of Mystic Seaport)*

Kirawan *out of water shows her long run to good advantage. (Courtesy of Mystic Seaport)*

shore boat, giving her a non-jerky motion and easing the strain on her rig. *Kirawan's* symmetrical hull, with rather full lines forward, can encourage pitching in certain conditions, but this symmetry, with moderate beam amidships, generally produces good balance and easy steering, even when the boat is well heeled. During her Bermuda Race conquest, *Kirawan* shortened down at one time to reefed mainsail alone, then to headsails alone when her mainsail was lowered for repairs. Under each sail combination her helm was easily handled, and this shows that her hull is exceptionally well balanced.

Kirawan's cockpit shelter affords perfect protection for the on-deck crew. Although a folding dodger allows removal in fair weather, the permanent doghouse is stronger, and its heavy glass windows allow better visibility than do the soft plastic windows found on the usual dodger. There is no companionway under the shelter, and this can be a drawback, but such an arrangement allows more

seating at the forward end of the cockpit and complete privacy for the owner's after cabin.

The cockpit shelter might have been a factor in *Kirawan's* success during that rugged Bermuda Race. It kept the crew dry and comfortable, thereby boosting its morale, and it also may have made the crew, thus protected, a bit less inclined to shorten down. *Kirawan* might well have been driven just a little harder than were her competitors without doghouses.

Kirawan's main companionway is on the cabin top, and its ladder is just forward of the owner's stateroom. There is a large enclosed head to port of the ladder. Farther forward is the main saloon, with an extension transom and pilot berths on each side, and ahead of this, a large galley. The fo'c's'le, with a pipe berth, its own head, and a separate companionway, is perfect for a live-aboard paid hand.

The English designer/author Uffa Fox was somewhat critical of *Kirawan's* galley in that it was so far from the cockpit. He pointed out that the cook would have a difficult time carrying a hot drink to the on-deck watch in heavy weather. This is true, of course, but the problem might be rectified, if it weren't blowing too hard, by mounting a portable one-burner Seaswing stove under the doghouse. This stove could easily be removed when not needed, but it could be set up quickly in cold weather to give the afterguard hot coffee or soup.

Rhodes alumnus Robert M. Steward recently reported that he saw *Kirawan* at Newport Beach, California, in about 1956. At that time her 20-year-old Buda gasoline engine was replaced with a Mercedes-Benz diesel. Steward wrote: ''The boat was in good shape — withdrawn planking fastenings showed no signs of corrosion.''

In 1986, I heard from *Kirawan*'s owner, Thomas R. Jones of San Diego, California, that his boat was being cosmetically restored. He said that her West Coast career had included two races to Hawaii and one to Tahiti. For the latter event she was changed to a yawl and she still retains that rig. At one time, he added, *Kirawan* had been owned by Tony Dow of the *Leave It to Beaver* TV show, who during his "affair with the lady" had given her some well-deserved "kind attention."

15

Arabella
Able and Fast

One of the most distinguished of Phil Rhodes' designs is the ketch *Arabella*. An outstanding salty-looking cruiser, never intended for serious competition, she nevertheless excelled in European racing, almost 19 years after she was designed. Her basic dimensions are 46 feet 3 inches LOA, 35 feet LWL, 11 feet 9½ inches beam, and 5 feet 5 inches draft.

Arabella was designed in 1936 for prominent yachtsman Elihu Root, Jr., and her evolution is rather complicated. Root had at one time owned a small, shoal-draft cruiser named *Dormouse*, which had the windward ability of a boat with much deeper draft. *Dormouse* made quite an impression on Paul Hammond (with whom Root had co-owned the famous schooner *Nina*), so he commissioned her architect, Starling Burgess, to design a larger version. This became the well-known singlehander *Barnswallow*, and Phil Rhodes was called in to help with many of her details.

In 1933, Phil designed a 24-foot-waterline boat named *Jingleshell* based on the *Dormouse* concept. It has been written that *Arabella* was a development of *Jingleshell*, and a comparison of their plans bears this out. Thus, the *Dormouse* concept of a shallow-draft keelboat without a centerboard but with good windward ability was carried through to *Arabella*.

In the interim between *Jingleshell* and *Arabella*, Root had Phil draw up the plans for a 28-foot-waterline version of the concept. Although this boat was never built for Root, the design was later picked up by Harry P. MacDonald of Gray Boats in Thomaston, Maine, and marketed by him as the Rhodes Cutter. MacDonald claimed that despite the boat's shallow draft, her "best point of sailing is actually when hard on the wind in a chop."

It is difficult to say why this family of shoal-draft boats performs so well on a beat to windward, but perhaps Phil Rhodes gives us a clue in a description of his early design *Volante* (see Part One), which has a related but deeper keel profile. Phil wrote, "*Volante* has been given the full rocker keel. This gives the entire keel length a chance to cut solid water." According to one theory, when the water flow runs aft rather than turning under the bottom of the keel, tip vortex, which robs a keel of much of its efficiency, is minimized. So perhaps *Arabella* and her forerunners derive some benefit from a keel slope angle and profile curvature that reduce the vortex and present a relatively long leading edge to non-turbulent water.

Elihu Root did not cruise offshore extensively in *Arabella*, although he sailed her to Bermuda in 1938. But the ketch became a long-distance voyager when

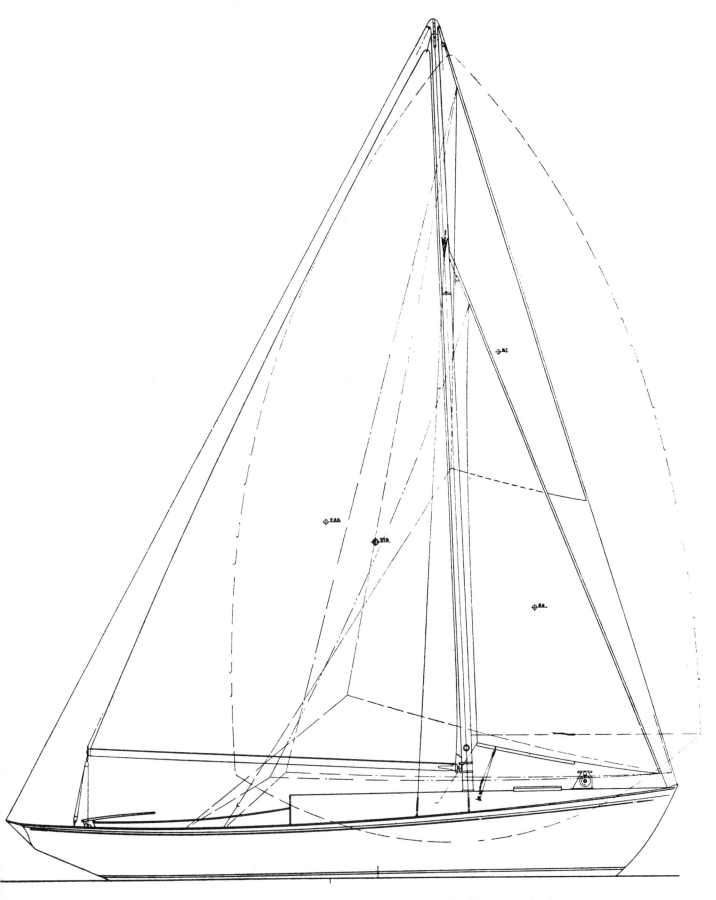

The Rhodes-designed 31-foot sloop Jingleshell, *based on the Burgess-Atkin-designed* Dormouse, *is a forerunner of* Arabella. (The Rudder)

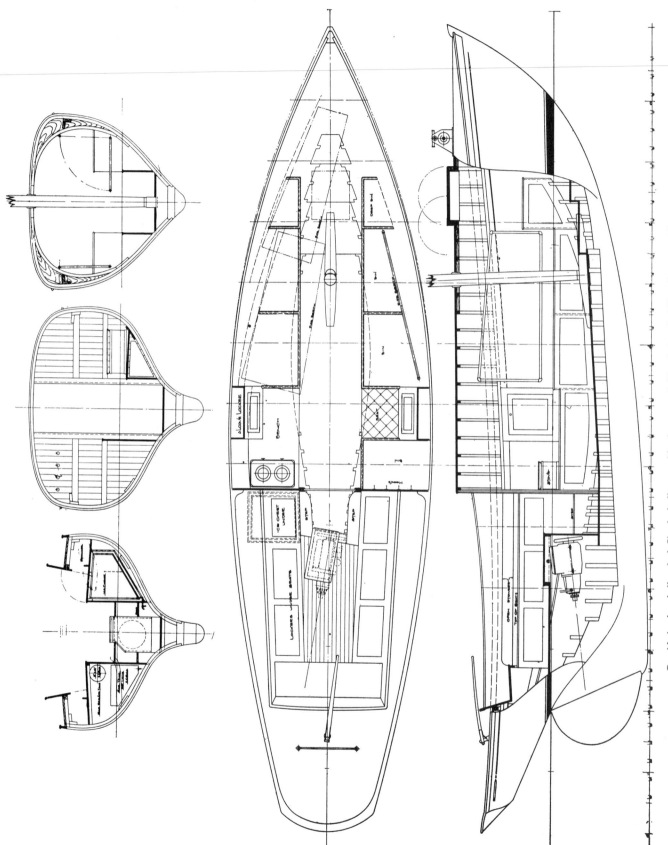

Considering her shallow keel, Jingleshell was said to have remarkable windward ability. An unusual feature is the turtleback deck. (The Rudder)

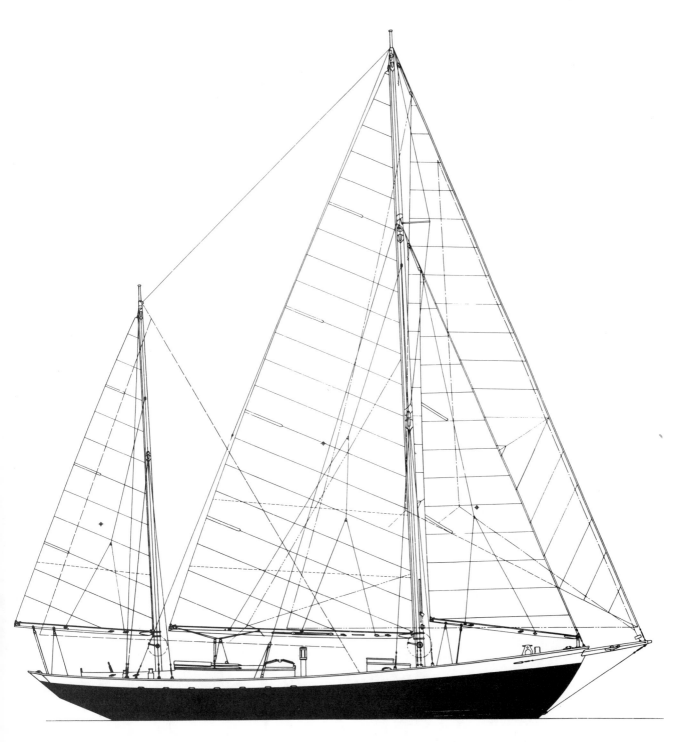

Arabella is a unique combination of able sea boat and fast cruiser. She is 46 feet 3 inches overall. Her unusual ketch rig with relatively small mizzen allows handiness with little sacrifice to power.

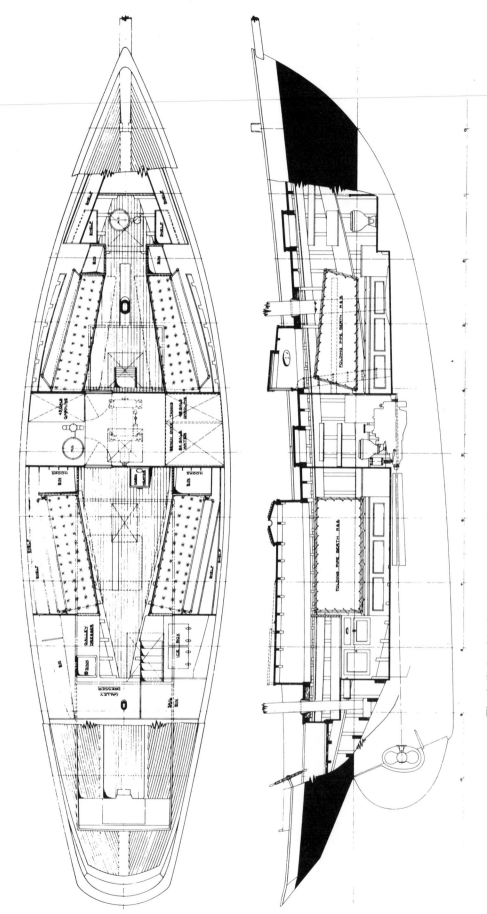

The similarity of Arabella's underwater profile to that of Jingleshell is easy to see. In her accommodations Arabella is undeniably a two-cabin boat.

This painting of Arabella *by Benjamin T. Stephenson graced the cover of* Yachting *magazine in September 1955.*

she sailed across the Atlantic in 1955 and back to the United States in 1956 under the ownership of Pehr Sparre. During her outward-bound passage she showed her speed by making good almost 600 miles in one three-day period, and on another occasion she covered 220 miles on a noon-to-noon run. Racing abroad under both the Swedish SHKR rule and the English RORC rule, against the most competitive European craft (including *Lutine, Foxhound,* and *Jocasta*), *Arabella* did amazingly well. Her victories included a class first in a long-distance Baltic race (the Gotland Runt); first in fleet in a race from Plymouth, England, to LaRochelle, France; and second in fleet, first in class, racing from LaRochelle to Benodet on the coast of Brittany.

Arabella gives an appearance of extreme saltiness, almost in the manner of Slocum's *Spray.* Two distinctive features that give her this character are her high bulwarks and her separate cabin trunks.

The bulwarks give security to the crew and help prevent lowered sails from washing overboard. To contrast with the dark hull, and thus lower the apparent height of freeboard, the bulwarks are painted white. The two cabin trunks allow plenty of deck space and permit the use of full-width deck beams and bulkheads amidships, which strengthen the hull.

The separated cabins ensure maximum privacy below. Each cabin has its own head and companionway and is a separate unit, although there is a low-headroom connecting passageway through the engine room. The central engine location requires a long shaft, but having the engine's weight amidships inhibits hobbyhorsing. The four berths, two aft and two forward, are canvas pipe berths, the kind first used by Elihu Root and often called "Root berths." They make sense on a real sea boat, since they can be adjusted for heel and are not excessively bouncy when hard mattresses are used. Light is provided by a skylight above the dining table, and the after galley gets reasonable air and light from the companionway.

Arabella has a small mizzen for a ketch, but it nicely balances the forestaysail, and these two sails alone or with a deeply reefed main make a good sail plan for heavy weather. Since the mizzen boom does not overhang the stern, any risk of the crew falling overboard while furling sail is reduced. The mizzen shrouds are quite far abaft the mast so as to support the forward pull of the mizzen staysail, and they will interfere with the boom when it is broad off; however, it is often preferable to lower the mizzen when running in a seaway to keep the center of effort forward and avoid blanketing the forward sails. The bowsprit is not long enough to be considered a "widow maker," and besides, with the roller-furling jib, there is no real need for a crew member to go out on it. Bending on the large genoa would require a man forward, but that sail would only be carried offshore in light to moderate winds when the sea would be reasonably smooth. Working sail area abaft the stemhead is only 770 square feet, but the roller jib adds another 192 square feet and the large genoa adds considerably more.

In her heyday, *Arabella* had numerous admirers, and let's hope that there are still sailors who can appreciate a handsome, functional vessel of such character. She is presently owned and cruised by Paul Pennoyer of Locust Valley, New York, Peter Ward of Darien, Connecticut, and David E. Place of Cohasset, Massachusetts. Interestingly enough, Pennoyer's cousin, Walter Page, owns *Barnswallow*.

16

The Lake One-Design and Related Classes
Accent on Racing

The Lake One-Design was Phil Rhodes' idea of an able one-design racer having minimal accommodations for three. The boat was conceived for class competition on the Great Lakes in events that included distance races in exposed waters, so it was important for her to be reasonably seaworthy. Phil drafted her plans in 1937 for a design competition sponsored by the Lake Yacht Racing Association, an organization formed by 10 yacht clubs located on Lakes Erie and Ontario. A selection committee, consisting of one representative from each club, carefully studied plans submitted by a number of the best Canadian and American yacht designers. After due consideration, they chose the Rhodes design — a speedy-looking sloop with harmonious waterlines; longish, balanced ends; wineglass sections; and, as might be expected, a lovely sheerline. Her dimensions are 34 feet by 23 feet 4 inches by 7 feet 9 inches by 5 feet 3 inches, and she displaces 9,450 pounds.

This selection probably resulted from the boat's beauty, her easily managed rig, and the presence of certain safety features, including a self-bailing cockpit, a bridgedeck, and perhaps even the small cabin-trunk ports. Her integral keel with full gar-

boards, reasonable freeboard for a racing boat of those times, and powerful 4-cylinder Gray Sea Scout engine suggested a one-design that would be suited to more than just closed-course racing.

The committee also might have been influenced by the Lake One's sound construction. The plans called for ⅞-inch mahogany planking and closely spaced frames (on eight-inch centers), which provide for good hull strength without excessive weight. The early boats were built at various yards on the Great Lakes, including the Skaneateles and Herman Lund yards, but others were constructed elsewhere after the class became well known and spread to various parts of the country. The original boats, adequately equipped, could be purchased for as little as $3,000.

Although the moderate freeboard and low cabin trunk help give the Lake One-Design a sleek, graceful look, her svelteness is a trade-off in below-decks comfort, for there is only five feet of headroom under the cabin top. Her layout is simple and open, with a rudimentary galley aft; an unenclosed head is tucked away forward. The three berths are located abaft the mast, and the forepeak has been left open for storage.

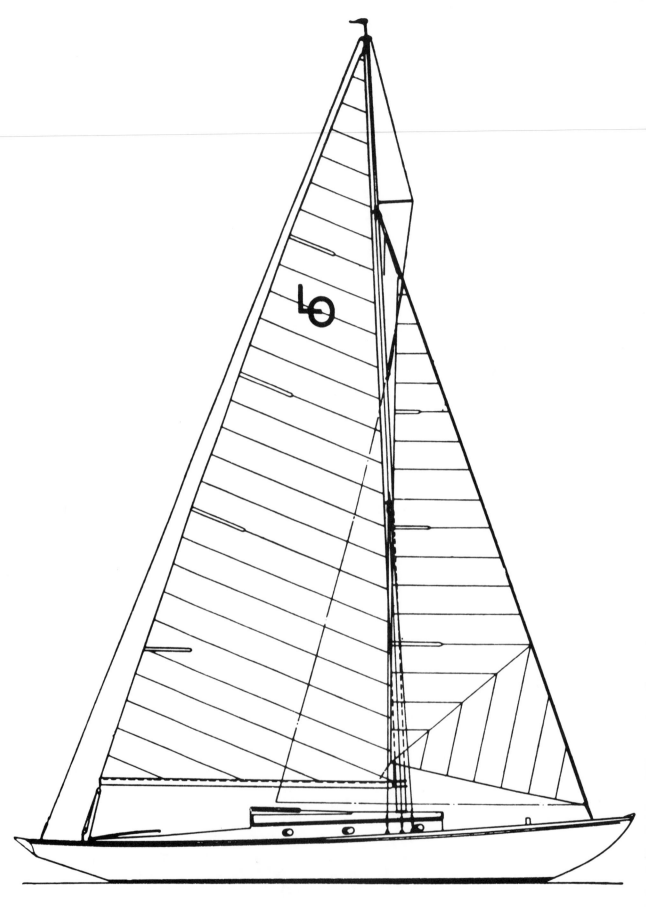

The 34-foot Lake One-Design is an attractive blend of sleek racer and reasonably able weekend cruiser. (Racing, Cruising and Design *by Uffa Fox*)

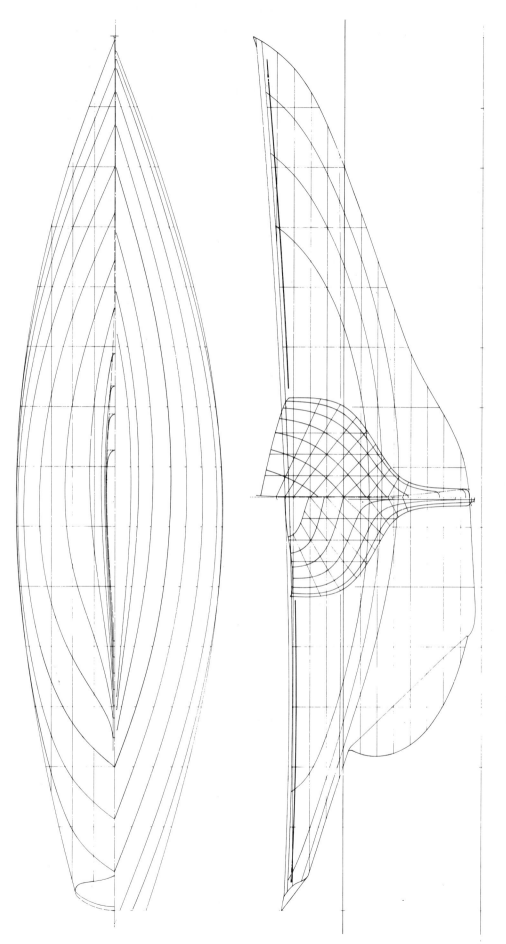

The lines of the Lake One-Design could almost be described as exquisite. They are not unlike those of many Rhodes ocean racers, but the LOD is a bit finer, and her keel is thinner and more salient.

Right: *The LOD* Night Cap *preparing to start a race on Chesapeake Bay.*
Below: *The Lake One's accommodations are adequate for overnighting or even weekending with a small racing crew or a couple with a child.* (Racing, Cruising and Design *by Uffa Fox)*

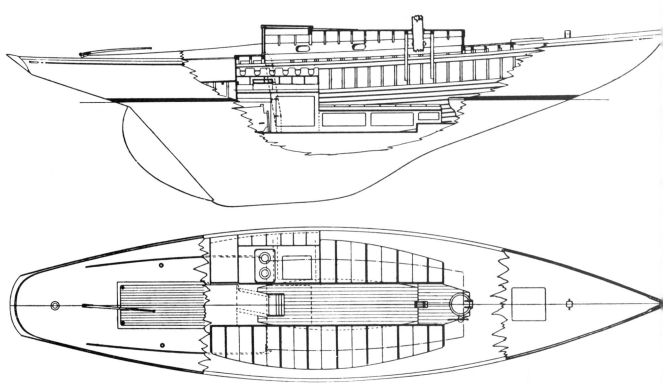

A Lake One showing her upwind ability in a moderate breeze. Note the number of crew her cockpit can hold.
(Courtesy of Mystic Seaport)

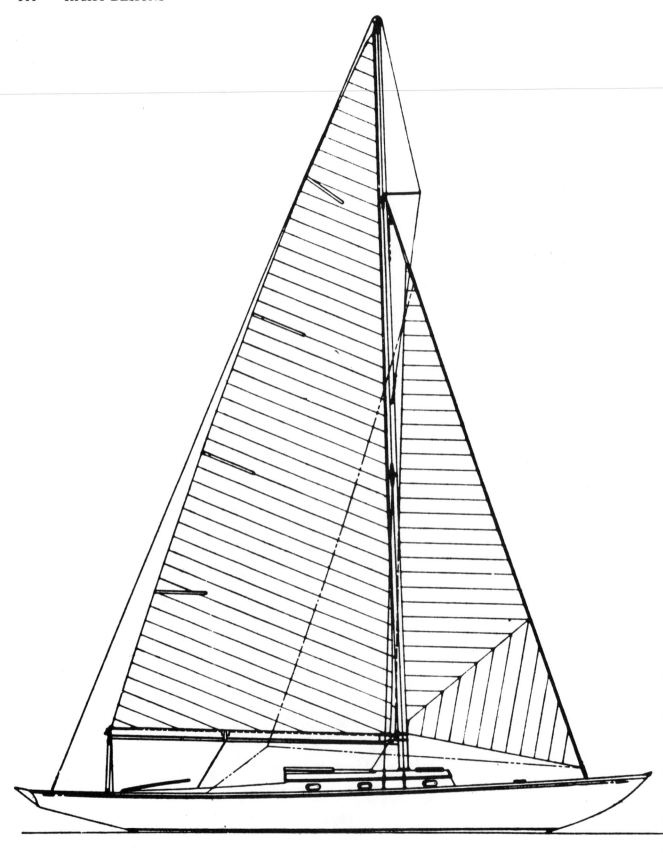

The Rhodes 33 is more of a racer than the Lake One-Design. Her rig is quite similar, but she lacks the LOD's forward lower shrouds, which provide better mast support in rough seas.

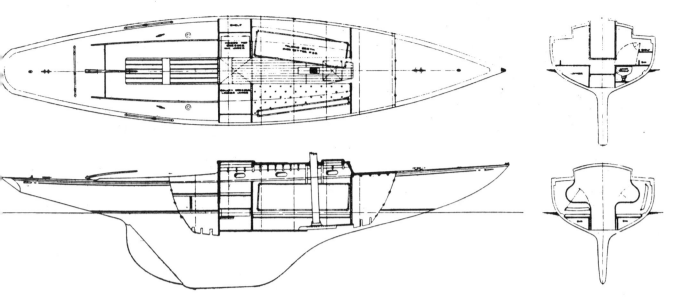

The Rhodes 33 lacks the accommodations and self-bailing cockpit of the LOD, but her cockpit is deeper and perhaps gives the crew a greater feeling of security.

The three-quarter rig, with only 444 square feet of sail, allows the boat to be handled by a crew of two, and one additional person if a spinnaker is carried. The mast is stepped well aft for a sloop, but the jib stay is set back from the bow. This provides more foredeck width for those setting and handing headsails, and it means that the spinnaker can be set up in a turtle ahead of the stay.

Back in the late 1930s and early 1940s, we used to race my father's 34-foot Alden yawl *Kelpie* against a lovely sloop called *Night Cap*. She was a Lake One-Design owned by Nathaniel S. (Cap) Kenney, formerly an avid Star-boat sailor and father of junior sailing at Gibson Island, Maryland. *Night Cap* had the same overall length as our yawl and almost exactly the same rating (one-tenth of a foot difference).

During her first year or so of racing, *Night Cap* was seldom beaten until she met William Crouse's speedy sloop named *Babe*, which resembled a bobtailed six-meter. In their first duel, *Babe* was beautifully sailed by Gordon Raymond (Chapter 2), and the Kenney sloop was soundly defeated for a change. Local sailors were amused when headlines in the *Baltimore Sun* proclaimed: ''Freak Boat Beats Night Cap.'' Our yawl finished third in that race, and my father remarked that the headline should have read, ''Two Freak Boats Beat Kelpie.'' Of course, *Night Cap* was no freak — she was simply a different concept, that of a cruising racer rather than a racing cruiser. At any rate, her beauty, as well as

her superb performance, has left a lasting impression on me.

The Lake One-Design was not Phil's first commission for a sleek, fast sailboat having simple overnight accommodations — nor was it the last. Phil had designed a somewhat similar boat as far back as 1929, when he produced a 32-foot knockabout sloop for daysailing on Little Traverse Bay, Lake Michigan. He carried this concept a step further toward the all-out racer when he designed the Rhodes 33 in 1938 and the Evergreen and Eastern Interclub classes in 1945. These later stock boats are approximately the same size, and they resemble the Lake One-Design, but they are a bit racier, with slightly longer overhangs, shorter keels, smaller cabins, and less auxiliary power.

The Rhodes 33 was originally designed for class racing in Southern California, where there were 20- or 30-mile races to offshore islands. These events required boats that could accommodate a crew overnight and that were weatherly and reasonably able, for the races were in open waters and often upwind. The Rhodes 33 measures 33 feet 8 inches by 22 feet 4 inches by 6 feet 10 inches by 5 feet, and she was given a sloop rig similar to that of the Lake One, but with only 386 square feet of sail area. She has a deep cockpit, but it is not self-bailing, and there is no bridgedeck or high companionway sill. Auxiliary power is supplied by an outboard fitted through a

At 36 feet overall, the Evergreen is basically a slightly larger version of the Rhodes 33. (The Rudder, February 1947)

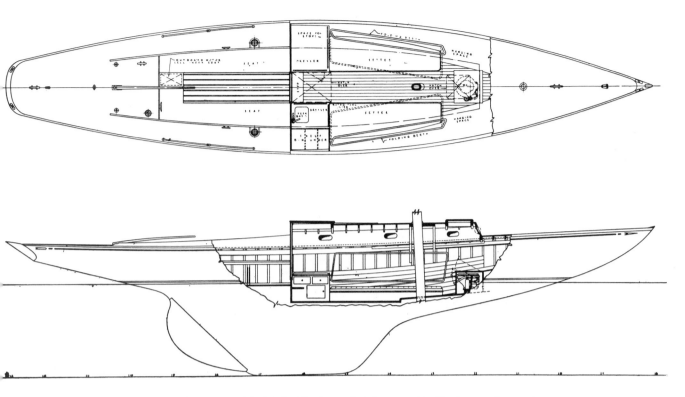

The Evergreen's profile, like that of the Rhodes 33, shows a keel that is considerably shorter and more cut away forward than that of the LOD. (The Rudder, *February 1947*)

This windward-side view of the Evergreen Prelude *illustrates one value of hollow sheer. With straight or reverse sheer, the boat might look somewhat hogged from the windward side when heeled.* (Courtesy of Mystic Seaport)

Above: *This picture of an Evergreen out of water gives an unusual view of her stem line and sheer. Unlike some sheerlines, the Rhodes sheer usually looks right from any point of view. (Courtesy of Mystic Seaport)* **Left:** *The Eastern Interclub is a later interpretation of a cruising racer. These boats were said to be "perfectly balanced."* (The Rudder, *January 1947*)

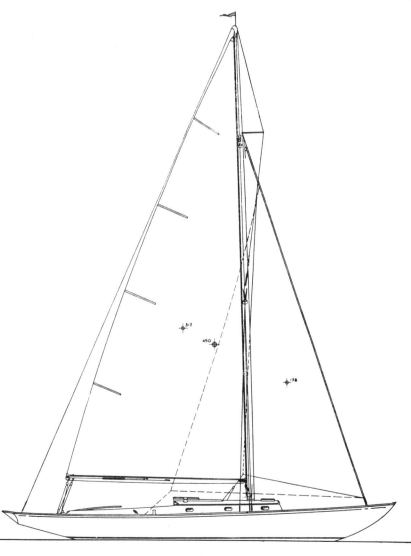

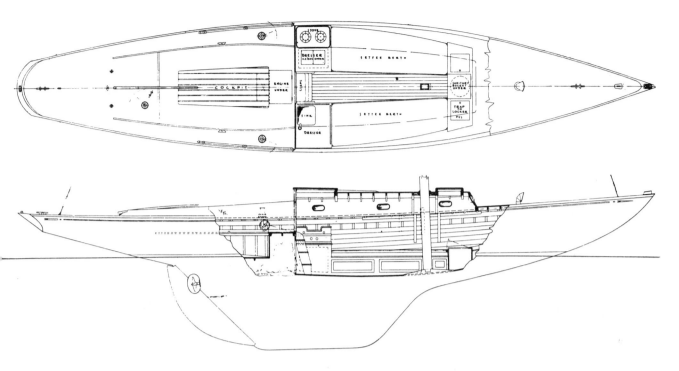

The Eastern Interclub resembles the Rhodes 33 and the Evergreen but is fitted with inboard auxiliary power.
(The Rudder, *January 1947*)

well in the counter. The 33s were built by the South Coast Boat Building Company of Newport Beach, California, and their construction is a bit lighter than that of the Lake One-Design.

Almost identical concepts are the Evergreen, a class racer designed for use in the Pacific Northwest, and the Eastern Interclub, commissioned by a group of prominent Connecticut yachtsmen for one-design racing. The former measures 36 feet by 24 feet by 7 feet 4 inches by 5 feet, has a three-quarter sloop rig with 472 square feet of sail area, and carries an outboard motor for auxiliary power. The Interclub measures 35 feet by 23 feet by 7 feet 2 inches by 5 feet 2 inches and has a rig similar to the Evergreen's, but with only 450 square feet of sail, and is fitted with a small 5-horsepower Kermath inboard engine.

These designs, as well as the Rhodes 33, are somewhat more lively sailers when compared with the Lake One, but the latter is more practical as a cruiser and is probably the best sea boat, with her longer keel, greater deadrise, easier sections, slightly shorter ends, and self-draining cockpit well. Then too, the LOD's more powerful engine gives her the ability to make good speed in calm weather, it enables all sail to be removed in a sudden squall, and it can be used more effectively to motorsail in extremely rough conditions.

All these one-designs, including the LOD, are primarily fast, responsive sailers. It is interesting to note that they are just about the closest Phil Rhodes came to turning out a sizable pure racing machine prior to his designing the 12-meter *Weatherly.*

17

Tamaris
First of a New Concept

The 81-foot ketch *Tamaris* is without a doubt one of Phil Rhodes' most important yacht designs. She was unique in her time and was hailed by yachting periodicals as the first of a new type. What really sets her apart from her predecessors is her unusual performance under both sail and power. She performs too well under sail to be called a motorsailer, but at the same time, her speed and range under power rival that of a displacement offshore motorboat. In close quarters, her twin screws provide better maneuverability than that of the normal single-screw trawler yacht. An example of her sailing speed is that she once covered 120 miles at an average speed of 10.5 m.p.h. under main and staysail alone. Under power, she makes about 13 m.p.h. at normal cruising speed. Combine these qualities with luxurious comfort and a six-foot draft that allows entry into almost any harbor and you have an exceptionally versatile cruiser.

Tamaris is also unique in her construction. Her entire hull is made of steel plates electrically butt welded instead of butt riveted, as was then common. She was reportedly the first yacht built using this method, which saves weight and also results in a

smoother hull. *Tamaris* has four full bulkheads, which form five watertight compartments, and she has a double bottom. Had she been built before the *Titanic,* she undoubtedly would have been called unsinkable.

Some interesting features of her construction were described in *The Rudder* magazine (November 1938) as follows: "The design of the ballast keel is a distinct innovation, being of cast steel so that it could be welded directly to the shell plating, floors, frames, centerboard trunk, etc. To get the proper weight without excessive width and length, the keel has been made deeper and projects up into the hull, contributing to a perfect welding job and unusual strength. Lead with steel would, of course, cause electrolysis, while iron cannot be successfully welded. It may be of interest to note that like all other materials in this hull, this keel was tested and showed a tensile strength of 80,000 pounds per square inch. The centerboard trunk and its streamlined centerboard are of steel, welded directly to the keel and structure, making perhaps the strongest such job ever produced."

This unusually solid yacht was built in 1938 by

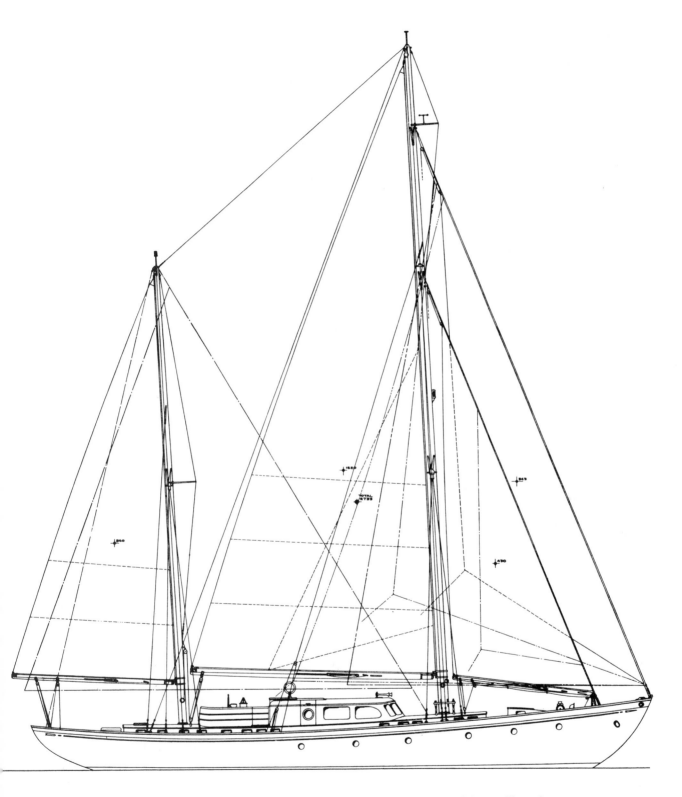

The landmark design Tamaris *is the first of a distinctive line of Rhodes heavily powered, large, sailing cruisers. She is 81 feet overall. The rig is nicely divided, and the huge mizzen staysail greatly helps her light-air reaching performance.*

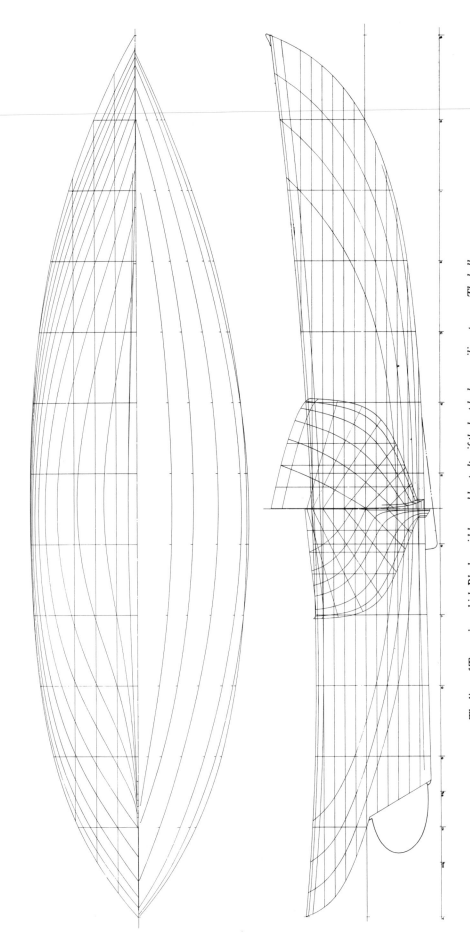

The lines of Tamaris, which Rhodes said he would not alter if the boat had no auxiliary power. The hull un-doubtedly has a higher prismatic coefficient than that of the typical Rhodes ocean racer, but its ends are finer than one might expect for this type of vessel.

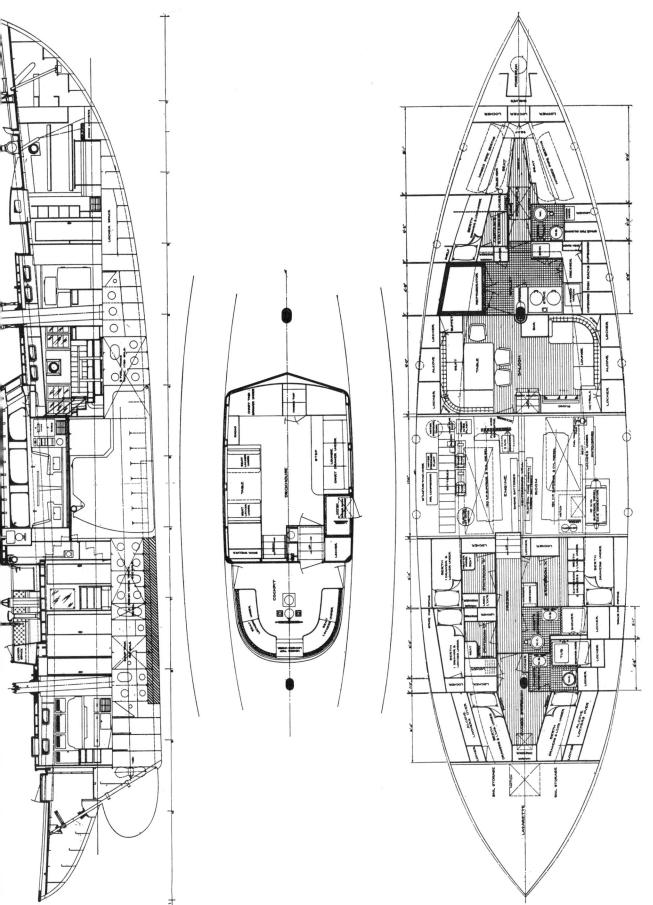

The accommodations plan of Tamaris includes what the author considers the ultimate feature: a music center with bar. The inboard profile plan shows the large, low-aspect-ratio centerboard that needs lowering only to a reasonable depth for sufficient lateral plane. (The Rudder)

Tamaris *under construction at the Burger Boat Company in Wisconsin. Her all-steel construction with butt-welded plates was a unique method of yachtbuilding in those times.*

This view of Tamaris *out of water emphasizes the shallowness of her hull. (Courtesy of Mystic Seaport)*

the Burger Boat Company at Manitowoc, Wisconsin. The welding was so well done that the hull had the smoothness of the best-made wooden yachts. To guard against corrosion, the steel was sandblasted, red-leaded, and then coated with a special cement to serve as a binder for paint. The hull's interior was lined with cork to insulate against sound and temperature and to prevent condensation. The deck and deckhouses were built of teak.

With a beam of 20 feet 3 inches and a waterline length of 65 feet, *Tamaris* has room for elegant accommodations. Abaft amidships, the original plans show four private staterooms (one of them later converted into a large walk-in storeroom) and two heads. The heads are so homelike that they are labeled bathrooms on the plans. Why shouldn't they be, when one head is fitted with a large shower and the other has a bathtub (with a shower head above)? Amidships, there is a large engine room (or actually two engine rooms, because the centerboard well divides the compartment in two) and directly above, there is a sunken deckhouse. This enclosed shelter, which is just forward of a raised cockpit, contains a dinette and a chart table, together with much navigation equipment. It is somewhat puzzling that the sail plan shows two large windows and a porthole on one side of the deckhouse, while the accommodation profile shows three windows.

A stairway at the forward end of the deckhouse leads down to the main saloon, which has a large settee with a table and stuffed chairs, and, across from the saloon, a lounge. The lounge might alternatively be called a music room, for in it are a record player (labeled "Victrola" in the plans) and a spinet piano (located between the stairs and the Victrola). Farther forward is the large galley and the crew's quarters, which includes a private stateroom for the captain.

In addition to being a comfortable "house boat," *Tamaris* was intended as a go-anywhere cruiser that could manage heavy weather offshore and, at the same time, negotiate the shallow waters of the Bahamas or elsewhere. The double-ended hull was thoroughly tank tested upright and at various angles of heel, and Rhodes claimed that he was able to make a number of improvements as a result of the tests. The high spoon bow helps keep water off the forward deck, while the overhanging canoe stern mitigates slamming and provides a reserve of buoyancy that is sometimes needed in boats with narrow, sharp sterns. The long, shallow keel helps *Tamaris* track well, and it allows good performance under power as well as the ability to enter shallow harbors with the centerboard up. The twin screws originally were driven by two 150-horsepower Superior diesels.

After studying this photo of Tamaris *on a close reach, who could question her sailing ability?*

One would think that numerous design compromises would be necessary for such an all-purpose boat, but Phil Rhodes said that if he were designing *Tamaris* as a pure sailer without engines, he would have used the same hull lines. Of course, there is some trade-off in stability range with such a shallow draft, but inclining experiments performed on *Tamaris* indicated that she has positive stability up to at least 115 degrees of heel. Furthermore, her large size, broad beam, and the weight (7½ tons) of her cast-steel ballast give her tremendous initial stability and sail-carrying power.

Her sail plan is well matched to her shallow hull. The non-masthead ketch rig spreads out her ample sail area of 2,733 square feet fore and aft and keeps it low, which provides a short heeling arm for a boat of this size.

Tamaris was designed for Ralph T. Friedmann of Milwaukee, Wisconsin, but was sold to D.C. Ellwood, who renamed her *Curlew II*. Later, Ellwood commissioned Phil Rhodes to design him a still larger yacht, which was named *Curlew III* (Chapter 33), and *Curlew II* was sold to James H. Kimberly.

At one time, both *Curlews* were docked in the same area at Palm Beach, Florida, and this leads to a rather amusing, possibly apocryphal story. A young boy, who apparently was a sort of waterfront urchin, wandered down on the dock at which *Curlew II* was moored and said to Kimberly, "I see you got one of those *Curlews* too." Apparently, the boy had recently seen *Curlew III* in the area. This irked Kimberly, who quite rightfully considered that he owned a very special and individual yacht; so he changed the boat's name to *Gray Fox*. This meant, or so the story goes, that all articles monogrammed or marked with *Curlew II,* such as linen, silverware, stationery, and so forth, had to be discarded and replaced.

Kimberly need not have worried, however, for his magnificent craft was unique in most every respect, regardless of her name.

18

Escapade
Queen of the Lakes

The 72-foot yawl *Escapade* is Rhodes' largest expression of the *Ayesha-Alondra* concept of a centerboard ocean racer (Chapter 8). She was designed for Henry G. Fownes, of Stamford, Connecticut, who wanted the largest boat that could fit under the size limit for the Bermuda Race, but with a draft shallow enough to negotiate the Intracoastal Waterway.

When Rhodes suggested a keel-centerboard model similar to *Ayesha* and *Alondra*, Fownes was at first opposed, perhaps fearing that the centerboard would be too troublesome on such a large boat. It wasn't until he was taken on a tour of *Alondra* by her first owner, Robert Noyes, that he became sold on her concept. Actually, her draft is relatively deeper than that of her predecessors, but she is otherwise much the same. Her dimensions are 72 feet 6 inches LOA, 54 feet LWL, 17 feet beam, and 7 feet 10 inches draft (board up).

She was built in 1937 to the highest specifications by the Luders Construction Company of Stamford, Connecticut, for $40,000, a considerable sum in those days. Her skeleton is of the best white oak and her outer planking is mahogany, while the decks are Burma teak. She has a centerboard of teak that is bronze-strapped to add strength and prevent warping.

Under Henry Fownes, she was not a particularly successful racer. Her best performance in her early years was a first-to-finish and second in class and fleet in the 1941 Miami-Nassau Race. Her early nemesis was the 72-foot yawl *Baruna*, designed by Sparkman & Stephens in the same year. *Baruna* was more often first to finish, and she seems to have been the better boat, upwind at least.

However, under Wendell C. Anderson, and successive skippers James Y. Camp, Baldwin M. Baldwin, Peter Grimm, and Robert Way (charterer), *Escapade* came alive, and she piled up an impressive racing record, which included the following: a course record in the Port Huron-Mackinac Race in 1950; third in class in the 1959 Honolulu Race; first to finish in the 1960 Transatlantic Race (with a 24-hour run of 256 miles); fleet first in the Miami-Jamaica Race in 1961; first to finish in the Channel Island Race in 1962; first overall in the 1963 St. Petersburg-Venice Race; first to finish in four other Miami-Nassau Races, including a course record in 1966 (breaking the 26-year-old record held by *Ticonderoga),* and setting a new elapsed-time record for the Annapolis-Newport Race in 1965.

Escapade's greatest achievement was her five fleet wins in well-attended Port Huron-Mackinac Races,

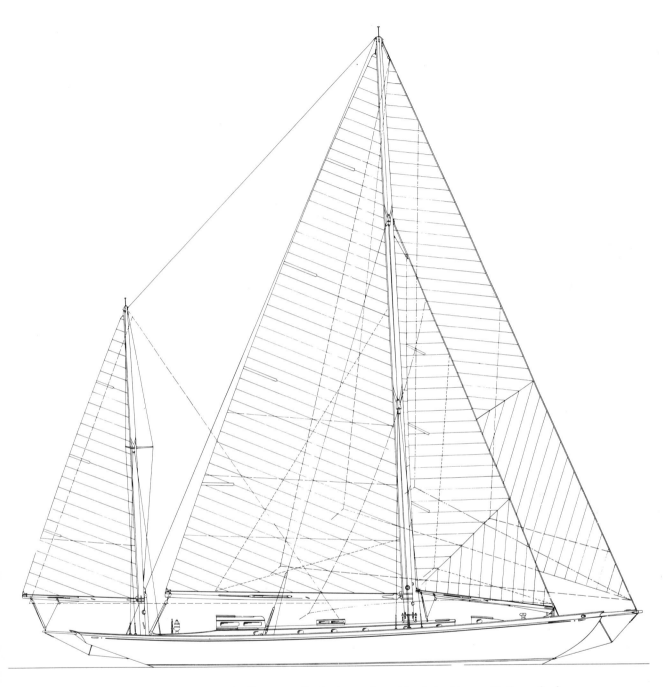

Escapade's double-head yawl rig allows easy sail reduction, yet it provides plenty of power with the masthead foretriangle and sizable mizzen staysail. Escapade is 72½ feet overall.

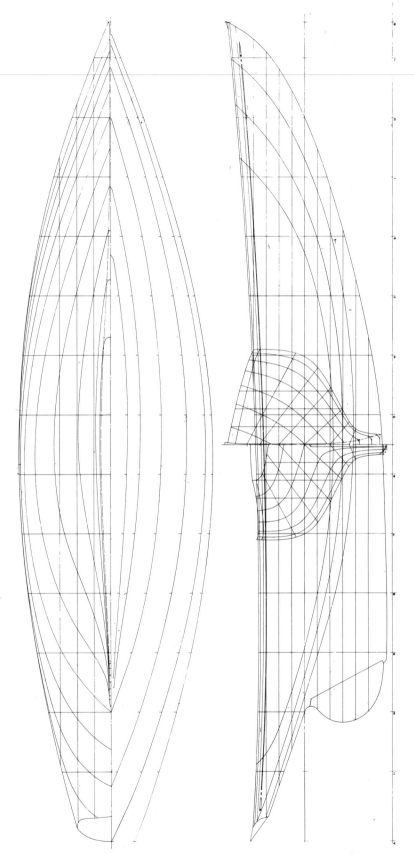

Escapade's sweet, well-balanced hull represents the Ayesha-Alondra concept brought up to the maximum size for ocean racing.

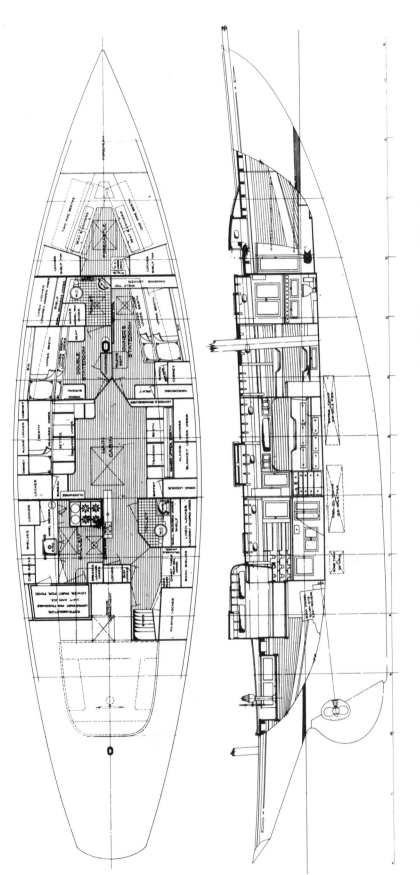

Although Escapade's staterooms are fairly far forward, where some motion will be felt, the accommodations afford privacy and convenience for the on-deck watch, with the galley, head, chart table, and oilskin locker easily available from the cockpit.

With her dark blue hull and maximum size for ocean racing, Escapade *might be called the "Blue Max." She also earned that name for shooting down her competition. (Photo by Beckner Photo Service. Courtesy of Mystic Seaport)*

four of them under Wendell Anderson and the last (in 1967) under Peter Grimm. The yawl's best year was undoubtedly 1951, when she scored a Great Lakes "grand slam" by winning the Chicago-Mackinac Race as well as the Port Huron-Mackinac, the Rochester Race, and the Mills Trophy (awarded to the victor of an important 65-mile race on Lake Erie). Her Great Lakes successes led to her being called the "Queen of the Lakes."

During the 1958 Acapulco Race, *Escapade*'s crew, under James Camp, rescued from life rafts the entire crew of John Hedden's ketch *Celebes*, which was destroyed by fire. *Escapade* continued the race with an additional dozen men on board, and the extra weight didn't seem to slow her down very much, for she still was second to finish and was second in her class.

Compared with today's successful ocean racers, *Escapade*'s long, overhanging counter may seem strange, but it makes sense on this kind of boat. Her relatively heavy hull may need some reserve buoyancy aft, and the extended end allows easy handling and efficient sheeting of the mizzen without the need of a very long boomkin. The chopped sterns of the modern boats of the IOR configuration can be laid, in part, to an effort to mitigate excessive pitching, which arises because of the fine ends, the extreme waterline beam amidships, and the deep, heavy keels and tall rigs of the modern boats, which adversely affect the moment of inertia. *Escapade,* however, does not have this problem, with her straighter midships waterlines, her shallower draft, and her moderate ballast ratio. She gets along very well with a drawn-out stern, which nicely matches her bow.

Her large size and generous beam allow comfortable quarters for a large crew. Because the beam is carried forward and the bow is not pinched in, *Escapade* has enough room for two completely private and roomy twin staterooms forward of the main cabin. The little nook abaft the main cabin's settee that has a locker, bureau, and glass rack seems to be ideal for a bar. There are two large heads, one convenient to the companionway and another serving the two staterooms. There is still another W.C. for a paid hand in the completely private fo'c's'le, which has its own companionway. The beam is also kept well abaft amidships, and this allows such a large, after, port-side galley that it has a centerline bulkhead with a sliding door, which can close off odors from the rest of the cabin. The galley is well ventilated with hatches, and it has a huge icebox-refrigerator. On the starboard side opposite the galley there is a good chart table and a large oilskin locker just where it should be, near the companionway. An unusual feature is the gun locker.

With her masthead rig and bowsprit, *Escapade* can spread a lot of sail — as much as 3,200 square feet with her big genoa. She carries quite a bit of rake in the mainmast, and this moves the center of effort of the large mainsail aft to help balance the huge foretriangle. Rake also helps keep the headstay taut, but *Escapade* has twin headstays to facilitate sail changing, and with this arrangement, it is difficult to keep the luff from sagging excessively. It is interesting that Carleton Mitchell deplored such an arrangement on his *Caribbee* (previously *Alondra)*. The bowsprit on *Escapade* is fitted with a dolphin striker to help prevent the sprit from bending upward.

Escapade is now more than 40 years old, but that doesn't mean that she still can't perform. As recently as the summer of 1980, she won the Opera House Regatta, held in Nantucket for classic yachts, beating a fleet of 34 boats. So, in a sense, "the Queen" still reigns. Long may she live.

19

Kirawan II
Unique at Both Ends

In 1938 Phil Rhodes came out with a distinctive ocean-racing double-ender that was markedly different from any of his previous designs. Her name was *Kirawan II,* and she was destined for great acclaim. This boat was commissioned by Robert P. Baruch, who had won the Bermuda Race in 1936 with his first *Kirawan,* discussed in Chapter 14.

About two years prior to the conception of *Kirawan II,* Phil designed for Baruch a beautiful 19-foot double-ended centerboard daysailer, which was roughly based on a northern European type known as the Kustenjolle. A number of these Rhodes boats were built by Abeking & Rasmussen in Germany. They were carvel planked and were beautifully constructed, and at one time, woodworking apprentices at Abeking & Rasmussen were tested and judged by the work they did on these double-enders. These boats draw only two feet with their boards up, although the outboard rudder extends to below the bottom of the keel.

Evidently Robert Baruch was pleased with the sharp stern on his Rhodes Kustenjolle, for when he ordered the much-larger *Kirawan II,* he asked Phil to make her, also, a double-ender. The sterns of both boats are fairly similar, although *Kirawan II* has a

more raked rudderpost. The sharp stern configuration also fit in well with Baruch's desire for a short-ended boat, thus reducing the L measurement under the CCA rule. Baruch first intended that *Kirawan II* be a deep-keel boat, but he settled on a shoal-draft centerboarder for gunkholing. Tank tests showed the performance of the centerboard model to be as good as that of the keel version. Her centerboard was streamlined in shape and was constructed of plate bronze over a cast bronze frame, with 1,000 pounds of lead shot to weight it down.

If *Kirawan II*'s stern is quite distinctive for an ocean racer, her bow is even more so. Rhodes originally designed the boat with a short bowsprit in order to give her a large foretriangle for powerful headsails, but for some reason this was not aesthetically right, so he drew the stem line into a concave curve, giving her an unusual kind of clipper bow. Recognizing that certain types of clipper bows tend to bury in head seas, Phil gave this one plenty of flare for reserve buoyancy and dryness. This configuration proved very successful and was used later on *Thunderhead* (described in Chapter 38), *Wunderbar,* and a class of motorsailers, the first of which was *La Belle Sole* (Chapter 30). All these boats proved dry in

The beautiful 19-foot Rhodes Kustenjolle, designed for Robert Baruch in 1936, may have offered some inspiration for Kirawan II. *The word* Kustenjolle *means "coastal jollyboat" in German. (Yachting, October 1956)*

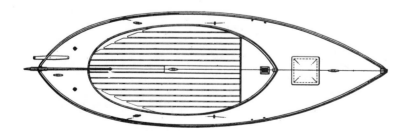

Hother *(formerly* Kirawan II*) on a spinnaker reach. Note her unusual backstay arrangement, helmsman's well, and permanent cockpit shelter. She is 46 feet 3 inches overall. (Courtesy of Paul Hoffmann)*

head seas, but Paul Hoffmann, a subsequent owner of *Kirawan II* and owner of *Thunderhead,* has noted that this bow worked most successfully on the double-ender, probably because the fine stern does not depress the bow but allows it to lift.

Kirawan II was built by the Kretzer Boat Works of City Island, New York. She has a length overall of 46 feet 3 inches and measures 37 feet 6 inches on the load waterline. Her beam is 12 feet 6 inches, and she draws only 4 feet 9 inches with the centerboard up. Her original cutter rig carried 898 square feet of sail (85 percent foretriangle).

Her deck layout and arrangement below are also unusual. On deck, she has a divided cockpit with a small well for the helmsman aft, a permanent cockpit shelter, and an amidships companionway on

An interesting model test for Kirawan II. *Stripes of wet paint indicate the flow pattern and areas of greatest skin friction. (Courtesy of Mystic Seaport)*

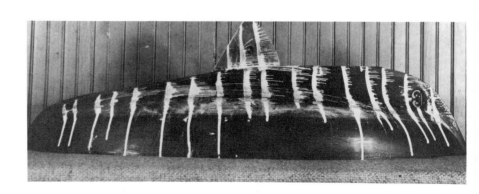

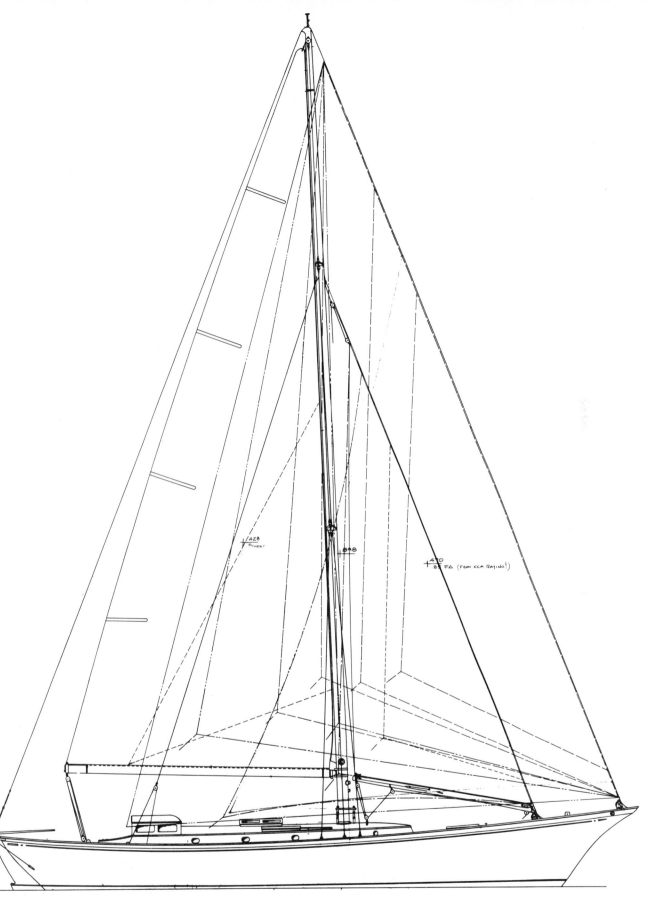

Kirawan II's tall cutter rig divides the sail area almost equally between main and foretriangle. This would tend to disprove the theory that boats with unequally divided sail plans are the most successful.

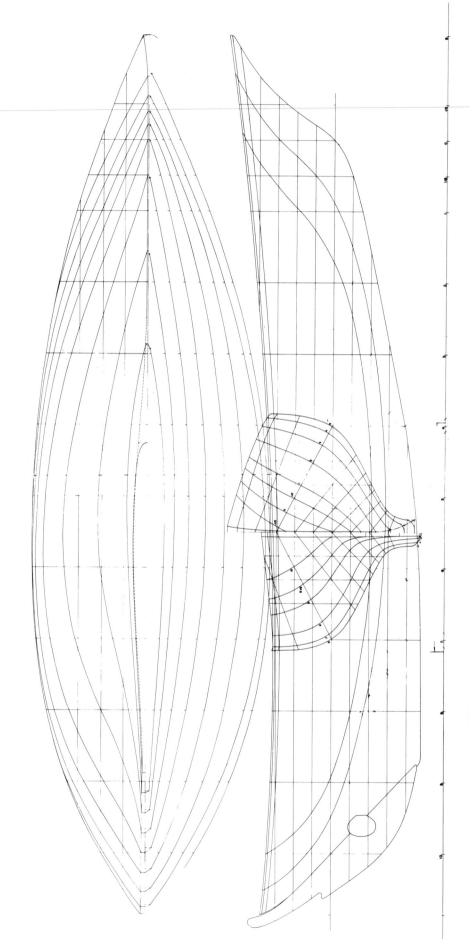

Kirawan II's clipper bow and double-ended stern produce, in a most graceful way, an extremely long waterline.
Note the almost powerboat-like flare of the forward sections.

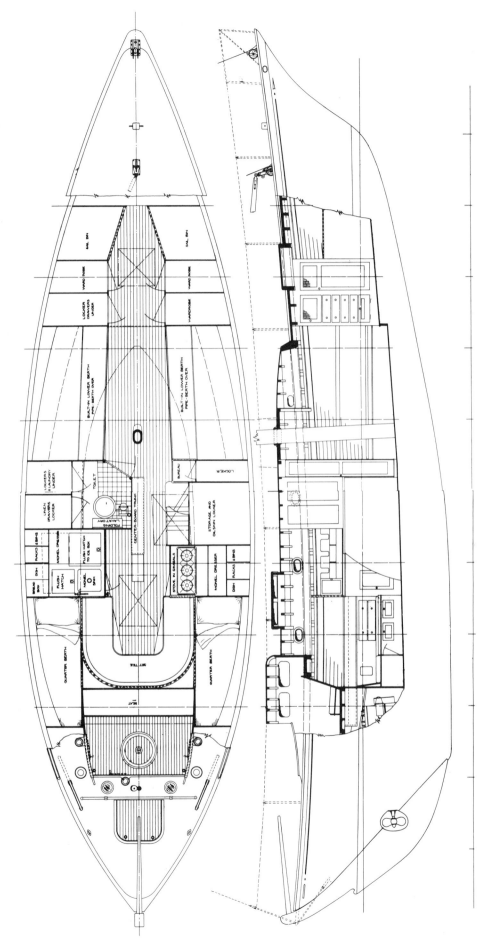

Even in her accommodations Kirawan II is strikingly unique. Note the convenience of the galley to the U-shaped
settee aft and the ample stowage area forward for sails.

the starboard side of the deckhouse. Below decks, moving from aft to forward, there is a U-shaped settee with outboard quarter berths in the saloon, then the galley on both sides of the boat, an enclosed head to port with a huge oilskin locker opposite, a cabin with four berths, and a tremendous stowage area forward with wardrobes and sail bins.

Robert Baruch had only moderate success racing *Kirawan II,* but he did attract attention with her. In an article on the 1938 Vineyard Race, in which she finished third, *Yachting* magazine noted that *"Kirawan II* showed conclusively that a centerboarder can close reach and go to windward." Sailing in the Halifax Race the next season, she took the Boston Yacht Club trophy for the best equipped yacht for ocean racing.

Kirawan II did quite well under her next owner, Jakob Isbrandtsen, who changed the boat's name to *Hother.* It wasn't until 1955, however, that *Hother* really started cleaning up on the race course. At that time she was bought by Paul Hoffmann, and during the next six years she won 29 prizes out of 33 races entered. These included two class seconds in Bermuda Races and two fleet wins in well-attended Stamford-Vineyard Races.

When Hoffmann bought the double-ender, she was fast but not perfectly balanced, for she carried considerable weather helm when heeled on a reach. In consultation with the Rhodes office, Hoffmann sought to alleviate her ardent helm by fitting a new rudder, with more area at the bottom, and shortening the main boom. With these changes the helm was greatly improved, and after internal stiffeners were added to the mast, enabling it to carry larger headsails, *Hother* became one of the fastest boats on the East Coast racing circuit. Paul Hoffmann has said that he thinks *Hother's* high-aspect-ratio mainsail, with its luff more than three times as long as its foot, was the forerunner of the typical modern racing rig.

Hother was later retired from racing and was taken gunkhole cruising on the Chesapeake Bay. With her shallow draft she is well suited for that use, but she could probably still race very successfully under a handicap rule such as the Measurement Handicap System.

20

Copperhead
Sheer Beauty

The lovely *Copperhead* is another Rhodes yawl that achieved fame on the Great Lakes. She was designed less than a year after *Escapade* and is perhaps even more handsome because of her more closely matched ends. Her design was commissioned by John T. (Bud) Snite, who went to Phil Rhodes for the design because he admired *Kirawan,* and he was particularly taken with the Rhodes sheerlines. Snite said that the initial sketches for *Copperhead* were drawn on the backs of coasters in a cocktail lounge. As was the case with many of Rhodes' clients, Snite became a lasting friend of Phil's.

Copperhead was well built by Sturgeon Bay Boat Works (now known as Palmer Johnson) in Wisconsin in 1939. She cost $14,000 to build; 8,338 hours of labor, at a cost of $1.00 per man-hour, went into her construction. Her mahogany-planked and Everdur screw-fastened hull was strengthened with bronze knees and straps, and she was given laminated bilge stringers for strength without excessive weight.

Snite tells a story about how one of Phil's assistants made a mistake in computing the weight of the lead ballast, which resulted in an excessively heavy keel. Rhodes caught the mistake, but a block of lead had to be cut out of the casting, and the cavity was filled with mahogany. According to Snite, Phil would later joke about the incident and say that *Copperhead* was the only boat he knew of that had mahogany keel ballast.

With dimensions of 47 feet 8 inches overall, 34 feet LWL, 11 feet 4 inches beam, and 6 feet 10 inches draft, *Copperhead* is similar in size to *Narada* and her sisters (Chapter 13), except that Snite's boat has slightly longer ends and a deeper keel. She was thoroughly tank tested, and her lines are said to be developed from *Narada's*. Originally, *Copperhead* was fitted with a *Kirawan*-type of cockpit shelter with opening windows, and the shelter could be completely screened in to keep out the Lake Michigan water flies. Later, under the ownership of Charles Kotovic, the shelter was taken off to reduce weight; its removal also enhanced the boat's appearance.

John Snite carried a paid hand, so *Copperhead* has a forward galley and a pipe berth for the hand in the fo'c's'le. Abaft the main saloon there is a large enclosed head and oilskin locker near the companionway and farther aft, the owner's double stateroom. Doors are nicely arranged so that the head can be used with maximum privacy from either the stateroom or areas farther forward.

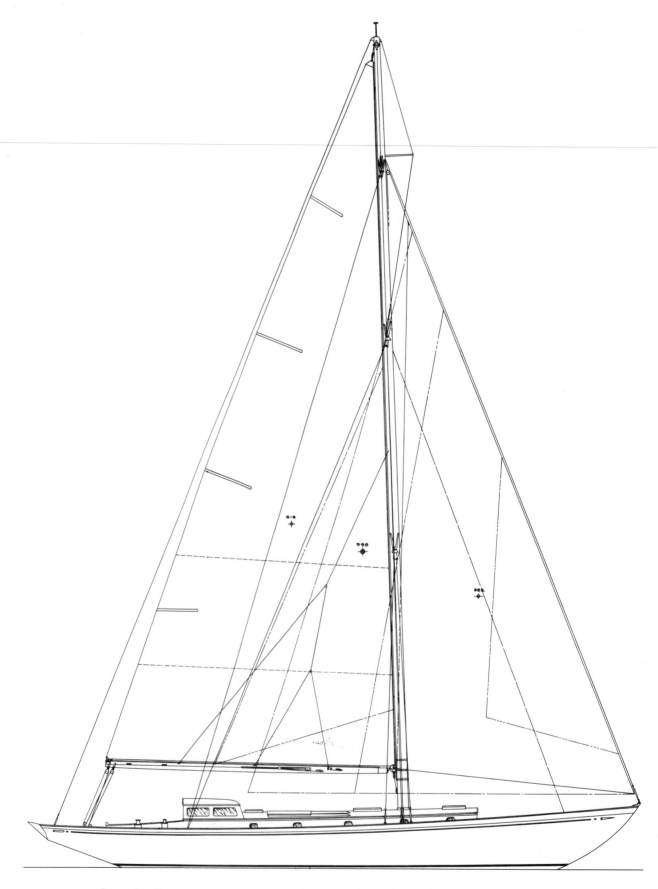

Copperhead's *original fractional sail plan has jumper stays that restrict the luff lengths of her large jibs. She is 47 feet 8 inches overall.*

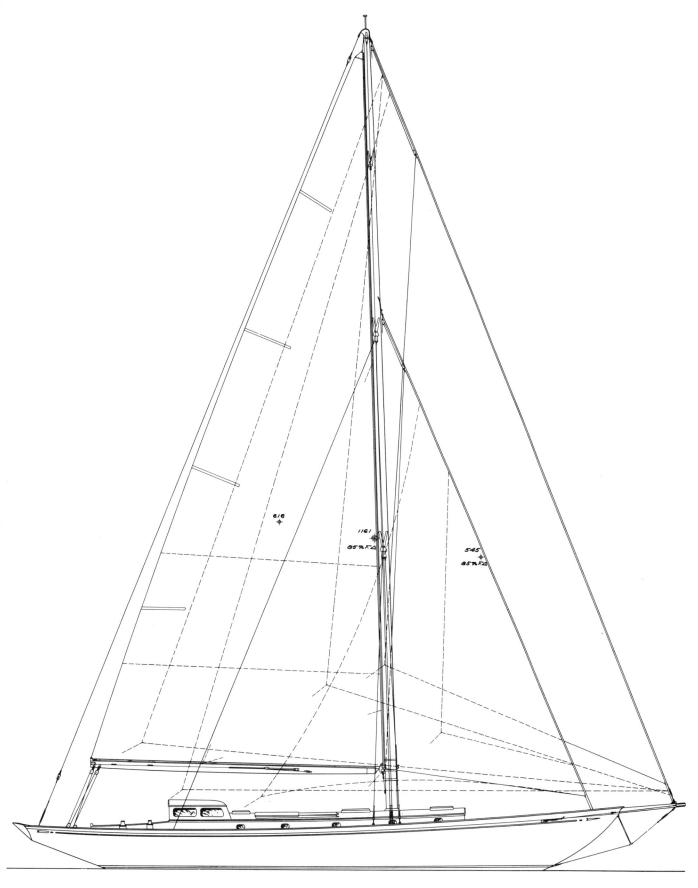

The 1941 rig change ordered for Copperhead *by John Snite provides a huge foretriangle. Note the reaching jib with its clew not far from the end of the main boom.*

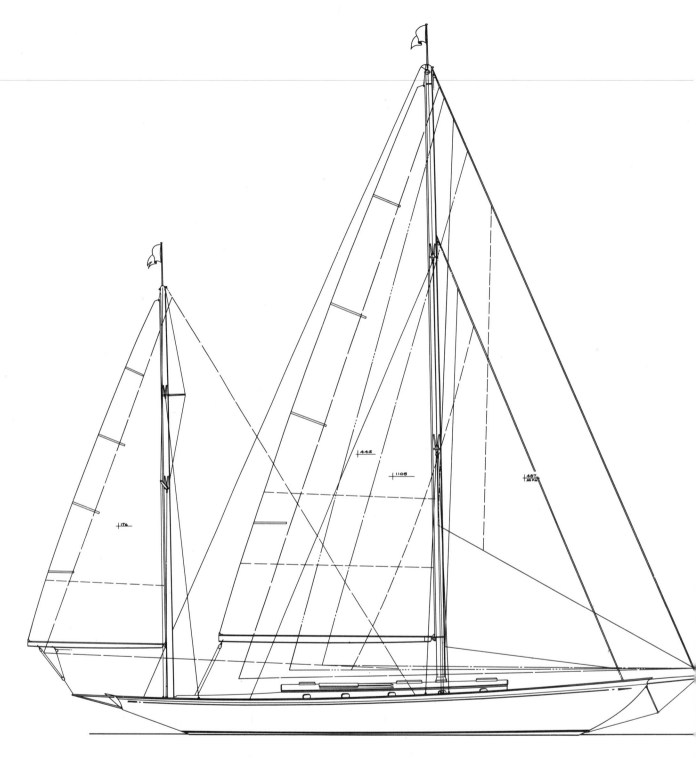

Copperhead's *yawl rig ordered by Charles Kotovic. The mizzen was made two feet shorter than the one shown on this plan. Removal of the cockpit shelter made her even more sleek in appearance.*

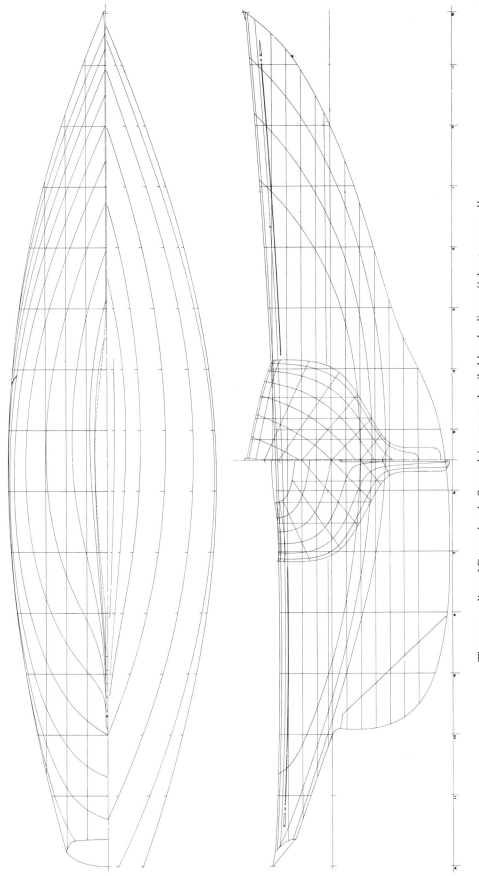

The gorgeous lines of Copperhead. *One yachting reporter described her sheerline as "almost sensuous."*

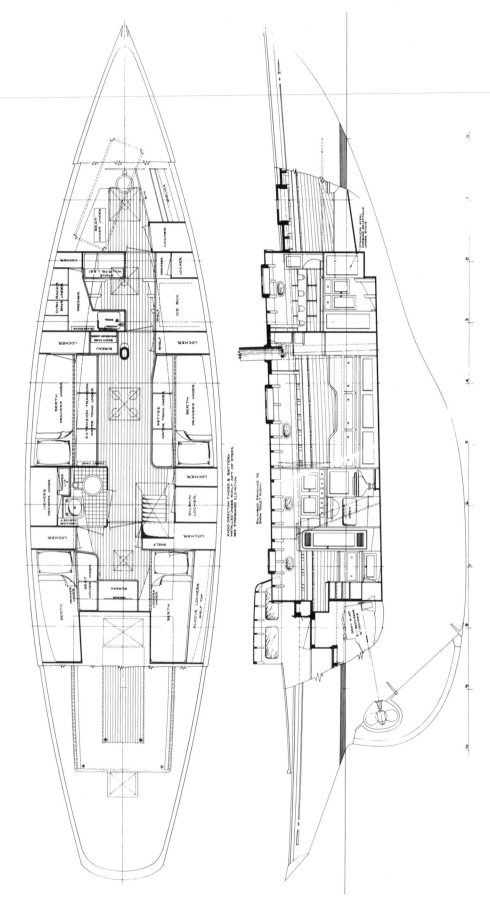

Copperhead's accommodations afford great privacy and are well arranged for a paid hand. Her deckhouse, inspired by that of Kirawan, could be entirely screened in.

Copperhead, *shown on a beam reach with her spinnaker pole nearly against the forestay. Her original rig kept her from setting a spinnaker from the masthead. (Courtesy of Mystic Seaport)*

Copperhead *with her yawl rig that made her one of the fastest boats on the Great Lakes during the mid-1950s. Notice the foot length of her genoa jib. (Photo by M.E. Denash. Courtesy of Mystic Seaport)*

Copperhead originally had a fractional sloop rig, and Snite felt she was a bit undercanvased for light weather, so he increased her sail area in 1941. The Rhodes office drew up plans for a new cutter rig, which extended the foretriangle with a bowsprit and a masthead jib stay, thereby increasing the sail area from 998 to 1,161 square feet. This made her more lively, and she took a class second in the Chicago-Mackinac Race that year. She was slightly over-burdened in a breeze of wind, but Snite and Rhodes worked out a jiffy-reefing system that was similar in some respects to present-day systems.

Copperhead was sold the following year to Philip Wrigley (of Wrigley chewing gum), and after that she had several owners, including the aforementioned Charles Kotovic, who in 1953 made some rather drastic changes in the boat. Besides removing the cockpit shelter, he stripped her of everything he considered unnecessary weight, converted from wheel to tiller steering, and changed the rig from sloop to yawl. *Copperhead* had always been a smart sailer, but after these revisions, she was even more competitive, especially in off-the-wind events. From 1953 to 1958 she won more than 50 prizes, including firsts in the Chicago and Port Huron-Mackinac Races.

After he sold *Copperhead*, John Snite owned another hot Rhodes design, the yawl *Tahuna*. This boat, which was somewhat lighter, was very competitive, and she won her division in the 1952 Chicago-Mackinac under the ownership of P.C. McNulty. Despite the virtues of *Tahuna*, it seems that Snite's first love was *Copperhead*. She is still going strong under the ownership of Thomas J. Perkins of Belvedere, California.

21

The Rhodes 27s
A Class with Class

The Rhodes 27 was Rhodes' first outstandingly successful class boat of the racing-cruiser type. This class came about as a result of a design competition sponsored by the Fishers Island Yacht Club in 1938. Leading naval architects submitted designs for a medium-sized class boat with good racing potential, yet with comfortable accommodations for cruising. After careful consideration, the club's selection committee chose the Rhodes design, which measures 39 feet 2 inches overall and 27 feet on the waterline. The boat has a beam of 9 feet 8 inches and a draft of 5 feet 10 inches, while the three-quarter sloop rig carries 635 square feet of sail.

A dozen of these boats were built by the Henry Nevins yard at City Island, New York, in 1939. Through the efforts of promoter Harry MacDonald, the boat became a standardized racer-cruiser available to the general boating public, and before the war, Rhodes 27s were also built on the Great Lakes and on the West Coast. Several were built abroad.

Her accommodations include at least one novel feature, namely, the disappearing galley. Under the raised portion of the cabin trunk there are uphol-

stered seats, but the area can be quickly converted to a galley by removing cushions to expose the icebox and sink and by pulling out from a cupboard the sliding stove, which moves on sail tracks. Another somewhat unusual feature is that the after ends of the transom berths in the main cabin are recessed under the galley dressers, and this opens up space forward for a large head and wardrobe. The arrangement also allows more floor space in the double stateroom forward.

The R-27s proved to be capable sailers and gave very good accounts of themselves wherever they raced, but in 1944 Phil Rhodes decided to modify the design. As he put it, "I made some changes in the design, which are not at once apparent to the layman's eye but which I consider were improvements." The new version of the boat was labeled "Super R/27" in the Rhodes design index, but later it became known as the New Rhodes 27. Without seeing the lines drawings of each boat for comparison, all the hull changes aren't evident, but an obvious modification is the keel profile. The new 27 is a little more cut away forward and there is a definite toe to the keel. It has been said that the New

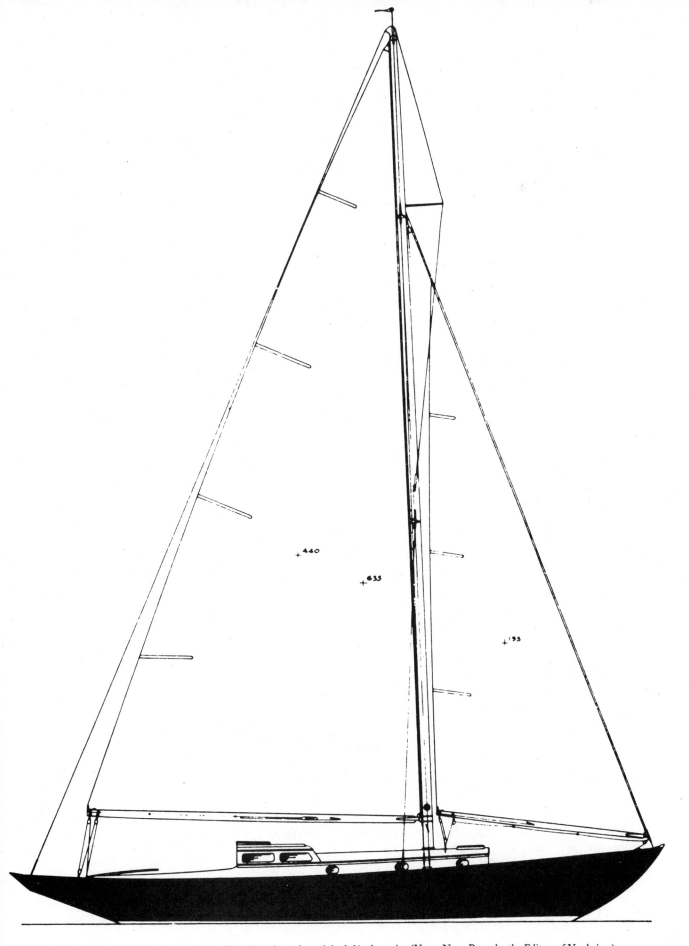

The outstandingly successful Rhodes 27. This plan shows her original ¾ sloop rig. (Your New Boat *by the Editors of* Yachting)

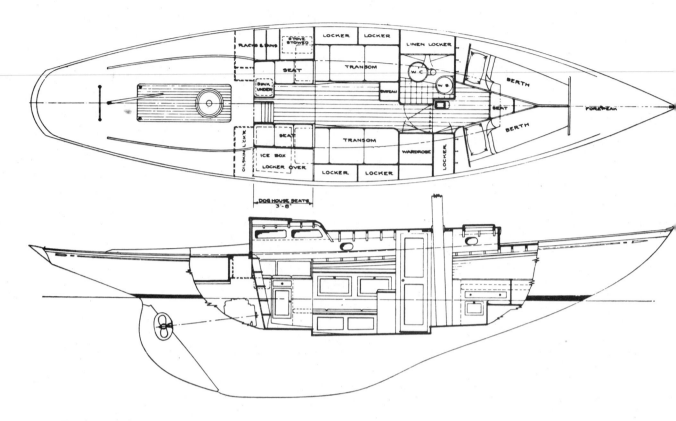

The accommodations plan of the Rhodes 27, which shows her offbeat hideaway galley. (Your New Boat *by the Editors of* Yachting)

Rhodes 27 had some influence on the design of the famous Owens cutter, which was designed in 1945. In comparing profiles, it is possible to note a similarity, except that the Owens cutter has been carried a step or two further, with the keel toe being more pronounced.

Although the accommodations of the original and the new R-27s are almost identical, there is a very noticeable difference in the appearance of the doghouse. On the original boat, the doghouse appears to be sitting on top of the cabin trunk in the manner of *Kirawan* and *Copperhead,* while on the new version the doghouse is an integral part of the trunk. This integrated form of doghouse was the type that Rhodes was to use in the future.

Both stock versions of the 27-footer were originally designed with fractional rigs, but the foretriangle height was increased slightly on the newer boats. This increased the total sail area by about 53 square feet. The non-overlapping working jib is fitted with a boom so that it is self-tending for easy tacking when sailing shorthanded. The boom was originally fitted

against the base of the forestay, but a revised plan showed the boom mounted on a foredeck pedestal. This latter arrangement has several advantages: among them, it induces less working stress against the forestay and its lower fittings; it allows overlapping racing jibs to be carried closer to the deck; and the working jib's draft is automatically increased as its sheet is eased. In the early 1960s the New Rhodes 27 was updated with a masthead rig that increased the foretriangle and decreased the mainsail's area.

In whatever version, Rhodes 27s were always a threat on the race course. To mention a few examples, the R-27s *Daphne* and *Rascal* excelled in racing on the Great Lakes, while the New R-27s *Patricia* and *Lancer* had exceptional records on Long Island Sound and San Francisco Bay, respectively. Perhaps the most famous R-27 is *Tiny Teal;* in 1949 she won the Southern Ocean Racing Circuit when co-skippered by Palmer Langdon and Richard Bertram. She also won the St. Petersburg-Havana Race against a competitive fleet. Under the rating rules such as the MHS and PHRF, which ensure reason-

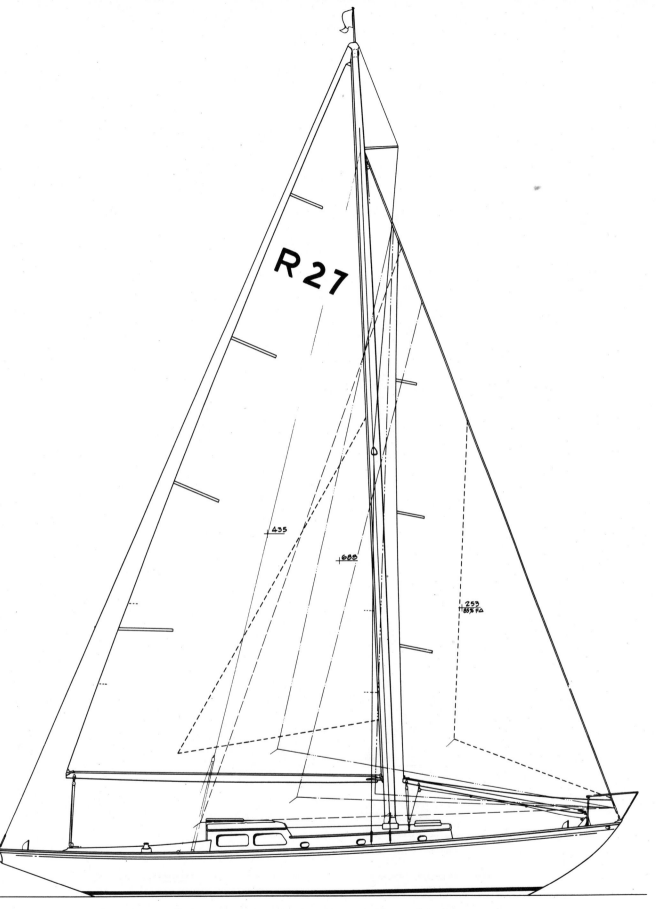

Sail plan of the New Rhodes 27, with her larger foretriangle and jib boom on a pedestal. Phil designed a number of yacht fittings, including a pedestal that is still in the Merriman-Holbrook catalog.

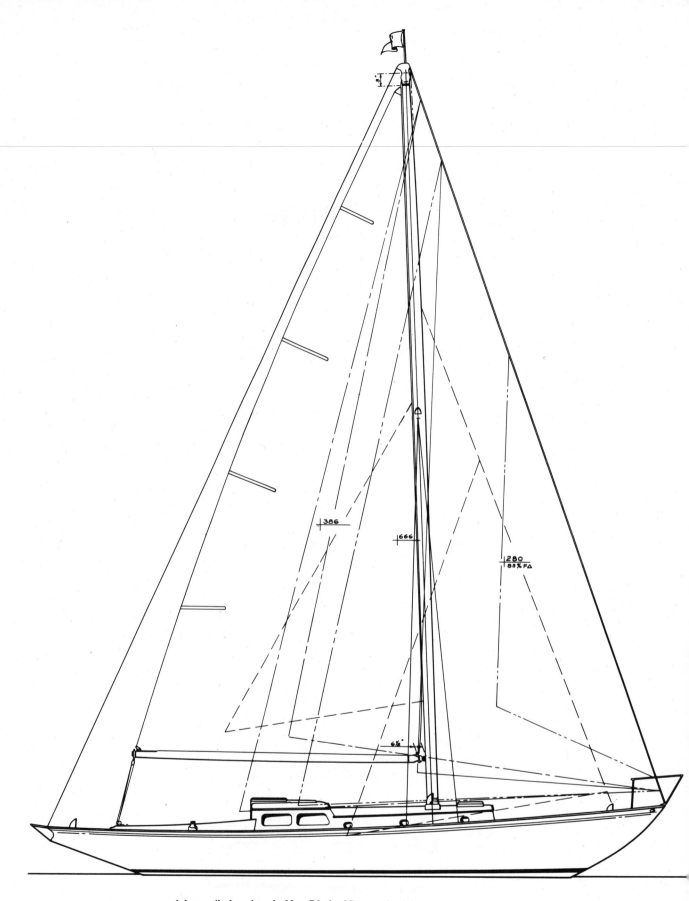

A later sail plan gives the New Rhodes 27 a masthead foretriangle and smaller mainsail.

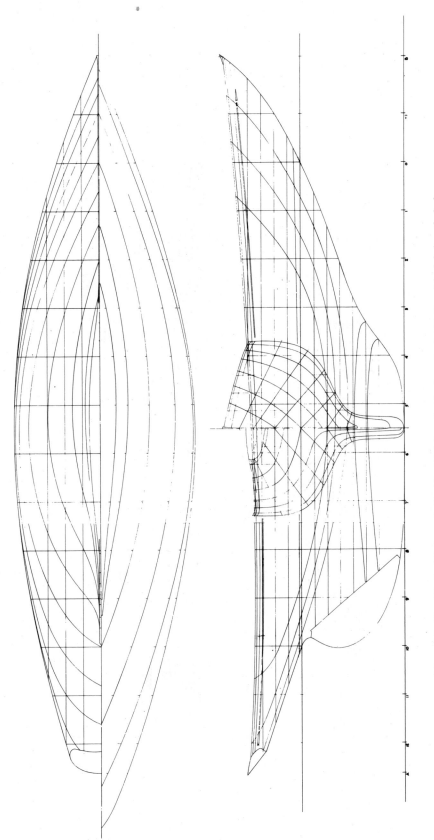

Lines of the New Rhodes 27 show a hull with well-balanced ends. In contrast with the original design, the keel has a definite toe.

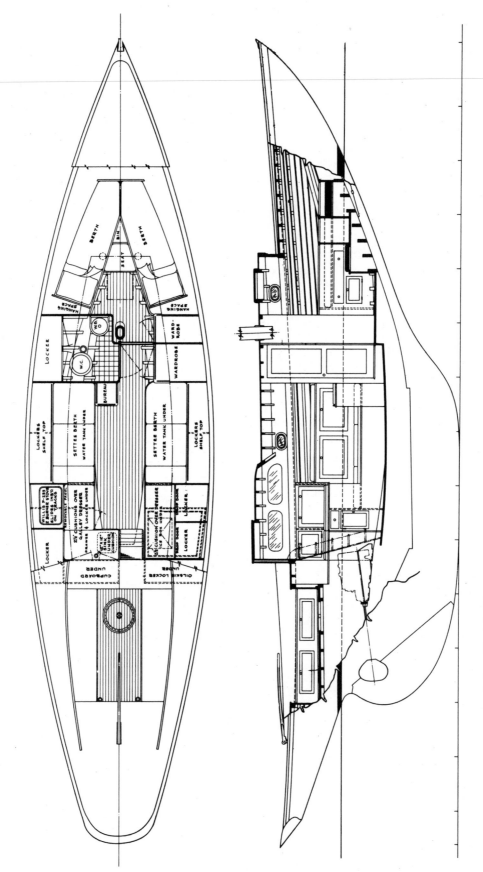

Both models of the Rhodes 27 are basically alike in their accommodations, but the newer one has the integrated doghouse with larger windows.

Phil Rhodes (forward) and his son Bodie (middle) sailing with A.P. Davis aboard his race-winning New Rhodes 27 Patricia. *(Courtesy of Mystic Seaport)*

ably fair handicapping, Rhodes 27s should still be competitive.

Most of the 27s were well built by respected yacht yards, such as Kretzer, Abeking & Rasmussen, Herman Lund, and, as previously mentioned, Nevins.

Phil Rhodes wrote, "They are built very strongly and will last forever if given ordinary good treatment." If a Rhodes 27 owner can bear the expense of maintaining a wooden boat, there is no reason why he should not want to keep such a lovely, comfortable, and nimble craft forever.

22

The Bounty
Semi-Mass-Produced

When the Rhodes-designed Bounty class was introduced in 1939, it caused no small amount of stir. In fact, an article in *Yachting* magazine said, "No sooner had Bounty appeared than the luncheon tables, gab-fests, and sundry other gatherings of yachtsmen were abuzz with gossip and discussion about her." The reason for this reaction was that this smart-looking, 39-foot stock cruising sloop was being offered at a price 35 to 40 percent below that of similar boats built by competitors. The Bounty's producer, the Coleman Boat Company, received hundreds of inquiries, and despite cautious skepticism from prospective buyers, a dozen firm orders were placed before the first boat was completed.

Builders and designers had been putting increasing emphasis on stock boats since the early depression years in order to keep costs down and to create a broader market, but the Coleman Company achieved a price breakthrough by using semi-mass-production methods. The first seven or eight Bountys were built in the Thomas D. Scott yard at Riverside, Connecticut, but space was limited, so Coleman set up a new operation in Medford, Massachusetts, devoted entirely to building these specific boats as efficiently as possible.

The Bountys were built upside down at stations along an assembly line. The structural members were cut and shaped with the aid of jigs and templates, and then the skeleton of each hull was assembled over a large jig called a "camel's back," which had individual metal-faced molds for each frame. After this operation, the hull was planked with strakes cut and beveled on steel-edged jigs. The shutter planks were the only ones that needed elaborate working to make them fit. Decks, bulkheads, and the cabin top were of waterproof plywood, while the cockpit sole was made of teak strips and holly "feathers" glued under pressure to sheet plywood. As much as possible, interior parts, such as cabinets and lockers, were assembled before installation. As a result of this building method, and the fact that equipment was kept simple and minimal, a Bounty could be purchased for around $4,000. (One owner told me he bought his boat for the unbelievable price of $2,800.)

There were some dire predictions that the Bountys would fall apart after five years, but a number of them are still sailing today, about 40 years after their launching. Furthermore, one 30-year-old Bounty passed through the eye of a hurricane at sea without

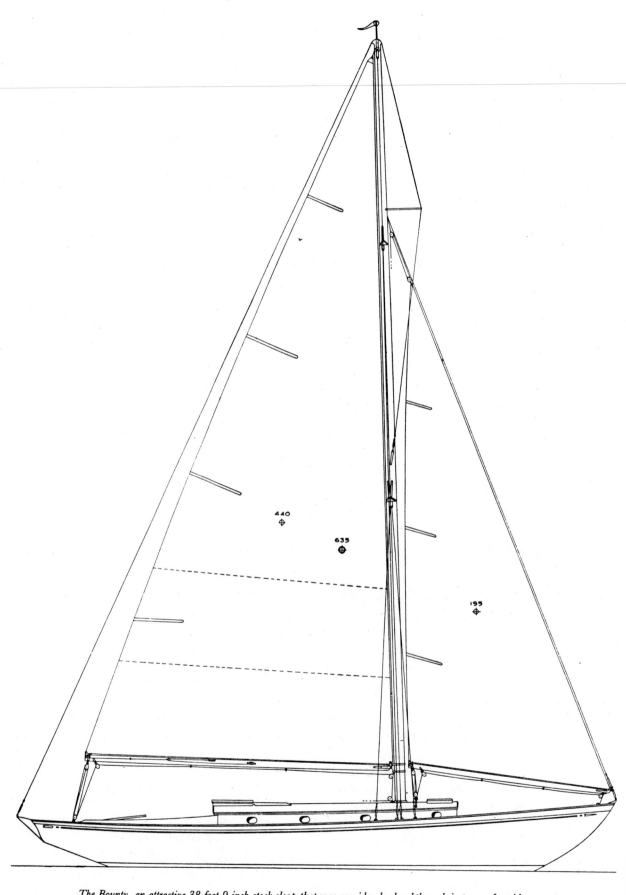

440

635

195

The Bounty, an attractive 38-foot 9-inch stock sloop that was considered a breakthrough in terms of rapid construction and low price. (The Rudder, *October 1939*)

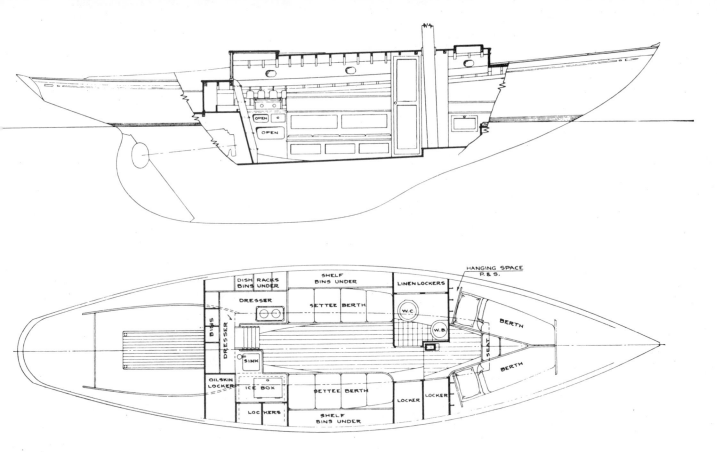

Above: *The Bounty has a large galley and plenty of stowage space below. An interesting feature is the hanging space for clothes abaft each forward berth.* (The Rudder, *October 1939*) **Below:** *A close-up view of the first Bounty shows not only how graceful she is but also how economy is achieved by trimming the genoa with a tackle.* (*Courtesy of Mystic Seaport*)

being seriously scathed. Many years earlier I was crewing on that boat when she was struck head-on by a Navy yawl sailing at top speed. Her toughness was shown by the fact that she suffered little more than a split rail.

Not only were the Bountys built strongly, considering their price, they were also quite fast for their time. John Sherwood's *Gibson Girl,* for example, had a fine record in local races on the Chesapeake Bay. In 1941 she won the Chesapeake Bay Yacht Racing Association's overall seasonal High Point Award. I crewed for Anne Palmer once or twice and was impressed by the performance of her father's Bounty, *Wyvern.* However, the boat had one occasional fault: she had a tendency to gripe when close reaching in a fresh breeze. Many years later, *Wyvern* was bought by Dr. Roy Scholz, who removed all mast rake, and this alleviated her weather helm.

The Bounty measures 38 feet 9 inches by 27 feet 6 inches by 9 feet 8 inches by 5 feet 8 inches. She has a three-quarter sloop rig with 635 square feet of sail area. Her rig is simple to handle, for her headsails are small, the boomed working jib is self-tending, and sail can be shortened in a blow without much difficulty by reefing the large main.

The accommodations provide four berths, two in the main cabin and two in a forward stateroom. The after galley extends across the width of the boat, and it has a number of desirable features, including an on-center sink (for good drainage when heeled), a lot of counter space, and a large icebox, the top of which can be used for a chart table. In addition, she has an oilskin locker conveniently located near the companionway. There is an enclosed head amidships, but original plans show the top of the head bowl below the load waterline, which necessitates that seacocks be operated every time the head is used.

Production of the Bounty was cut short by the war. It was sufficiently successful, however, for the Coleman Company to introduce a stock fiberglass sloop, the Bounty II, in 1956. The fiberglass sloop is often considered to be a fiberglass version of the original Bounty, but as will be explained in Chapter 31, the two Bountys are not alike except in name.

23

Merry Maiden
Versatility at Its Best

Of all the ocean racers moored in Hamilton Harbor after the 1950 Newport-Bermuda Race, the most interesting to me was H. Irving Pratt's 52-foot ketch, *Merry Maiden*. She had handily won first place in Class B, she was handsome, and she had an unusual deck plan, with an amidships cockpit, an arrangement rarely seen in those days.

Measuring 52 feet 4 inches LOA, 38 feet LWL, with a beam of 13 feet 3 inches and a draft of 6 feet 6 inches, *Merry Maiden* was built by Palmer Scott & Company of New Bedford, Massachusetts, in 1947. She is a virtual sistership of *Jane Dore III*, which Phil Rhodes designed for Hobart Ford in 1945. These sisters were originally designed to be shoal-draft keelboats, but *Merry Maiden* had a centerboard added during the winter following her Bermuda triumph. Owner Irving Pratt, a prominent yachtsman, former commodore of the New York Yacht Club, and a major force behind the leading handicap rules, was a noted experimenter; he reasoned that *Merry Maiden*'s upwind performance could be improved with the centerboard. Later, a bowsprit was added, and still later the mizzen was enlarged to improve speed off the wind.

Undoubtedly these changes did improve the boat's performance, but it is hard to say just how much, for she did well both before and after the changes. She seemed to perform as well in light weather as in strong winds. For example, she won the 1951 Monhegan Island Race off the coast of Maine in heavy weather that caused 11 out of 22 starters to retire, yet in 1953 won her class in the same race in light-air conditions.

Phil Rhodes called *Merry Maiden* a ketch, but she might be considered a yawl, since her mizzen is so far aft. Regardless, her rig spreads plenty of canvas, and it is well divided for easy handling by a small crew. In addition, her sheets and winches are arranged so that all sails can be handled without difficulty from the helm. This made it possible for Commodore Pratt to sail her in a number of single-handed races sponsored by the lighthearted but earnest organization known as the Cruising, Snoozing and Boozing Club. The plans show some cruising labor-savers, such as the anchor davit, lazyjacks, and the self-tending forestaysail. The mizzen boom might be handy for a lone sailor in lifting the dinghy aboard to its stowage place abaft the mizzenmast.

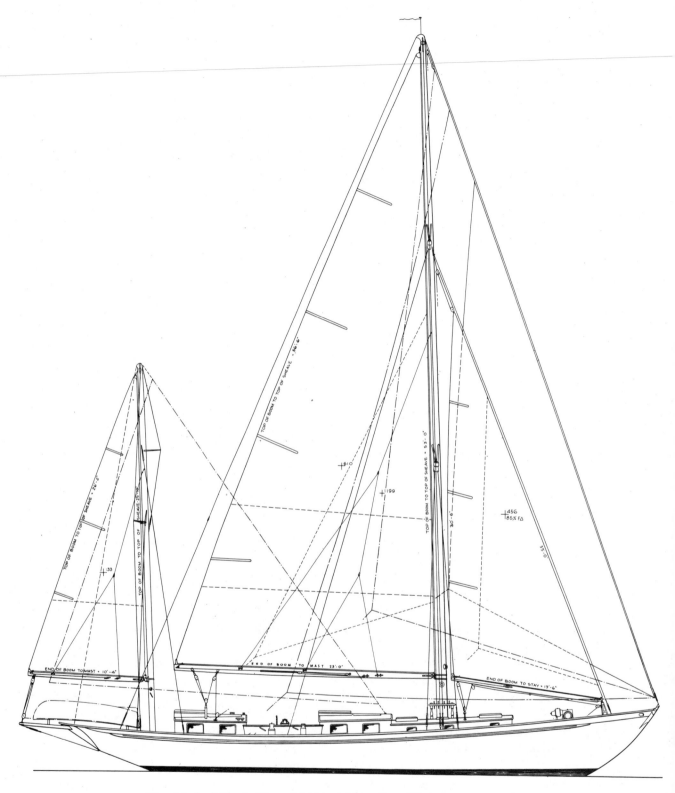

The original sail plan for Merry Maiden *and* Jane Dore III, *both 52 feet 4 inches overall.*

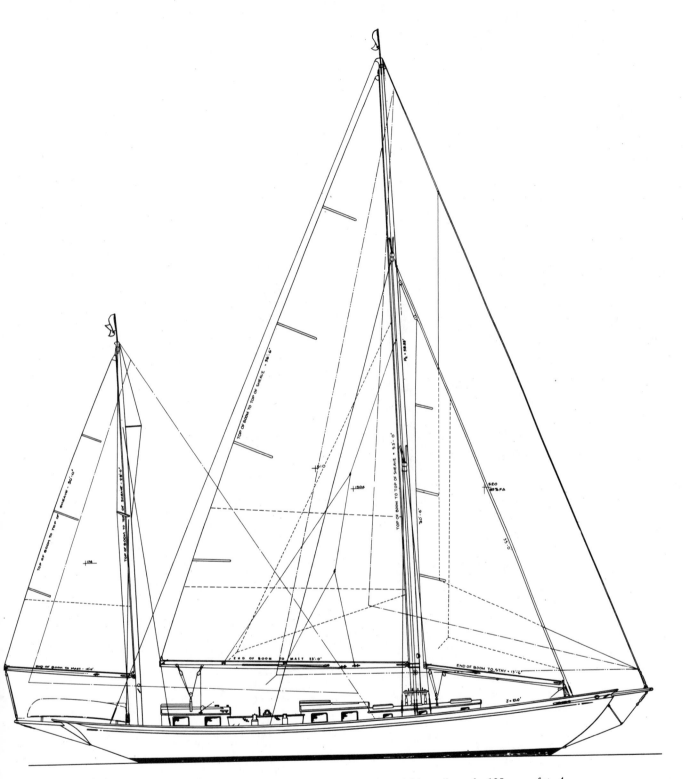

Merry Maiden *with her bowsprit and larger mizzen, which increased her sail area by 105 square feet. A centerboard was also added to improve her windward ability.*

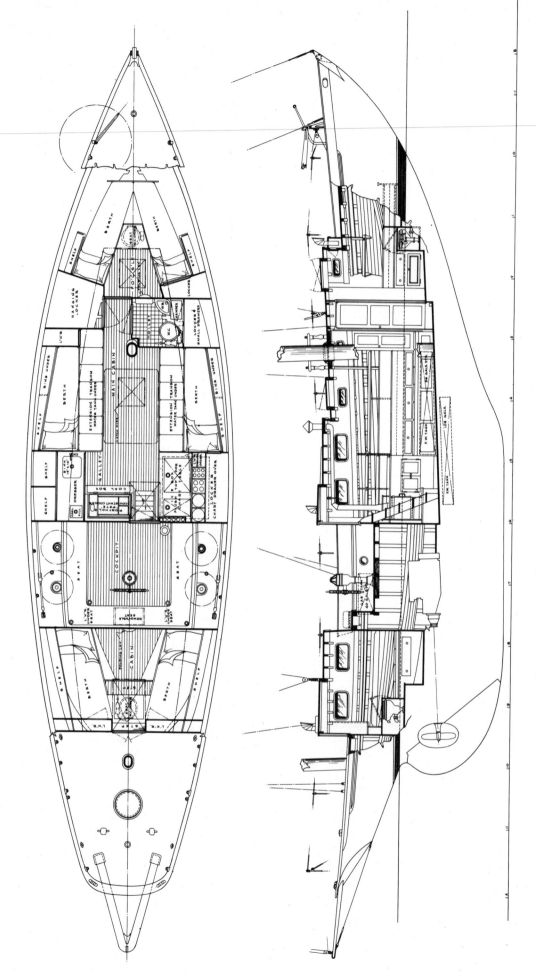

The innovative layout of Merry Maiden and her sister affords maximum privacy.

Although this photo of Merry Maiden *shows a number of crew in the cockpit, she was rigged so that she could be singlehanded. (Photo by Roll Photo Service. Courtesy of Mystic Seaport)*

Even though her double cabin trunks and center cockpit were novel at the time, the configuration does not sacrifice *Merry Maiden's* graceful appearance. This arrangement is now quite common, but the specific layout on *Merry Maiden* is still unusual in some respects. Her two-berth after cabin is relatively far forward, and there is a large after deck, which allows room for stowage of the dinghy. Also, the companionway to the after cabin is at the after end of the trunk rather than at the forward end. This is desirable on a boat with freeboard as low as *Merry Maiden's* because with a forward-facing companionway, spray might be blown into the after cabin when the boat is beating into a choppy sea.

One drawback of *Merry Maiden's* particular arrangement is that there is no below-decks passageway between the after and forward cabins, which means that one has to leave the cockpit to enter the after cabin and one is unprotected when going from one cabin to the other. Compromises are always necessary, and in this case some convenience and possibly some safety are traded for extra privacy. A definite plaudit for the after cabin's farther-forward-than-normal location is that its two bunks are not far from the boat's pitching axis, so sleepers will not be rocked unduly in rough weather.

The forward cabin has a large after galley, two pilot berths, two extension transoms, and a large enclosed head, as well as a fo'c's'le with two bunks and another W.C. Although there is no navigator's desk, charts can be spread out on top of the icebox, which is conveniently located alongside the companionway ladder. The engine room is under the cockpit, and it houses a 105-horsepower gasoline auxiliary, which drives a 24-inch feathering propeller. This, and her nearly horizontal shaft, give *Merry Maiden* outstanding performance under power.

The arrangement plans show a large "Porthole Pete" coal stove, which can be used for heating and drying the cabin as well as for cooking. The stove is named for its inventor, Phil's old friend Porthole Pete Chamberlain. Bodie Rhodes has said, "For a long time, he [Porthole Pete] produced a very superior coal stove which included pots with machined bottoms that promoted heat transfer . . . . It was a heavy but very efficient item that to the best of my memory sold very well."

Merry Maiden is a very able boat, an assessment that has been borne out by the fact that she is presently on her second circumnavigation. With such unique versatility, she might be called a total all-arounder.

24

The Rhodes 77s
Handsome Full-Powered Sailers

At the end of World War II, Phil Rhodes designed a slightly smaller variation on the theme of *Tamaris* known as the Rhodes 77. This design is similar to *Tamaris* (Chapter 17) in concept, arrangement, rig, and construction but has a counter stern instead of a canoe stern. Like *Tamaris,* the Rhodes 77 has good performance under both power and sail. Although the 77 was referred to by some as a motorsailer, Rhodes emphatically rejected this label, saying, "While she has accommodations that would dispirit the average motorsailer, she is a true sailer in the best seagoing tradition."

The Rhodes 77 design was drawn near the end of 1945 for Henry B. Babson, the former owner of *Maruffa* (Chapter 11), and there were four boats built in 1947 by the Burger Boat Company of Manitowoc, Wisconsin. Their basic measurements are 77 feet 2 inches by 55 feet by 19 feet by 6 feet 6 inches. Although their decks are of Burma teak, the hulls, and even the deckhouses, are of electrically welded steel. These yachts were built to the exacting requirements of the American Bureau of Shipping, and they have certificates of the Bureau's highest classification, which ensures that construction is top drawer.

In hull shape, these yachts fall somewhere between *Tamaris* and *Escapade* (Chapter 18). Compared with *Escapade,* the 77s have a longer, shallower keel, and they are a bit fatter, with slightly more rounded sections. Their windward performance is undoubtedly better than that of *Tamaris,* because the 77 has a deeper keel and more efficient lateral plane for upwind sailing, and she is dragging only one propeller.

The deck and arrangement plans are almost identical to those of *Tamaris,* with the after cabins, raised cockpit, sunken deckhouse with engine room beneath, saloon just forward of amidships, galley farther forward, and crew's quarters in the bow. The only major difference in the accommodations is that the 77s lack *Tamaris'* large storeroom aft, and their after heads are opposite, rather than adjacent to, each other. And instead of the Victrola and piano, there is simply a radio. (No doubt some of these boats are now fitted with stereo systems that pipe music to most cabins.)

The accoutrements for comfort and convenience on the 77s include hot and cold running water, blowers in all quarters, an oil-fired hot-water heating system, a refrigerator and deep freeze, and

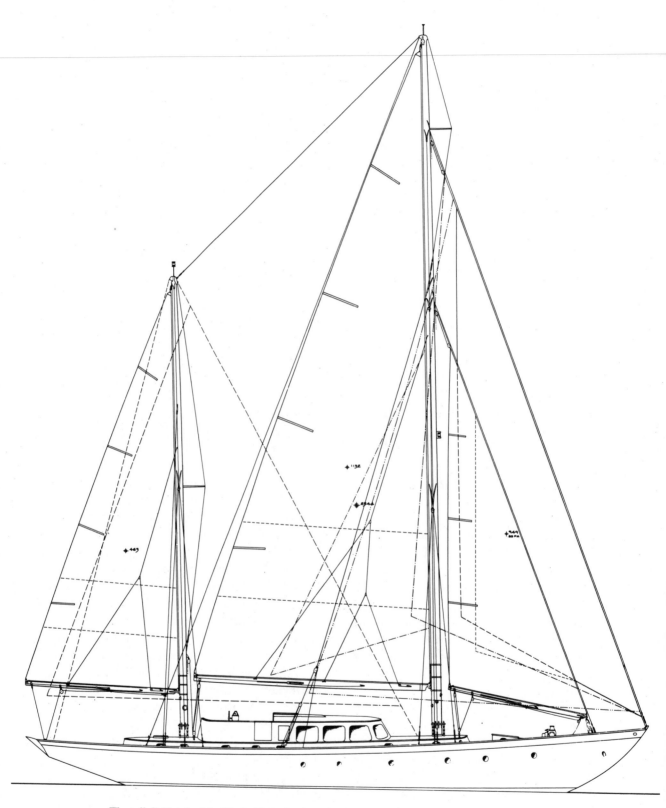

The well-divided rig of the Rhodes 77. Phil Rhodes rightfully called her "a true sailer in the best seagoing tradition."

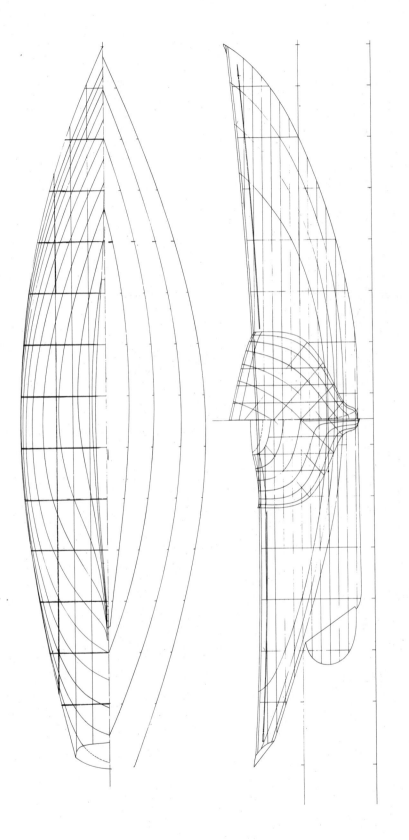

The lines of the Rhodes 77 show the Tamaris influence, but the forefoot and counter stern are more closely related to the typical Rhodes centerboard ocean racer.

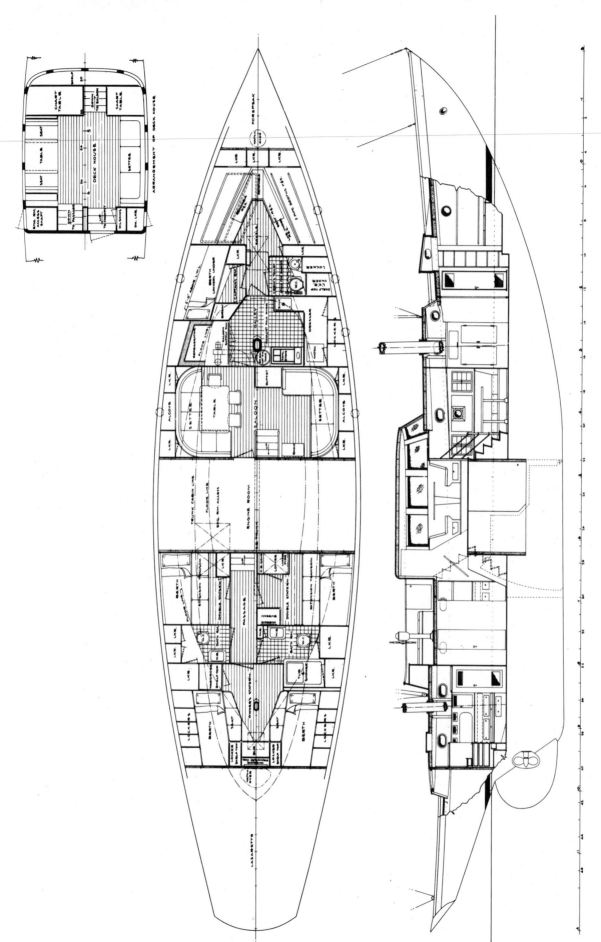

Except for the lack of a music center, the Rhodes 77's accommodations are as elegant as those of Tamaris.

The Rhodes 77 Windjammer II *just prior to launching. The fact that the rudder is effective, considering its lack of depth and large aperture, indicates a well-balanced, easily controlled hull for her size and type. (Photo by Glander Art Studio. Courtesy of Mystic Seaport)*

an electric garbage disposer. Other electrical equipment includes numerous pumps (for the bilge, fire, sumps, deck wash, etc.) and a powerful anchor windlass. As a precaution against breakdowns, most gear is provided with dual electrical or mechanical back-up systems.

Unlike *Tamaris,* the Rhodes 77 has only one engine, a 200-horsepower General Motors diesel. The 77 sails so well that she has no need for a back-up engine. Twin screws would provide better maneuverability, but the 77 steers just fine, with her large rudder located directly behind her good-sized propeller.

The fractional double-headsail ketch rig seems to be a logical sail plan for a boat this large, because the divided sail area simplifies handling. The only sizable sail is the mainsail, and that can be left up, fully hoisted or reefed, in most conditions. It should not be too difficult to hand the mizzen and jibs when it breezes up, because those sails are much smaller. With a listed sail area of 2,544 square feet (85 percent foretriangle) and some large light sails, such as

the huge mizzen staysail, the Rhodes 77 has plenty of canvas for speed off the wind.

These yachts weren't raced often, but one of them, *Windjammer II,* won the 1948 St. Petersburg-Havana Race against a good fleet of racers, including the venerable *Stormy Weather.* This performance takes on added significance when it is realized that about half the race was to windward. Writing in his *Yachting* column shortly thereafter, Alfred Loomis took note of this and speculated that she would be a real threat in that year's Bermuda Race if she were qualified to enter. (Her overall length was four feet over the size limit.)

Aside from Henry Babson's 77, which he called *Maaroufa,* and *Windjammer II,* originally owned by Garner H. Tullis of New Orleans, the two other sisterships were *Dragon Lady,* originally owned by William A. Parker of Boston, and *Bosun Bird* (later *Alondra II*), built for Burwell Smith of York, Pennsylvania. These boats were extensively cruised in northern as well as southern waters.

Windjammer II is perhaps the best known of this

Left: *Garner Tullis'* Windjammer II *shows her power under sail in a fresh breeze. (Photo by R. Kendall Williams Studios. Courtesy of Mystic Seaport)* **Right:** *Inside the deckhouse of a Rhodes 77. (Courtesy of Mystic Seaport)*

design. Soon after completion at the Burger yard, she traveled south from Wisconsin down the Illinois and Mississippi Rivers to New Orleans in the dead of winter. She encountered ice that might have been the undoing of a wooden vessel, but her sturdy steel hull was unscathed. Once south, *Windjammer II* was used mainly for cruising, and she roamed the entire Caribbean. During one cruise lasting 101 days, she reportedly covered 3,850 miles and visited 54 different ports.

Under subsequent owners, the yacht's name was changed to *Scimitar,* then to *Bahama High,* and after that to *Barrendo.* Horace W. (Hod) Fuller bought *Barrendo* in San Diego, California, in 1964, renamed her *Velila,* and sailed her to Greece. Until the beginning of the 1970s, she was extensively cruised and she explored almost every nook of the eastern Mediterranean, especially the Aegean, Ionian, and Adriatic seas. Fuller sold *Velila* in 1971; renamed *High Barbaree,* she is now a charter boat operating in the West Indies.

One of the 77s, *Maaroufa,* had a tragic end. While cruising off the West Coast, a fire broke out in her

engine room. The Coast Guard was called to quell the fire and upon arrival, they flooded her engine room. Unfortunately, her engine room ports had been left open, and when the water that had been pumped into her sank her to the level of the open ports, sea water poured into the vessel and she went to the bottom.

There are many large motorsailers that have very efficient engine power, luxurious comfort, and great cruising range. The Rhodes 77 has all of these features, but in addition she is very graceful and she is a pure sailer. The only criticism I have heard about her behavior under sail is that in the roughest conditions the helm can become a bit heavy and the centerboard may thump rather severely against its trunk, a common occurrence in many centerboarders, especially large ones. W. Mason Smith, a veteran Cruising Club of America sailor, summed up *Velila's* performance when, after cruising on her in the Aegean, he wrote, "*Velila* is a rather tremendous vessel, but she is a fine sailer, responsive to the helm, and a delight to handle."

25

Criterion and Two Developments
Seventy-Thirty Motorsailers

Phil Rhodes may have disapproved of any reference to the Rhodes 77s as motorsailers, but this didn't mean he disliked the type of yacht that is part sailboat and part powerboat. In fact, Phil was noted for his motorsailer designs. One of his most successful concepts was *Criterion* and two later developments, *Sea Prince* and *Bar-L-Rick*. These yachts might be considered 70/30 types, meaning that about 70 percent of their propulsion was in their sails and 30 percent in engine power.

Criterion was designed in 1951 for Charles H. Cuno of Meriden, Connecticut, and she was built by Abeking & Rasmussen the following year. Like *Tamaris* and the Rhodes 77s, she is constructed of welded steel and has four integral bulkheads that divide the boat into five watertight compartments. An interesting detail of *Criterion*'s construction is her off-center centerboard, located slightly to starboard of the keel. This arrangement detracts a little from sailing performance, but it adds to the boat's strength and protects the centerboard slot from being clogged with mud and shells and the like during a grounding.

With an overall length of 77 feet and a beam of 18

feet 8 inches, *Criterion* is about the same size as the Rhodes 77, but there are many differences between the two designs. *Criterion*'s waterline length of 65 feet is 10 feet longer, and her draft of 5 feet 9 inches (with board up) is somewhat less than that of the Rhodes 77. *Criterion* is double-ended, with a long keel, and has a more pronounced sheerline than the 77. She carries less sail, having shorter masts and a single-head rig. Another feature that gives her the look of a motorsailer is the permanent windshield and cockpit shelter.

The below-decks arrangement of *Criterion* is quite similar to that of the Rhodes 77, except that the motorsailer has a much larger deckhouse and there is no lower saloon. Meals on *Criterion* are taken at a dining area on the port side of the deckhouse rather than in a dining saloon. The disadvantage of this arrangement is that meals prepared in the forward galley must be carried up a stairway to the deckhouse, but on the other hand, the dining table is quite convenient to the cockpit, and the large deckhouse windows provide plenty of light and a good view. It would be mighty pleasant to be able to lean back with a second cup of coffee after breakfast

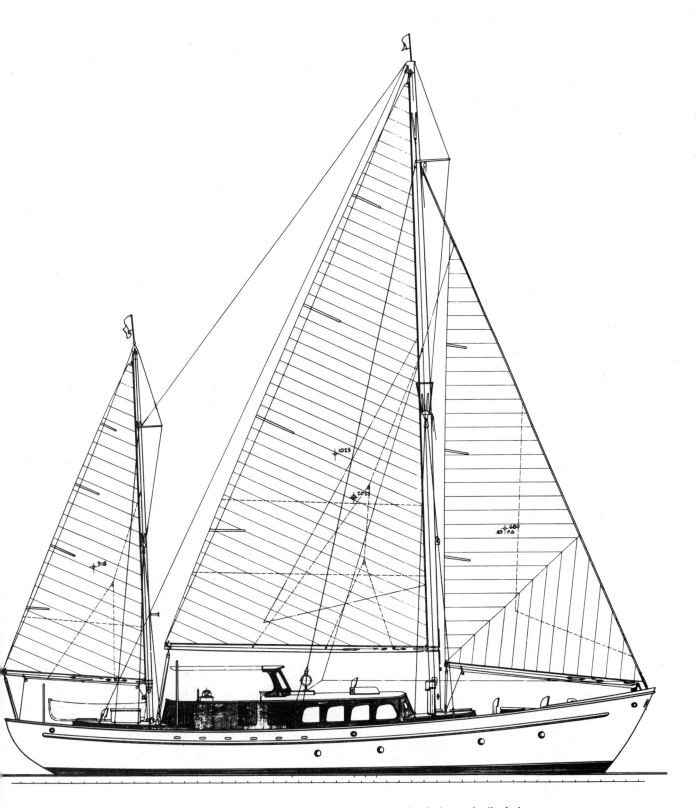

The modest sail area puts the 77-footer Criterion *in the motorsailer class, but she is a good sailer for her type.*

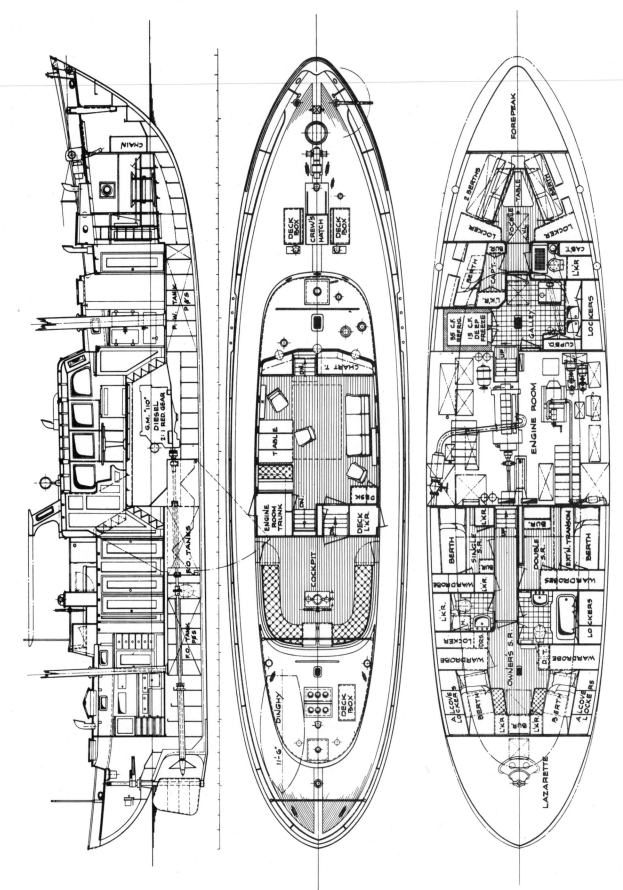

Criterion is exceptionally comfortable and seakindly. The yacht-deliverer Patrick Ellam said, "Of all the boats that we handled, the most comfortable at sea was

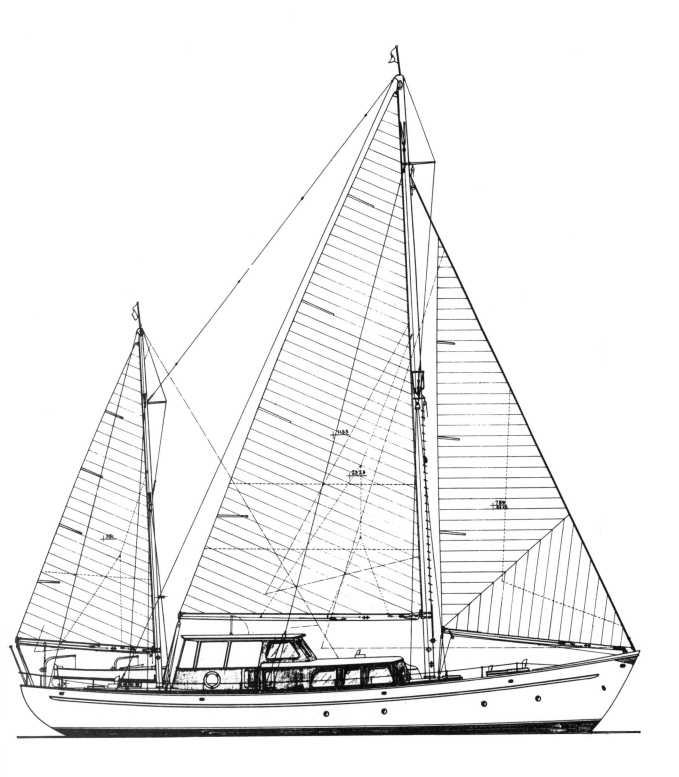

Sea Prince, *a larger (82 feet 11 inches) version of* Criterion *with a permanent cockpit shelter.*

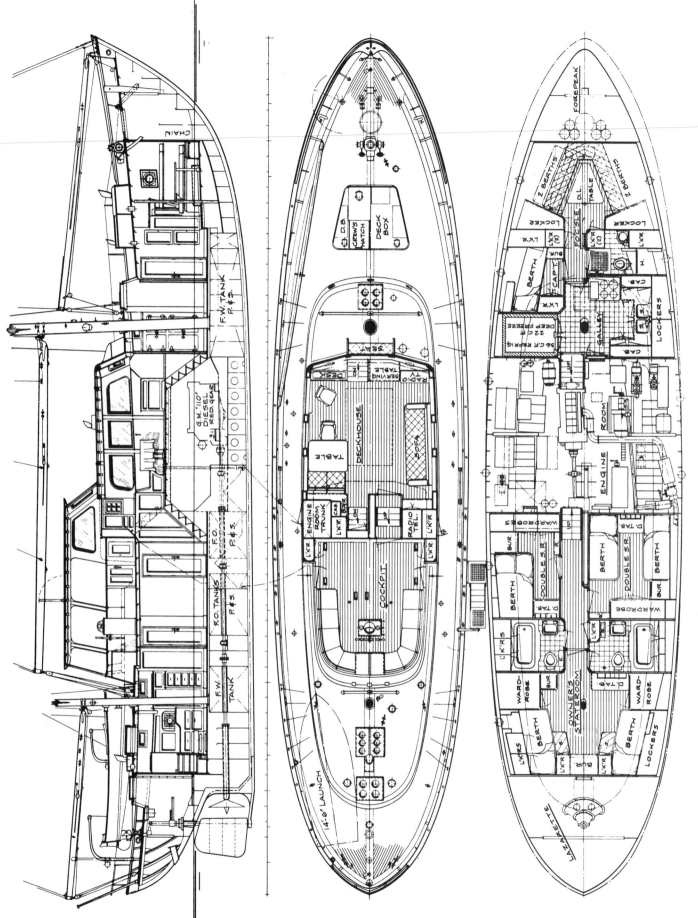

Sea Prince's accommodations are a bit roomier but almost identical to those of Criterion.

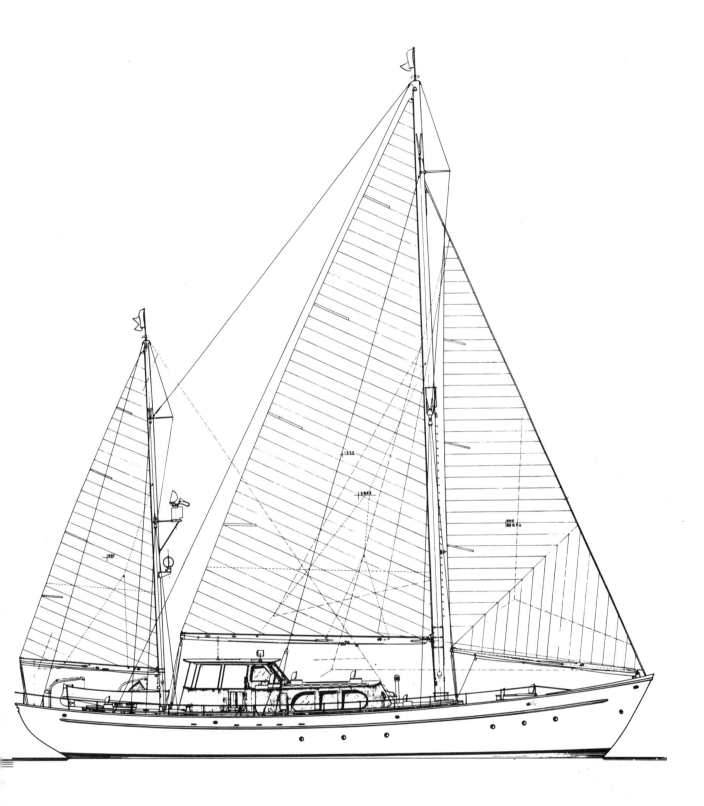

Bar-L-Rick, *the 90-foot motorsailer of the* Criterion *type. The antennas on the mizzen give a hint of her lavish navigation equipment.*

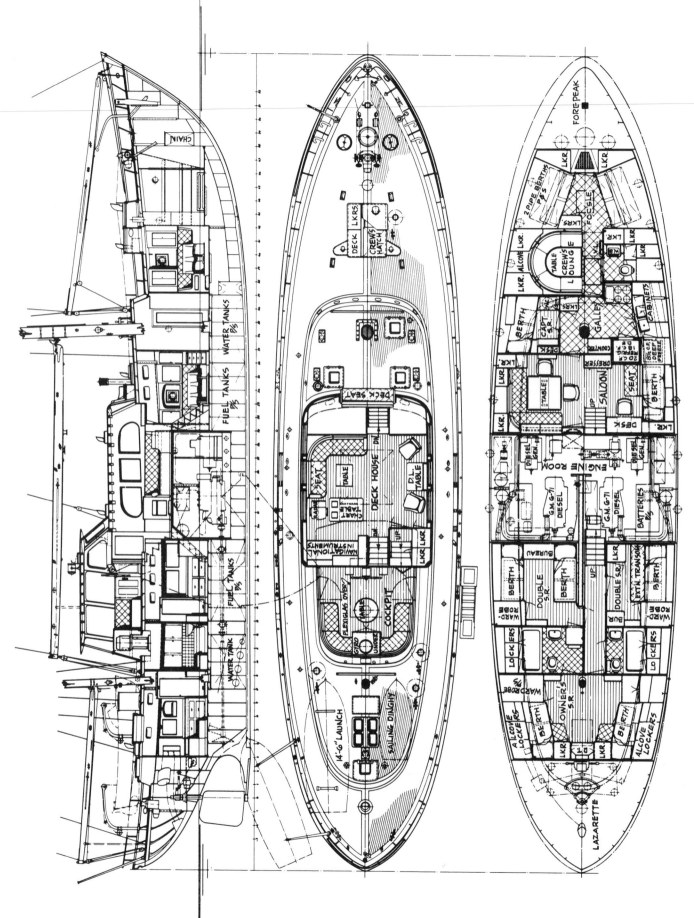

Bar-L-Rick's accommodations are almost the last word in comfort for a boat of her size.

This photo of Bar-L-Rick *demonstrates that she can sail even in a light breeze. (Photo by Niel C. Nielsen, Jr. Courtesy of Mystic Seaport)*

and gaze out at a spectacular seascape or harbor scene.

Even though *Criterion* has a somewhat modest sail area of 2,023 square feet, she is fast, given a little wind. She can make 9.5 knots reaching under working canvas in a 25-m.p.h. breeze. The boomed headsail and relatively short rig permit easy sail handling. There are mast steps leading up the forward side of the mainmast to crosstrees crow's nests, which are particularly valuable for conning the vessel through reefs in tropic waters. Cockpit shelters restrict the helmsman's view of the sails, so Rhodes specified plastic windows in his shelter tops.

Obviously, *Criterion* does not sail upwind as well as the Rhodes 77, but she does beat reasonably well with her board down. She can always improve her progress to windward by motorsailing, with the engine turning over just fast enough to augment the thrust of the sails and reduce leeway without drawing the apparent wind too far ahead. The yacht is powered by a six-cylinder 110 General Motors diesel, which drives her prop through a 2:1 reduction gear.

Criterion is an exceptionally seakindly vessel. Her heavy displacement gives her an easy motion, and the full, canoe-type stern prevents slamming, while the high, flaring bow helps keep water off the decks. Such high bows often restrict the helmsman's visibility, but the helm on *Criterion* is well elevated.

A larger, almost identical version of *Criterion* is *Sea Prince* and she, too, was constructed of steel by Abeking & Rasmussen. Her dimensions are 83 feet 10 inches by 70 feet by 20 feet 2 inches by 6 feet 1 inch (board up). Built for Canadian yachtsman John Conroy, *Sea Prince* was completed in the summer of 1953. She is like *Criterion* in almost every respect except that some of her cabins are a little more roomy. For example, the port stateroom just abaft the deckhouse is a double rather than a single stateroom, and its head compartment is big enough for a bathtub. The after deck on *Sea Prince* is sufficiently large to carry a 14½-foot motor launch.

A still-larger version of the *Criterion* design is *Bar-L-Rick,* which was built in 1955-1956 by Abeking & Rasmussen. Also of steel, she was built for Henry D.

Belock of Kings Point, New York, a marine electronics manufacturer, who spared nothing in equipping his yacht with the finest in navigation instruments. A description of *Bar-L-Rick* in *Motorboating* magazine (January 1958) described her equipment as follows: "Her navigation department has the works — everything from loran to rudder angle indicator, from radar to 700-fathom range depth finder, from automatic steering devices to her owner's very own dead reckoning analyzer. There are globe-girdling freighters and passenger liners whose bridges and chartrooms are neither as well thought out or equipped as *Bar-L-Rick*'s."

With dimensions of 90 feet overall, 75 feet on the waterline, 21 feet 6 inches beam, and 6 feet draft, this yacht is a size that allows both a large deckhouse and a lower dining saloon. Even the crew's quarters are posh on this vessel, for the captain's cabin has its own W.C., and there is a comfortable crew's lounge. The owner's luxurious after cabin and the two guest staterooms are air-conditioned, and, as might be expected, there is also a heating system for cold weather.

Needless to say, *Bar-L-Rick* has a voracious electrical appetite. The enormous electrical demands are supplied by two General Motors diesel generators, each providing 12 kilowatt 110-volt DC and 4 kilowatt 110-volt AC. A Constavolt rectifier converts AC shore power to DC boat power and allows battery charging with shore current. Unlike her two smaller sisters, *Bar-L-Rick* has twin screws, which give her great maneuverability and standby power in the event that one engine breaks down. Twin General Motors 6-71, 6-cylinder diesels supply the power, and turning over at 1,800 r.p.m., they drive the yacht at 10.7 knots.

Having a spare engine for standby power on one of these motorsailers is like putting on an extra pair of suspenders when you already are wearing one pair and a belt, since performance is satisfactory under one engine and sail when there is any breeze. At any rate, you're bound to reach your destination, and you'll do so in luxurious comfort in almost any kind of weather conditions.

26

Dolphin
Past and Present

Phil Rhodes must have considered the motorsailer *Dolphin* to be one of his most interesting design commissions, for she is a unique combination of old and new. Rhodes wrote: "What we have done in this design is to accept all that is modern and new in the basic elements having to do with the vessel's performance, but to give her sheer line and decorative motif the engaging personality of the older ships. It is a simple matter to develop an exact copy of an antique, but it is equally foolish. What we feel we have successfully accomplished is a melding of the latest design developments as far as efficiency and performance are concerned with the unquestionably pleasing flavor of the old-timer. After all, this interesting craft is not so radically different from the customary motorsailer except in the treatment of the sheer and the beautiful hand carving that decorates the trail boards, transom, and the quarter windows."

Her topsides are like those of a 17th-century caravel, and her ornate raised poop aft was copied from Lord Nelson's *Victory*. The hand-carved motif referred to above shows real dignity and craftsmanship and features gilded dolphins. While such elaborate ornamentation would be flamboyant on most modern yachts, it very well suits such a character vessel as *Dolphin*.

Dolphin was designed in 1951 for H. Nelson Slater of New York and San Raphael, Italy, and she was intended for use on the Mediterranean; she didn't visit the U.S. until after Slater's death. She was built of steel by Abeking & Rasmussen, and launched in late 1952. Her dimensions are 79 feet 2 inches by 68 feet by 18 feet 2 inches by 6 feet 6 inches.

Dolphin has the same basic arrangement plan as the *Criterion,* with the owner's cabin and guest staterooms aft, a sunken deckhouse amidships with engine (a 220-horsepower diesel) beneath, a galley forward, and crew's quarters still farther forward. Unlike the owner's quarters on *Criterion,* however, those on *Dolphin* take the form of a "great cabin." Located under a raised quarter deck, it is fitted with large stern windows and quarter windows in the old tradition. Plans show a large table, a U-shaped transom, and two berths, but later, a canopied double bed was installed in this stately cabin. The blending of old and new is apparent even in the two heads, for in each case, side by side with a modern electric

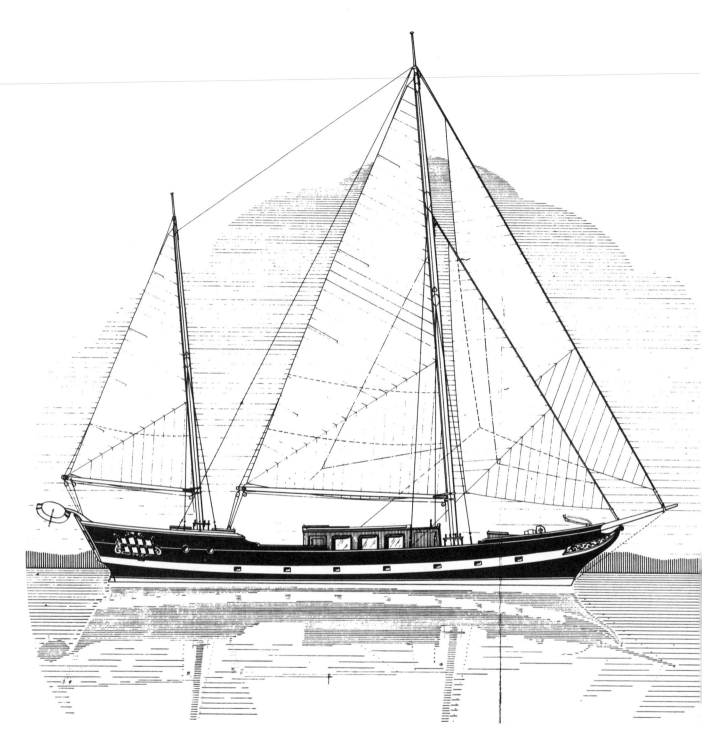

The distinctive motorsailer Dolphin, *79 feet 2 inches overall. Even her rig is a blend of nostalgia with modernity.*

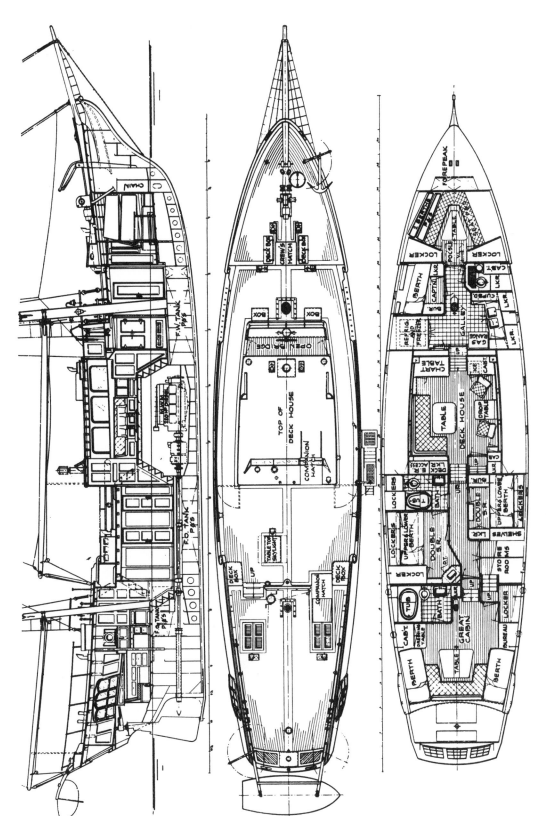

Dolphin's accommodations are infinitely more comfortable than those of the early vessels she resembles. (The Rudder, January 1954)

This dockside view of Dolphin *shows some of the beautiful hand-carved decorations around her quarter windows. (Foto Maack. Courtesy of Mystic Seaport)*

toilet, there is an 18th-century staved teak bathtub. The large deckhouse contains a dining area, a bar and sitting area, and a chart table.

Above deck, *Dolphin* has an unusual layout, for her helm is located at the forward end of the deckhouse in what Rhodes terms in the plans an "open bridge." This arrangement is not ideal, for the helmsman doesn't get a good view of the mainsail and mizzen and the visibility forward is partially blocked by the mast. However, it does provide for plenty of deck space aft, and one interesting feature there is the high skylight, which doubles as a table.

One would not expect outstanding performance from *Dolphin* under sail, but Phil Rhodes has written

that she sails well. With a sail area of 2,230 square feet on a masthead rig, she spreads a lot of canvas for a motorsailer. She has no centerboard for windward work, but her full-length keel is deeper than that of the *Criterion* type, and she is most likely motorsailed to windward anyway. For this reason, *Dolphin*'s mainsail and mizzen are loose-footed, emphasizing off-the-wind efficiency. With outhauls eased, the sails can be given a lot of draft, yet they can be flattened quite easily when motorsailing to windward. Despite her modern jib-headed ketch rig, *Dolphin* has some traditional details that allow the rig to harmonize with the hull, including deadeyes and lanyards, ratlines, and a "fighting top" on the

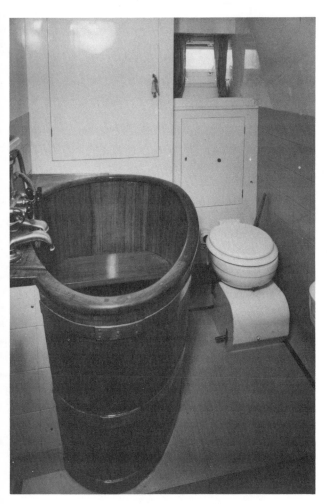

Above: *The interior view of Dolphin's great cabin, with its many stern and quarter windows.* **Left:** Dolphin's *famous teak-staved bathtub alongside her modern W.C. (Foto Maack. Courtesy of Mystic Seaport)*

mainmast at the spreaders. The latter makes a good conning and lookout station.

Unless her large stern and quarter windows were fitted with storm shutters, it might not be wise to take *Dolphin* offshore in the most rugged conditions, but her high quarter deck does make it seem unlikely that she would be pooped. She must have good form stability, because at some time during her career, with a great deal of her ballast having been removed, she was tossed on her beam ends during a meltemi and she righted herself, even after taking on a lot of sea water. With so much ballast gone, it is a wonder that she didn't capsize or turn turtle.

In 1980, *Dolphin* lay in bad shape at an Italian yard, needing new electrics, replacement of her teak deck, and many new plates. But a year later she was bought by Californian Maurice Taylor, who spared no expense in restoring her to a condition of classical elegance, while adding almost every conceivable electro-mechanical device. The Taylors have taken her to the Caribbean, and in 1986 I had the pleasure of seeing her underway on the Chesapeake Bay.

When Phil Rhodes designed the schooner *Mary Jeanne II* (Chapter 1), he wrote, ''In her we created an atmosphere mildly suggestive of romance reminiscent of *Treasure Island,* perhaps.'' *Dolphin* is an even more romantic vessel, and although she may not evoke Stevenson's novel, she certainly can prod the imagination and take one back to the days of iron men and wooden ships.

27

The Virginia Reels
"Practically Perfection"

Among the better known of Philip Rhodes' many motorsailer designs are the *Virginia Reels*, two sea-going, sloop-rigged, cruiser-fishermen designed for Arthur M. Stoner of Madison, Connecticut. These boats might be considered 30/70 types, with roughly 30 percent of their propulsion sail and about 70 percent, power.

The first *Virginia Reel* was designed in 1954 to Stoner's requirements for a comfortable offshore fishing boat sufficiently seaworthy to stay out and take it in heavy weather. She was built of welded steel by Gebr. Dolman in Muiden, Holland, and her measurements are 44 feet by 40 feet by 13 feet 1 inch by 4 feet 6 inches. You might call her a moderately heavy, highly modified trawler-type yacht, with high freeboard and a sweeping sheer. She has a raised flush deck forward, while aft, she has a fairly low deckhouse and a sunken after deck, with two fighting chairs and a transom door for boating large fish. Unlike many trawler-yachts, *Virginia Reel* has twin engines, which ensure power reliability and good maneuverability. Fuel consumption is high, but *Virginia Reel* has a tank capacity of 700 gallons, and she can save fuel by sailing some of the time.

Virginia Reel's basic hull form is very possibly a development of that of an offshore cruiser and sport-fisherman that Phil designed for Luis Puig of Santiago, Cuba, in 1927. The dimensions of the earlier boat are 45 feet by 42 feet by 11 feet 3 inches by 5 feet. With her narrower beam, deeper draft, and single screw, Puig's boat seems to be based more on the idea of an old-style displacement powerboat than is *Virginia Reel*. Her sails are merely for steadying and trolling.

Virginia Reel could by no stretch of the imagination be called a smart sailer, but Phil Rhodes made the point that she really *can* sail. This brings to mind Dr. Samuel Johnson's remark about the dancing bear. He said, in effect, that it is not how well the bear dances, but a wonder that it can dance at all. *Virginia Reel* might be somewhat like that bear when beating, but with 546 square feet of sail, she can reach remarkably well in a decent breeze. The sails are also very effective in steadying the boat when she is rolling to beam seas.

The deckhouse, sunken quite far below the main deck level, contains a galley and dinette, which can also be used for navigation. Farther forward and at a lower level there are an enclosed head and a stateroom with two berths and a seat. Still farther for-

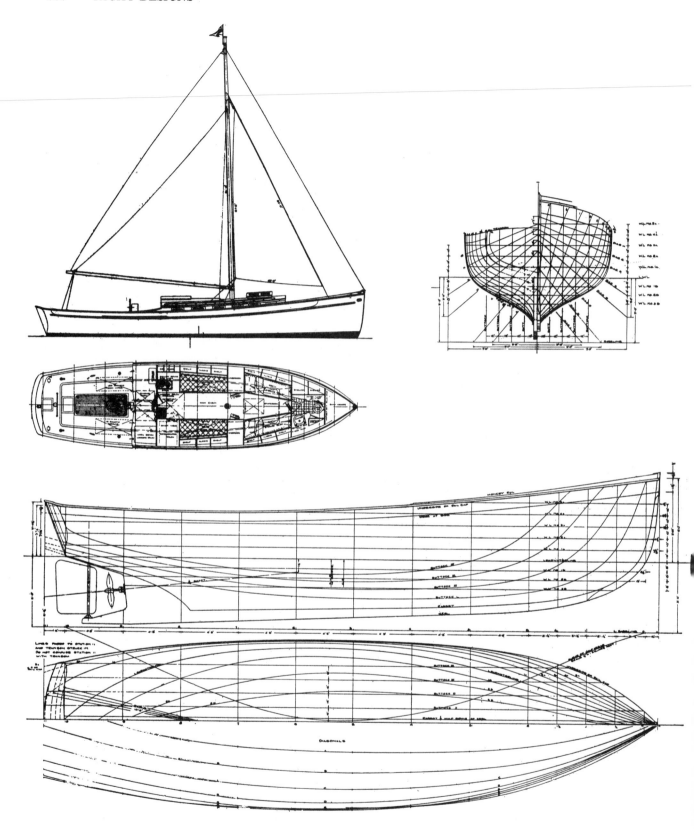

This 45-footer was an early forerunner of the Virginia Reel *concept. The owner asked Phil Rhodes for the most seaworthy boat possible for offshore fishing.* (The Rudder)

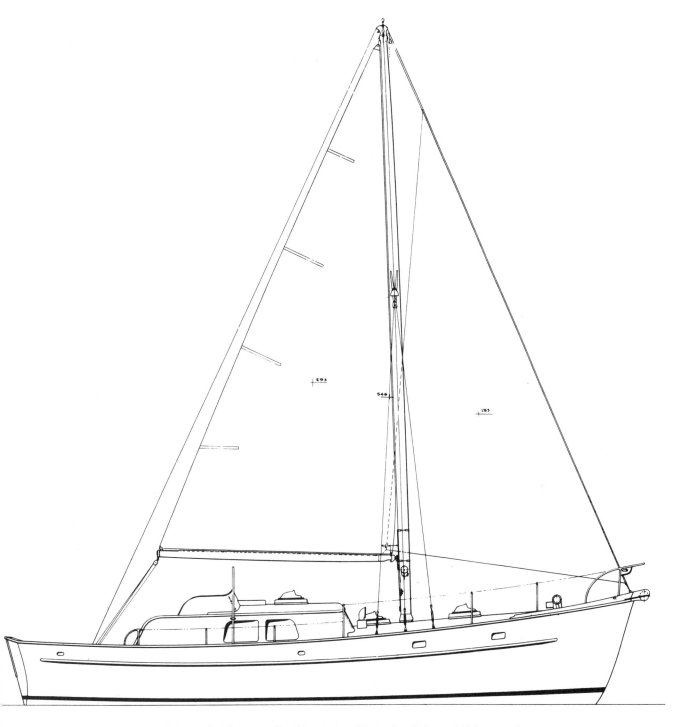

The first Virginia Reel, *44 feet overall. Although she might be classified as a 30/70 motorsailer, Rhodes claimed, "She really can sail."*

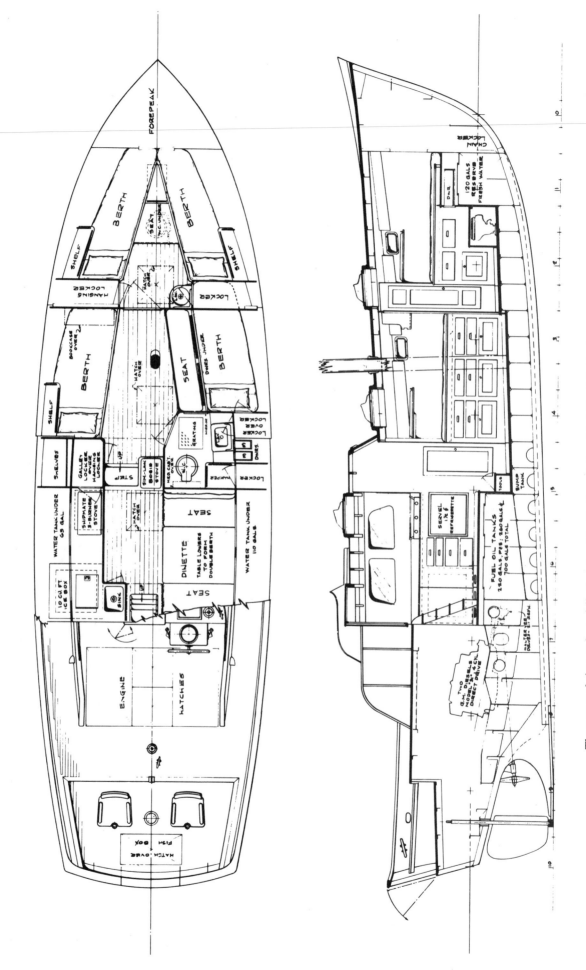

The accommodations and especially the inboard profile plans of the original Virginia Reel show some interesting details, such as the V-drives for her two 4-cylinder GM diesels, the numerous drawers and lockers in the after stateroom, and the fishing cockpit with fighting chairs and hinged transom door.

Virginia Reel *(I) seems to be showing that she can make some progress to windward under sail alone if her sheets are well eased.* (Motor Boating, *May 1956)*

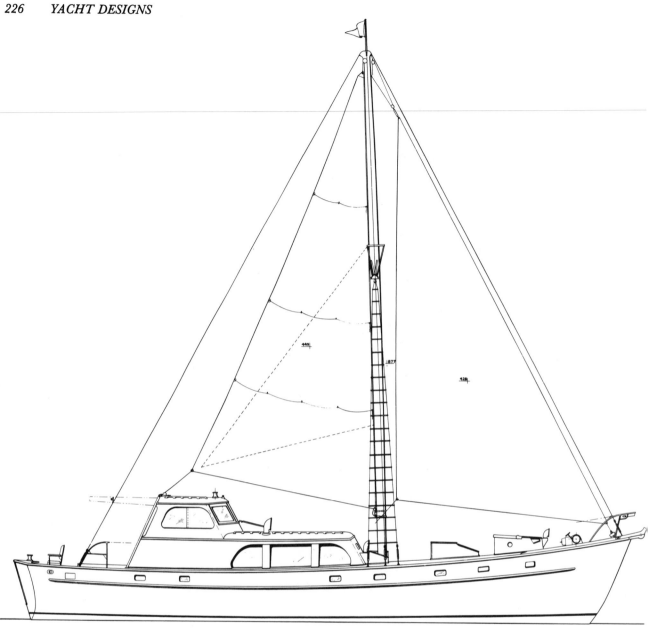

Above: *The second* Virginia Reel, *65 feet 1 inch overall, has a slightly less efficient but easier-to-handle sail plan than her predecessor had.* **Below:** Virginia Reel *(II) is basically an enlarged version of the first* Virginia Reel *with extra accommodations and a pilothouse.* (The Yachtsman, *December 1960*)

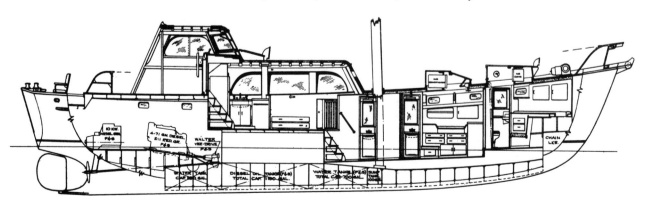

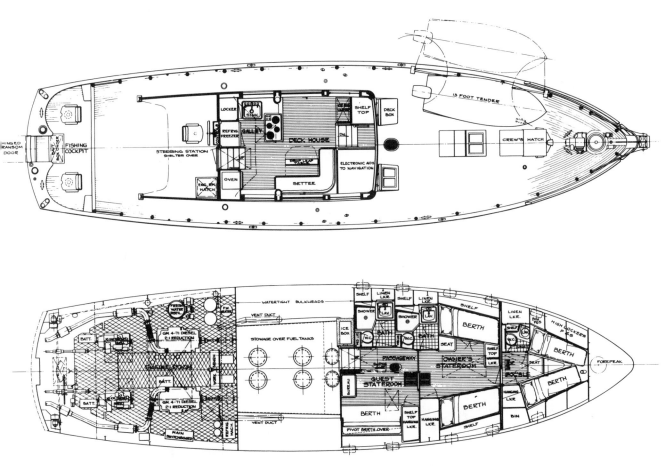

The larger size of the second Virginia Reel *allows a much roomier deckhouse and another stateroom as well as an extra head below.*

ward is another stateroom with two berths and a W.C.

Seven of the boats were built. The early ones had no shelters over the helmsman's station abaft the deckhouse, but evidently the owners felt the need for better protection in foul weather, because Phil Rhodes wrote in an article for *Motor Boating and Sailing* (March 1970), "Every single one of the owners installed a shelter before he had the boat very long." In the same article, Phil also made the interesting general comment that many prospective owners of motorsailers wanted steering stations inside the main deckhouse, for use in bad weather, but that he felt this was undesirable. He expressed his reasoning as follows: "Now, I consider this [an inside steering position] a considerable mistake in a small boat: the simple reason is that on a motorsailer type, with any given amount of sheer, you can't see forward out of the house well enough to steer safely. I have found that not a single one of those owners of boats so

equipped that I have ever done has ever used the inside steering. It's a little added expense, and it also takes up room. The real answer to it is that when it's nice, you want to be outside to steer; and when it's nasty, you've damn well *got* to be outside."

After Arthur Stoner had used *Virginia Reel* for about four years, he decided he wanted a larger version of the boat. Phil Rhodes and his organization drafted plans for an offshore fishing cruiser that measured 65 feet 1 inch overall, 59 feet on the waterline, with a beam of 17 feet 2½ inches and a draft of 5 feet. In many respects this boat, also named *Virginia Reel,* was similar to the 44-footer, except she was larger, roomier, and more comfortable. This satisfied Stoner's request that the new boat be as close as possible to the first one in every way except size. She was built of steel by the Amsterdam shipyard G. DeVries Lentsch, Jr., and was launched in 1960.

The main difference between this boat and her

Virginia Reel *(II), with her high freeboard, rugged hull, steadying sails, and other seagoing features, appears to be the ultimate offshore, long-distance fishing cruiser.*

predecessor is that she has an elaborate pilothouse, the deckhouse is much roomier and has a U-shaped galley (better for offshore work), and there is another stateroom and another head. A nice feature is the sliding partition between the off-center guest stateroom and the passageway, which allows a large, open cabin when there are no guests aboard but provides privacy when the stateroom is occupied. The heads are arranged so that no guest or crew need ever use the owner's head, and even the W.C. in the fo'c's'le is enclosed.

She, too, has a fishing cockpit aft with fighting chairs and a sunken bait box, but unlike her smaller sister, she has a curved taffrail in way of each chair to provide a good foot brace for fighting the big ones. She has a hinged transom door for boating fish, and it folds down in a manner that forms a step and lower platform that is also handy for swimming and dinghy boarding. (Incidentally, there are davits forward that can handle a Boston Whaler.) Her functionalism for fishing is capped off by her spreader-mounted lookout stations, from which fish can be spotted.

Mechanics often curse a boat's designer because of the inaccessibility of the engine, but that would never happen on this boat, which has from 5 feet 3 inches to 6 feet of headroom around her twin GM 4-71 diesel engines. At one time Stoner claimed his

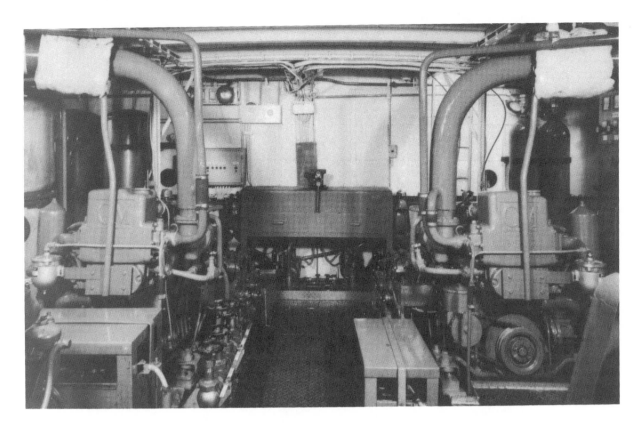

The unusually large engine room of the second Virginia Reel, *which encourages and facilitates meticulous maintenance.*

boat had never had a cruise interrupted by a mechanical failure, and three of these cruises lasted over 12 weeks each. Undoubtedly, the large, well-lighted and well-ventilated engine room encouraged thorough engine maintenance. With tanks capable of carrying 1,380 gallons of fuel, this boat has a cruising range under power of about 1,500 miles. Her water tanks carry 700 gallons; a Maxim seawater evaporator, which operates on the engine exhaust, can provide pure drinking water at a rate of 18 gallons an hour.

This yacht has a lot of electrical equipment, such as refrigeration, deep freeze, autopilot, pumps, blowers, a windlass, and so forth. In addition she has an electric stove, electric heating, air conditioning, and an electrolysis control system that uses an impressed electrical current flowing from five platinum anodes to protect all underwater structures from corrosion. One-hundred-fifteen-volt alternating current is supplied by two exceptionally quiet Mercedes-Benz/Onan diesel generators.

The second *Virginia Reel* is not as good a sailer as is the first, and she probably could be considered to be a powerboat with steadying sails. But even so, her longer waterline and greater sail area (887 square feet) make her faster than her little sister on a broad reach in fresh winds. In conjunction with bilge keels, her sails have an excellent steadying effect on the boat's motion.

A fair amount of efficiency in the sail plan is traded off for ease of handling. The mainsail is boomless so that it need not be manhandled when taking it in. The original plans show that the main was brailed to the mast, but later it was set on a roller-furling drum mounted a couple of feet abaft the mast. This leaves a wide gap between the luff and mast, but it helps assure that the sail will not bang against the spar when it is furled. The jib likewise is roller furled.

Arthur Stoner evidently was pleased with both of his *Virginia Reels*, especially the larger version. Some of his comments to Phil Rhodes about the latter include: "A wonderful boat — superb at sea. Everyone comments about the spaciousness . . . and comfort. They all say it is the last word in an offshore fishing boat. This is practically perfection."

28

Carina (II)
Phil's All-Time Favorite

Phil Rhodes said many times that of all the yachts he had designed, the 53-foot yawl *Carina,* built in 1955, was his all-time favorite. It is not hard to see why, for *Carina* is a versatile, fast, and beautiful boat, and she had a truly exceptional racing record under the capable management of Richard S. Nye and his son Richard B. Nye.

The elder Nye did not start sailing until quite late in life, but he took to it like a duck takes to water. In 1945, with little if any sailing experience, he bought a 40-foot Rhodes-designed sloop, which served as a basic trainer for him and his son. Later, he bought a 46-foot keel yawl, the first *Carina,* designed by Rhodes for James Rider in 1941, and began racing in earnest. The Nyes were fast learners, and this *Carina* won the Marblehead-Halifax, the Vineyard, and the Block Island races, as well as the 1952 Bermuda Race — a remarkable achievement after such a short sailing career. The following year, Nye and his son sailed this boat across the Atlantic to England in the fast time of 18½ days, and there they won the Cowes-Dinard, the Cross Channel, and the Cowes Week Britannia Cup. She also took a class second in the Fastnet Race. By the next year, the Nyes had succumbed to the ocean-racing bug to such a degree

that they decided to build a new *Carina,* which would be raced in the 1955 Transatlantic Race. The first *Carina* continued to have a successful career, and as late as 1970, with her name changed to *Chee Chee V,* she won her class in the St. Petersburg-Fort Lauderdale Race.

Phil Rhodes was asked to design the new *Carina,* and the Nyes told him that they wanted a larger version of a 52-foot Rhodes centerboarder named *Blue Water,* a boat whose performance had impressed them, especially upwind. It is also true that the second *Carina* is very similar to a steel centerboard yawl named *Kuling,* which Phil designed in 1954. Of course, each of the aforementioned centerboarders is a development of the *Ayesha-Alondra* concept (Chapter 8).

Compared with *Blue Water, Carina* (II) has a longer waterline and less-drawn-out ends. Her relative draft is slightly less, and to compensate for the loss of lateral plane, her rudderpost has less rake. She also has more relative beam.

Although the hull design was left to Rhodes, the boat's arrangement and sail plan reflect the Nyes' own thinking. *Carina* is essentially flush decked, except for a very short cabin trunk just forward of the

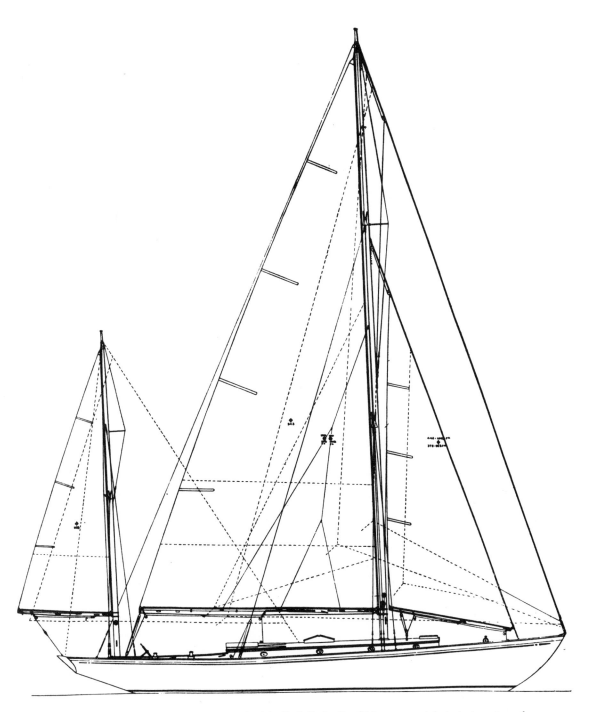

The first Carina, *a 46-foot 4-inch yawl originally built for Jim Rider, won such important events as the Detroit-Mackinac, Marblehead-Halifax, Block Island, Bermuda, and Britannia Cup races.* (The Rudder, *November 1953)*

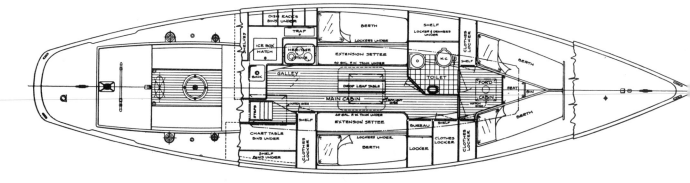

The first Carina's *accommodations are identical to those of* Pavana *and* White Squall, *the postwar sisters of* Narada. (The Rudder, *November 1953*)

cockpit. A flush deck provides great hull strength and a lot of deck space, and combined with a slight increase in freeboard, it gives a greater feeling of spaciousness below. The flush deck has one main drawback, according to Richard B. Nye, namely, that the cabin sole sits directly on the floors, which prevents the use of a large water tank under the sole.

Without a bilge tank, a boat's water supply must be carried higher up in the boat, and this can detract from sail-carrying power, but *Carina* does not suffer in this department, for she has excellent form stability, due primarily to her 13-foot beam. She also has a high range of positive stability for a centerboarder — up to 128 degrees of heel. This comes from her relatively deep draft of 6 feet, her heavy bronze centerboard and trunk, and the low-down concentration of her ballast.

Her generous beam and her waterline length of 36 feet 3 inches give enough room below decks for accommodations for a full crew. In port (when the most bunks are needed), she can sleep eight — there are two forward berths, four in the saloon, and one aft, with the chart table serving as an auxiliary berth by extending it into an after locker. Underway, the entire off-watch can sleep abaft the mainmast, where the motion is not pronounced.

The galley is placed in the saloon near the dining table, yet it is fairly convenient to the cockpit. There are several other nice features of her accommodations layout, among them the large chart table, the heating stove (most desirable for North Atlantic racing in the early summer), and the oilskin and bosun's lockers. She has few partitions below, which gives a feeling of great spaciousness, the lack of strengthening bulkheads being compensated for by her full-width deck beams and extensive hull strap-

ping. A minor drawback, perhaps, is that there are no ports or windows in the saloon, but a large skylight provides plenty of light and air.

Carina originally had a seven-eighths foretriangle. Rhodes had used this rig successfully on *Blue Water* and *Kuling,* and the Nyes liked the idea of having reasonable-sized headsails that would not require a coffee grinder for trimming. With a fairly modest sail area of 1,194 square feet, *Carina* was quite stiff, and she excelled beating to windward in a breeze, but she sometimes suffered from lack of sail in light airs. In 1965 she was given a masthead rig to compensate for this weakness, and it was felt that the boat was stiff enough to carry the bigger jibs in fresh winds as well. (The design of cockpit winches had, by that time, been improved sufficiently to handle large headsails.) The masthead plan also simplified the rig by eliminating a set of running backstays.

Carina was built by H. Heidtman of Hamburg, Germany, in the record time of four months. (There were still a dozen men working on her as she was lifted aboard the ship bound for the United States.) Finishing touches were supplied by the Kretzer Boat Works of City Island, New York, and 12 days after she was delivered to America, *Carina* started the 1955 Transatlantic Race to Sweden. She proceeded to win her maiden race on both elapsed and corrected time, but that was just the beginning. At Cowes Week, she won three coveted awards: the Britannia Cup, the Sir Walter Preston Trophy, and the New York Yacht Club Challenge Trophy. She then capped her foreign expedition by winning the 605-mile Fastnet Race.

The following year, *Carina* won her class and was third in fleet in the Bermuda Race, and in 1957 she had racing successes that rivaled those of her first

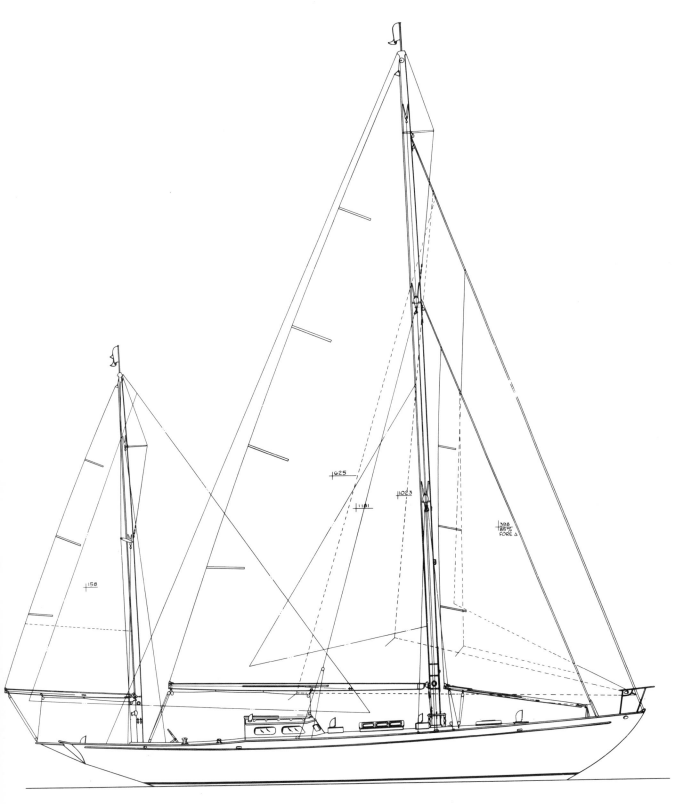

Kuling, *a steel forerunner of the second* Carina.

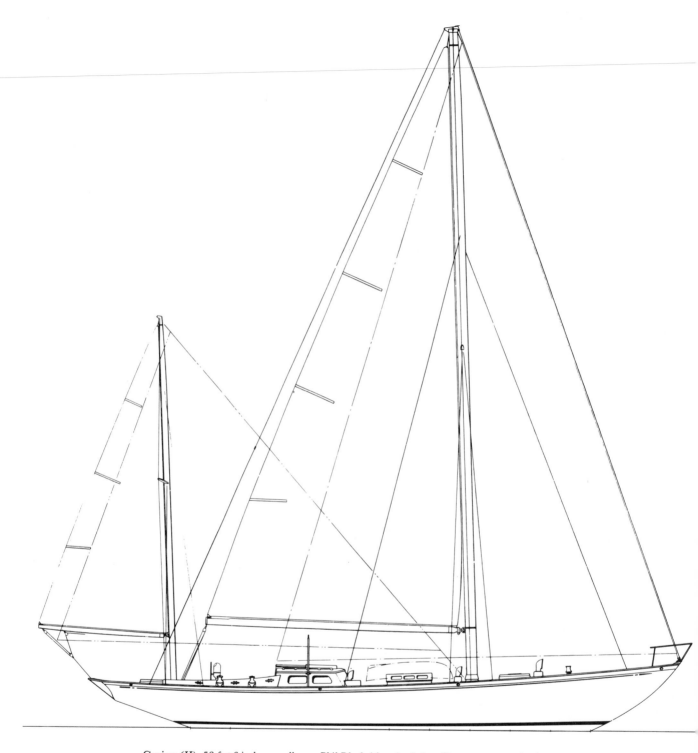

Carina *(II), 53 feet 6 inches overall, was Phil Rhodes' favorite design. She won, among other important events, two transatlantic and two Fastnet races. This plan shows her 1965 rig.*

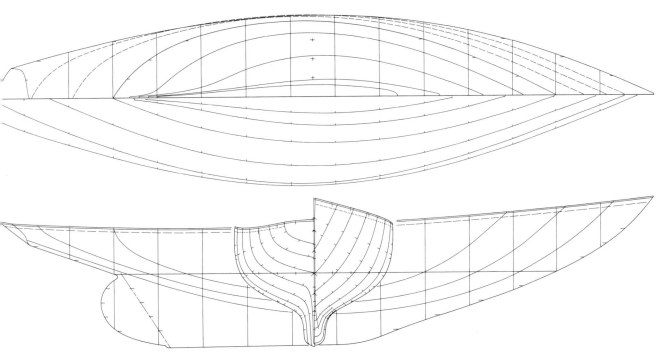

Carina (II) has a fairly fine afterbody for a centerboarder, but her quarters are firm. Wetted surface is low, yet the keel is somewhat deeper than those of the early Rhodes ocean racers of this type. Although the keel is quite thick, it is nicely streamlined.

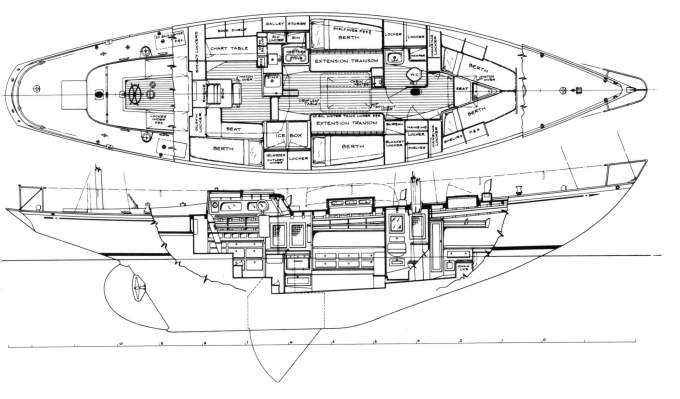

The Nyes had considerable influence on the second Carina's accommodations, and the arrangement suited them well for ocean racing.

year. She started off by winning the Edlu Cup on Long Island Sound and then won the Transatlantic Race from Newport, Rhode Island, to Santander, Spain. Her most dramatic triumph came when she again won the Fastnet, this time in what was then described as one of the toughest races ever.

Dick Nye drove his yawl so hard that she cracked three frames and started her deck. It was necessary to man the pumps almost continually, and after *Carina* crossed the finish line her skipper said to his crew, "O.K. boys, you can let her sink now." Only nine boats finished out of 43 starters, and *Carina* won every possible prize, including first to finish.

Not content to rest on their laurels, the Nyes went back to England for the next Fastnet Race. As Nye said: "After twice, you've gotta be there to take your licking." During the Atlantic crossing, *Carina*

averaged 182 miles per day. She did not quite pull off another Fastnet fleet victory, but she did win her class, and she took third overall in a fine fleet. *Carina* was still doing well as late as 1966, when she took her class in both the Bermuda and Transatlantic races.

In 1968, Richard S. Nye ordered a third *Carina,* which was designed by Phil's son Bodie and another Rhodes alumnus, James McCurdy. This lovely boat won the 1970 Bermuda Race and other important events, such as the Bermuda-to-Spain race in 1972, but it is doubtful that she will ever quite have the record of the second *Carina.* It was once written in *The Skipper* magazine that, "the only item designer Philip Rhodes seems to have overlooked on Richard S. Nye's new *Carina* is a permanent masthead fitting for a clean-sweeping broom."

Left: Carina *(II) racing in British waters. Notice that she gains extra sailing length from her overhanging stern. (Photo by Beken of Cowes. (Courtesy of Richard S. Nye)*

29

Rara Avis
A Thames Barge Yacht

The 99-foot, three-masted motorsailer *Rara Avis,* which Phil Rhodes designed for Paul Hammond in 1956, is well named, for she is indeed a rare bird. She has a hull shaped like a Thames barge, as well as an unusual rig, which includes two yardarms and brailing or roller-furling sails. Her accommodations would put a large houseboat to shame. Furthermore, she has a number of unique features, such as a rudder drop-plate, two galleys, fireplaces, and even a wheelchair lift.

Paul Hammond was one of the most illustrious of Phil's clients. He was an early patron of the six-meter class, skipper of the J-boat *Whirlwind,* and owner-skipper of such famous yachts as *Nina, Landfall,* and *Barnswallow.* He also assisted Samuel Eliot Morison in his transatlantic expedition, which researched and retraced the voyages of Christopher Columbus. Hammond built *Barnswallow* with his own hands, and it may be recalled from Chapter 15 (on *Arabella),* that Rhodes was called in to help with many of her design details. Phil later drew up some alterations for Hammond's *Landfall,* and he designed the sturdy ketch *Mary Otis,* which accompanied Morison's flagship on the Columbus expedition. Thus, Hammond knew well and respected

Phil's ability, so he selected the Rhodes firm to produce the plans for his dream cruiser, *Rara Avis.*

Paul Hammond chose the Thames barge hull for his ultimate boat because he had long admired the looks of this picturesque working craft, and its hull provides maximum volume with shoal draft and respectable sailing speed in the right conditions. Some of the large working barges have been clocked at 10 to 12 knots in fresh breezes.

The lines of *Rara Avis* show a rather rectangular box-shaped hull, in typical barge fashion. Nevertheless, the vessel has a graceful, sweeping sheer, bulwarks that slightly tumble home, an almost heart-shaped transom, and an outboard rudder that suggests the character of a workboat. The tandem centerboards shown on the plans provide good lateral resistance and can be adjusted to obtain perfect balance under a variety of conditions. The drop-plate in the rudder enhances steering control in deep water. The shallow hull allows amazing gunkholing ability for such a large vessel, and the flat bilges allow her to remain fairly level when grounded in regions of extreme tide. The dimensions of *Rara Avis* are 99 feet by 94 feet 6 inches by 23 feet, with a draft of only 4 feet.

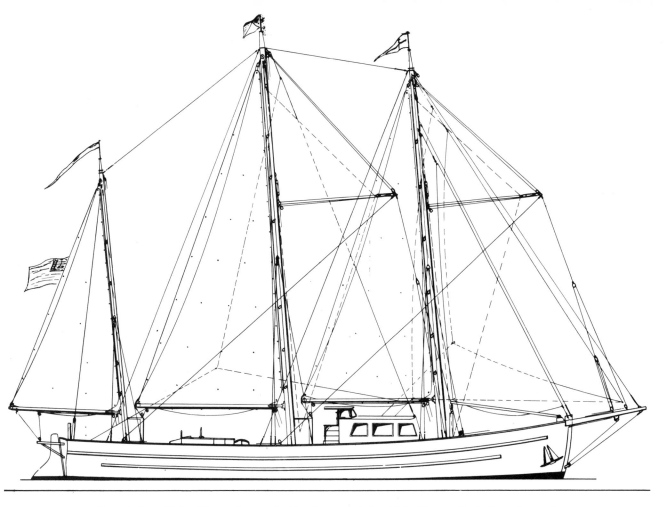

Rara Avis, *a 99-foot Thames barge yacht. Her three-masted rig with brailing or roller-furling sails was designed with the emphasis on manageability. A Rhodes office writeup said, ''It is doubtful if any boat of her size was ever so easily handled.''*

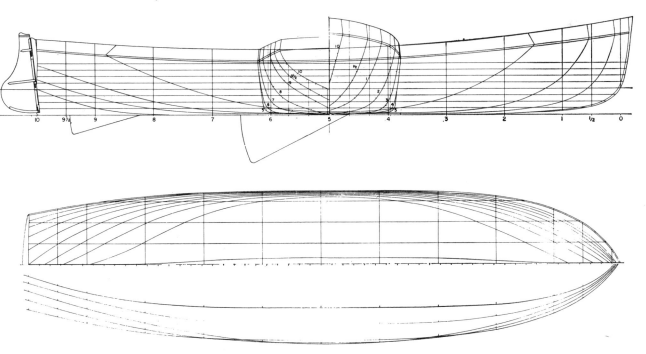

The lines of Rara Avis. *The square sections amidships provide a lot of hull volume for accommodations while allowing very shoal draft. Compared with a true working barge, the bow of* Rara Avis *appears to be less bluff, but her fine lower waterlines aft are somewhat typical.* (Yachting, *May 1960*)

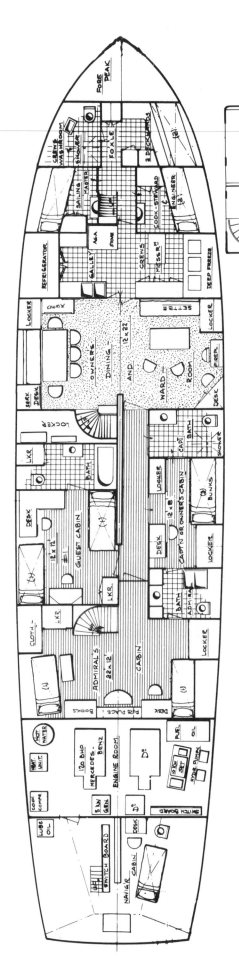

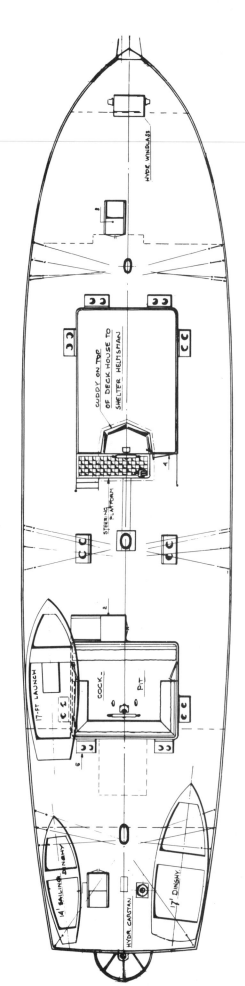

Phil Rhodes said that the requirements for the accommodations of Rara Avis were "comfort for continuous living," and undoubtedly they met the owner's high expectations.

Rara Avis has a lot of deck space, and it is kept as uncluttered as possible with such devices as walk-under travelers.

Rara Avis *under sail showing a lot of character with her Thames barge appearance, high bulwarks, and tanbark sails.* (The Rudder, *June 1959*)

The barge hull is certainly not the most ideal for extensive ocean sailing from the standpoint of ultimate stability, but *Rara Avis* has enormous initial stability by virtue of her flat bilges, great size, broad beam, and 160-ton displacement. Also, her short, spread-out rig keeps the center of effort low. In really heavy weather she could run off under bare poles, with her after centerboard partway down, or she could possibly power very slowly into the seas. She would have little difficulty keeping her head up to the seas hour after hour, for her two 120-horsepower Mercedes-Benz diesels provide ample power, her fuel supply is great, and her twin controllable-pitch propellers give her excellent control.

Rara Avis' three-masted rig nicely divides her 3,500 square feet of sail area. Handling is simplified by brailing the foresail, main, and mizzen against their masts, while the jib and forestaysail are fitted with roller-furling drums. Yardarms can be sent up the two forward masts, and each yard supports a pair of triangular "twins" for trade-wind sailing. Even these latter sails are roller furling so that they need not be hoisted or lowered — nor do they require that a man be sent aloft to tend them. Travelers for the foresail and main are on steel gallows frames elevated seven feet above the deck to reduce clutter.

The accommodation plan shows quarters in vary-

ing degrees of comfort for sailors of every grade from "deckhand" to "admiral," and the latter's cabin certainly befits his rank. It measures 12 feet by 22 feet, and aside from two comfortable berths, it has a desk, bookcase, three lockers, bathroom with tub, and a fireplace. Farther forward, there are two only slightly less luxurious staterooms, a guest cabin to port and a "capt'n's" or owner's cabin to starboard. Each of these staterooms has a bathroom, with a tub in one and a shower in the other. Next forward is the owner's huge dining and ward-room, which has two tables, two desks, a settee, and another fireplace. Above this cabin is a large deckhouse with a table, a settee-berth arrangement, and a small galley. Stairs connect the deckhouse with the cabin below, but there is also a large dumb-waiter and, according to the plans, a wheelchair lift. The main galley, forward of the dining room, has a refrigerator, deep freeze, and everything one would expect, including a crew's mess. Still farther toward the bow, two staterooms accommodate the sailing master and cook-steward, while the fo'c's'le houses two deckhands and contains an enclosed head with shower for the crew. The navigator is well cared for with his own cabin all the way aft, which contains a chart desk and a bunk.

The weather decks are spacious, despite the deckhouse and cockpit. There are no fewer than five companionways and three boats, including a 17-foot power launch. Two steering stations provide advantageous positions for the helmsman under sail or power. The after station, in a cockpit abaft the mainmast, is the best position for sailing in open waters and in fair weather, while the forward station, which is elevated and protected by a shelter, is the best location for steering under power in crowded waters or in bad weather. A large hydraulic windlass forward handles two 500-pound anchors, a Danforth and a plow, which are stowed in hawsepipes.

Rara Avis was built between 1957 and 1959 by Gebr. de Klerk and the Terneuzen Shipbuilding Company in Holland. She is constructed of electrically welded steel, with inner bottoms and three watertight bulkheads. The exterior surface of her bottom is shod with 12 tons of steel strips, which serve as ballast and offer protection when grounding. Her steel spars and rigging were installed by Grove and Guttridge of Cowes, England.

After her commissioning, *Rara Avis* spent two full seasons in the Mediterranean and Aegean Seas. Later, she crossed the Atlantic via the trade-wind route to the West Indies. Her passage from the Cape Verde Islands to Martinique, a distance of almost 2,400 miles, was made in 11 days, which is indeed respectable for this type of vessel. After a season in southern waters, she was taken to her home port at Oyster Bay, New York.

To say the least, *Rara Avis* is a very unusual, interesting, and versatile vessel.

30

La Belle Sole and Meltemi
A Successful Cruising Concept

The Rhodes concept of a large motorsailer with comfortable deckhouse, elevated cockpit, completely separated staterooms, and good performance under sail as well as under power was brought down to a size well under 70 feet when Phil designed *La Belle Sole* in 1956. This yacht measures 64 feet by 47 feet 6 inches by 17 feet 4 inches by 5 feet 6 inches, and some might consider her too small for such an elaborate concept. It may be true that she pays a small price aesthetically for her big deckhouse with its large windows, but this affords a kind of comfort and luxury seldom found on that size boat. It is also true that people in the cockpit seem unusually high above the water, but they have excellent visibility, and the arrangement allows a full-headroom, spacious cabin beneath the cockpit sole. *La Belle Sole* is not just a comfortable houseboat, though; she is a long-range cruiser that can go almost anywhere, thanks to her generous tankage and shoal draft. Her seakindly hull can be driven remarkably well under both sail and power. This boat attracted considerable interest, and her acceptance is illustrated by the fact that five sisters were ordered.

La Belle Sole was built for H.M. Dancer by Burmeister in Germany, and she has an exceptionally strong hull of welded steel. There are four watertight steel bulkheads, and some have double walls with soundproofing in between. Tanks are integral, which adds to the hull strength, and they have capacities of 505 gallons for fuel and 304 gallons for water. The superstructure is also steel, but the decks are of teak.

For two couples, *La Belle Sole* is about the last word in comfort and privacy. The owner's stateroom aft is huge, and it is far away from the guest quarters. The large, well-lighted deckhouse amidships has a chart table that converts to a bar, an L-shaped settee with dropleaf table, an oilskin locker, and even a Winthrop desk. Farther forward and at a lower level are: the galley with stainless steel dressers, Shipmate gas stove, refrigerator, and deep freeze. Opposite the galley is the guest stateroom, which has a berth and extension transom. This room, as well as the owner's stateroom, has a private head with shower, and as a matter of fact, even the crew's quarters in the fo'c's'le has an enclosed head with shower.

Under the deckhouse amidships there is a tremendous engine room housing considerable machinery, including a General Motors 4-71 diesel, which can drive the yacht at 9 knots for 1,000 miles when her

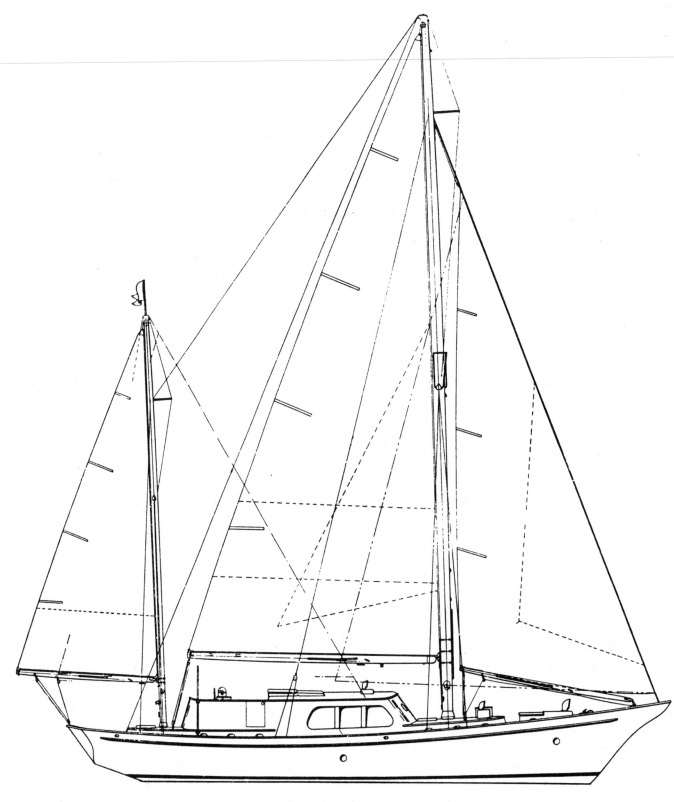

La Belle Sole *has a generous sail plan for a motorsailer. She is 64 feet overall. Unlike many double-head-rig ketches, which have large foretriangles with small forestaysails,* La Belle Sole's *single headsail nicely matches her mizzen, so that she is well balanced with main lowered.* (The Rudder)

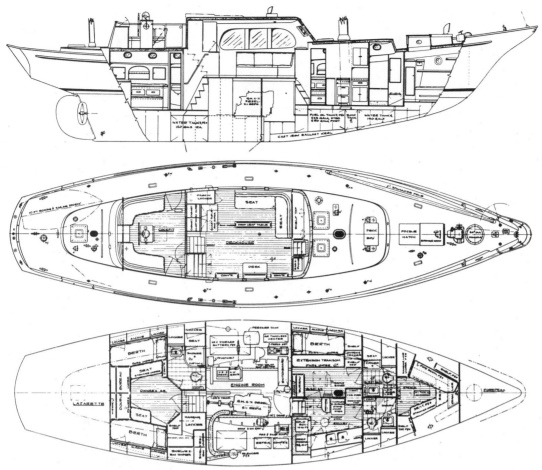

La Belle Sole's accommodations are ideal for maximum privacy for two couples. The boat's underwater profile is like that of a pure sailer.

tanks have been filled. Although this boat has been used mostly in southern waters, especially in the Bahamas, she is fitted with hot water heating for chilly weather. A blower system provides excellent ventilation when it's hot.

Phil Rhodes wrote that even though *La Belle Sole* was intended as a motorsailer, he gave her the underwater shape of a pure sailer. She has a somewhat cutaway forefoot for good balance and helm response and a centerboard to enhance her windward ability. Her bow is the unique clipper type that Phil first developed for *Kirawan II* (Chapter 19). Actually, *La Belle Sole* might be considered a forerunner of the famous racing-cruiser *Thunderhead,* for not only do both boats have clipper bows, but they also have similar short transom sterns, and their underwater profiles are very much alike.

It must have come as no surprise to Phil Rhodes that *La Belle Sole* turned out to be a good sailer, for besides having an efficient hull, she has an effective ketch rig supporting a sail area of 1,703 square feet,

which is generous for a motorsailer. *Alegria II,* a sistership, was cruised extensively in European waters, especially the Mediterranean, and her owner wrote Phil about her performance as follows:

She has met just about every weather condition from dead calm to gale force wind, mostly on the latter side, especially in Greek waters. Everyone who has been aboard, including two crews, marvel at her performance. When hove to for six·hours in a storm between Malta and Athens she rode beautifully. The most amazing thing about her is her sailing ability: she is a really able sailboat. In force 4 winds between Aegina and Athens she made between 7½ and 8½ knots all the way under sail.

In a few words, Phil, your office has designed one of the best cruising boats possible. And with a good allowance she might do alright in an ocean race.

Apparently the *La Belle Sole* concept was successful enough to justify a miniature version, and in 1964

La Belle Sole *sliding along under spinnaker and making remarkably little fuss moving through the water.*
(Photo by Niel C. Nielsen, Jr. Courtesy of Mystic Seaport)

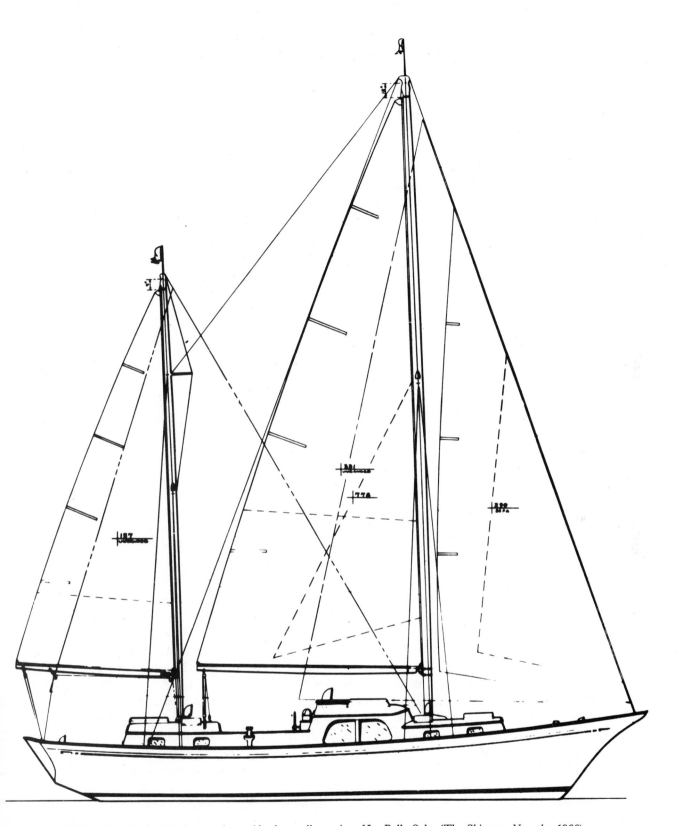

Meltemi, *at 45 feet 2 inches, can be considered a smaller version of* La Belle Sole. (The Skipper, *November 1966*)

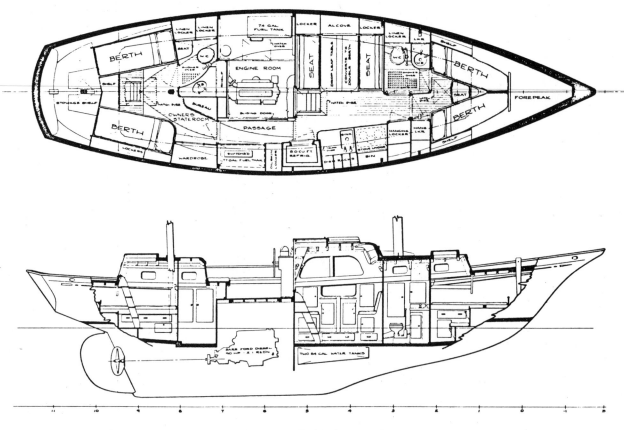

Like La Belle Sole, Meltemi *has separated staterooms, but, of course, she is not large enough to have a real deckhouse.*

Phil designed a closely related but much smaller ketch named *Meltemi*. This boat measures only 45 feet 2 inches by 33 feet 4 inches by 12 feet 8 inches, but she has a relatively deeper keel drawing 5 feet 3 inches, because she is not fitted with a centerboard.

Although *Meltemi* can be considered an enlargement of the small motorsailer the Vagabondia 38, which Phil designed in 1961, her hull above water more closely resembles *La Belle Sole*. Obviously, *Meltemi* is too small for *La Belle Sole*'s type of deckhouse, but her layout is similar in that it has the owner's stateroom aft, a fairly high cockpit forward of the mizzenmast, and a raised cabin trunk with large windows forward of the cockpit. Also, of course, these two boats are much alike in their rigs, counter sterns, drawn-out clipper bows, and concept as a comfortable cruiser with maximum privacy for two couples, yet with the ability to sail well.

Meltemi was built by the Cheoy Lee Shipyard in Hong Kong for Martin Fenton of Wilmington, Delaware. Some exotic woods such as ipol and yacal were used for her skeleton, and she was planked with Philippine mahogany, while Burma teak was used for her decks and joinerwork. She was fitted with a 90-horsepower six-cylinder diesel engine driving a large, three-bladed propeller, which gives her the power performance of a motorsailer, although Phil Rhodes preferred to call her a "full-powered auxiliary" because of her good sailing ability.

Her ketch rig is not large, but it is ample for a pure cruising boat, and it is easy to handle. *Meltemi* has 732 square feet of working sail; in addition, a large, overlapping masthead jib can be carried when the wind is light or moderate. The sail plan also shows a sizable mizzen staysail, which should give her a real kick in the flank on a reach. This sail has more area than the mainsail, so it might be preferable to have running backstays on the mizzenmast to carry the load of the staysail, which tends to pull the mast mostly forward. Powerboat skippers would probably like the helm where it is located, at the after end of the doghouse, but sailors would no doubt prefer it on the boat's centerline at the after end of the cockpit.

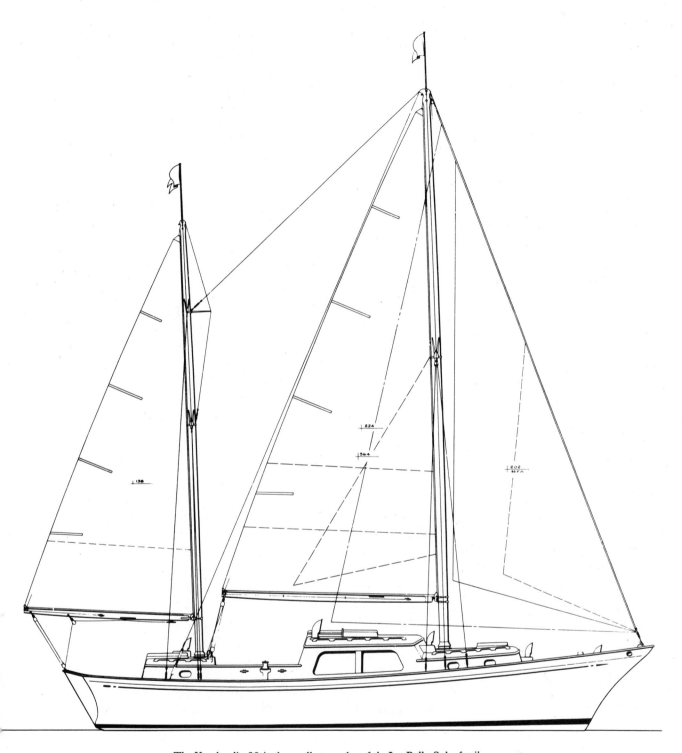

The Vagabondia 38 is the smallest member of the La Belle Sole *family.*

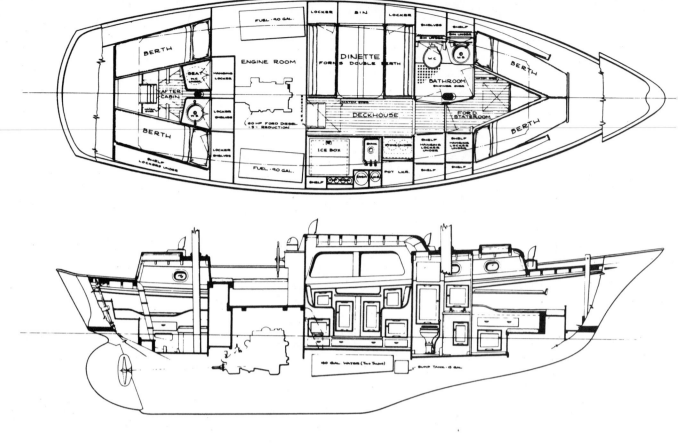

The Vagabondia 38 *is basically similar to* Meltemi *in her accommodations, but her smaller size precludes an enclosed head aft and a passageway between cabins.*

Meltemi is about the smallest-size boat that can have a large owner's stateroom aft with its own enclosed head and a passageway below connecting the forward and after cabins. An unusual feature, which adds to the privacy of the owner's cabin, is that its companionway is located at the after end of the cabin trunk. Another benefit of this location is that the owner's companionway is well protected from spray and rain blowing aft.

Up forward is an ample galley to starboard and a raised dinette with athwartship seats on the port side. This is not the best arrangement for cooking and eating on board an ocean racer when the boat is well heeled, but on a heavy air beat or reach, the crew of *Meltemi* could always drop the main and turn on the kicker prior to a gourmet meal. Farther forward is a large enclosed head with a shower and a guest stateroom just abaft the forepeak.

Soon after this boat was introduced, Phil Rhodes wrote: "We feel that *Meltemi* is a smart, amiable little ship that will be well received by yachtsmen everywhere." She was indeed well received, for a number of sisters were built, in addition to the *Branta,* an aluminum variation on the original model. Even today *Meltemi* is a very desirable cruiser in a size that is not too large for a couple who want all possible creature comforts and also like their privacy when guests are on board.

31

Bounty II and the Rhodes 29-Footers
From Wood to Fiberglass

The Bounty II class is one of the best known of all the stock racing-cruiser designs by Phil Rhodes. She is a landmark boat, for she was the first large stock auxiliary to be built in fiberglass. Her dimensions are 40 feet 10 inches overall, 28 feet on the waterline, 10 feet 3 inches beam, and 5 feet 9 inches draft.

Her builder was the Coleman Boat and Plastics Company (later Aeromarine Plastics Corporation) of Sausalito, California. Before World War II, Coleman had built on the East Coast a similar-sized boat known as the Bounty (Chapter 22), and there is a prevalent misconception that the Bounty II is somehow related to this earlier boat. Actually, the two are distinctly different designs, being related in name only. Production of the earlier Bounty was cut short by the war.

After World War II, suitable woods and highly skilled woodworkers began to become scarce, and fiberglass had been developed as a boatbuilding material for small boats. Thus, when the Coleman Boat Company decided in 1956 to produce another stock auxiliary, these factors induced them to build it in fiberglass. Rhodes had designed small craft for fiberglass construction as early as 1950 but of course had no experience with the material in boats the size

and type of the Bounty II. To help work out the scantlings, Coleman enlisted the aid of naval architect William Garden who, likewise, had previous experience building small fiberglass boats. According to Garden, the project was a joint venture, with the Rhodes office producing the lines and Garden providing the structural details, such as the lay-up and the tooling. The deck mold was actually built under Garden's direction. The scantlings were pretty much guess-work, and as a result the boat was overbuilt and perhaps unnecessarily heavy.

According to Bodie Rhodes, who was working for his father at the time, the Bounty II is a scaled-down version of a 29-foot-waterline sloop named *Altair*, which had been designed for Bradford Smith, Jr., in 1955. Bodie himself reduced the lines, and she was an exact reproduction.

The Bounty's layout is a fairly standard one, with four berths in the main cabin and two in a forward stateroom. There is an enclosed head amidships and an after galley that extends across to both sides of the boat, thereby providing a good amount of counter space. The cabinhouse has a modern look to it, with a raised doghouse and large windows.

Bounty II was originally rigged as a seven-eighths

The first rig of the Bounty II. This 40-foot 10-inch boat was the first large stock auxiliary sailboat produced in fiberglass, and originally even her mast was made of the material.

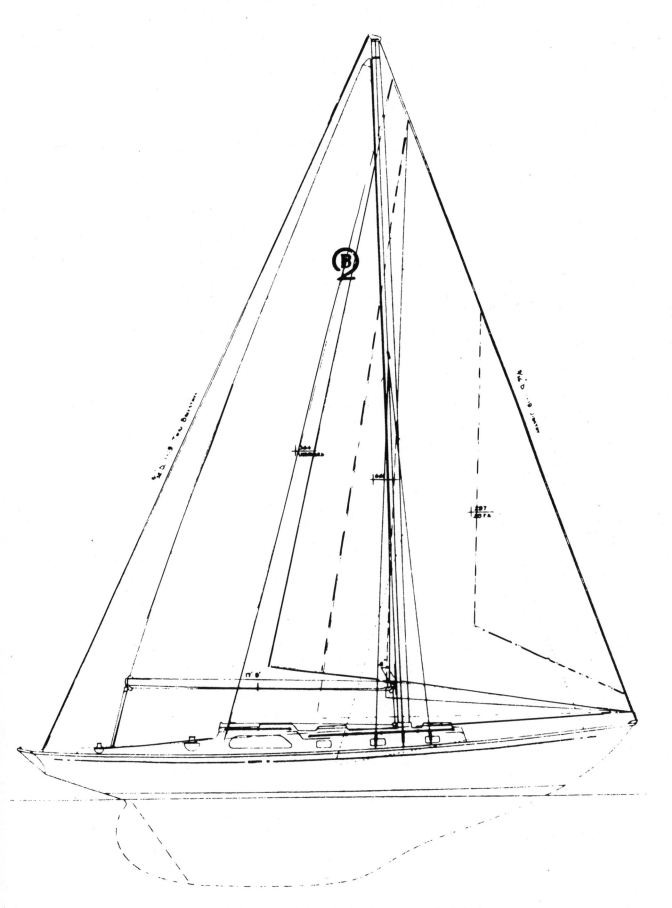

The Bounty II's later masthead sloop rig with shorter mast made of aluminum.

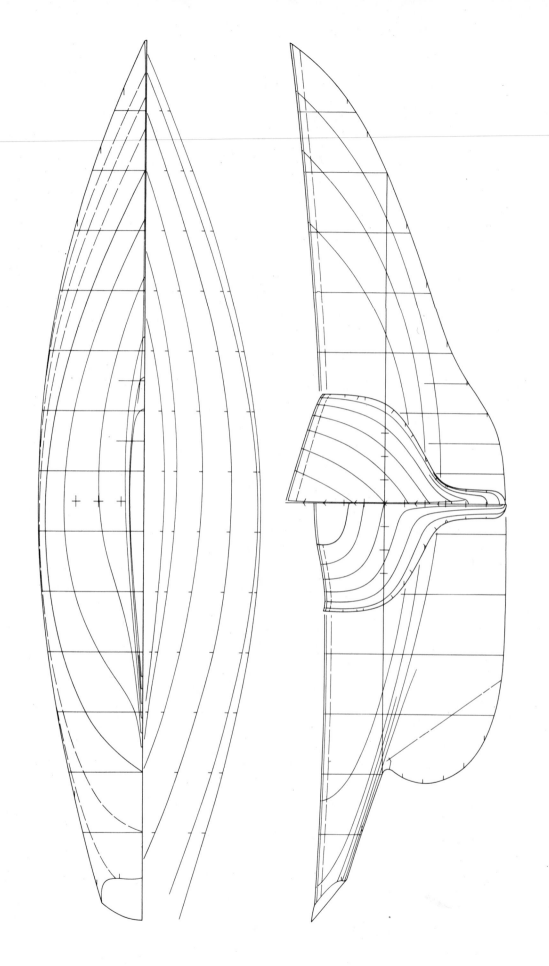

In her hull shape, Bounty II is an exact reduction of Altair, the first boat of a class measuring 29 feet on the waterline.

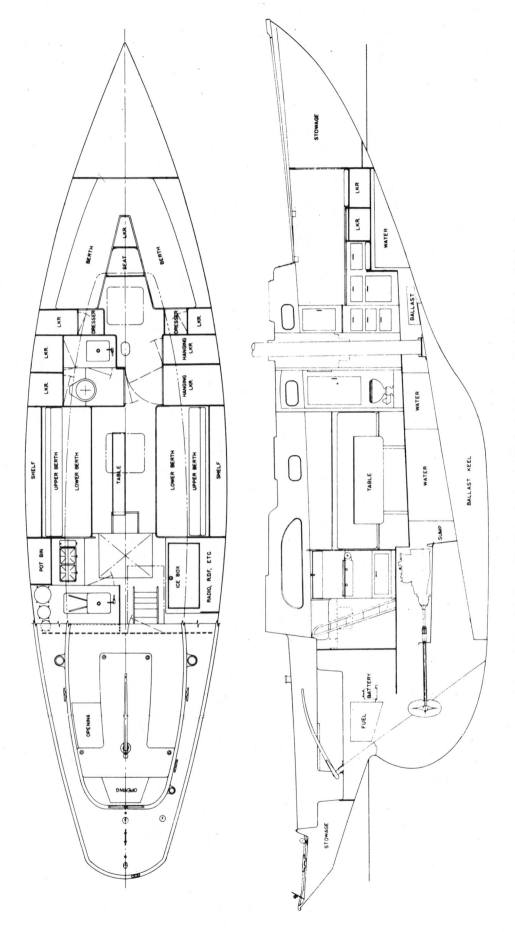

Accommodations of the Bounty II. The engine is quite deep in the bilge, but at least it keeps the weight low and provides a horizontal shaft. Unfortunately, the head is below the load waterline.

The Bounty II Alert *racing on the Chesapeake Bay in 1964. (Photo by Fred Thomas)*

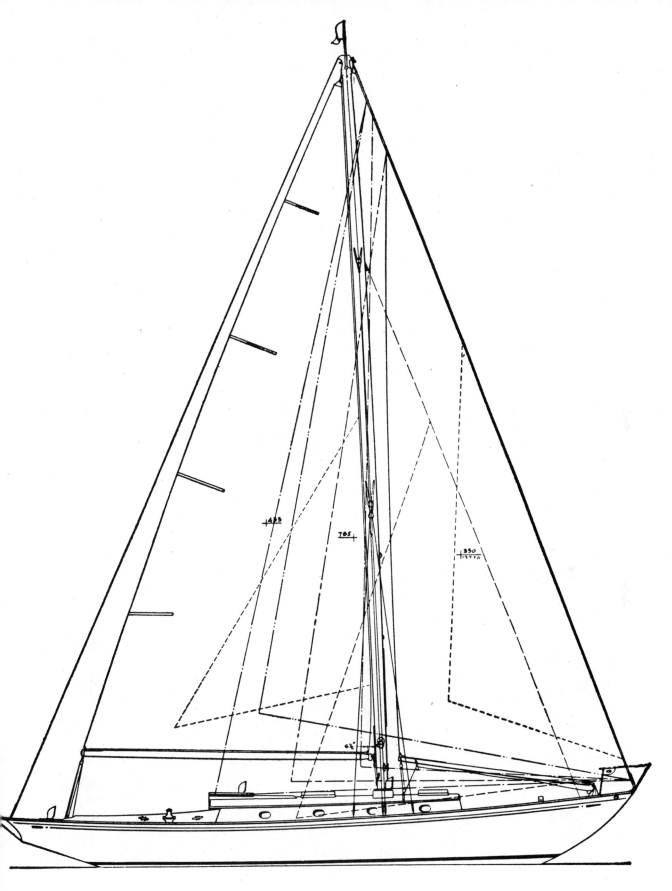

Altair, *the 42-foot 3-inch sloop from which the Bounty II was derived, has been very successful in her own right.* (Yachting, *March 1956*)

Albert W. Fribourg's Erewhon, *the first of Altair's centerboard sisters. (Courtesy of Mystic Seaport)*

Thor, *a well-known centerboard version of* Altair *and her sisters. Her owner, Ed Thurber, raves about* Thor's *perfect helm balance. (Courtesy of A.E. Thurber, Jr.)*

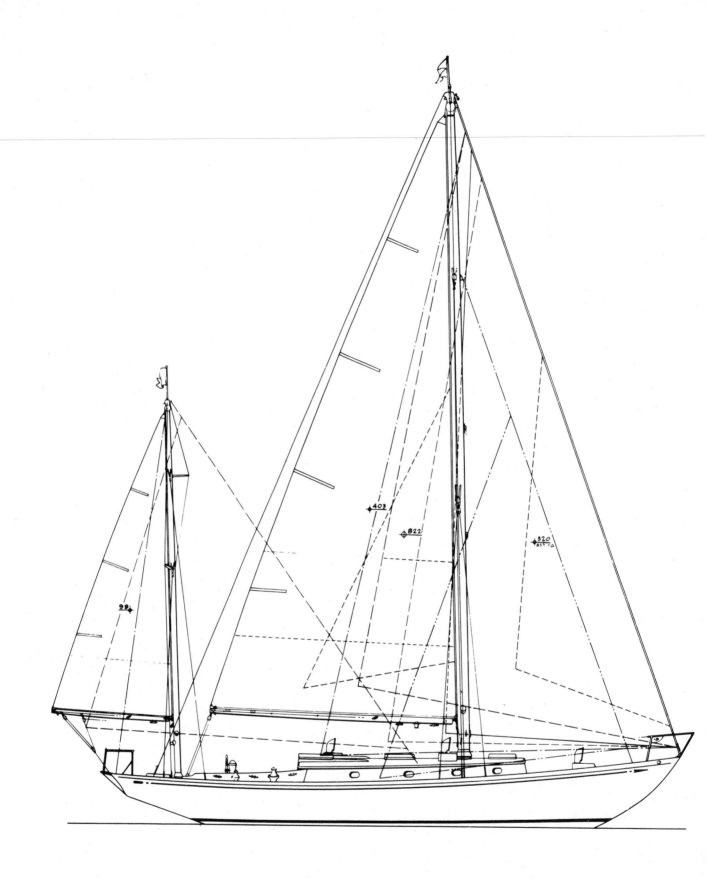

Sail plan of Fair Winds, *a sister of* Thor.

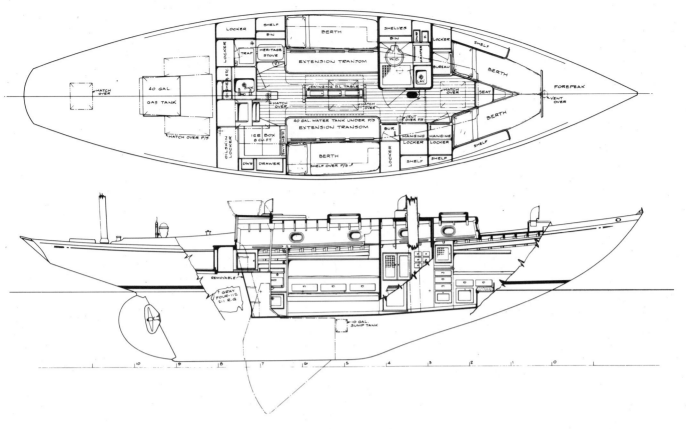

Labels on plan view (top): LOCKER, SHELF, BIN, BERTH, SHELVES, BIN, LOCKER, SHELF, HERITAGE STOVE, HEAD, W/C, LOCKER, BERTH, EXTENSION TRANSOM, BUREAU, SHELF, HATCH OVER, 40 GAL GAS TANK, SWINGING DL TABLE, LAV, SEAT, FOREPEAK, HATCH OVER, HATCH OVER, HATCH OVER, VENT OVER, VENT OVER P/S, BERTH, ICE BOX 8 CU FT, 40 GAL WATER TANK UNDER P/S, EXTENSION TRANSOM, BUR, HANGING LOCKER, HANGING LOCKER, SHELF, HATCH OVER P/S, OILSKIN LOCKER, DWR, DRAWER, BERTH, SHELF OVER P/S, LOCKER, SHELF, SHELF
Labels on profile view (bottom): REMOVABLE, GRAY FOUR-112 2:1 R.G., 10 GAL SUMP TANK

Fair Winds' *arrangement plan. Indicative of this boat's comfort is the fact that Ed Thurber has lived aboard* Thor, *a sister boat, every summer for many years.* Thor, *however, has many minor modifications and innovations.*

sloop, with a tall mast made of fiberglass that supported 737 square feet of sail area. The boat seemed to be a bit tender, so it was given a slightly shorter rig with a smaller total sail area but with a masthead plan for carrying larger genoas in light airs. The fiberglass mast was replaced with a lighter, stiffer aluminum mast, which likewise improved stability with little sacrifice in sail power. To be as stiff as an aluminum mast, a fiberglass mast has to be heavier or larger in section, and since aluminum extrusions were becoming more available and cheaper at that time, it made sense to go that route.

The Bounty II also came with a yawl rig, which provided more sail area without raising the center of effort.

The 29-foot-waterline (and 42-feet 3-inch LOA) sloop from which the Bounty II evolved was successful in her own right. In her first long-distance ocean race, the 1957 Annapolis-Newport Race, *Altair* won her class. The design proved to be so attractive that 12 sisters, or "supplement" designs, were built. These "supplement" designs had the same hull lines as *Altair* but often had slightly dif-

ferent cabin trunks, arrangements, or rigs.* Three of the boats were rigged as yawls.

One of these "supplement" designs is the sloop *Santander*, owned by the famous British actor Richard Greene. She was often written up in British yachting magazines, not only because her owner was a celebrity, but also because her appearance (generous beam, masthead rig, long ends, and pronounced sheer) differed so much from that of most contemporary English yachts. *Santander* was greatly admired abroad and her designer was highly praised. In a write-up on *Santander*, *Yachting World* (May 1957) stated that "Philip Rhodes is without question among the finest designers in America, if not the world."

Immediately after designing *Altair*, Phil designed a centerboard "counterpart" to the 29-footer. This

*S-1, William A. Burkey, *Cleo IV;* S-2, Richard Greene, *Santander;* S-3, Charles Britton II, *Tenba;* S-4, Milton O. Cross, *Whisper;* S-5, J.C. Tibbetts, *Spartan;* S-6, T. Sgt. A.W. Hicks; S-7, Col. Clayton Claassen, *Ta'aroa;* S-8, Riembold; S-9, William F. Page; S-10, Jacques Ouellet; S-11, Gherardo Zamorani (not built); S-12, Peter J. Lewis.

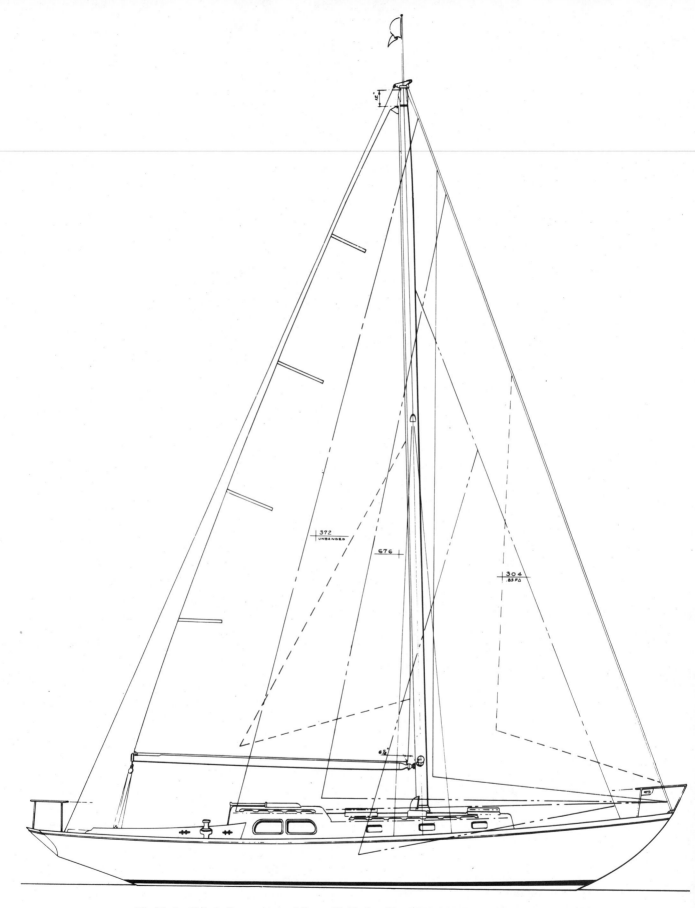

The Rhodes 41 is the Pearson-produced Bounty II. Freeboard has been raised slightly and the doghouse has been given smaller windows in pairs. Advertisements claimed that the mast was moved farther aft, but the base of the R-41's foretriangle doesn't look much greater than that of the Bounty II.

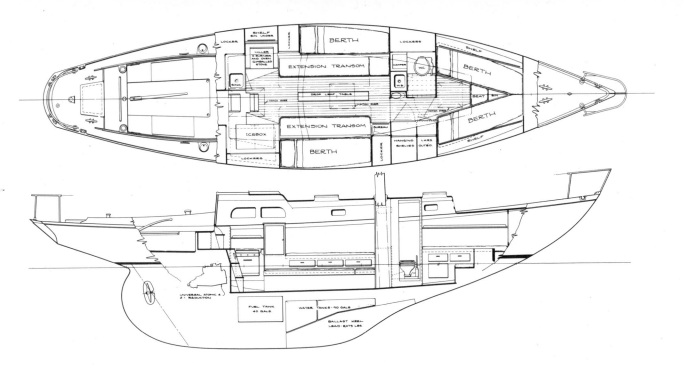

The Rhodes 41's accommodations plan. The Bounty II's dressers in the forward stateroom have been traded for extra lockers and a bureau in the main cabin. Also, the R-41 has pilot berths and sliding transoms aft rather than fixed lowers with folding upper berths.

was the sloop *Erewhon,* for Albert W. Fribourg, and she had 12 sisters.** She is beamier and, of course, shallower (11 feet 3 inches beam versus *Altair's* 10 feet 6 inches beam, and 4 feet 7 inches draft versus *Altair's* 6-foot draft). Actually, the centerboard version is more closely related in hull form to the famous ocean racer *Carina,* and Phil called the design *Carina's* "small sister."

One of *Erewhon's* sisters is *Thor,* owned by A.E. Thurber, Jr. Although she is listed in Phil Rhodes' records as *Erewhon's* first "supplement" design, Thurber exchanged ideas with Phil concerning the design as early as 1954. Like a number of her sisters, *Thor* was beautifully built by Abeking & Rasmussen in Germany. In her gear and her accommodations, she has many unique innovations, and some of these have been featured in *Yachting* magazine's "Gadgets and Gilhickies" column. Thurber raves about his boat's sailing performance, claiming that she is about the best-balanced boat he has ever sailed. He also says that she is marvelously comfortable, and he

has lived aboard her for two months each summer for many years.

During the early 1960s Aeromarine Plastics Corporation was bought by Pearson Yachts, located in Rhode Island. The plant and all of Aeromarine's molds except those for the Bounty were liquidated. The Bounty's hull mold was shipped east, and Pearson resumed production in its Bristol plant in 1962.

The Pearson version, called the Rhodes 41, has the same hull as the Bounty II, but with slightly more freeboard. Rhodes also made several improvements in the deck plan, arrangements, and installations. The engine was moved up out of the bilge; the single window on each side of the doghouse was replaced by two smaller windows, thus increasing the integrity of the cabinhouse; the cockpit was made less subject to flooding through its drains; lead was substituted for iron as ballast; and the main cabin was given a better arrangement with pilot berths and extension transoms.

Production was stopped by Pearson in 1968, after nearly 50 boats had been built. While she certainly did not establish any records for number produced or time span of production, Bounty II will always be regarded as an important boat. She helped usher in the age of fiberglass and mass production that enabled many sailors of limited means to acquire sizable yachts of reasonably high quality and competitive potential.

**S-1, A.E. Thurber, *Thor;* S-2, Hank McCune; S-3, George T. Fleitz, *Fair Winds;* S-4, David Easton, *Honey;* S-5, Henry Chance III, *Hirondelle;* S-6, Raymond Rosenfeld; S-7, B. Lanwell (not built); S-8, Vincent Canon; S-9, Paul R. Bartlett, *Sky Wave;* S-10, no information; S-11, Dr. Rogers Riedel, *Cara Mia;* S-12, Glenwood S. Weinert, *Snow Bunny.*

32

Caper
A Deep-Keel Winner

The sleek 56-foot *Caper* is an ocean racer that made Phil Rhodes extremely proud. She was designed in 1957 for H. Irving Pratt to replace *Merry Maiden* (see Chapter 23), and she compiled a fine record in ocean racing. *Caper* started off well, winning her class in her offshore debut, the 1957 Annapolis-Newport Race, and collected silver in two Bermuda Races, with a class third in 1960 and a class second in 1964. Her most impressive performances were a first in fleet of 102 starters in the 1958 Block Island Race and first overall in the 1959 Annapolis-Newport Race. These and other successes led to her selection for the 1964 Admiral's Cup team, in which she was the second-best boat on an American team that also included *Windrose* and *Figaro IV*. Even as late as 1972, after having been donated to the Coast Guard Academy, *Caper* won the Gulf of Maine Ocean Racing Championship, a season-long series of overnight and day races along the Maine coast.

Caper is quite different from the beamy centerboarders often associated with Rhodes, for she is a relatively narrow, deep-keel boat, with a hull more like that of a meter boat. The choice of this hull form may have been influenced by changes in the 1957 CCA and Storm Trysail Club rules, which made the

centerboarders less competitive. Also, Pratt liked a boat that would excel upwind in all conditions, and *Caper*'s hull and sloop rig are reflective of this. In fact, she represents a trend toward designing with racing efficiency in mind. This can be seen in her spacious deck, with a coffee grinder for trimming large headsails; her aluminum mast; her wide-open layout below, with numerous bunks for crew; an extensive array of instrumentation; and a sail storage area forward with a hatch large enough to accept all her sails.

Caper was built of wood by the Thomas Knutson Shipbuilding Company of Halesite, New York, using top-grade materials, including Honduras mahogany planking, Everdur bronze fastenings, and lead keel. According to Jim McCurdy, who was then head of the Rhodes yacht section, *Caper* was practically designed on Knutson's loft floor. Commodore Pratt was anxious to have *Caper* in time for the 1957 season, so to hurry things along, McCurdy oversaw the lofting from a rough set of preliminary drawings. By dispensing with the usual process of drawing up a finished set of lines, three weeks' time was saved, and *Caper* was launched on May 1.

Caper's dimensions are 56 feet 3 inches long

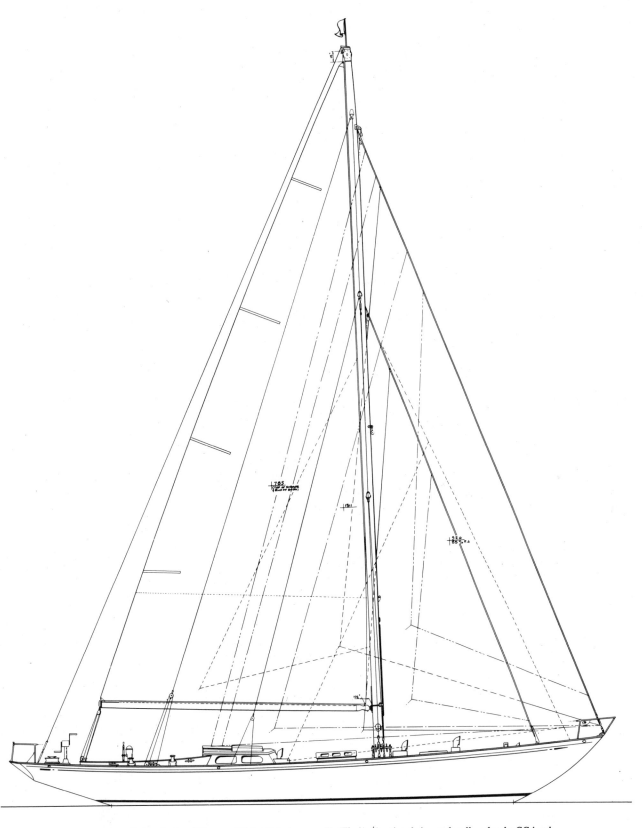

The beautiful, tall-rigged Caper, *56 feet 3 inches overall. The ⁹/₁₀ fractional rig rated well under the CCA rule yet still allows powerful headsails.*

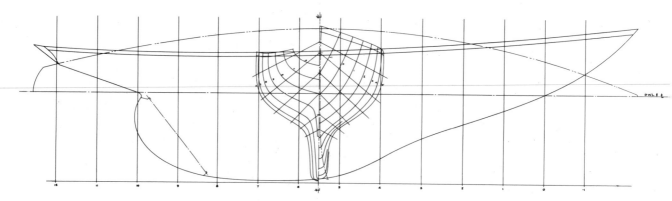

Caper *was practically designed on the loft floor. These lines were reconstructed especially for this book by Philip H. Rhodes.*

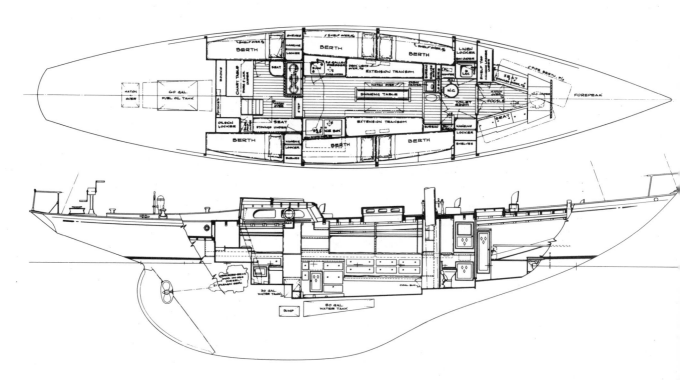

Caper *is laid out below decks as well as above for maximum racing efficiency.*

overall, 38 feet on the waterline, 12 feet beam, and 8 feet draft. As with many boats, her measured waterline length turned out to be considerably longer than her designed waterline due to the addition of heavy gear for distance cruising and ocean racing.

Caper is essentially flush-decked like *Carina,* but being larger and deeper than *Carina,* she has room enough for a water tank under the cabin sole. Her open layout has already been mentioned. This allows four fixed berths (two end-to-end on each side) and two extension transoms in the main cabin.

The ends of the fixed berths are recessed into the head and behind the galley. With two more bunks in the after cabin, eight people can sleep abaft the mast, where the motion is least. In addition, there are folding pipe berths in the fo'c's'le, but as noted previously, that area is used mostly for stowing sails when ocean racing. The galley is almost amidships, and the outboard bunks push it inboard toward the boat's centerline. The cooking stove seems to be facing the wrong way for gimbaling, but it is labeled "swinging" on the plans, so perhaps it is made to turn about its shorter fore-and-aft axis.

Considering her fairly heavy displacement (for a racer), Caper is a good ghoster, with momentum to carry her from puff to puff. (Courtesy of Mystic Seaport)

Even though she does not have a masthead fore-triangle, *Caper* carries plenty of sail, 1,311 square feet of it. Her large-section aluminum mast is stiff enough to obviate the need for jumper stays, thus the luffs of the largest genoas can be almost as long as the jib stay. *Caper* also has a forestay that can be set up or disconnected with a lever, and this enables her to carry a very effective doublehead rig when it really blows. One trouble with this rig is that two sets of running backstays are needed. Her old-fashioned pinrail at the base of the mast seems somewhat incongruous with the rest of her more modern gear.

I had the pleasure of sailing aboard *Caper* in a race out of North Haven on Maine's Penobscot Bay back in the mid-1960s, and it was an experience I shall never forget. Boarding the great blue sloop before the rest of the crew, I arrived in time to help Commodore Pratt prepare his boat for the race. It was the first time I had ever seen or heard of rigging being adjusted with the use of tuning forks. The skipper used them in setting up the stays as though he were tuning a piano. Little wonder we speak of tuning the rigging.

Irving Pratt had the reputation of being very demanding of his crew, so I tensed up when he asked me what I did best. I looked around at the unfamiliar deck gear, including the coffee grinder aft, and stammered that I usually steered my own boats. "Very well," he said, "you'll be the relief helmsman." Before the Commodore turned the helm over to me, he would say something like, "Just keep her at seven knots, 18 degrees heel, and 27 degrees wind angle." Actually, steering was probably the easiest job on the boat, for *Caper* really sailed herself. All I did was to sail her by the seat of my pants, ignoring her battery of instruments. I found her to be well balanced, sure-footed, and easy to keep in the groove. In short, she was a joy to steer. It was easy for me to understand why *Caper* was such a success and why she bolstered Phil Rhodes' pride.

33

Curlew III and Variations
"The Best of Both Worlds"

Curlew III was ordered in 1956 by D.C. Ellwood of Houston, Texas, to replace *Curlew II* (ex-*Tamaris*). Said to be the largest steel sailing yacht built in the United States during the postwar period, *Curlew* measures 97 feet 7 inches by 72 feet 6 inches by 23 feet 7 inches. She is a tandem centerboard ketch and has a designed draft of 6 feet 6 inches with boards up, but her recent draft is figured at over 7 feet, indicating that she is really loaded down with equipment.

She is similar in concept to her forerunner *Tamaris* (Chapter 17) and might be considered to be a larger version of that design. She has the same long, shallow keel as her forerunner and an overhanging canoe stern, but she has slightly less forefoot, a more modern, squared-off rudder, and as previously mentioned, two centerboards in tandem rather than a single one. Like *Tamaris,* she was built of butt-welded steel by the Burger Boat Company of Manitowoc, Wisconsin.

Her tandem centerboards allow her to achieve perfect balance under any sail combination. With her after board down, steering is eased when she is running before strong winds and high seas. The large main board is operated electrically. Steering characteristics under power can be regulated to some extent with the centerboards, but her twin screws provide very effective control and excellent maneuverability.

Her mainmast towers 100 feet above the deck, and the total sail area is a whopping 3,775 square feet. In 1958 her sailmaker, G.W. Valentine, of City Island, New York, claimed that her sails were the largest at that time ever made of Dacron. A good testimonial to the fact that this large, heavy cruiser can really sail is given by Patience Wales in an article that appeared in the September 1979 issue of *Sail* magazine. After a short cruise in the Caribbean (at that time she was named *Fandango* and was a crewed charter boat), Wales wrote: "*Fandango* is a flying cloud. I had thought that her 112 tons would make her dull to sail, but that is not true. I take the wheel and she responds wonderfully."

Her accommodations are sumptuous. The basic layout is similar to that of *Tamaris,* although there are many minor differences, as a study of the plans will show. Obviously, the biggest difference is that *Curlew III* has a permanent cockpit shelter that can

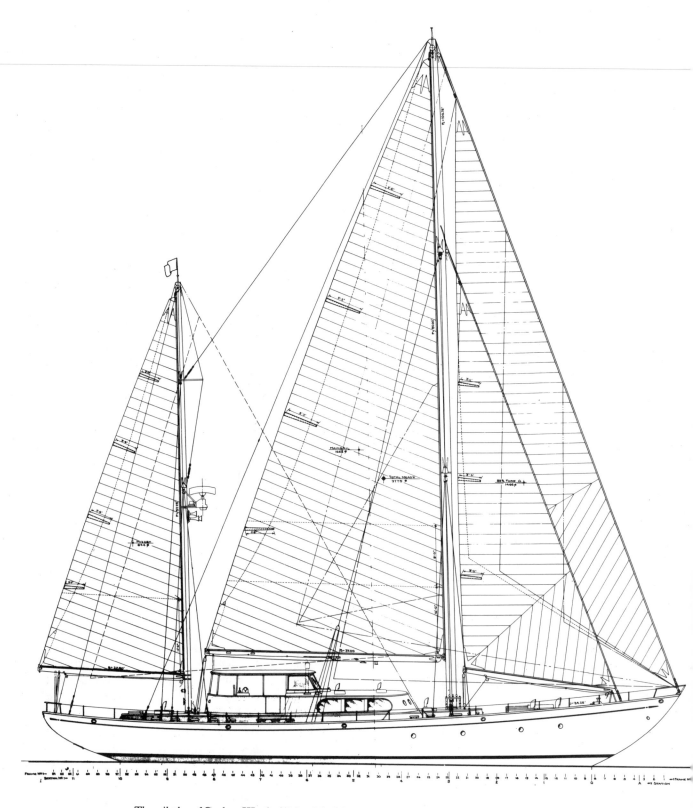

The sail plan of Curlew III, *the 97-foot 7-inch ketch perhaps better known by her later name of* Fandango.
When she was built, her sails were said to be the largest ones ever made of Dacron.

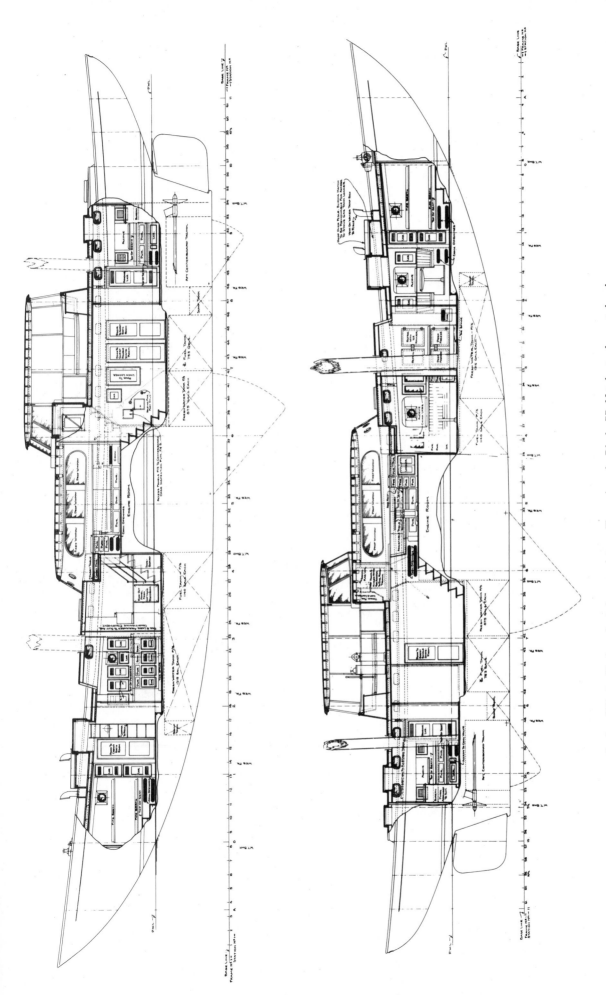

Curlew III's profile shows her to be a cross between Tamaris *and a* Rhodes 77. *Note her tandem centerboards, which offer great flexibility of balance.*

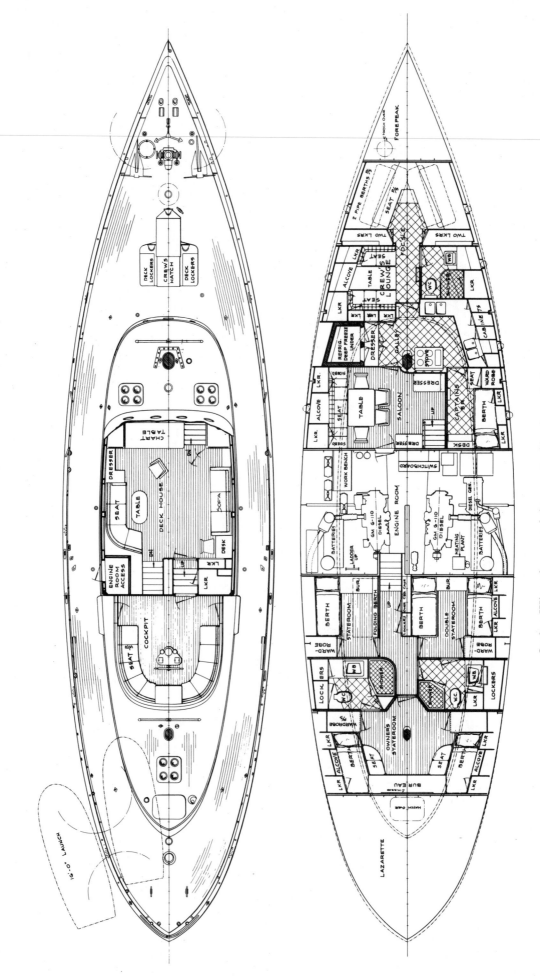

Curlew III's posh accommodations even provide a lounge for the crew.

This photo of Fandango (Curlew III) *under sail helps explain why the yacht has been called ''one of the crown jewels of crewed boat chartering.'' (Courtesy of Travel Inc.)*

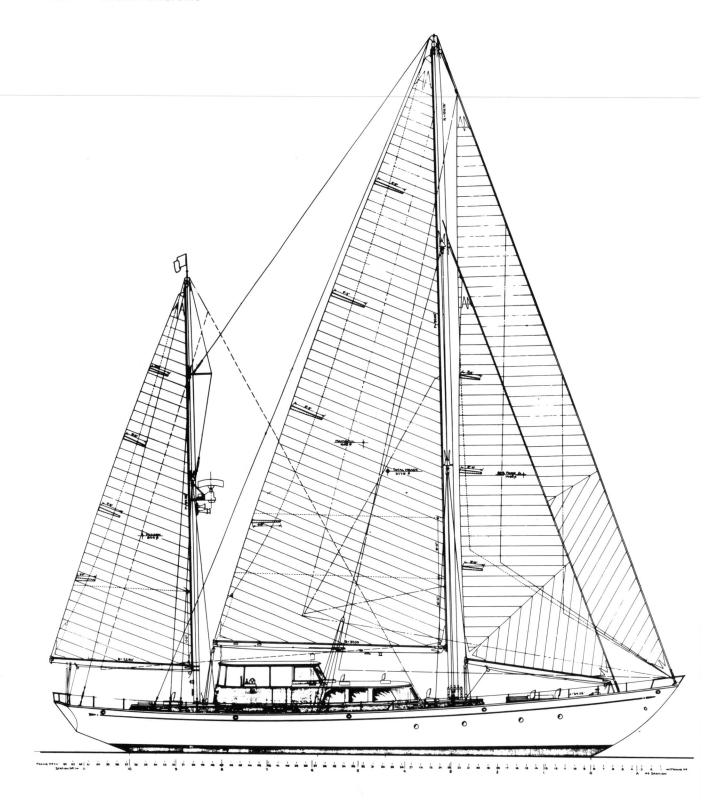

Astral, *a 98-footer presently owned by the U.S. Naval Academy, is essentially* Curlew III *with a counter stern.*

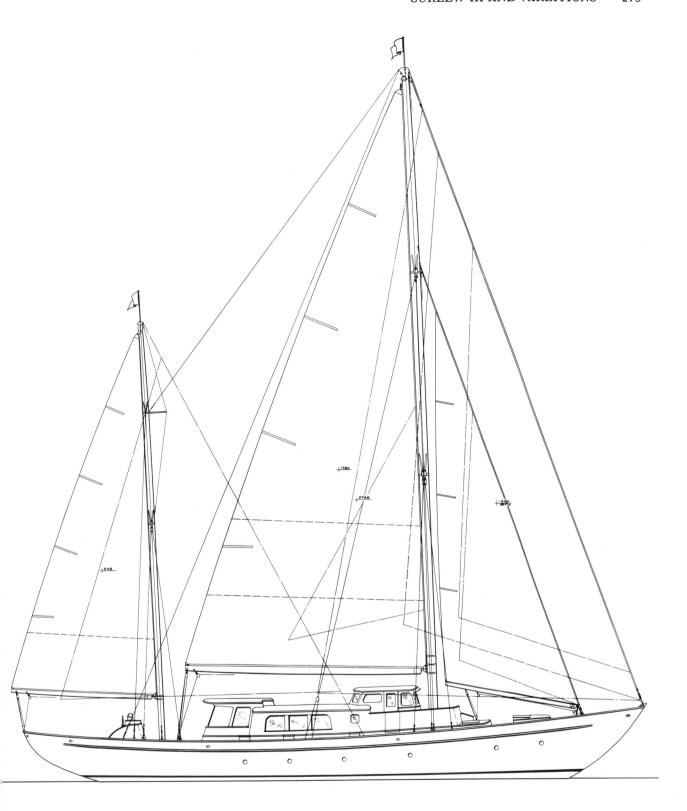

Fei-Seen, *a close relative of* Curlew III *but with different deckhouses and layout below. She is 98 feet 11 inches overall.*

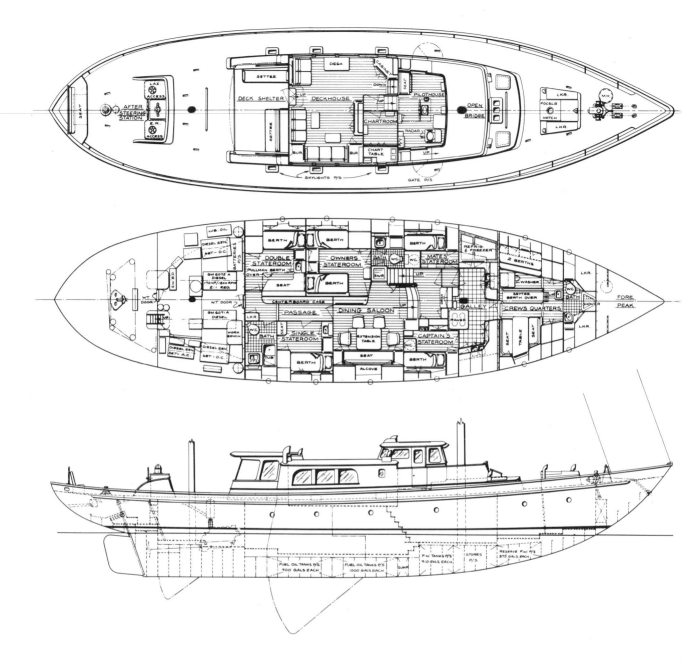

There is not much lacking in Fei-Seen's *accommodations. Few yachts have a huge, walk-in chartroom.*

be completely enclosed with transparent curtains, which in effect makes a large pilothouse. The major drawback of this feature for a sailboat is that the helmsman cannot see the sails very well, but Rhodes provided a small viewing window in the shelter's top. The lounge/music center in the saloon of *Tamaris* has been traded on *Curlew III* for a crew's lounge forward. This vessel has been kept immaculate, and Patience Wales described her as "one of the crown jewels of crewed-boat chartering."

Curlew III has a near sister, *Astral*, built by Krogerwerft of Rendsburg, Germany, in 1970 for C.C. Vanderstar of Monterey Park, California. The two vessels are almost identical except that *Astral* has a counter stern. She has recently been owned by the U.S. Naval Academy and was used extensively offshore for training the academy midshipmen.

A close relative of *Curlew III* in hull form and rig is *Fei Seen*. This vessel is slightly larger, however, with dimensions of 99 feet by 75 feet by 25 feet by 6 feet 9

Fei-Seen under working sail in a moderate wind seems to be moving well even without her jib. *(Courtesy of Mystic Seaport)*

inches. Also, her accommodations and deck plans are entirely different from those of *Curlew III,* for she has a pilothouse forward and an enclosed deck shelter abaft the amidships deckhouse. *Fei-Seen* was designed in 1960 for Robert D. Huntington of Palm Beach, Florida, and she was built in Germany by Abeking & Rasmussen.

The unusual deck plan is at once apparent after a look at the profile of the superstructure. The slightly sunken top of the amidships deckhouse makes a snug place to stow a tender. The problem of steering under sail from the pilothouse is at least partially solved by having an after steering position. It would seem prudent to use the after helm in crowded waters only with a careful bow watch kept, because the view ahead is partially obstructed by the high superstructure.

Fei-Seen's engines, two 170-horsepower General Motors diesels, are fairly far aft rather than amidships, and this, coupled with the fact that there is full headroom under the deckhouse sole, allows a below-decks arrangement that is different from many of the large Rhodes sailers and motorsailers. The owner's stateroom with private head and the dining saloon are under the deckhouse, while two guest staterooms and a large head compartment with a bathtub are aft. A wide galley and spacious quarters for the crew are up forward. There is even a stateroom for a mate as well as one for the captain. The cabins on deck afford plenty of lounging space, and the navigation facilities are outstanding. The original owner was a retired naval officer, and he must have felt right at home with the elaborate pilothouse, bridgedeck forward, and good-sized chartroom just abaft the helm.

Fei-Seen is now a crewed charter yacht working both the Caribbean and Mediterranean Seas in alternating seasons, and she has proven ideal for this use. In referring to her accommodations and dual means of propulsion, a recent charter advertisement called her the "best of both worlds."

The same could be said of *Curlew III* and *Astral,* for these vessels, too, combine the comfort, luxury, and sustained speed of a large motor cruiser with the fun and excitement of big-boat sailing.

34

The Idler Class and Firande
An Atypical Approach

Phil Rhodes didn't normally advocate light displacement for cruising yachts, and he seldom used the fin-keel configuration, except for fairly small craft. Thus the two designs in this chapter, especially the larger one, represent departures from his usual sailing cruiser interpretation. Of course *Firande* and the Idler are not really true fin-keelers, in that their rudders are attached to their keels, but their keels are less integrated with the hulls than in most Rhodes sailing cruiser designs, and their bilges appear quite flat.

The Idler was designed in 1946 as a stock boat for the Kargard Boat and Engine Company of Marinette, Wisconsin. She has an oak skeleton with mahogany planking and cabin trunk, while her decks are plywood covered with canvas. Her dimensions are 25 feet by 20 feet by 8 feet by 3 feet 10 inches.

Originally she had a fractional sloop rig with 293 square feet of sail area (one plan shows 296 square feet), but after a dozen boats were built, the Idler was given a masthead plan with a shorter mast. Either rig makes her a cinch to handle with her small

sails and a permanent backstay, which obviates the need for runners.

The original model had a low trunk cabin, which was very handsome, but headroom below was only 4 feet 5 inches, so later boats were given a doghouse, which not only improved headroom but also allowed the installation of a large window on each side for a brighter cabin. There are two comfortable berths in the cabin and a good-sized galley for such a small boat. On the original model the head is aft, and not enclosed, but in the doghouse version the head is forward, just abaft the forepeak, so a curtain could be rigged for limited privacy.

Although she doesn't appear to be a hot racer, the Idler is said to be a smart sailer. With her short ends, ample freeboard, and moderate rig, she seems to be a seaworthy craft, especially the early non-doghouse model, for it has a small cockpit well and bridge-deck. The fairly short keel reduces wetted surface and allows good maneuverability, while its shoal draft permits exploration of most shallow gunkholes without the bother of operating and maintaining a centerboard.

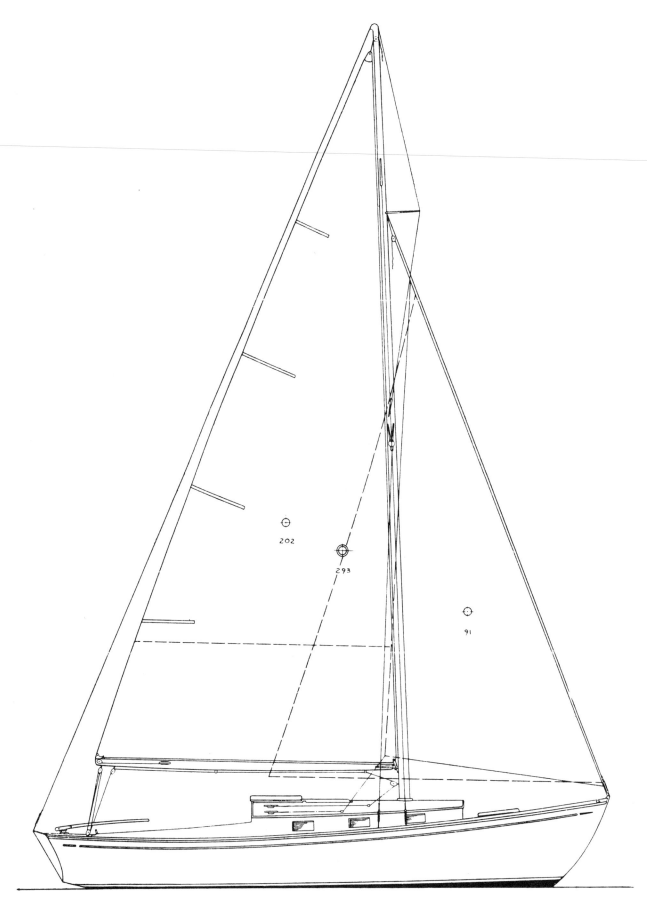

Sail plan of the popular 25-foot Idler class. On larger boats intended for shorthanded sailing, it is not a good idea to have the mainsheet cleat far from the helm, but on the Idler the helmsman can reach the sheet without much difficulty.

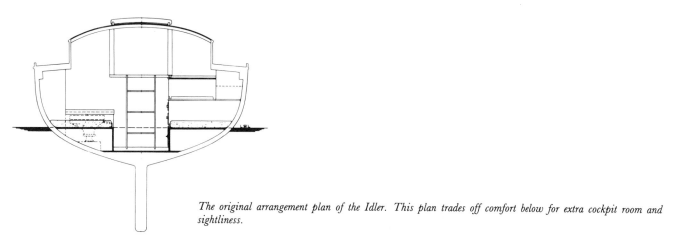

The original arrangement plan of the Idler. This plan trades off comfort below for extra cockpit room and sightliness.

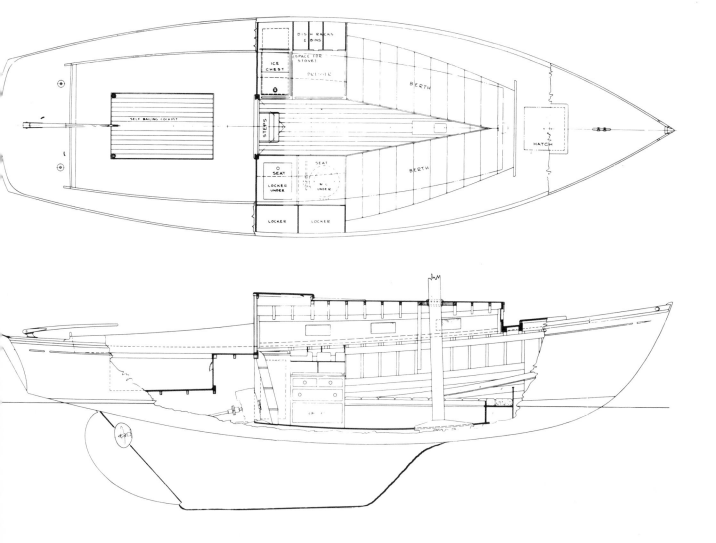

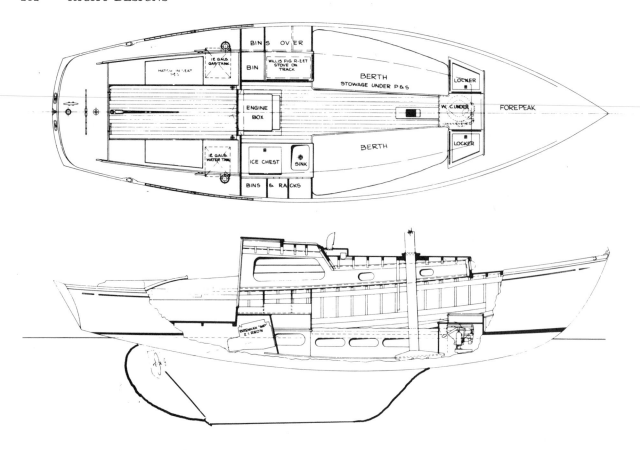

The doghouse model of the Idler detracts some from the boat's good looks, but it provides headroom aft, and the longer cabin trunk allows a far better location for the head.

The Idler proved to be a popular design that was built all over the world — countless numbers of plans were sold to individuals. Phil's son, Bodie, owned and was very happy with one of these boats for a number of years.

Firande is basically a larger version of the Idler, but with her ends drawn out a bit more and a little shorter but deeper keel. She is 38 feet 6 inches by 28 feet 6 inches by 9 feet 10 inches by 5 feet 9 inches. Despite fairly flat bilges, she has well-rounded sections that, in addition to reducing wetted surface, lessen any tendency to pound in a seaway. Her displacement is 12,960 pounds and she has a displacement-length ratio of 248, which is on the light side for that era. The Idler's displacement is not given, but judging from the depth of hull shown on the profile plan and the size of the rig, it would seem that *Firande* is relatively lighter. Another minor difference is that the larger boat has her propeller above and abaft the rudder rather than in a rudder aperture.

With folding blades, *Firande*'s propeller and its installation probably causes less drag under sail, but some control might be sacrificed under power.

Designed in 1957 for Franklin M. Gates, *Firande* was built of wood by Johann de Dood in Bremen, West Germany. She was planked with mahogany over oak frames, and her decks are plywood scored to simulate teak. She is a handsome boat with moderately short but shapely ends, a low cabin trunk, and the lovely sheerline one normally associates with Rhodes.

She has a rather short rig, only 555 square feet of sail area, but this is sufficient for her modest displacement (the lighter the hull, the less sail needed to move it). Gates wanted a reasonably small rig that he and his wife could handle alone. After sailing the boat for a number of years, Gates further simplified handling by installing a roller-furling jib and mainsail. By today's standards especially, *Firande*'s sloop rig would be considered a very low-aspect-ratio type; but the base of the foretriangle is

Philip H. (Bodie) Rhodes and his family enjoying a sail in his Idler. (Photo by Philip L. Rhodes. Courtesy of Mystic Seaport)

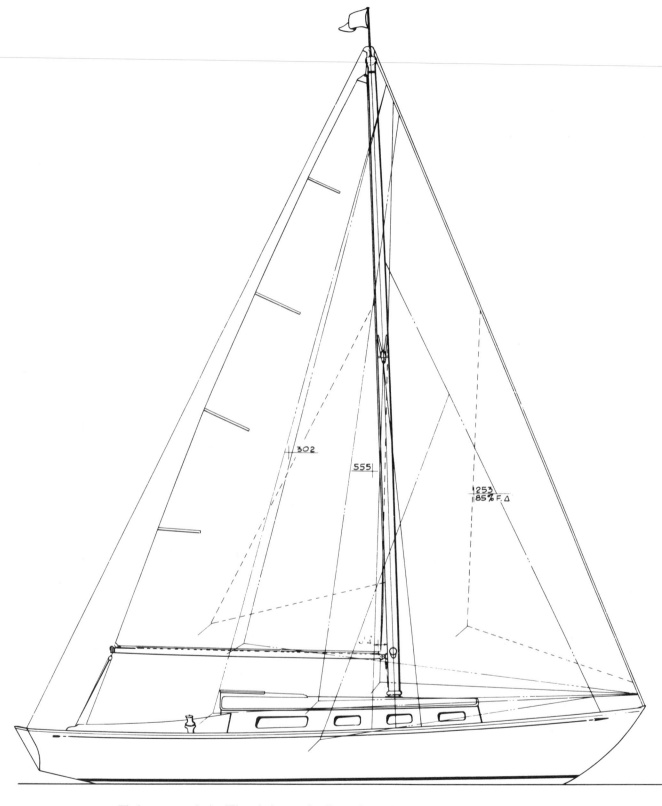

302

555

253
85% F. △

The low-aspect-ratio rig of Firande *is easy to handle yet adequate for her moderately light-displacement hull. She is 38 feet 6 inches overall.*

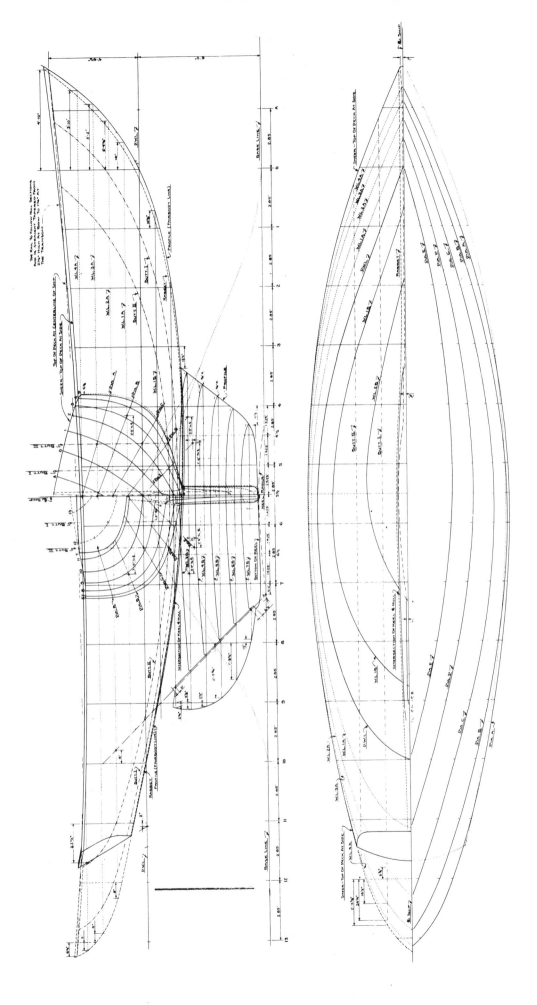

Firande's lines indicate a kinship with the Idler. With both boats the keel is less integrated with the hull than is normal for a Rhodes cruising hull. Note Firande's tight garboards, long flat run, and almost semicircular sections amidships.

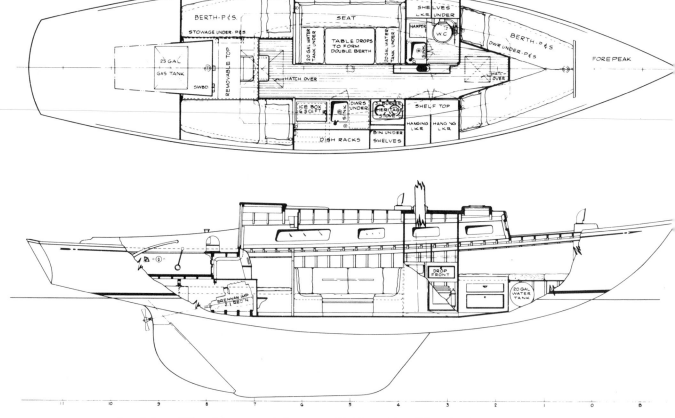

Some features of Firande's *accommodations are not ideal for cruising offshore, but the layout is fine for harbor living and weekend cruising.*

sizable, and the jib stay goes to the masthead, so it is possible to carry a large jib and a well-shaped spinnaker.

Gates had definite ideas about the kind of boat he wanted, and he was entirely responsible for the interior arrangement. The galley, stretching along one side of the main cabin, would be somewhat difficult to use when the boat is well heeled, especially on the starboard tack, while it would not be easy to use the dinette at large angles of heel on the port tack. Of course, the arrangement is splendid for harbor use. Quarter berths are good sea berths (when there is a dodger or curtain to keep out spray from the companionway), but those in *Firande* are a bit wide for use when the boat is rolling, although they are first rate when the anchor is down. There is a comfortable stateroom forward, and the enclosed head affords good privacy, even if it is slightly cramped.

Firande's home port is North Haven, Maine, and she has spent most of her life in Penobscot Bay, but Gates did not ship her home from Germany right after she was built. He left her abroad for three years so that he and his family could cruise the waters of Scandinavia. After being shipped to Maine, she did

a lot of cruising Down East, going as far as the St. John River in Canada.

The sloop was never campaigned, but she sailed in one prestigious event abroad, the Scandinavian Skaw Race, and took third in her class. In the United States, *Firande* participated in a few Monhegan (Maine) Races but never did very well, primarily because she had a poor sail inventory. Gates' three children now own the boat; his son Kenneth tells me that her roller-furling sails hurt her performance, which is not at all surprising, but he says the boat is a smart sailer, stiff, fast, and maneuverable. In the summer of 1981 they removed the roller-furling mainsail in order to improve her performance. One of her few faults, which she shares with many modern fin-keelers — even those with separated rudders — is a tendency to broach when sailing under spinnaker in fresh winds and rough seas.

Not only does *Firande* illustrate Rhodes' ability to satisfy a client, but she and the Idler show the versatility of Phil and his design team in handling almost any type of boat.

35

Kamalii
Pacific Princess

Edward L. Doheny III, of Beverly Hills, California, and Honolulu, Hawaii, needed a versatile boat. He wanted a handsome, seakindly, heavily powered sailer with the smallest hull that would have enough room for three double staterooms, a deckhouse, and a main saloon. He also sought good performance for long-distance cruising and deep-water racing. The Rhodes 77 had a proven track record along these lines, and it was natural that Doheny should look to that design for ideas. Along with the 77's larger sister *Constellation* (later *Sorrento)*, she served as the inspiration for Doheny's boat *Kamalii*.

"Kamalii" is the Hawaiian word for princess, and this ketch is truly worthy of the name. Designed in 1957, she is 75 feet 3 inches overall, 54 feet on the waterline, and has a beam of 18 feet 2 inches. Although similar in most respects to the Rhodes 77 type, she differs in that she has much greater draft — 9 feet with the board up. She really could be considered to be a deep-keel boat, with a centerboard added for extra efficiency to windward. Her deep draft puts a damper on gunkhole cruising, of course, but she was not designed with this in mind. The keel depth gives her plenty of reserve stability and the

ability to make good progress to windward, even without the centerboard. Her deep rudder makes steering easy and gives good control off the wind in rough conditions.

The arrangement plan is very similar to the 77's, except that there is no separate captain's cabin. There are adequate quarters for paid hands in the fo'c's'le. Two appealing details at variance with the 77 are the splendid bar with water and ice in the saloon, and the separate companionway provided for the owner's cabin. The deckhouse windows are perhaps a bit large, and it might be wise to bolt sheets of Lexan over them for the very worst weather at sea. However, they certainly make the interior of the deckhouse bright and attractive, while providing a grand view.

Kamalii was built of wood by the Wilmington Boat Works, of Wilmington, California, who had built Doheny's previous boat. It was very difficult to find top-quality oak for bent frames and naturally shaped structural members for such a large boat, so the backbone members and the frames were laminated of oak, following procedures used on Rhodes-designed Navy minesweepers. A write-up of *Kamalii*

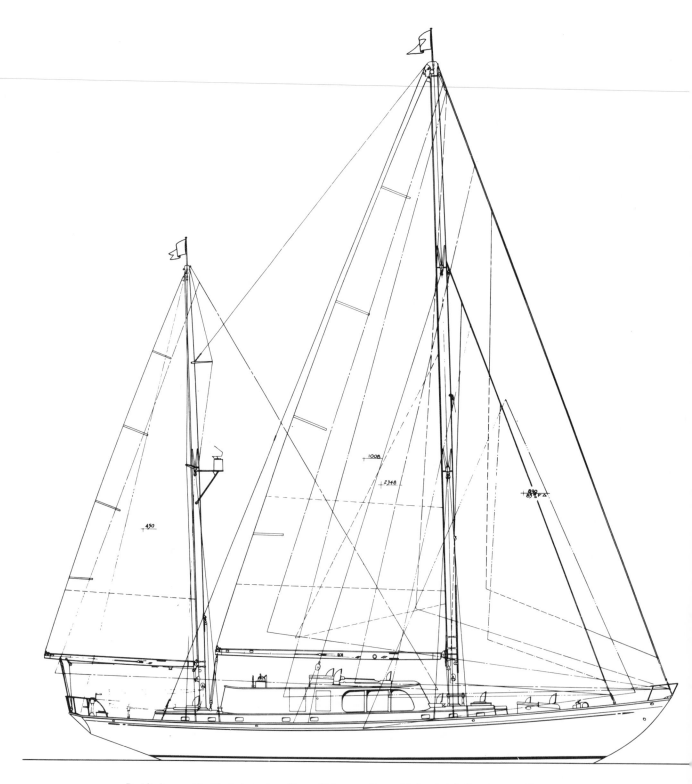

Despite her considerable deck structure, Kamalii is appealing with her sleek hull and tall, well-raked masts. She is 75 feet 3 inches overall.

KAMALII

LOA—75' 4"	Beam—18' 6"
LWL—54'	Draft—9'

Draft (centerboard down)—14'
Displacement—143,000 lbs.
CCA Rating—54.4
Power—Mercedes-Benz 185-hp diesel
Cruising Speed—9½ knots
Working Sail—2940 sq. ft.
Fuel Capacity—894 gal.
Water Capacity—615 gal.

Rendering specially prepared for SEA by Blaine Seeley

An open perspective painting of Kamalii dramatically presents her deck layout and accommodations. (Sea and Pacific Motor Boat, *September 1958*)

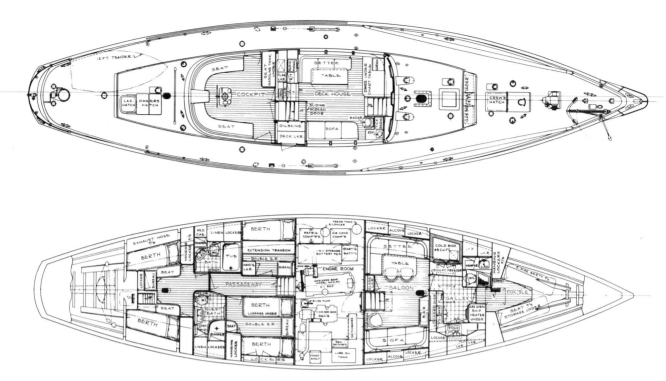

The accommodations of Kamalii *show her kinship to the Rhodes 77.*

from the Rhodes office stated, ''This construction provides absolutely sound timbers free from natural defects. The frames, having been bent from many thin strips, have no locked-in stresses, and each one is perfect.''

Built to withstand a lifetime of ocean sailing, *Kamalii* is double planked with mahogany, and her decks, cabin trunks, and exterior trim are of teak. She is fastened with Everdur screws and also carries 10,000 pounds of sheet Everdur in her mast step, engine bed, floors, diagonal strapping, centerboard trunk, and structural bulkheads. Her ballast is 37,800 pounds of lead. With heavy equipment such as a Mercedes-Benz (Model OM-315) diesel engine, a 110-volt D.C. diesel generator, a heating system, and abundant refrigeration added to her hefty hull, *Kamalii* weighs a whopping 143,000 pounds.

Despite her heavy displacement, the ketch moves and handles well, for she carries a lot of sail. Her masthead rig provides for powerful jibs and spinnakers, while her mizzenmast is tall enough to support a huge staysail (or mizzen spinnaker). The sail plan shows 2,348 square feet of sail area, and this figure includes a headsail area that is only 85 percent of the foretriangle.

In regard to *Kamalii*'s sailing performance, Larry Doheny writes: ''She handles well on all points of sail and, of course, loves a close reach. She drives well in heavy winds, but her favorite velocity is 18-20 knots — she flies for a heavy displacement ship. She ghosts beautifully in extra-light air and accelerates in the puffs like a Star.'' Further testimony of her owner's satisfaction comes from such remarks as, ''*Kamalii* has to be the most seakindly vessel afloat,'' and ''We *never* made an inadvertent jibe while racing.'' The latter remark probably refers to *Kamalii*'s ability to track while running in blustery winds with sizable following seas. She experienced those conditions often in the west coast northers and Pacific trades.

Although *Kamalii* is heavy for competing against light-displacement boats in downhill, fresh-wind races, she participated in seven Transpacs and in 1959 was the fourth boat to finish and second in her class. She also sailed in a number of Mazatlan and Acapulco races and was cruised extensively along most of the North American west coast and among the Hawaiian islands.

Undoubtedly, the yacht's greatest adventure occurred when she was hijacked in 1971. While the

Kamalii under sail in a good breeze with everything but her spinnaker flying. Larry Doheny says, ''She loves a close reach,'' but she also seems to excel at sailing a bit farther off the wind. (Courtesy of Edward L. Doheny III)

ketch was berthed at Honolulu with three professional crew members on board, three armed hijackers made their way aboard and forced the crew at gun-point to get underway. The vessel was taken to a point 160 miles or so southwest of Oahu, where the captives were ordered to jump overboard. Naturally they pleaded for their lives, and the pirates agreed to cast them adrift in a life raft. Apparently the decision to let the crew live was made by the flip of a coin, for one of the pirates tossed a dime into the raft with the casual comment that the coin had saved their lives.

This scene, almost from the pages of *Mutiny on the Bounty,* took place in a region remote from shipping lanes, and the castaways were most fortunate to be rescued by a passing ship only hours after being set adrift. The incident was reported by radio immediately after the rescue, and *Kamalii* was soon being tracked down by an Air Force rescue plane and an armed Coast Guard cutter with Doheny on board. The yacht, enroute to Thailand on a dope mission, was overtaken by the Coast Guard four days after she was hijacked, and after some cat-and-mouse maneuvering, but without gunfire, *Kamalii* was recaptured and taken safely back to Honolulu.

This experience must have been almost as shocking for the boat's owner as it was for her captured crew, for Larry Doheny wrote me that he loved *Kamalii* like a wife.

36

Weatherly
Defender of the Cup

The 12-meter *Weatherly* is perhaps Philip L. Rhodes' best-known design because of her participation in the America's Cup races, yachting's most publicized and glamorous event. Although unsuccessful in her effort to defend the Cup in 1958, she was selected as the defender in 1962 and turned back one of the stiffest challenges ever. *Weatherly* was Rhodes' only design to the International Rule (the meter-boat design formula), and until 1987 she was the only Twelve to have defended the Cup that wasn't originally designed by Olin Stephens.

Despite Rhodes' unfamiliarity with the 12-meter rule, the Henry D. Mercer Syndicate considered him to be the logical choice as *Weatherly*'s designer when they put together an effort to defend the America's Cup in 1958, the first such postwar competition. He was well known for his successful ocean racers and one-designs, his outstanding versatility, and his meticulous attention to detail. The Syndicate stipulated that Phil himself should handle every detail of the design and the supervision of the building.

In designing *Weatherly*, Rhodes sought first to familiarize himself with *Vim*, the prewar Stephens design that was to date the most advanced and suc-

cessful Twelve afloat. Using *Vim* as a yardstick, Phil opted for a slightly longer waterline length at a small cost in sail area, shooting for greater speed potential and improved stability. He tested three different models in the Stevens Institute test tank and settled on the third one, which was smaller and lighter than the other two.

Weatherly's original dimensions were 69 feet overall, 46 feet on the waterline, with a beam of 11 feet 10 inches and a draft of 9 feet. She has moderately full waterlines forward and almost wineglass sections amidships. Her U-shaped sections aft appear to be less flat at the bottom than those of her principal rivals (with the exception of the Ray Hunt-designed *Easterner)*, and her original keel seems to be a little thicker. She is one of the prettiest of the Twelves.

Weatherly was built by the Luders Marine Construction Company in Stamford, Connecticut, and she was built with bronze floors and web frames in way of the mast, alternating laminated wood frames, and double planking of African mahogany. Her builder, A.E. Luders, Jr., has said that she might have been built a little heavier than need be, for Phil was always concerned with building a strong boat.

Although she did not earn the right to compete against the British challenger for the America's Cup in 1958, she provided good competition in the trials. Racing against rival Twelves *Vim, Easterner,* and *Columbia,* Stephens' new design that year, *Weatherly* actually had the best record in the August observation trials. Skipper Arthur Knapp, Jr., and his crew compiled a record of six wins and only two losses in that series of match races. In the final trials, *Columbia* was selected to defend, after a tight battle with *Vim.*

After the 1958 season, *Weatherly* was raced quite successfully under Knapp, particularly in port-to-port races. Her performance kept improving until, in 1961, she was beating both *Columbia* and *Easterner* with some regularity. (*Vim* had been sold to the Australian syndicate challenging for the America's Cup in 1962.) In fact, she won both the Queen's Cup and the Astor Cup on the New York Yacht Club Cruise that year. *Weatherly*'s owners were sufficiently encouraged by her performance to feel that she had a reasonable chance for selection to defend the America's Cup against the Australian challenger in 1962. Arthur Knapp decided to retire from 12-meter racing, but a worthy replacement was found in Emil (Bus) Mosbacher, Jr. Mosbacher had shown his outstanding match-racing talents during the 1958 Cup trials as skipper of the then-19-year-old *Vim.*

Weatherly had always been fast running and reaching in light airs, but she was tender on a fresh-air beat. In fact, during the 1958 trials, Knapp would sometimes have his crew hang over the side like Star sailors to help her stand up better. To prepare her for the 1962 races and make her more true to her name in a breeze, it was decided that *Weatherly* should have a new keel, one that was heavier and perhaps deeper forward. The keel work, as well as other hull modifications and a complete retuning of the rig, was done at the Luders yard.

Bill Luders was instrumental in *Weatherly*'s revitalization. Besides executing the changes, he also provided a substantial amount of the input upon which the changes were based. He had been involved in *Weatherly*'s development program between the 1958 and 1962 Cup races and was able to devote a great deal of time to conducting experiments aimed at improving the boat.

Commenting on some of the changes and how they were made, Luders wrote:

> A new team was formed, which consisted of Bus Mosbacher as skipper, Ed Bainbridge representing the Syndicate, Jim McCurdy representing Phil Rhodes, and myself. Everybody contributed to the effort. The first project was to lighten the boat, which was done throughout, including cutting two feet off the transom. In the meantime, I had made a model of the boat and was model testing it at Stevens Institute, trying to make improvements in the hull, and I found by altering the keel and making other small improvements the tank indicated, that better performance could be achieved.
>
> In the meantime, Phil Rhodes had a model which he was experimenting with at the Stevens tank, and when the final authorization was made for hull changes, Phil Rhodes' alteration (which was rather extreme with a torpedo-shaped keel) was selected. No sooner had it been selected than an error was found in the tank test calculations, so after a hasty meeting it was decided to adopt the keel changes that my model indicated, and from there on everything went pretty smoothly.

The new keel turned out to be lighter than anticipated, for it was thinner than the original, presumably for the sake of reducing head resistance. What really made the difference was the attention given to lightening the hull and rig, for every bit of weight saved could be transformed into an equal amount of weight in inside ballast. According to Bodie Rhodes, even the crew got involved in the weight-saving campaign, and "some of them spent days either removing nonessential weight themselves, or suggesting to higher-ups where weight could be eliminated." In all, 4,500 pounds of inside ballast was added.

One of the biggest weight savings was achieved by stripping *Weatherly*'s accommodations. Due to a rather literal interpretation of Lloyd's rules for construction, with which the Cup defenders were supposed to comply, *Weatherly* was originally designed with complete accommodations as specified by Lloyd's. When first built, she had berths for eight (including three pipe berths and two swing-up pilot berths), a head, a galley, and such amenities as a folding table and cabinetwork. In addition, her accommodations were compartmentalized, with three

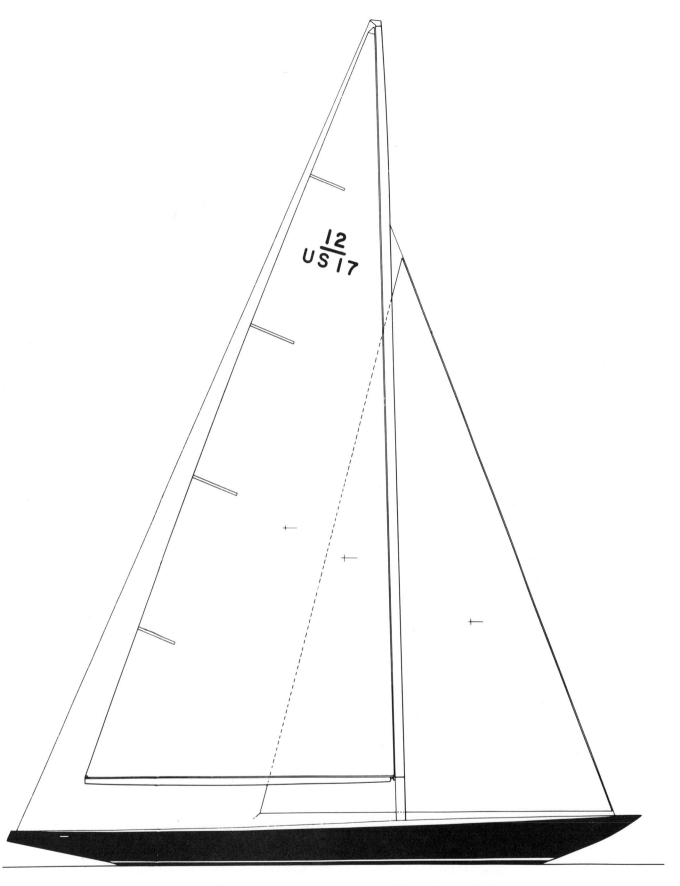

Weatherly's sail plan. Although a drawing was made for jumper struts, Jim McCurdy does not believe struts were ever used. Of course, their elimination allows a longer jib luff length and some mast bend.

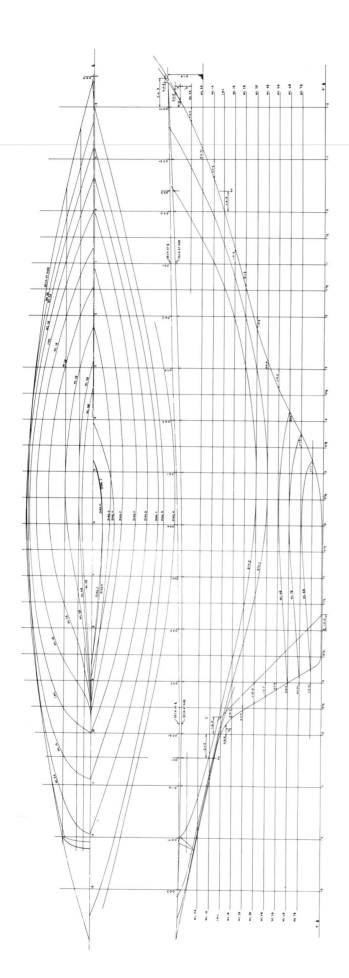

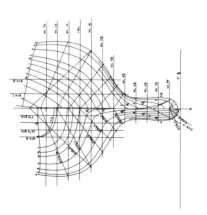

The lines of **Weatherly** showing her as modified for the 1962 America's Cup defense. Her keel has been slimmed a bit, the rudder squared off, and the transom shortened by 2 feet. (Tracing by Eugene A. Bossie)

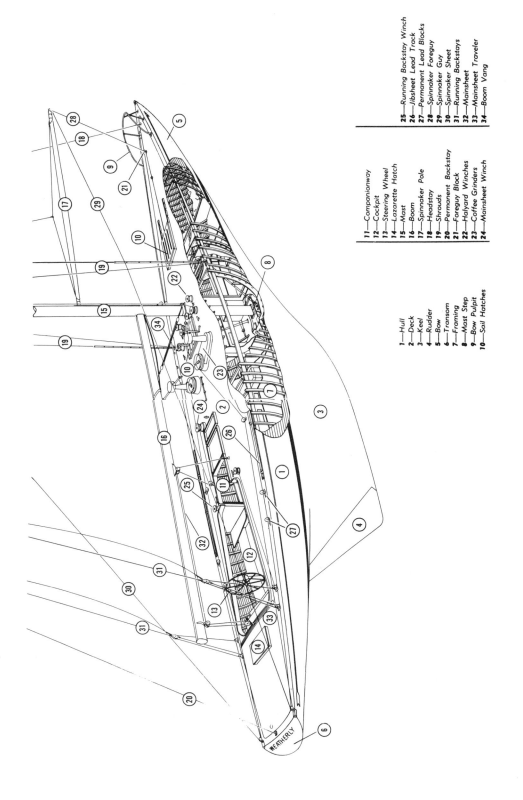

1—Hull
2—Deck
3—Keel
4—Rudder
5—Bow
6—Transom
7—Framing
8—Mast Step
9—Bow Pulpit
10—Sail Hatches

11—Companionway
12—Cockpit
13—Steering Wheel
14—Lazarette Hatch
15—Mast
16—Boom
17—Spinnaker Pole
18—Headstay
19—Shrouds
20—Permanent Backstay
21—Foreguy Block
22—Halyard Winches
23—Coffee Grinders
24—Mainsheet Winch

25—Running Backstay Winch
26—Jibsheet Lead Track
27—Permanent Lead Blocks
28—Spinnaker Foreguy
29—Spinnaker Guy
30—Spinnaker Sheet
31—Running Backstays
32—Mainsheet
33—Mainsheet Traveler
34—Boom Vang

This perspective drawing shows not only Weatherly's deck layout but also certain details of her construction. Judging from the angle of the sheet, the spinnaker's clew must be awfully high. (Yachting, September 1964)

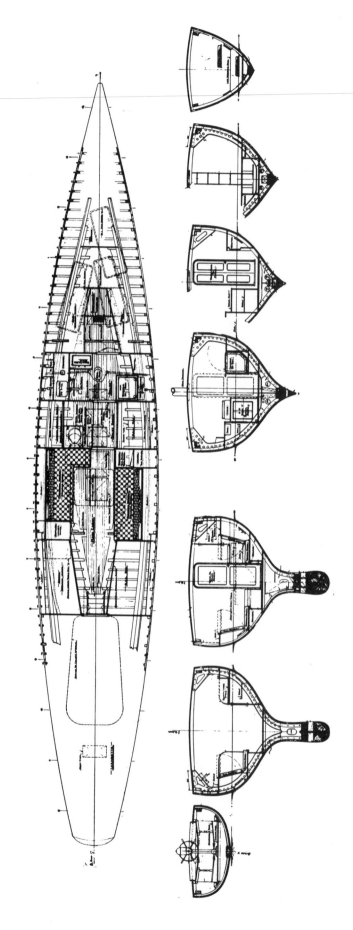

In the beginning, Weatherly had rather complete accommodations primarily because of some ambiguity in Lloyd's requirements for 12-meter boats. (Yachting, May 1958)

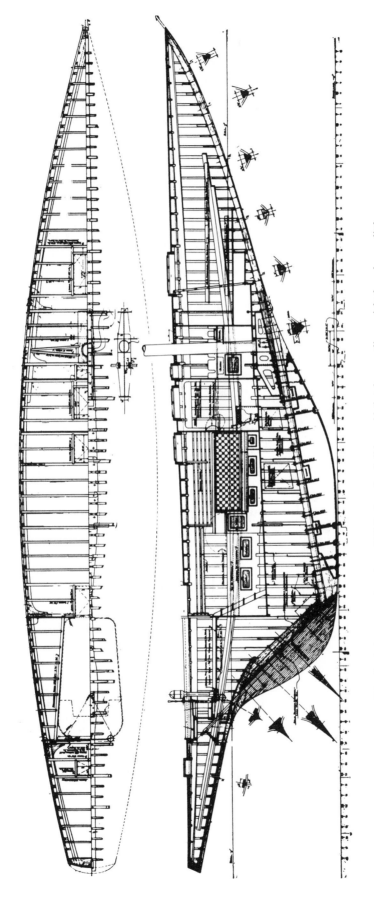

Weatherly's construction plans. Bill Luders, her builder, said that her scantlings might have been a little heavier than necessary, because "Phil always liked to build a strong boat." (Yachting, May 1958)

Weatherly *under construction in the Luders Connecticut yard in late March 1958. (Courtesy of Mystic Seaport)*

full-width bulkheads, each having a swinging door. Later, it became apparent that a great deal of flexibility in that part of Lloyd's rules governing accommodations was allowed for Cup defenders. Thus there was much below decks that could be removed and simplified to save weight.

Considerable thought was also given to making *Weatherly*'s rig more efficient, and the Luders/Rhodes combination achieved a simple yet effective breakthrough here. Before the 1962 campaign, Bill Luders, working in conjunction with the Rhodes office, conducted a number of experiments on the rig, with the result that they were able to reduce the length of the upper spreaders. This enabled *Weatherly* to carry larger genoas, for there was no need to hollow out the leeches to fit under the upper spreaders. She was thus able to increase her sail area (with no tax from the rule) from 1,778 square feet to 1,840. *Weatherly* was the only Twelve in 1962 to have such a spreader configuration, and according to George O'Day, Mosbacher's relief

helmsman, this was ''a secret weapon that virtually no one caught on to until too late.''

The fine team effort of retuning *Weatherly* paid off, for her all-around performance was decidedly improved. She had the edge on all the other 1962 candidates for the defense, *Columbia, Easterner,* and *Nefertiti,* a new, unconventional Twelve designed by Ted Hood. After a series of elimination races lasting throughout the summer, *Weatherly* was finally selected as the defender. A large measure of the success was due to the skillful handling of the boat by Bus Mosbacher and his crew.

Weatherly went on to defeat the Australian challenger in one of the most exciting series of races for the America's Cup. The Australian Twelve *Gretel* was fast. Indeed, some experts said she was faster than *Weatherly,* but she was not quite as stiff as the rejuvenated American Twelve, and she seemed to make a little more leeway, or at least be slightly inferior in windward ability. Many observers also felt that she was relatively weak in light airs.

Looking up into Weatherly's *bow during construction. (Courtesy of Mystic Seaport)*

The second race warrants a brief description here, for some observers have called it the most exciting race in America's Cup history. The two Twelves were almost dead even at the start, but after about 10 minutes of sailing close-hauled in a fresh breeze, *Weatherly* squeezed up and backwinded her opponent. This forced *Gretel* about, and *Weatherly* promptly tacked to cover. Shortly thereafter, the Australians began a tacking duel in an attempt to break cover. After about a dozen quick tacks, *Gretel* closed some distance between the boats, so Mosbacher abandoned his tight cover and broke off to sail his own race. He reached the weather mark a hair before the Aussies.

The next leg of the triangular course was a reach too tight for spinnakers, and the boats stayed close together. Chutes were broken out on the final leg, and *Gretel,* setting her chute a bit sooner, worked up to windward of *Weatherly,* partially stealing her wind. The challenger was then struck by a hard puff, and she surged ahead, surfing on the face of a big sea. The crew from Down Under whooped out their jubilation as *Gretel* tore into the lead, sending up billows of foam. Mosbacher immediately countered by steering across *Gretel*'s wake to steal her wind, but at

that moment *Weatherly*'s spinnaker guy parted, and her pole slammed against the jib stay and broke. *Weatherly*'s crew promptly rigged another pole, but by that time it was too late. *Gretel* crossed the finish line 47 seconds ahead of her rival amid a din of cheers, horns, and sirens.

Despite the fact that *Weatherly* beat the challenger four out of five times, the competition had been at times extremely close, and *Gretel*'s performance provided some thrilling moments. *Weatherly*'s victorious defense of the baroque silver pitcher, sailing's most coveted award, was tremendously satisfying to all associated with the American effort — including, of course, Phil Rhodes.

In 1965, *Weatherly* was donated by Henry Mercer to the United States Merchant Marine Academy at Kings Point, New York. There, she was used for a number of years as a training boat by the Merchant Marine cadets.

This didn't mean that her racing days were finished, however. In the 1967 Cup campaign, she was used briefly as a trial horse by the *Columbia* Syndicate. This time, she was completely outclassed, as she was not campaigned seriously, and all her rivals, including *Columbia,* had either been substantially

Phil Rhodes (left) with the Mercer Syndicate and skipper Knapp (second from right) standing in front of Weatherly. *(Photo by Philip H. Rhodes. Courtesy of Mystic Seaport)*

upgraded or were newer boats. This was the year that *Intrepid* achieved the breakthrough in 12-meter design, with her divided keel and rudder.

It was therefore somewhat of a surprise that *Weatherly*, again in the role of a trial horse, should have been competitive in the 1970 series. Sailing against a new Stephens boat named *Valiant*, a Britton Chance-reworked *Intrepid*, and a new boat named *Heritage* designed by Charlie Morgan, *Weatherly* gave the newest boats absolute fits. She was never very far off the pace, and she actually beat both *Heritage* and *Valiant* in a couple of races. In the

Weatherly *under spinnaker with her crew in action. In those times it was accepted practice to lead the sheet all the way aft, even on boats with long, narrow sterns. (Photo by Norman Fortier)*

September 1970 issue of *One-Design and Offshore Yachtsman,* Olin Stephens lamented, ''Heck, we should be beating *Weatherly* by 10 minutes around a 24-mile course, and we're lucky to beat her at all.'' It was generally acknowledged that all three designers had misread the test tank data and had produced boats that were too big with too little sail area. *Weatherly*'s presence as a yardstick was invaluable, and her good showing was an absolute delight to Phil Rhodes.

That fall, *Weatherly* was sold by the Merchant Marine Academy, and her new owner converted her into an IOR racer. A diesel engine was installed, as well as accommodations for eight people. In the 1970s, she compiled a successful racing record on the Great Lakes, and later, on Puget Sound.

Phil Rhodes was very proud of *Weatherly,* although he modestly downplayed his own contribution by saying that the designer of a Cup defender is less important than her crew and sailmaker. *Weatherly* was not only a successful defender, she was a contender for much longer than she had a right to be.

37

Barlovento II
"Technically Superb and Beautiful"

Barlovento II, a smaller version of the Rhodes 77, was conceived as a comfortable auxiliary sailing cruiser that could also ocean race, with a reasonable chance of doing well given her conditions. Designed in 1958 for Pierre S. duPont of Wilmington, Delaware, she is 71 feet 8 inches overall and comes in just under the upper size limit for the Bermuda Race. It can safely be said that she is one of the most comfortable boats ever to sail in that race. She has luxurious accommodations, and her size, weight, and easy-shaped underbody make her unusually seakindly — a good match for the Gulf Stream at its roughest.

Barlovento II's record confirms the validity of the Rhodes concept of going anywhere in comfort with good sailing performance. She has been extensively cruised along the Eastern seaboard, her 5½-foot draft allowing her to negotiate easily the shallow waters of Delaware and Chesapeake Bays and the Bahamas. Her ability in fresh winds on the race course has been proven. Although not at her best in light airs, she really comes to life in a blow. In her first race on the Chesapeake, the 100-mile Skipper Race, she topped a fleet of 31 competitive ocean racers. Then, in 1960, she earned a very respectable fourth in class out of 22 boats in the Bermuda Race. She did not fare well in the light going early on in the race, but she made it up later when the wind increased, gusting up to 60 knots. While other craft were well shortened down, *Barlovento* stormed toward the finish with full main and staysail. The powerful ketch had her greatest triumph in the spring of 1961 when she won the Block Island Race, which was sailed in such heavy weather that over half of the 103-boat fleet withdrew.

Perhaps more than any other Rhodes design of this type, she also demonstrates that a sailing cruiser with luxurious accommodations need not be the least bit unattractive. Despite her 18-foot beam and her deckhouse, she has a sleek appearance. Rhodes achieved this primarily by drawing out her ends, giving her only a 50-foot waterline. In addition, Rhodes' treatment of her deckhouse, with only a moderate amount of window area, makes her look like the pure sailer that she is rather than a motorsailer. The British magazine *The Yachtsman* opined: *"Barlovento II* is about the smallest yacht that can carry without disfigurement a deck cockpit." (Rhodes did use this cabin configuration on smaller vessels, such as *La Belle Sole* and some smaller versions of *Barlovento,* and the results were definitely not as appealing.)

Like the Rhodes 77, *Barlovento II* was built of

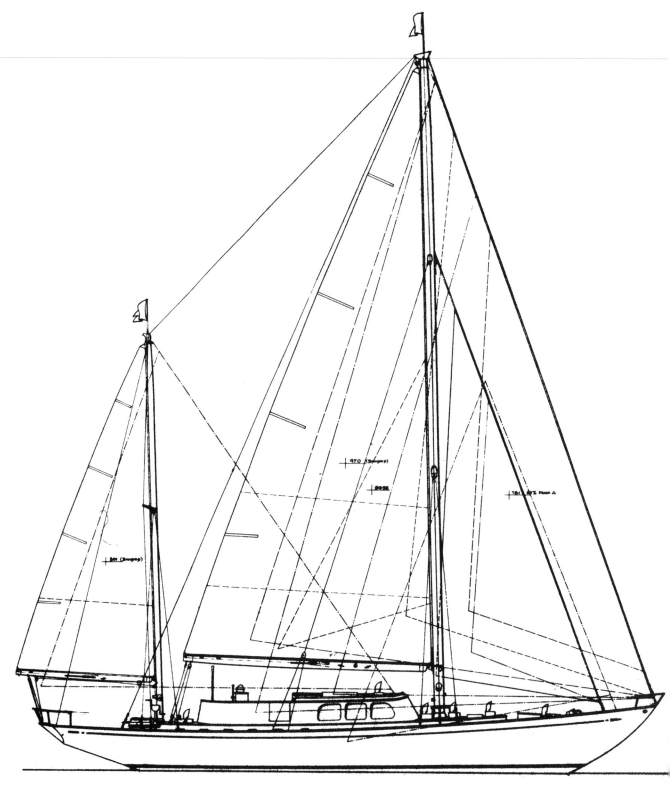

At 71 feet 8 inches, Barlovento II *might be considered a modified Rhodes 77 reduced to the size of a maxi ocean racer.*

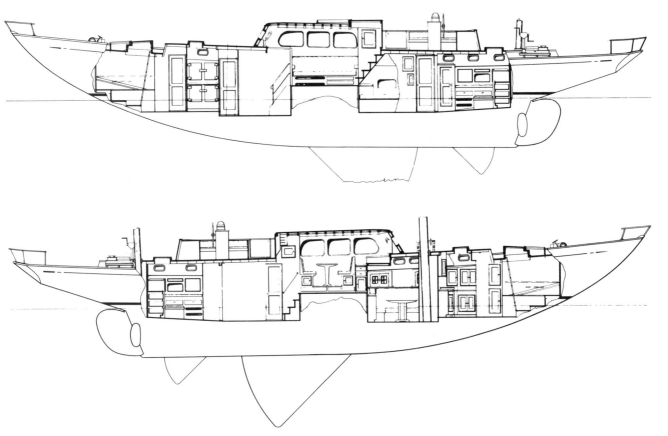

These profile views of Barlovento II *show her shallow hull with tandem centerboards and some interesting details of her accommodations.*

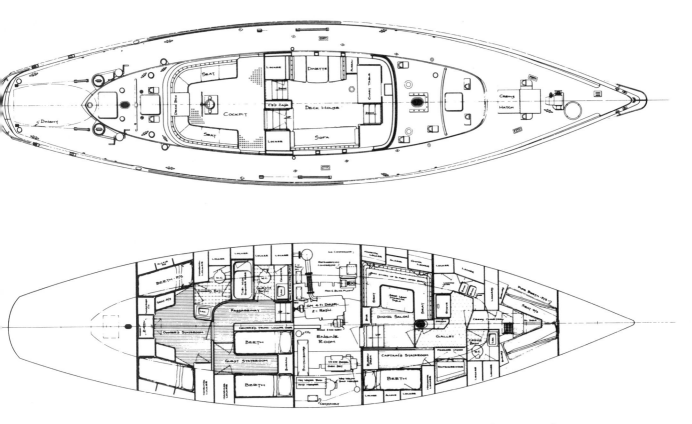

Barlovento II's *arrangement plan shows a number of clever innovations, such as the double entrance to the bathtub. Note the pointed after end of the cabin trunk and the engine room, which rivals that of a motorsailer.*

Barlovento II *showing her power and stiffness in a "breeze o' wind." (Photo by Bermuda News Bureau. Courtesy of Mystic Seaport)*

welded steel, with four watertight bulkheads. Her builders, Abeking & Rasmussen, did a beautiful job with her joinerwork, both above decks and below. Besides being smaller, *Barlovento II* differs from the Rhodes 77 in a couple of ways. She is fitted with tandem centerboards and has a masthead rather than a fractional rig. This sail plan provides 2,052 square feet of working canvas, which is a relatively greater amount than the Rhodes 77's 2,250 square feet.

The tandem centerboards in conjunction with the ketch rig afford excellent helm balance under virtually any condition. In theory, a reduction of sail forward can be compensated for by lowering the after board, or vice versa; a reduction of sail aft can be compensated for by retracting the after board and perhaps lowering the forward one. The primary reason for specifying tandem boards for such a shoal-draft boat is to ease steering problems in hard downwind steering conditions. With the after board down, any tendency to broach or yaw is mitigated. DuPont reported that he was pleased at how well *Barlovento II* tracked off the wind, especially compared with most other shallow boats. The tandem boards also improve self-steering characteristics, although it is not a major consideration on *Barlovento II*, since she has an autopilot. Of course, you do get twice the number of problems with jamming, worn pins, broken pendants, and the like, even though

such mishaps are not likely when the systems are well designed and maintained.

Barlovento II's layout below is in a general way like that of a Rhodes 77, with owner's and guest quarters located just abaft amidships, an amidship deckhouse with engine room beneath, and the dining saloon with galley and crew's quarters located forward. Obviously, a few compromises in room must be made on the smaller boat, and these take the form of one less guest cabin aft and a smaller dining saloon so that the professional captain's stateroom can be worked into the space immediately forward of the deckhouse. Aft there is a clever arrangement whereby the owner's and guest bathrooms each allow use of the bathtub and shower compartment. The deckhouse is a large, comfortable sitting area with navigation facilities, and its windows are fitted with heavy plexiglass storm shutters for rugged offshore conditions. The engine room contains a GM 4-71 diesel that works through a 2:1 reduction gear and gives the boat a top speed of 9½ knots.

Barlovento II has all the amenities for the most comfortable live-aboard cruising, such as refrigeration, deep freeze, running hot water, mechanical ventilation, and so forth. The aforementioned article about this boat in *The Yachtsman* rightfully said: "No vessels in the history of sail have been technically so superb as the best modern yachts. Nor, as it happens, glancing at the profile, so beautiful."

38

Thunderhead
An Innovative Champion

In 1959 Paul Hoffmann went to Phil Rhodes for the design of a replacement for his Rhodes-designed double-ender *Hother,* ex-*Kirawan II* (Chapter 19). *Hother* had been a particularly successful racer under Hoffmann, taking 14 first places and 11 second places in 33 races, and he wished to retain her good features while improving on others. Above all, Hoffmann desired a similar-sized boat that would be roomier yet even faster than *Hother.* A long period of design work and extensive tank testing produced a design that both Hoffmann and Rhodes felt would live up to her owner's requirements. The boat was named *Thunderhead,* and she was beautifully built of wood by Abeking & Rasmussen. She measures 48 feet 9 inches overall, 37 feet on the waterline, and has a beam of 13 feet and a draft of 5½ feet.

Like *Hother, Thunderhead* is a short-ended, cutter-rigged keel-centerboarder having a distinctive clipper bow. A basic similarity can also be found in the deck and accommodations plans of the two boats. Her basic hull form, though, is actually closer to that of the *La Belle Sole*-type of motorsailer (Chapter 30) and the smaller cutter *Wunderbar,* designed by Rhodes in 1957 for Hoffmann's brother George.

Besides being deeper, the biggest difference between the newer cutter and *Hother* is in the stern configuration. *Thunderhead* has a broad transom, which gave Hoffmann added roominess at the stern, more bearing aft, and a wider sheeting angle for her large headsails.

Thunderhead fully lived up to her owner's expectations, for she proved to be tremendously comfortable, extremely handsome, and highly competitive. Between 1961 and 1972, she collected a mine of silver and pewter mugs, which is remarkable when you consider that she is a heavy, comfortable cruising boat.

It is not an easy task to get *Thunderhead*'s racing record from Paul Hoffmann. Whether this is because Hoffmann is overly modest, or because *Thunderhead* has had so many successes that it is difficult to remember the record, is not clear. At any rate, suffice it to say that *Thunderhead* did well, and a sample year illustrates the point: in 1966 she was first in class and second overall in the Vineyard Race; first to finish, first in class, and first overall in the City Island Day Race; first to finish, first in class, and first overall in the Port Washington Two-

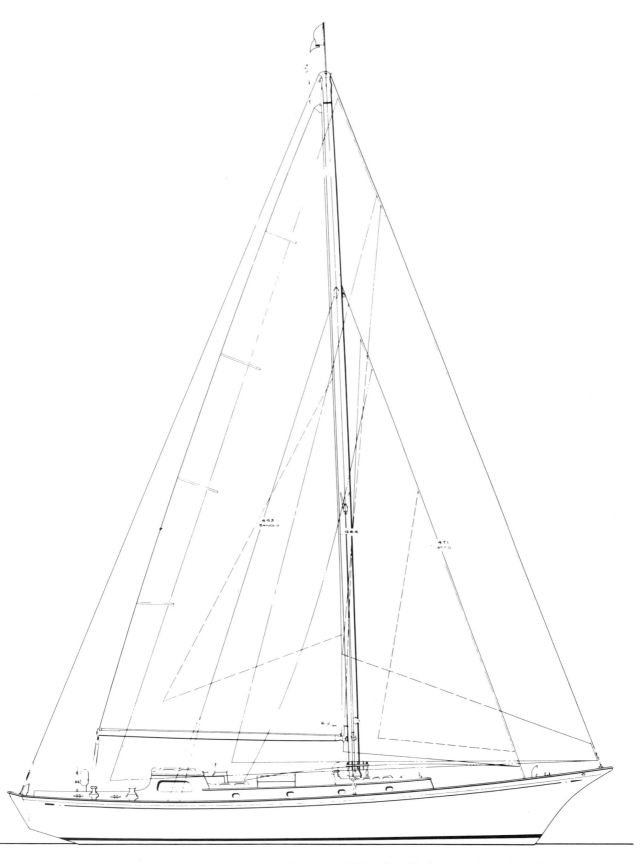

The original sail plan of Thunderhead, *48 feet 9 inches overall. Her sail area/displacement ratio was designed to agree closely with that of* Hother, *but it was later discovered that* Hother's *assumed displacement was incorrect, and this meant that* Thunderhead's *rig was relatively modest.*

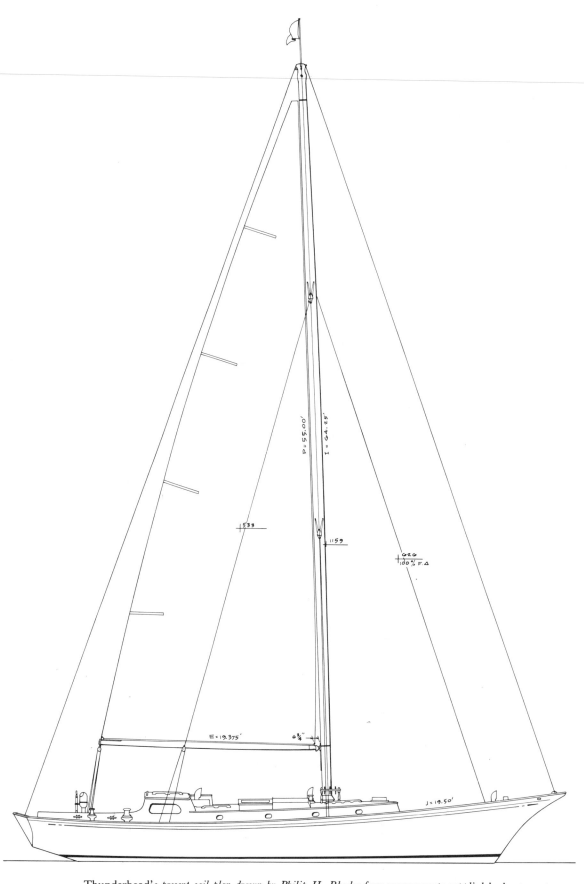

P = 55.00'

I = 64.25'

533

1159

626
100% F.△

E = 19.375'

6¾"

J = 19.50'

Thunderhead's present sail plan drawn by Philip H. Rhodes from measurements supplied by her present owner, John D. Riddell. Paul Hoffmann's revised rig was just as tall, but the main boom was longer.

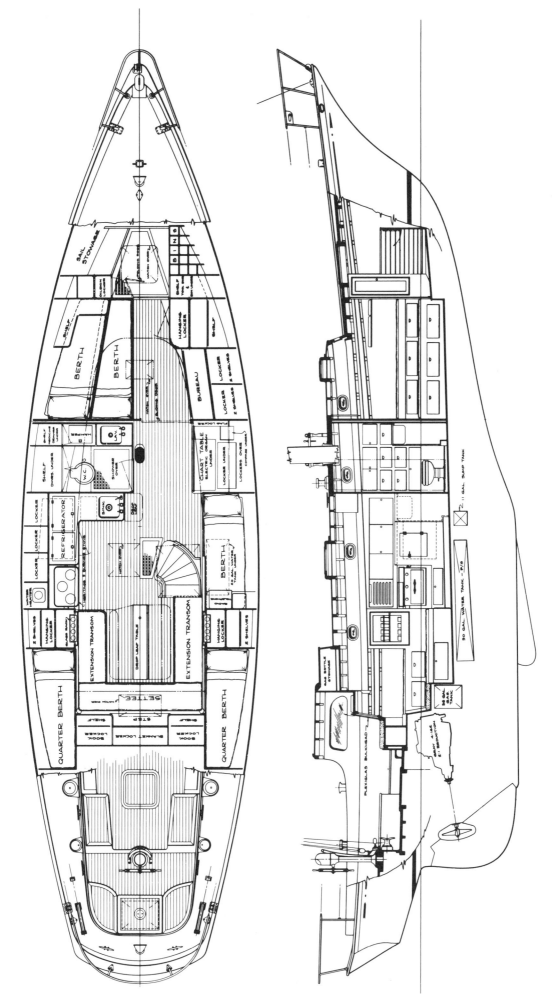

Thunderhead's accommodations, which Phil Rhodes described as producing the effect of a "vista."

Thunderhead *on her way to Bermuda carrying a roller-reefed main, no. 2 jib, and genoa staysail, a combination that supplies power with a low center of effort.* (One Design Yachtsman, *November 1968*)

Day Race; first overall (for 2 days) and first in class in the Manhasset Bay Two-Day Distance Race; first to finish, first in class, and first overall in the Huntington Over-Night Race; and first to finish, first in class, and first overall in the Edlu Trophy Race. Perhaps her most successful year was 1968, when she won all three of the East Coast high-point distance prizes: the De Coursey Fales Trophy, the Stamford Ocean Racing Trophy, and the Storm Trysail Ocean Racing Trophy.

Her below-deck arrangement is a development of *Hother*'s. As Phil Rhodes expressed it, "When we built the *Kirawan II [Hother]*, she had a unique layout, with a U-shaped after cabin, flanked by wing bunks (or built-ins, as some people call them), and a galley at the forward end, which increased the overall length of the main cabin space, and then a stateroom forward. The owner, Paul Hoffmann, expanded on this layout when we built his *Thunderhead,* and the result is one of the most wide-open and amiable layouts ever put on a boat. When you walk below on this boat, you think she's twice the size she is: it has a tremendous vista."

The vista effect is enhanced by a transparent

heavy plexiglass bulkhead between the after cabin and cockpit, which, in effect, opens up the cabin out to the cockpit. At the other end of the main cabin there is a wide passageway leading forward through the owner's stateroom to a large fo'c's'le. This also adds to the feeling of spaciousness, yet there is a big sliding door at the after end of the owner's cabin to afford privacy.

The large U-shaped settee, which Phil Rhodes called a "triclinium," provides plenty of sitting room in the main cabin. The disadvantage of this arrangement is that it requires having an off-center companionway forward, which is vulnerable to spray and could be flooded during a severe knockdown. However, a dodger protects the side hatch from taking spray, and the emergency or secondary entrance from the cockpit to the after cabin can be used in the very worst conditions so that the side companionway can be closed off.

The location of the main companionway, leading below from the starboard side of the cabin trunk amidships, does allow for a distinctive circular stairway with an attractive chrome balustrade. Outboard of the stairway is the navigator's berth, with a large chart table at its forward end. There is even an electric organ under the table, used for entertainment in port (or perhaps hymns during a race?)

On deck, there are other unique features. The most prominent is the permanent cockpit shelter with a comfortable seat running full width and a fold-down chart table. This was an idea taken from *Hother*. In addition, there is a split-level cockpit, the forward end sunken to give the crew good leverage at the winches, and the after cockpit sole at a higher level to give the helmsman good visibility over the shelter. With her scrubbed cedar decks, gleaming brightwork and polished brass, and the fancy pinrail at the base of the mast, *Thunderhead* has all the elegance of an old-time yacht, yet her performance is competitive with the best of her racing contemporaries.

She was designed with a large masthead cutter rig that carried 964 square feet of sail. This was replaced in 1964 with a much taller rig to improve her light-air performance. Apparently the decision for this change came about as Paul Hoffmann was having a few drinks with his crew and they decided that the cutter would go better with a new mast about eight feet taller than the original. The Rhodes office was consulted, but when the designer in charge of the project looked over the preliminary drawings, he felt the increase in mast length was about twice what it should be and refused to endorse the change. Hoffmann, however, insisted on the extra-tall mast, with the result that *Thunderhead* became a hot contender in even the lightest weather.

A year or so later, that same designer congratulated Hoffmann on his boldness and admitted that the new rig had been extremely effective. "Hell," said Hoffmann, "if we'd had one more drink we would have added 10 feet to the mast."

39

Pilgrim and A and Eagle
Colossi of Rhodes

During the last truly active decade of Phil's life (between 1959 and 1969, approximately), the Rhodes firm designed a number of luxury power yachts that exceeded 100 feet in overall length. These included *Ivara, Chambel III, Manu Kai, Pilgrim,* and *A and Eagle.* The latter two will be featured in this chapter. Since these colossi of Rhodes each may have cost between half a million and a million dollars *(A and Eagle,* for example, cost $850,000), the design fee was sizable. The net profit from these jobs was not really tremendous, however, for vast amounts of time were required for engineering, drafting, and all aspects of the design work. At any rate, these vessels were prestigious, and the Rhodes name became as well linked with this type of yacht as with the others previously discussed.

Pilgrim was designed in late 1962 for General Robert W. Johnson, who wanted an able yacht with all the comforts of home — one that could go anywhere and carry a number of guests in complete privacy. Her length measurements are 140 feet 8 inches overall and 122 feet 6 inches on the waterline, while she has a beam of 26 feet and a draft of 7 feet 6 inches (mean half load).

Pilgrim is a very handsome power yacht, and she illustrates Rhodes' artistic touch. The rounded canoe stern, clipper bow, flowing lines, and well-proportioned deckhouse seem to harmonize in a most pleasing manner. Although many of the components show a lot of rake and certain cut-out portions of the bulwarks and window areas have rounded or oval shapes, the whole effect is one of function and sleek modernity rather than of tasteless flamboyance.

Pilgrim was built by Hall, Russell & Company in Aberdeen, Scotland, and she meets Lloyd's highest classification for yacht service. Her hull and main deckhouse are of welded steel, but the pilothouse is welded aluminum, which helps keep the center of gravity low. With the exception of the boat deck (which is covered with fiberglass), the decks are planked with Burma teak. Five steel bulkheads form six completely watertight compartments, and they make the yacht almost unsinkable.

Her round-bottomed form gives *Pilgrim* a seakindly hull, while her shallow draft enables her to enter almost any harbor into which she can fit. To inhibit rolling in beam seas — a characteristic common to

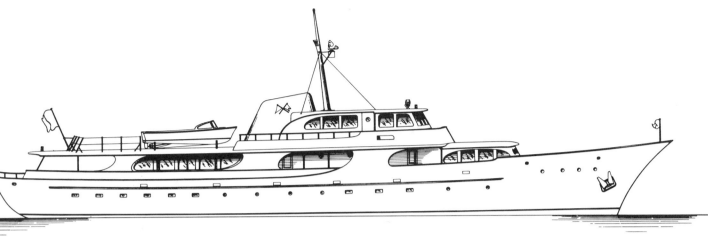

Pilgrim, at 140 feet 8 inches, is a study in sleek modernity. There is a fluid, rhythmic harmony in the shape of her profile lines and cutouts.

many round-bottomed powerboats — *Pilgrim* has two fixed Vosper fins.

She is powered by twin 650-horsepower Caterpillar V-8 diesel engines, which drive two controllable-pitch propellers, thereby eliminating the need for reverse gears. Her top speed is about 15 knots, and she can maintain a continuous cruising speed of about 13 knots. With her fuel capacity of 38 tons, carried in 12 double-bottomed tanks, she has a cruising range of from 7,000 to 8,000 miles traveling at a speed of 8 knots. Exhausts from the main engines, the diesel generators, and the hot-water heater are led to the top of an aluminum mast so that fumes and smoke will be carried well over the heads of people seated on the upper deck. This mast is hinged so that it can be folded down for clearance under low bridges.

Pilgrim is a triple-decker, with cabin space on all three levels. In the large lower level, she has spacious crew's quarters forward. This area has 10 berths in five staterooms, a toilet room with two heads and two showers, a large lounge, and two storerooms. Abaft the crew's quarters is the owner's huge cabin, which takes in the entire width of the vessel and has two private bathrooms, with a shower in one and a tub in the other. The engine room is amidships on this level, and even though the engine room bulkhead is well insulated, the two heads and a wardrobe have been placed in such a way as to form a further sound barrier between the owner's stateroom and machinery space. Abaft the engine room are the guest quarters, with three double staterooms

and three bathrooms. Here again, the bathrooms have been positioned next to the engine room bulkhead to ensure that guests may sleep undisturbed by engine noise. All berths have box springs, which, in rough waters, might be too bouncy in a smaller yacht, but which would probably be comfortable in almost any kind of seaway in *Pilgrim*.

On the main deck, going from aft to forward, there is a tremendous saloon, the captain's stateroom and head, a large dressing room and head for day guests, the galley, and the dining saloon. The boat deck, the highest deck level, has a pilothouse, and abaft that, a deck lounge. In the latter, there is a portion given over to electronic gear and counter space where, according to the Rhodes office write-up of this yacht, "guests may enjoy the art of navigation without bothering the helmsman."

As one might expect, *Pilgrim* lacks almost nothing in the way of equipment and support systems. She has a dishwasher, garbage disposal, clothes washer and dryer, two Maxim evaporators for making fresh water from sea water, hot water and electric heating systems, and air-conditioning. She even has a deck flushing system to remove atomic bomb fallout.

Pilgrim would not be a bad boat in which to escape from an atomic holocaust. It might be preferable if she had some sailing capability, but if her tanks were topped off before the blast, you could get to some remote tropical island, where she would make a luxurious houseboat, even without fuel for her engines and generators.

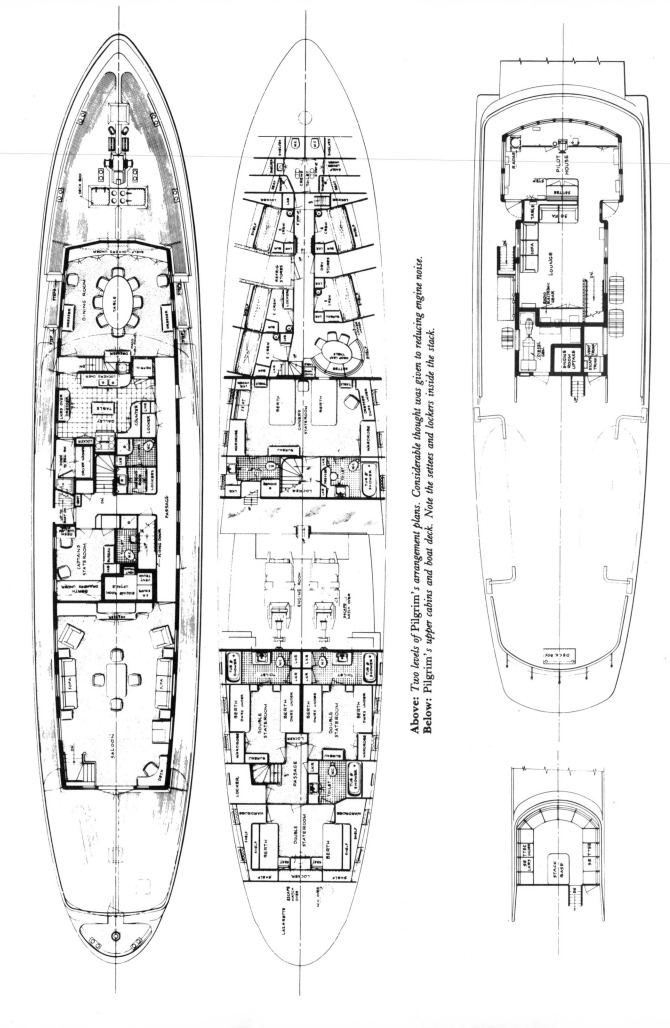

Above: *Two levels of Pilgrim's arrangement plans. Considerable thought was given to reducing engine noise.*
Below: *Pilgrim's upper cabins and boat deck. Note the settees and lockers inside the stack.*

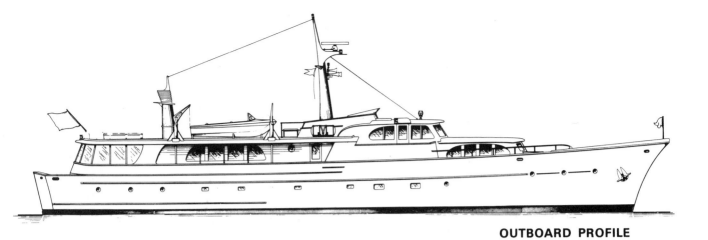

OUTBOARD PROFILE

A and Eagle is 119½ feet long and not as aesthetically fluid as Pilgrim, *but she is well proportioned and has a pleasingly functional look.*

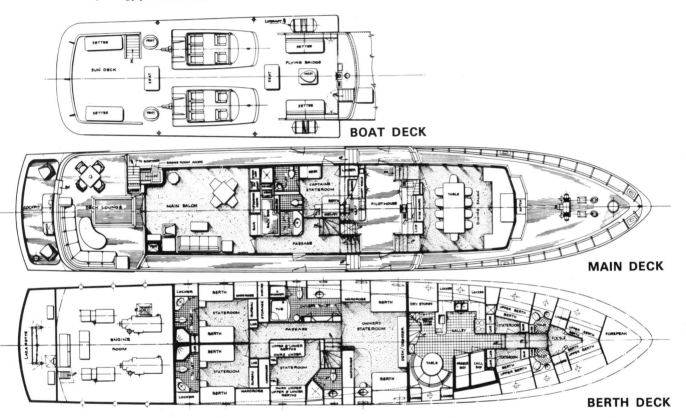

BOAT DECK

MAIN DECK

BERTH DECK

The deck plans of A and Eagle. *Her layout differs from that of* Pilgrim *primarily in that her engines are aft rather than amidships.*

Though not quite as large as *Pilgrim, A and Eagle* is comparable in about every other way. This vessel was designed in 1964 for the Anheuser-Busch Corporation, and her unusual name was derived from the company's trademark. The A-and-eagle symbol appears on the bulwarks amidships and also on the transom, where the eagle has a wingspan of eight feet.

A and Eagle has an overall length of 119½ feet, a beam of 22½ feet, and a draft of only 5½ feet, which allows her to cruise the Mississippi and Ohio Rivers and other shallow southern waters. She was built by Abeking & Rasmussen, of welded steel, except for her superstructure, which is welded aluminum. Four transverse bulkheads form five watertight compartments. Her decks, rails, and deck joinerwork are of Burma teak.

A and Eagle has a rather sophisticated underbody shape, resulting from extensive testing at the Stevens Institute tank. The forward half of the hull has a rather normal round bottom, but moving aft, the bilges become more shallow and flat to allow the use of large propellers while keeping draft to a minimum. Near the stern, the bottom flattens out to such an extent that a soft chine is formed at the juncture of the bottom and topsides, and this configuration tends to dampen rolling.

Power is supplied by a pair of 460-horsepower Caterpillar diesels, which provide a smooth and quiet cruising speed of 13½ knots. Upon the insistence of the Caterpillar company representatives, both engines were fitted with governors that hold the engine's RPM below 2000. The twin funnels aft serve the engine-room blowers, and one carries the stack for the hot water heater. According to Philip H. Rhodes, the funnels also serve as engine and generator air intakes. He explained that the two big Cats "and at least one 75-kilowatt generator take a *lot* of air. Very seldom is enough provided."

Unlike *Pilgrim*'s engines, which are amidships, *A and Eagle*'s engines are aft. While this arrangement doesn't allow as wide a separation between the owner's stateroom and the guest quarters as in *Pilgrim,* it permits the owner's stateroom to be located where there is minimal noise and vibration from the engine room. The three guest staterooms each have their own heads, two of which are positioned next to the insulated engine-room bulkhead to act as a buffer against noise. The galley is located in the crew's quarters, which puts it below the main-deck dining saloon, but there is an electric dumbwaiter to transport food and dishes up and down.

The main deck has an elevated pilothouse, and abaft that, the captain's stateroom and head plus

A and Eagle *underway and a closeup view of the Anheuser-Busch company symbol. Whoever said, "He who goes to sea for pleasure would go to hell as a pastime," could never have taken a cruise on a Rhodes luxury power yacht.*

another head. Farther aft is the main saloon and a deck lounge, which can be closed in with transparent plastic storm curtains. In addition to the fully equipped pilothouse, there is an upper flying bridge with a removable Bimini top, and there are controls on the bridge wings to facilitate docking. The boat deck holds two 16-foot inboard-powered launches, and the after end of the deck is arranged for lounging and sunbathing.

Equipment includes full air-conditioning, heat, refrigeration, independent ice makers, a washer-dryer, two radio systems, an intercom between quarters, record and tape players to all quarters, television for passengers and crew, water evaporators, and retractable stabilizers. Even if a guest were to become bored watching the sea and lounging on the sun deck, there is a cockpit with facilities for fishing, swimming, and trap shooting. Undoubtedly, *A and Eagle* is well stocked with beer.

Phil Rhodes once remarked that the modern naval architect is expected to be a hotel and industrial designer as well as a creator of yachts. All these skills and more are certainly well demonstrated in *Pilgrim, A and Eagle,* and other Rhodes luxury power yachts.

40

Froya II
Late Thinking in Ocean Racers

The lovely yawl *Froya II* is one of Phil Rhodes' last ocean racers, and she represents his thinking about that type during his final years as an active designer. She is a highly refined, sensible boat that is in no way extreme. Designed in 1966 for Oivind Lorentzen, Jr., she was built of wood by Grimsoykilen Batbyggeri, near Fredrikstad, Norway. Her dimensions are 50 feet 2 inches by 35 feet by 12 feet 7 inches by 7 feet 1 inch.

Froya's underwater profile shows the hull to be a fairly low-wetted-surface type, but with the rudder attached to the keel. This provides good rudder strength and protection, while allowing the blade to act as a trim tab for additional keel lift when beating to windward. The underwater hull profile aft has a slightly concave shape, and the rudder's trailing edge is straight, with its greatest area at the bottom. This general shape was partly a result of tank tests conducted for the 1964 crop of 12-meters. Olin Stephens, who carried this profile almost to the extreme with the 1964 Twelve *Constellation,* said that in addition to allowing reduced wetted surface with little or no harm to steering control, the profile reduces weather helm resulting from the keel tip vortex flowing up and against the head of the rudder.

There is no doubt that *Froya* is a good sea boat. Her proportions are moderate and wholesome, she is capable of fast passages, and she has the windward ability to work her way off a lee shore in heavy weather. Her keel is of sufficient length for reasonable tracking ability, and its depth provides a low center of gravity, thus assuring a high range of stability. Freeboard is ample for dryness, and the ends are long enough to afford some reserve buoyancy, but not so long as to slam. The low cabin trunk with small windows and the on-center companionways are also good features for offshore work.

The rig is well suited for blue-water sailing. It is inboard, sail area can be reduced quite easily, and the main boom is high so crew members are not apt to be beaned. The widely spaced lower shrouds give good support to the mainmast, and the pipe rails are a great help to crew working at the mast. The sail area of 1,117 square feet is not tremendous for a 50-footer, but the masthead foretriangle allows some large headsails for racing and light-weather cruising. The sail plan shows a storm trysail and storm jib with an area that nicely matches that of the small mizzen, so good balance can be maintained in a blow. It is interesting that so late in his career and on

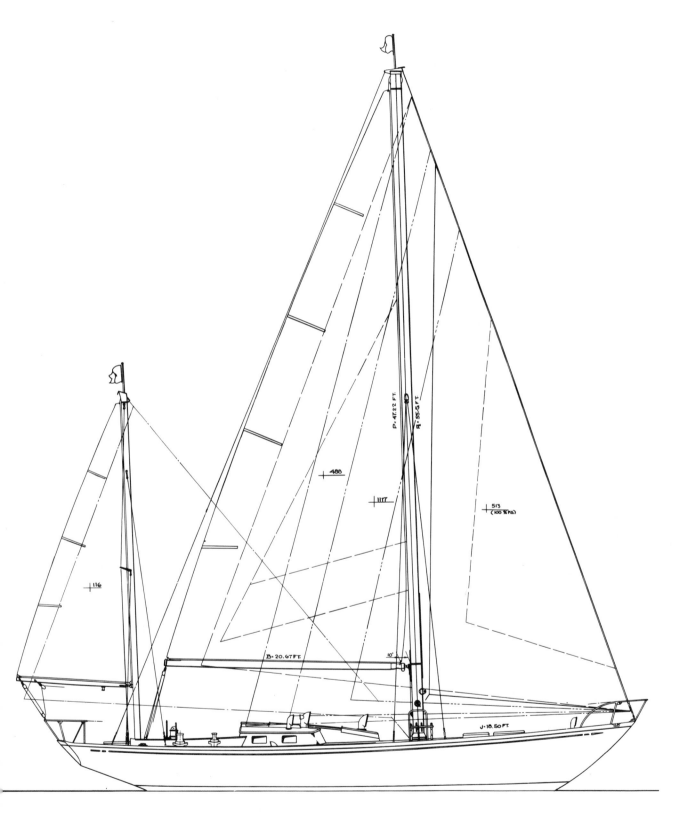

Froya II's *sail plan is fairly modest but in line with Rhodes' conservative thinking regarding boats that are designed primarily for blue-water sailing. Note the high main boom and "sissy bars" at the mainmast. She is 50 feet 2 inches overall.*

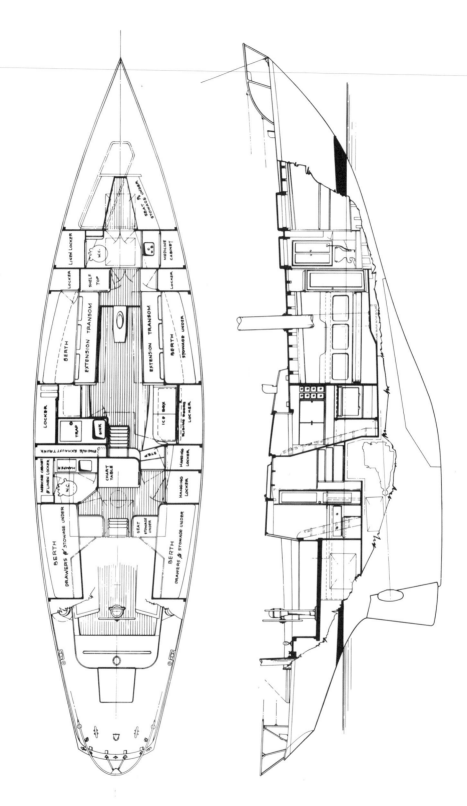

Froya II's profile shows a moderately short keel and modern rudder. Her layout below is to some extent convert-ible for use in port or at sea.

such a modern boat, Phil Rhodes still included the pinrail at the base of the mainmast. As well as being functional, it gives the boat a salty look.

With her two companionways, *Froya* has a very flexible below-decks arrangement. In port, the after companionway can be closed off, which allows a completely private after cabin for the owner, but at sea in rough weather the amidships companionway can be closed off for maximum safety. Then the after cabin, with its two good sea berths, large chart table, oilskin locker, and convenient enclosed head, becomes a useful shelter for the on-watch crew. Forward of the after cabin are the galley, which extends across the entire width of the boat, and the main saloon, which has two pilot berths and two lower extension transoms. Still farther forward, an enclosed head stretches across the boat, and its doors allow use from either the saloon or the fo'c's'le.

Froya was not campaigned to any great extent, but she did sail in a Bermuda Race and in at least one Buenos Aires-Rio de Janeiro Race. She never did outstandingly well, although she took a class third in the Skaw Race in Scandinavian waters soon after she was built. According to Oivind Lorentzen, she was tank tested, but her actual performance was not as good as her model's performance promised. Nevertheless, Lorentzen said she was an extremely seakindly boat, well balanced and well behaved under all conditions. She is presently located in Brazil.

Froya may not represent the culmination of a lifetime of design experience, for she is a special boat for a particular client, but it is certainly true that she benefits from Phil Rhodes' many years of producing successful ocean racers.

41

Sea Star
A Three-Masted Gold-Plater

One of the last and most impressive of the Rhodes luxury yachts is the three-masted sailing yacht *Sea Star*. She was built at a reported cost of two million dollars for Laurance S. Rockefeller, who wanted a thoroughly comfortable, seagoing yacht capable of good performance under either sail or power. Deluxe accommodations for as many as 10 guests was also a requirement, so that the yacht could be used for charter when the Rockefellers were not using her. A further requirement was that there be extensive deckhousing to afford protection from the sun, for Rockefeller was sensitive to the sun's rays, and *Sea Star* was to be used primarily in the Caribbean and the Mediterranean.

Her generous dimensions are 122 feet 10 inches by 97 feet 6 inches by 28 feet 6 inches. Although her original designed draft was 6 feet, the vessel turned out to be about 45 long tons overweight (about a sixth of this was in the form of trimming ballast), and this and her abundant gear loaded her down so that she actually drew about 7 feet.

Built by Goudy and Stevens of East Boothbay, Maine, *Sea Star* was launched in 1970. A Rhodes office write-up described her construction as follows:

"*Sea Star* is built of all-welded steel in excess of Lloyd's requirements. Her flat plate keel, for example, is one inch thick and the wide garboards are ½ inch. Although not required, she has a solid ⅜-inch steel deck beneath the 2-inch Burma teak decking. She is a vessel of great strength, with five transverse steel bulkheads, i.e., six individual compartments.''

In her general arrangement below decks, *Sea Star* is quite similar to *A and Eagle* (Chapter 39). Her original accommodation sketches were based upon the *Tamaris* concept of amidships engines, but after discussion, the layout was rejected by the Rhodes office in favor of having her machinery aft.

Moving from aft to forward, there are: the engine room, the guest quarters, the owner's stateroom, the galley, and the crew's quarters. On the main deck, however, *Sea Star* differs considerably from *A and Eagle*, although *Sea Star*'s dining saloon is also directly above the galley, and it, too, is served by a dumbwaiter. The main difference in layouts is that the pilothouse is, understandably, aft on the sailing yacht, permitting the main saloon to be immediately abaft and adjoining the dining saloon. *Sea Star* has a

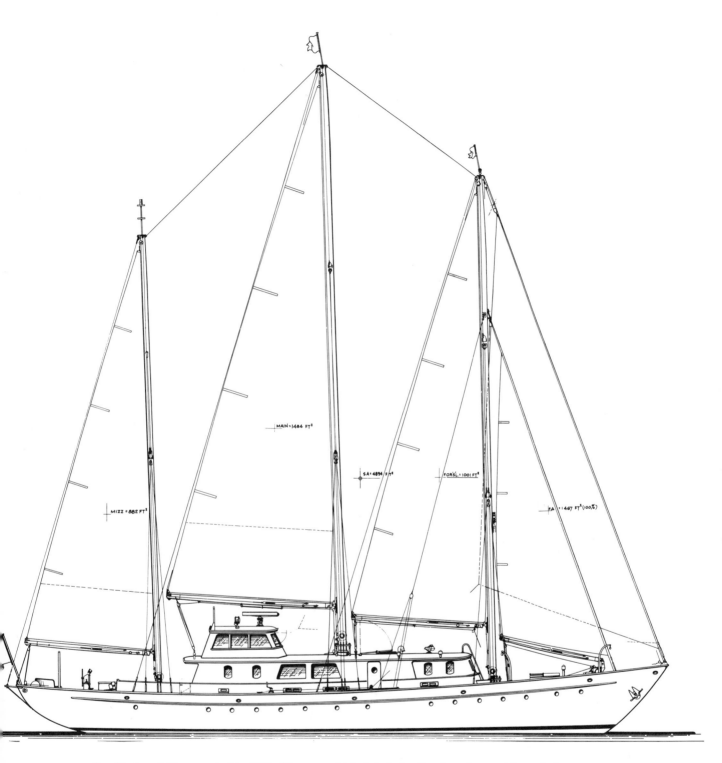

Sea Star's *sail plan as revised in 1974. Changes consisted of shortening the mizzen boom, adding a short boomkin, and installing a permanent backstay to obviate the need for mizzen runners. She is 122 feet 10 inches overall.*

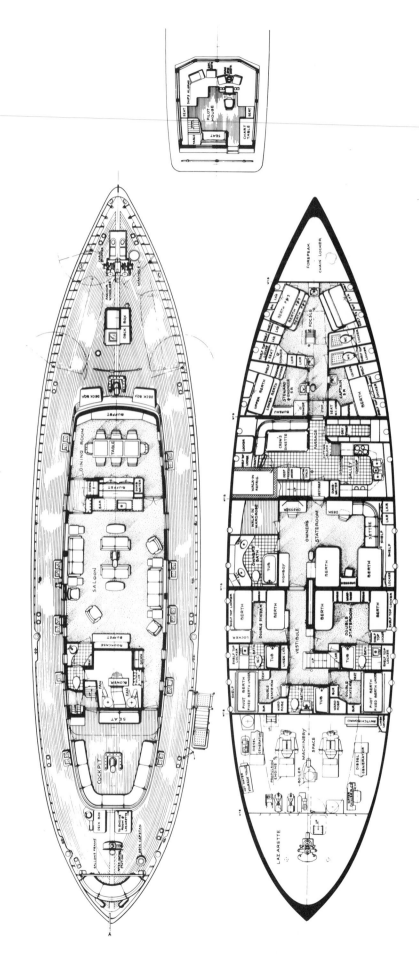

Sea Star is arranged somewhat like A and Eagle except that her pilothouse is aft at a higher level, and this allows an unusually large saloon on the main deck.

Sea Star *making "a big splash" at her launching at East Boothbay, Maine, in 1970. (Mickles Photo. Courtesy of Robert E. Wallstrom)*

large, open (but partially sheltered) cockpit abaft and below the pilothouse. Toward the stern there is an outside steering station.

The crew's quarters contain, in addition to a fo'c's'le for the deckhands, a stateroom for the captain and another for the steward and engineer. In the guest quarters there are four double staterooms and three heads, each with a shower and bathtub. There is also another head/dressing room on the main deck.

The three-masted rig nicely divides the enormous sail area of 4,930 square feet, and it allows great flexibility when shortening down. *Sea Star* should balance well under main and forestaysail or main and foresail, under mizzen with foresail and ˮrestaysail or jib, or under foresail or main alone in real blow. Of course, many more sail combinations are possible when you begin reefing, especially since balance can be adjusted with the yacht's tandem centerboards.

The original plan shows mizzen running backstays that don't look very efficient, since they are quite close to the mast, but a boomkin and permanent backstay were added later. This change improves the angle between the mast and backstay and obviously saves the work of tending a set of runners. Her long spreaders provide generous shroud angles, thereby minimizing mast compression. Although Richard O. Davis did most of the design work on *Sea Star*, James Bister, another Rhodes employee, did nearly all the work on her rig. This was a sizable job, because almost all the fittings, including turnbuckles and toggles, had to be custom made.

Despite her high cabinhouse and tremendous dis-

Sea Star *under sail at her trials making five knots despite not having much wind. (Photo by E.L. Boutilier)*

placement of 403,814 pounds, *Sea Star* was said to be a surprisingly good sailer. For example, it was reported that on her trials she sailed at 5 knots in a light breeze. It was also said that she can be tacked without too much difficulty, even though she has a very long keel and drags two propellers. Although she is certainly a far cry from a 12-meter boat when beating to windward, her size alone assures good speed on a reach when there is a fresh breeze.

The usual way of figuring a heavy-displacement boat's hull speed is to multiply the square root of her waterline length by 1.34, and this calculation for *Sea Star* would give her a theoretical top speed of slightly over 13 knots. (I am told, however, that Phil Rhodes always used the factor 1.36 rather than 1.34. Perhaps he did so with his sailboats because they normally have generous overhangs and pick up a lot of extra sailing length when heeled.)

In rough waters when the wind is close to being abeam, *Sea Star*'s sails also steady the yacht. For those times when the wind is aft or very light, there are articulated anti-roll stabilizers, but apparently they never could be made to work very well.

Sea Star's hull form and her divided rig, which keeps the center of effort reasonably low, give her a lot of initial stability. Bob Wallstrom, who did a great deal of work on this yacht, notes that the original plan was to build the spars and superstructure of aluminum, but when preliminary stability calculations indicated a very long GM (metacentric height), the decision was made to have steel spars and superstructure. This additional weight aloft, of course, raised the vertical center of gravity and slightly shortened the GM. Wallstrom wrote, "The decision was well founded, for I recall she had an easy motion. I don't recall her exact roll period, but I'm sure it was over six seconds."

Sea Star is powered by two V-8 General Motors diesels of 350 horsepower each, driving controllable-pitch propellers. She was designed to cruise at 11 knots under power, but the yacht's first captain, Lester Hallett, wrote that she could not make that speed, and that the power transmission that operated the feathering gear would not work properly. Bob Wallstrom maintains, however, that the yacht lived up to performance expectations on her trials, so perhaps the feathering malfunction and thus the wrong propeller pitch accounted for the decrease in speed later on. According to Wallstrom, "The system [for feathering] worked correctly on trials, for we were going down the Kennebec River at hull speed, and I asked Captain Hallett about going from full ahead to full astern in one motion by changing only pitch, as I had heard that could be done on the Coast Guard cutter *Hamilton*. Well, he tried it, and she slowed instantly and came to reverse smoothly, getting up to 6 or 8 knots within 15 seconds or so."

It is common for yachts as large and complicated as *Sea Star* to have plenty of engineering bugs, but this vessel had more than her share. Phil Rhodes was in his twilight years when she was built, and he probably was not able to devote his usual meticulous attention to the myriad of details. A number of the systems that malfunctioned, such as the electrical and sewage systems and the centerboard hoisting gear, were designed by subcontractors who were not even selected by the Rhodes office. A somewhat amusing, but perhaps exaggerated, story is that on one occasion when Rockefeller was giving an important party, the sewage system "burped" and sent effluent out of the vents high on the mast and down onto the assembled guests.

At any rate, the bugs were eventually worked out, and *Sea Star* proved to be a real queen. She is certainly one of the grandest and most luxurious fore-and-aft-rigged sailing yachts in use today.

42

Some Sailing Cruisers in Fiberglass
Classic Plastics

Near the end of the 1950s many yachtsmen were coming to appreciate that fiberglass, as a material for yacht construction, had definite advantages in maintenance, longevity, and watertightness. By that time the material had been well proven in small boats and even in some fairly large ones, and these craft could be produced quite economically when sufficient numbers were made from a single mold. As mentioned in Chapter 31, Phil Rhodes' Bounty II was a landmark fiberglass boat. Although there had been at least one similar-size one-off sailboat and smaller stock auxiliaries produced in fiberglass prior to the Bounty II, the 1956 Rhodes-designed 40-footer was the first large stock cruising auxiliary sailboat made of the material.

One of the new companies that became well known for marketing and then producing fiberglass auxiliaries was Seafarer Yachts, which commissioned several designs from Phil Rhodes. The early Rhodes Seafarer classes have a reputation for being among the better-built stock fiberglass boats. In 1958 Seafarer commissioned Phil to design the first of its products, a 33-foot-overall keel-centerboard class sloop called the Swiftsure. With her good looks,

smart performance, roomy interior, and shallow draft, this sloop became one of Seafarer's most successful boats. About 150 Swiftsures were sold before 1965.

These attractive, mahogany-trimmed sloops were built in Amsterdam at the well-known DeVries Lentsch Shipyard. I recently attended a survey of a Swiftsure, and she was impressive even though she had had more than 20 years of hard use and abuse. The only faults seemed to be a few installation details, such as the fuel line leading from the bottom of the gas tank (the Coast Guard now recommends that the line lead from the tank's top).

For a boat that is only 22 feet 11 inches on the waterline, the Swiftsure has an amazing amount of room below. This is due partly to her wide beam of 10 feet and partly to some clever planning. Some well-thought-out features are: a stove on tracks so that it may be slid out of the way when not in use for greater counter space, the foot of the port berth recessed into the head compartment to allow an extra locker, and a convenient grab post that houses the centerboard pendant. On the boat I examined, there was also a folding extension to allow the icebox

The Swiftsure sail plan shows a well-raked mast, which gives the rudder some bite in light-to-moderate winds.

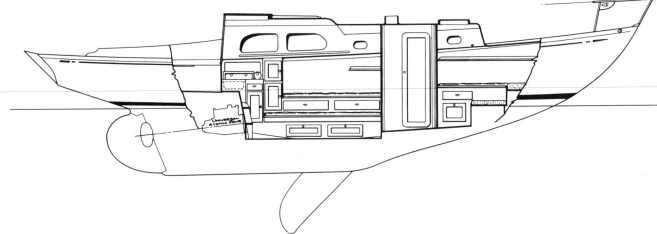

The Swiftsure's profile shows an attractive sheer and stern, a fairly cutaway forefoot, and a narrow centerboard.

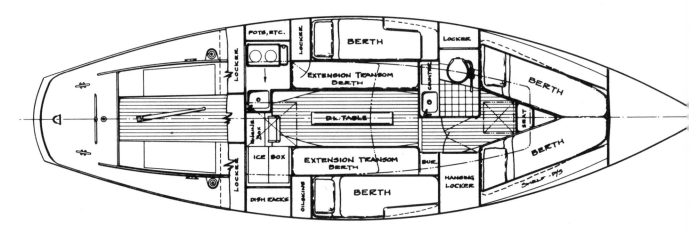

The interior of a Swiftsure is relatively roomy.

top to serve as a good-sized chart table. There are bunks for six, if the need arises, and a lot of privacy is provided with the ample enclosed head and forward stateroom, which can be closed off with a door.

Compared with many of the larger Rhodes centerboarders, the Swiftsure has less deadrise, and her hull is well rounded, with a large radius at the turn of the bilge. For a beamy centerboarder she has fairly full waterlines forward, and her hull is quite symmetrical compared with some of the beamy, wedge-shaped boats of her era and later. Her shallow draft of 3 feet 6 inches with the centerboard housed is ideal for gunkhole cruising, yet the high-aspect-ratio, streamlined board affords good lift for windward work.

She carries a simple masthead sloop rig with 472 square feet of sail area. The fairly short rig, in combination with the boat's broad beam, ensures that she will not be tender, despite the moderate softness at the turn of the bilge. Considerable mast rake is shown on the plans; one Swiftsure sailor told me that this rake is necessary to overcome a lee helm in light to moderate winds. There is ample area in the foretriangle for powerful headsails in light weather.

Two other early Rhodes designs for Seafarer Yachts are the Ranger and Meridian classes. The latter, unfortunately, tries to crowd in too much for its size. It attempts to accommodate four people and give them 5 feet 11 inches of headroom — an awful lot to ask of a boat under 25 feet in overall length. On the other hand, the Ranger, with an overall length of 28 feet 6 inches, takes care of four people quite well and allows headroom without unduly compromising the boat's appearance. Indeed, this is a handsome little cruiser despite her high doghouse.

Under sail, the popular Swiftsure shows off her attractive lines. (Photo by Fred Thomas)

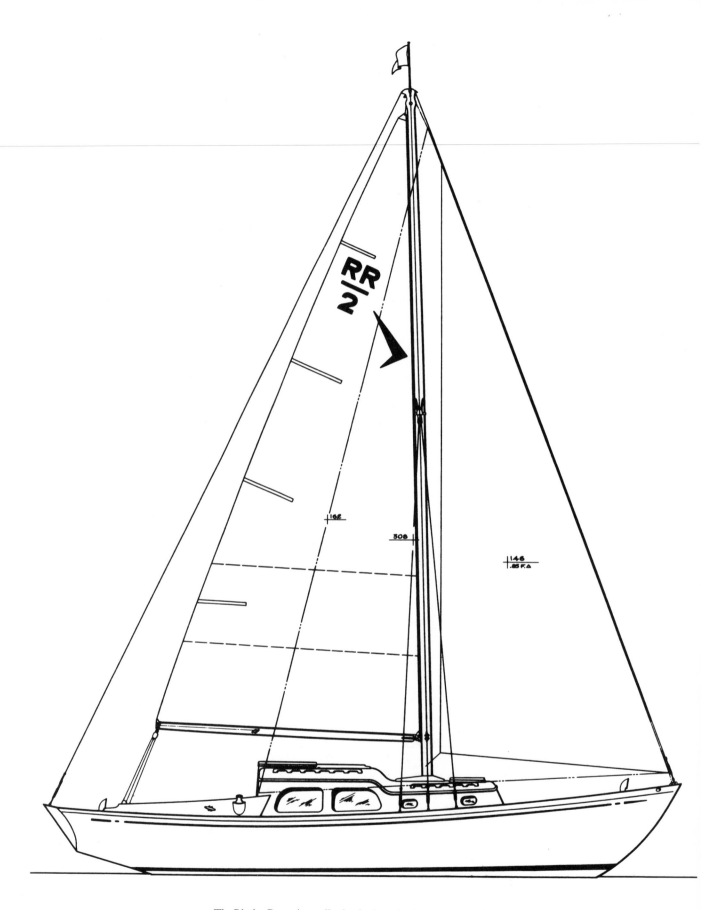

The Rhodes Ranger's small, simple rig makes her very easy to handle.

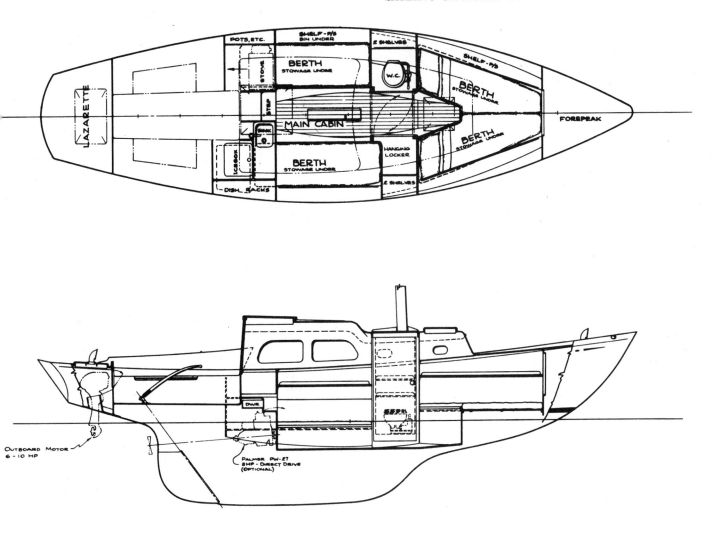

The Ranger's below-decks layout gains a lot of space by means of the after berths running under the galley.

She has a saucy sheer, moderate freeboard, and attractive overhangs. The raked transom is not only pleasing to the eye but it also keeps the permanent backstay well clear of the mainsail's leech. The short masthead sloop rig, with only 334 square feet, is a "breeze" to handle.

Although she is only 20 feet on the waterline and has a beam of just 8 feet, the Ranger has a complete galley aft, two bunks and a fixed table in the main cabin, a forward stateroom with two bunks, and a head that may be closed off from both cabins. With the lazarette, cockpit seat lockers, and a hanging locker below, there is a lot of stowage space for this size of boat. Auxiliary power takes the form of either an outboard in a well or an inboard engine. Condi-

tions can be cramped on any small boat, but the Ranger provides surprising comfort and privacy for a couple; and a nice feature is that a shallow draft of 3 feet 10 inches is achieved without a centerboard.

Perhaps one of the most successful Rhodes fiberglass cruisers is the Vanguard, which was designed in 1962 for Pearson Yachts of Warren, Rhode Island. She looks quite a bit like a larger version of the Ranger, except that her windows are smaller. The smaller windows are preferable not only for aesthetic reasons, but also for extra strength if the boat is taken offshore. The Vanguard's measurements are 32 feet 8 inches by 22 feet 4 inches by 9 feet 3 inches by 4 feet 6 inches. Her layout

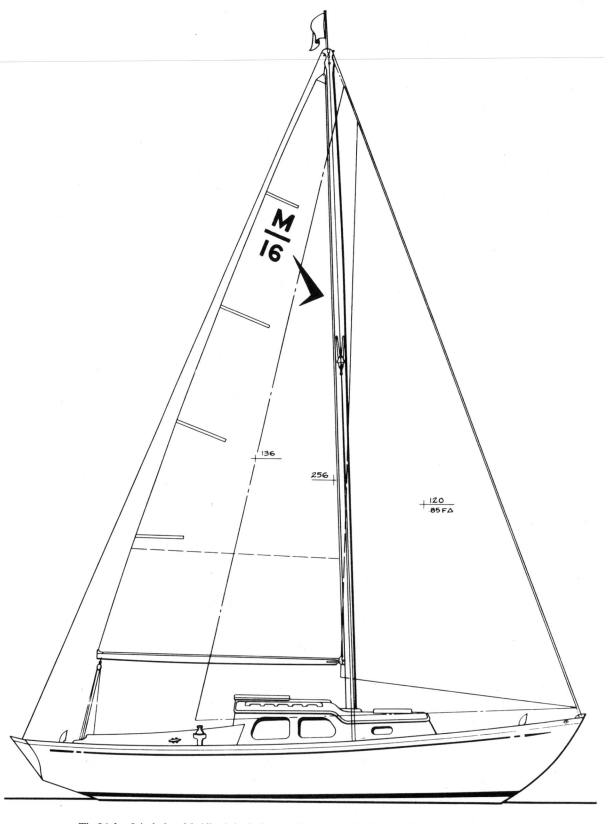

The 24-foot 9-inch sloop *Meridian* is basically a smaller version of the Ranger. Her mainsheet has a slightly better lead angle than that of the Ranger.

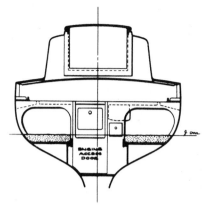

...cause of her smaller size, the Meridian's head cannot be closed off from both cabins. Compared to the Ranger's ...tional inboard auxiliary, the Meridian's is slightly deeper in the bilge, where it is more subject to bilge water, ...t it drives a prop that is forward of the rudder for better steering control under power.

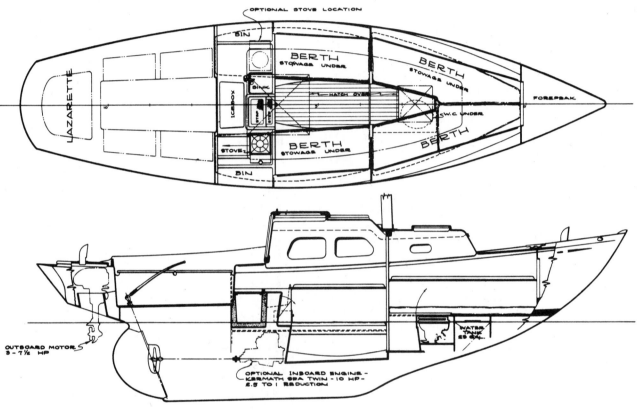

below is similar to the Ranger's — except, of course, that there is more room and the galley is considerably larger. Also, the main cabin has two extra berths in the form of an extension transom on the port side and a fold-up berth to starboard. An optional arrangement has two quarter berths, a dinette to port, and the galley stretched out along the starboard side of the main cabin.

The standard Vanguard had a masthead sloop rig with 470 square feet of sail (a yawl rig was also made available). The mast is stepped on deck, and there can't be a vertical pipe under the step without blocking the doorway to the head. However, there is a metal girder on deck that transfers the mast load to

posts on each side of the doorway. Several times I have sailed alongside Vanguards and have been impressed with their performance, especially in a fresh breeze.

An attractive sloop of about the same size as the Vanguard is the Chesapeake 32, which Rhodes designed for the George Walton Company of Annapolis, Maryland, in 1959. This boat — which is 32 feet overall and 22 feet 1 inch on the waterline — does not quite have the form stability of the Vanguard, since her beam is only 8 feet 9 inches, but she carries her ballast a bit lower with her deeper draft of 4 feet 9 inches. The narrower beam also

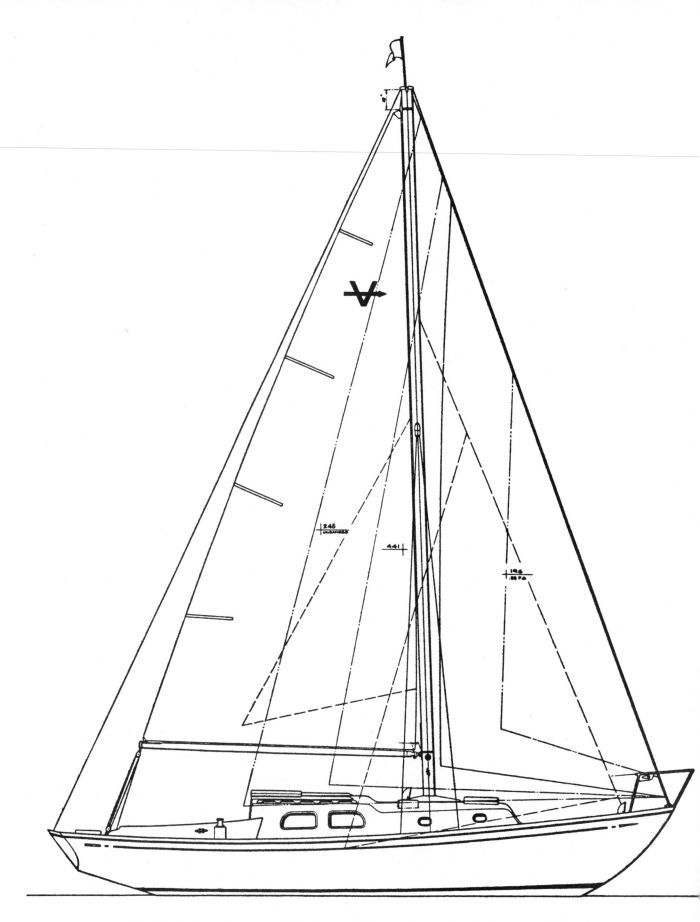

The Vanguard, a popular and successful enlargement (32 feet 8 inches overall) of the Ranger concept designed for Pearson Yachts.

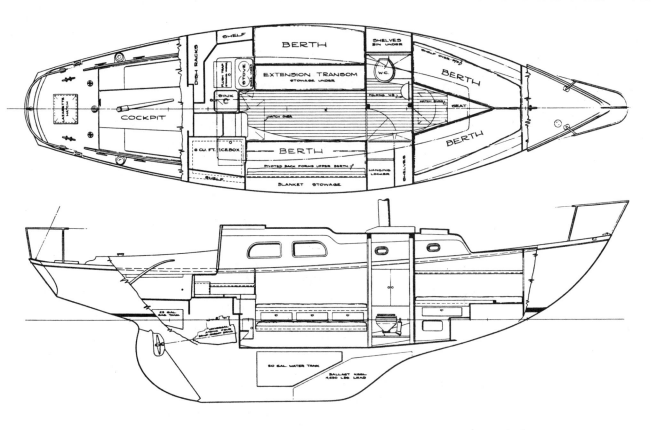

Standard arrangement plan for the Vanguard. Another plan features a dinette and quarter berths.

restricts the accommodations in the main cabin, but three people can sleep there if the need arises, for the port berth's backrest swings up to form an upper berth. An interesting feature in the marketing of these boats is that they were sold almost completely equipped, with few if any extras offered.

Chesapeake 32s were originally built by Danboats, Inc., in Denmark, and, as George Walton admitted, the first seven boats were prone to some oilcanning when driven into heavy seas. Even the eighth boat had some related problems. Later boats (and also some of the originals), however, were reinforced with longitudinal stringers, and this effectively strengthened the hulls. After boat number 25, the Chesapeake 32s were built by Sandersen's Plastic Boats in Copenhagen, and I understand that the construction was improved.

In their sailing ability, the 32s were quite smart, but they had a tendency to hobbyhorse at times when working to windward. George Walton sought advice from the Rhodes office, and yacht section head James McCurdy advised the addition of 250 to 500 pounds of inside ballast amidships. This change

improved the boat's motion and her sail-carrying ability, and she became a competent performer upwind. At least two 32s, those owned by James List and Paul Abbott, had good racing records on the upper Chesapeake Bay.

The last boat owned by Donald Sherwood (Chapters 2 and 13) was a Chesapeake 32, and she was named *Sea Witch* after the yawl featured in Chapter 2. Donald himself did not sail her a great deal, but his son Arthur, one of my best friends, used her quite a bit, so I spent many a pleasant hour aboard this boat.

Perhaps the most admired and sought-after fiberglass boat from the board of Phil Rhodes is the Rhodes Reliant, a keelboat measuring 40 feet 9 inches by 28 feet by 10 feet 9 inches by 5 feet 9 inches. I have sailed on and against this boat in races, and she handles extremely well. In addition, she has great aesthetic appeal, for she seems to be just the right size for the sweeping Rhodes sheerline and drawn-out, balanced ends. Her low, wood-covered cabin trunk with small windows also

The Vanguard is a smart, well-behaved sailer, especially in a fresh breeze. (Courtesy of Annapolis Yacht Sales)

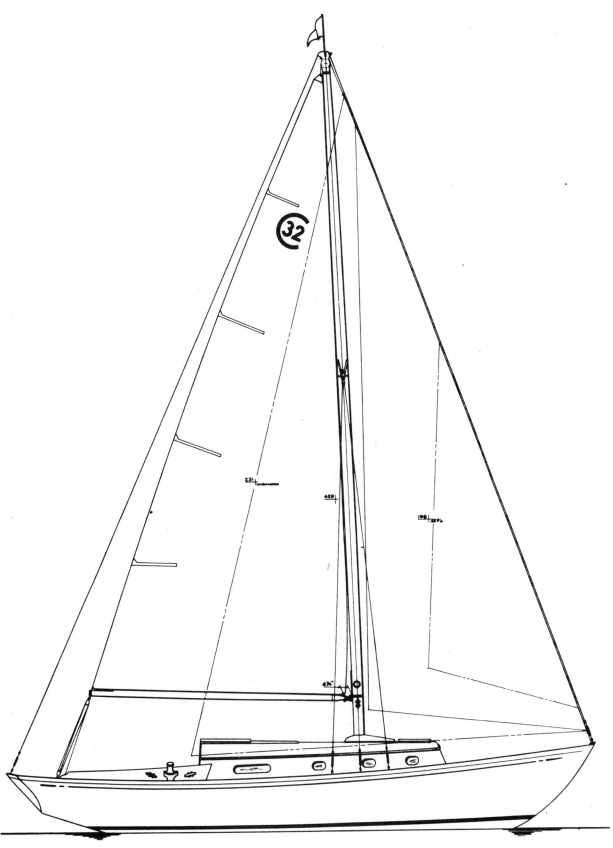

The Chesapeake 32's looks are enhanced by her small windows aft and lack of a doghouse.

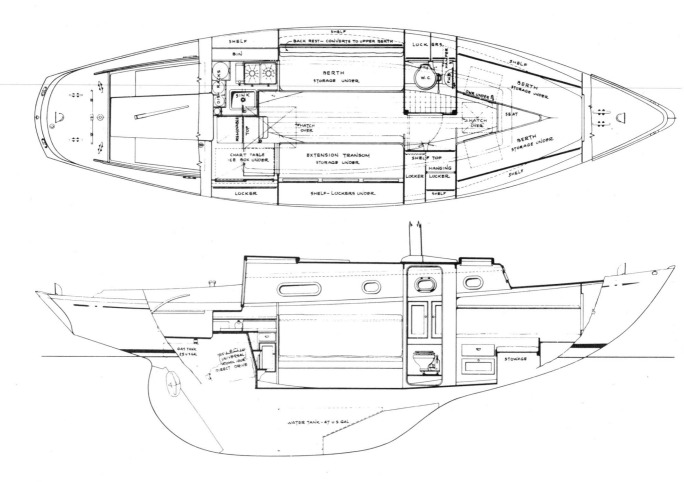

The Chesapeake 32 is not quite as comfortable below as the Vanguard, primarily because of her narrower beam. However, the head can be used without closing off the passageway between cabins.

enhances her looks. But the most distinctive feature of this 1963 design is her deck layout and arrangement below.

In a letter to Phil Rhodes, my friend Dr. Roy Scholz, who owns the Rhodes Reliant *Calypso,* described her arrangement as "the most beautiful layout of any ship ever built." Starting aft and going forward, there is a two-berth owner's cabin, then the saloon with a U-shaped dinette to port and galley on the starboard side, and a private stateroom forward. The head compartment is nicely arranged with two doors so that it may be used from either the owner's cabin or the saloon. There is another head between the bunks in the forward cabin.

This layout affords remarkable privacy for a 28-foot-waterline boat, but it requires that the main companionway lead into the saloon from the side, a feature that is less than perfect on an oceangoing boat. Although the companionway is inboard of the cockpit coaming, which is extended forward, the hatch is quite far off-center, which makes it vulnerable to flooding during a severe knockdown on the port tack. One model of the Reliant has two sliding companionway hatches, with one aft, close to the boat's centerline, and leading into the owner's cabin. Even though this plan may detract from the privacy of the after cabin, it would seem to be a better arrangement for ocean sailing, since it allows the side hatch to be closed off when necessary. If more privacy is desired when sailing in sheltered waters or moderate conditions at sea, then the after companionway can be closed with louvered slides, perhaps, and the side entrance can be used.

The Reliant is rigged either as a masthead sloop with 686 square feet of sail or a yawl carrying 750 square feet. *Calypso* has the yawl rig, which is powerful enough to drive her well in light airs. I have heard reports that the Reliant is a bit tender in a

The Chesapeake 32 Sea Witch *seems to be running well, but her standard narrow-shouldered spinnaker is far from ideal. (Photo by Fred Thomas)*

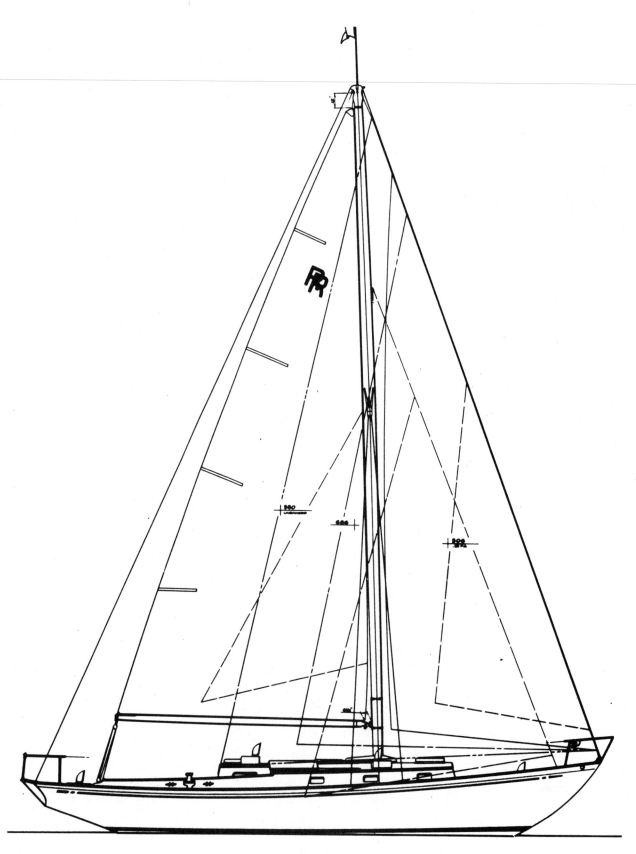

The 40-foot 9-inch Rhodes Reliant is undoubtedly one of Phil Rhodes' most successful fiberglass cruisers.

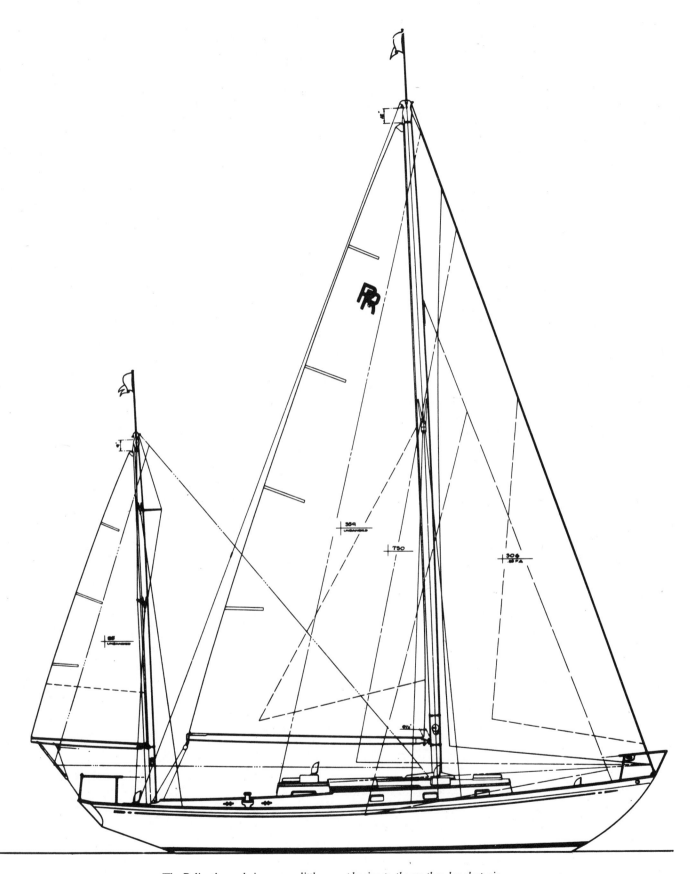

The Reliant's yawl rig seems a little more pleasing to the eye than her sloop rig.

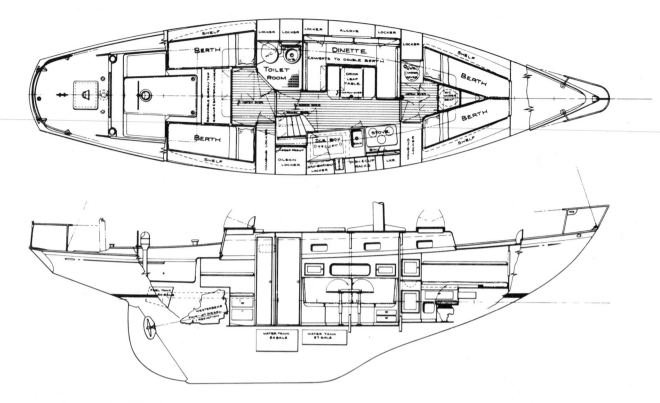

The Reliant's arrangement trades off a small amount of safety, because of her side companionway, for a lot of privacy below.

blow, but in a fresh wind, *Calypso* seems to have ample stability, partly because she carries about 900 pounds of extra ballast in the bilge, which apparently was recommended by Phil Rhodes. During one fresh-weather race in November, when the cold air had plenty of weight, *Calypso* was able to carry her spinnaker without much difficulty, although the crew had their hands full handling the sail. I was steering, and this turned out to be the easiest job on the boat, for she tracked like a locomotive compared with many of the modern short-keel racers, which a sailmaker friend describes as being ''squirrelly'' downwind.

The Reliant was built by the Cheoy Lee Shipyard of Hong Kong. With her generous wood trim and teak cabin trunk sides, as well as a laid teak deck over fiberglass, she gives the appearance of a wood boat. Cheoy Lee also put out a slightly modified version of the Reliant called the Offshore 40. This boat has several alternative arrangements, including a flopped tri-cabin plan similar to the Reliant's. About the only other differences between the Reliant and the Offshore 40 are that the latter has a slightly shorter overall length, a redesigned rudder, and iron rather than lead keel ballast. Evidently the builder

felt that sufficient changes in the boat had been made to circumvent the need for royalty payments to Rhodes, and obviously the designer was not overjoyed.

Two very successful but smaller Rhodes fiberglass boats introduced in the early-to-mid-1960s are the Tempest and Outlaw classes. Both these boats were produced by the O'Day Corporation of Fall River, Massachusetts.

The Tempest, designed in 1963, was a rather modern development of the Rhodes fin-keelers, discussed in Chapter 9. She has dimensions of 23 feet 2 inches overall, 17 feet on the waterline, 7 feet 6 inches beam, and 3 feet 9 inches draft. Instead of having an outboard rudder, which is characteristic of the 1932 fin-keeler *Nixie,* the Tempest has a completely submerged rudder attached to a shallow skeg, Star-boat fashion. Her keel does not have the Star-boat type of bulb, but the bottom of the keel is swollen somewhat to keep the ballast low. The cabin is very small, but it has two bunks, a stove, and a head. A large, self-draining cockpit extends quite far forward, and this not only allows plenty of comfort and room for daysailing, but it also helps keep the

The Rhodes Reliant Calypso. *(Courtesy of Dr. Roy Scholz)*

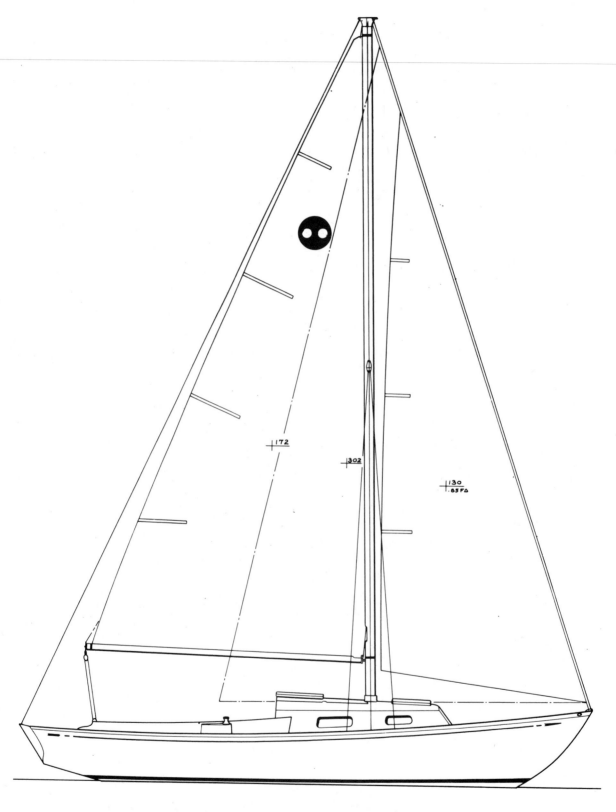

The standard sail plan for the 26-foot Outlaw. The champion Outlaw Turkey *had her stern and her boom bobbed.*

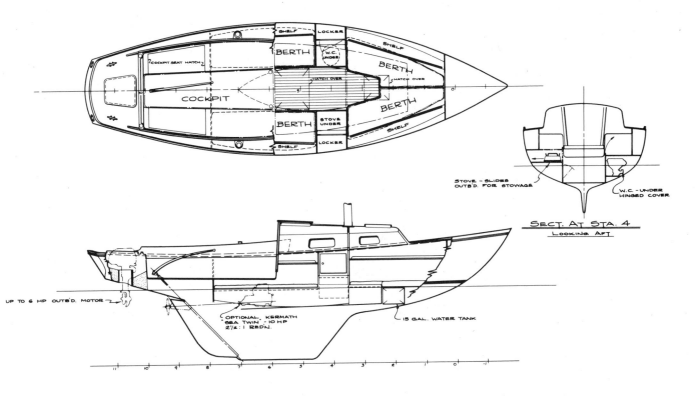

The Outlaw is quite roomy below, considering her small size and large cockpit. A lot of room is gained by running the after bunks under the cockpit seats, quarter-berth fashion.

crew weight amidships, an important consideration in this size of boat. Auxiliary power is supplied by an outboard motor, which fits in a well through the counter. The Tempest is unusually handsome, and she is fast with her masthead sloop rig, which supports 211 square feet of sail. An early O'Day ad claimed that "she won about everything she entered in her first year."

Although the Outlaw has been called a fin-keeler, she has a conventional but very short integral keel with attached rudder. The shortness of the keel reduces wetted surface area almost as much as a fin, but it has ample area for good lateral resistance under all conditions and sufficient size to carry plenty of ballast (more than half the boat's weight). Even if the rudder is not as far aft as a typical separated rudder, it is well protected, it will not stall easily, and the rake makes it efficient at high angles of heel.

With an overall length of 26 feet 3 inches, a waterline length of 19 feet, and beam of 8 feet, the Outlaw is large enough for simple weekend cruising, yet her eight-foot-long cockpit makes her ideal for daysailing. Her draft of 4 feet 3 inches allows gunkholing without the need for a centerboard. In

the cabin are four berths and a modest galley. The head, which is in the middle of the cabin on the port side, might have allowed more privacy if it had been located between the forward berths with a curtain rigged at the after ends of those bunks. An outboard in a well in the after lazarette supplies auxiliary power, but the boat could be obtained with an inboard engine.

What really sets the Outlaw apart from many other boats of her size is her good looks. As a result of her moderate freeboard, overhangs, and low cabin trunk, she gives the appearance of a fairly large yacht in miniature. The sheerline is attractive, and the stern seems a little finer and more shapely than those of many modern craft of this size. Tremendous buoyancy aft is not really necessary, because the cockpit is fairly far forward and the crew weight can be kept nearly amidships.

There is no doubt that the Outlaw is a smart sailer. One of these boats, named *Turkey*, skippered by Walter Fink, had a truly remarkable racing record under the MORC (Midget Ocean Racing Club) rule. It is true that *Turkey* was slightly modified, but not in a way that really upgraded her

*The 23-foot Tempest, which has an underwater configuration
not unlike that of a Star boat, is one of the few
boats Phil Rhodes designed with an inboard separated rudder.*

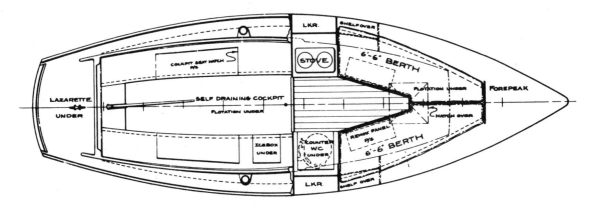

With her huge cockpit and limited accommodations, the Tempest might be considered a daysailer rather than a cruiser. (Yachting, *April 1965*)

speed potential. Her stern was bobbed nearly two feet for the primary purpose of improving her handicap rating. James McCurdy had a major hand in the design of the Outlaw, and he drew the *Turkey* modifications, which also included minor changes in her rig.

The standard Outlaw has a masthead sloop rig with 291 square feet of working sail area. *Turkey* had her boom shortened primarily for the purpose of allowing a well-roached mainsail that would clear the backstay for some rating advantage with little reduction of sail area. Also, her spreaders were shortened a bit to permit close genoa trim.

Turkey was finely tuned and well sailed by Walter Fink, so she all but dominated her class in a highly competitive region of Long Island Sound. In 1967, for example, she won eight first prizes and took four seconds and a third in 14 races sailed that season. I don't know why the boat was named *Turkey*, but she did indeed gobble up the competition.

Phil Rhodes was a pioneer in the use of fiberglass for cruising sailboats, and he was never one to shy away from new, unproven materials if he thought they had potential. He once made the remark that he would continue using fiberglass "until something better comes along." If Phil were alive today, I'm sure that he would still be using fiberglass, although he would undoubtedly be experimenting with the latest weight-saving construction techniques.

43

Small Fry
One End of a Long Scale

As anyone knows, you can't always believe advertisements, but you certainly could depend on the Rhodes slogan, which claimed that the firm could produce boats of any size, any type, and for any service. In the matter of size, Phil's yacht designs went up to at least 182 feet (much larger in commercial vessels), and at the other end of the scale, down to stock sailing dinghies only seven feet long.

Phil designed a great many small, open-cockpit daysailers, including a 15-foot-waterline one-design class in 1928 for the Junior Yacht Racing Association (it was never built), but undoubtedly his two earliest extremely popular small boat classes were the Penguin dinghy, created in 1933, and the Class D Dyer Dink, designed the following year. Many of America's top sailors either learned to sail or sharpened their skills by frostbiting during the winter months in these Rhodes dinghies.

Frostbiting was started at Port Washington, New York, in January 1932, when a group of avid sailors, who didn't think they could hold out 'til spring without sailing, decided to brave the winter weather and conduct a series of short course races in dinghies under 14 feet long. The sport caught on in a big way, and soon there was a demand for one-design class boats, so that the racing would be a truer test of sailing skill rather than a matter of who had the fastest boat.

Although the first frostbite one-designs were 11½ feet long, with 72 square feet of sail area, many sailors felt that smaller classes, which could more easily be cartopped and could better serve as yacht tenders, would be more desirable. One of the most popular classes to grow out of these requirements was the Class D Dyer Dink, a small, round-bottomed centerboard dinghy designed by Phil Rhodes and built by William Dyer of Providence, Rhode Island.

Originally a lapstrake boat with Philippine mahogany planking, most Dyer Dinks are now made of fiberglass. The original rig was a sliding gunter type with a short mast and yard that supported a single sail of 66 square feet, but now the Dink has a two-piece pole mast. The hull is 10 feet long with a beam of 4 feet 3 inches and a draft of 3 inches — 2 feet 6 inches with the board down. Weighing only 140 pounds, the Dyer Dink is not too difficult to lift, and she tows well behind a cruiser. An early advertising folder claimed: ''As a tender she's the nuts.''

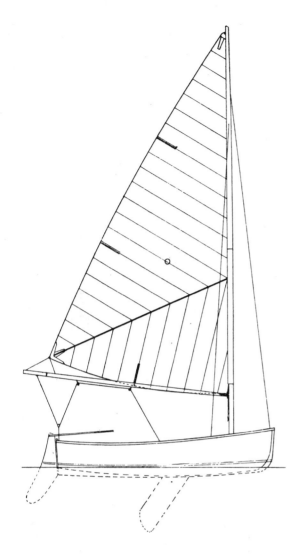

The famous Rhodes frostbiter, the 10-foot Class D Dyer Dink built by The Anchorage in Warren, Rhode Island. (Your New Boat by the Editors of Yachting)

When this dinghy was first introduced at a prominent frostbite regatta, she was a sensation. Headlines in the New York *Herald-Tribune* proclaimed: "*Squid,* 10-Foot Dinghy, Beats Larger Craft." The accompanying article by William H. Taylor, an avid frostbiter and later one of the great editors at *Yachting* magazine, described the Dyer Dink's performance: "*Squid* proved a surprise to all hands, including some of the B skippers who watched the little boat sail past them and couldn't do much of anything about it. She is a new boat which Bill Dyer brought down from Providence yesterday, and this was her first appearance in local waters. With a tall jib-headed rig carrying sixty-five feet of sail — only

seven feet less than the larger A and B boats — she ghosted along remarkably, even with the two persons aboard. She was sailed in various races by Dyer, Baker, and Arthur Knapp, but whoever sailed her, she stepped out just the same. Starting with the A boats, she easily outdistanced them and part of the time overhauled some of the Class B craft which had started several minutes earlier."

An even more popular dinghy used for frostbiting, junior training, and adult and junior summer regatta competition is the larger Penguin. The official history of the class (as expressed in the *International Penguin Class Dinghy Association Handbook*) states: "In 1938-39 a small group of Potomac and Chesapeake Bay sailors, near Alexandria, Virginia, wrote to the leading naval architects for plans of a dinghy which could easily be built by an amateur. Philip Rhodes came up with the 11½-foot dinghy, which could be built of waterproof plywood." In actuality, however, the Penguin prototype was designed in July 1933, after Bill Dyer asked Phil to draw plans for a simple frostbite racer. In a letter to *One Design Yachtsman* magazine (January 1964), Dyer wrote: "This was in the days before plywood came into use, and the original (we called it the Frostbite dinghy) was built of quarter-inch mahogany, two panels to a side and four panels on the bottom, batten-seamed." Unfortunately, the early model of the boat did not catch on, even though she was a successful racer. Dyer added: "In spite of the boat's performance, there was absolutely no interest among the frostbite group, since it was flat-sided and not in keeping with the nice round-bilged dinghies then in vogue."

The Penguin did not really become popular until May 1940, when *Yachting* magazine published plans of the boat. At that time the hard-chine, arc-bottomed hull form became perfectly acceptable, because the dinghy could be built so easily with marine-grade sheet plywood. Interest increased to such an extent that a national class organization was formed in the fall of that year.

Today the Penguin class is international, and there are well over 10,000 of the boats in America alone. Most of the newer Penguins are now made of fiberglass. Although the flat-sided hull form is not the ideal shape for fiberglass, and the original plastic boats tended to be too flexible, producers soon

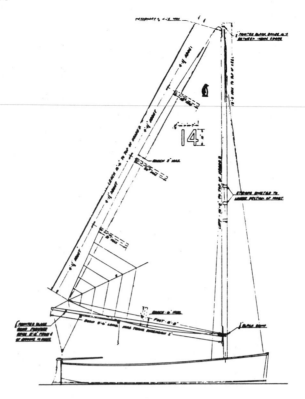

The Penguin, 11 feet 5 inches overall, is one of the most popular small boat classes in America. Her hull shape is ideal for plywood construction. (Your New Boat *by the Editors of* Yachting)

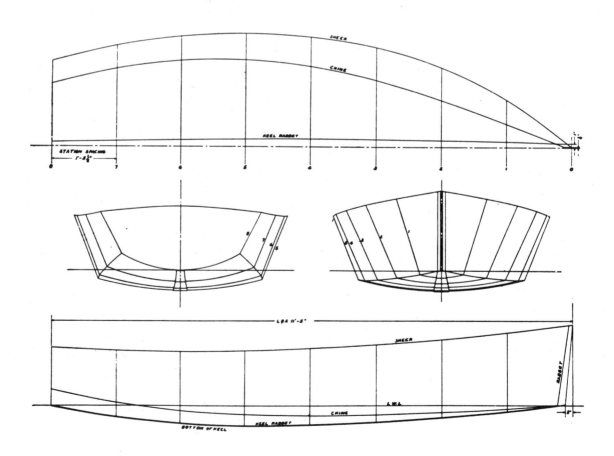

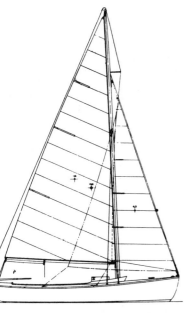

*One of Rhodes' most handsome small (17 feet) sailers is
the Edgartown (Massachusetts) Rover. The cutaway
skeg affords some tracking ability without sacrificing
maneuverability.* (Your New Boat *by the Editors of* Yachting)

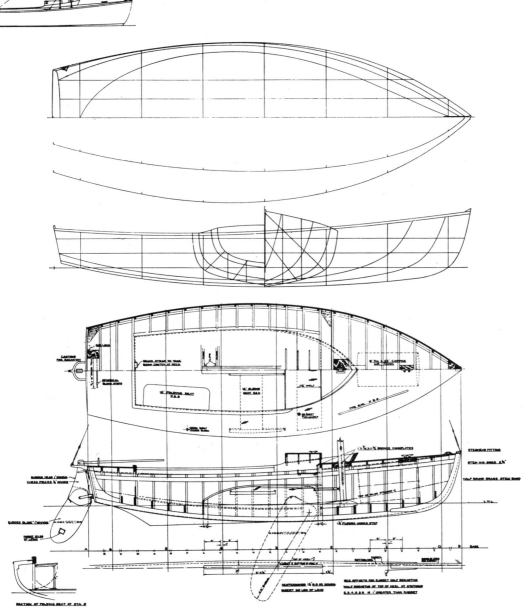

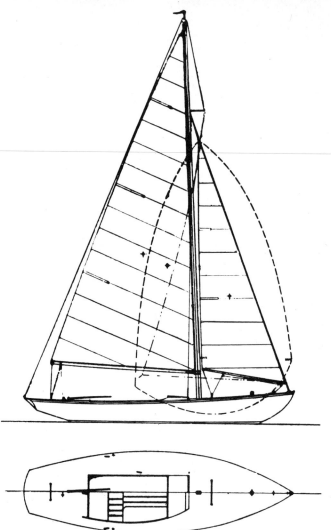

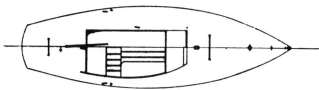

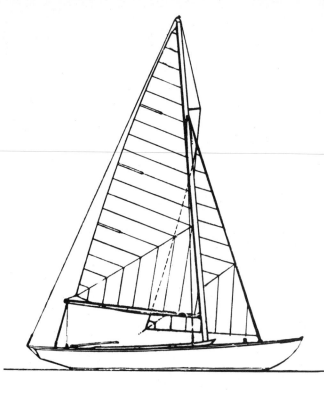

A pretty daysailer, the 18-foot Marlin, designed for Bill Dyer, offered an interesting optional heavy-air rig.

learned how to stiffen them. The hull dimensions are 11 feet 5 inches by 4 feet 8 inches by 4 feet (centerboard down). The mast, supported by a forestay and two shrouds, which attach to the gunwales with slides on tracks, carries a single loose-footed sail with an area of 72 square feet.

My son, Rip, learned to sail in a Penguin, and a number of times I had the opportunity to sail his boat, named *Ripple*. She impressed me as being smart, responsive, and roomy — at her best in light to moderate winds. As our local junior training boat, the Penguin has now been replaced by the fast and sporty Laser, but I think the Penguin is a better trainer: the Rhodes dinghy seems more like a real little boat to sail ''in,'' not ''on.'' Also, there seems to be more opportunity to practice seamanship and basic boat maintenance in a dinghy such as the Penguin.

Later in the 1930s Phil designed quite a few dinghies and daysailers. One fine-looking boat, designed in 1937 as a class for the Edgartown (Massachusetts) Yacht Club, is the 17-foot Rover sloop. Although not a great many were built, the Rover is a handsome craft, with a nice sheer, curved stem, and slightly raked transom. Her hollow entrance lets her knife through a chop, and her shallow draft — together with a fully retractable centerboard and kickup rudder — allow beaching and trailering. The sloop rig with 155 square feet of sail area is a handy one, for the permanent backstay, secured to a bracket abaft the rudder head, obviates the need for runners. The small working jib is easy to handle, while an overlapping genoa supplies more power in light weather. Hull dimensions are 17 feet by 15 feet by 6 feet by 11 inches with the board up and 4 feet 3 inches with the board down.

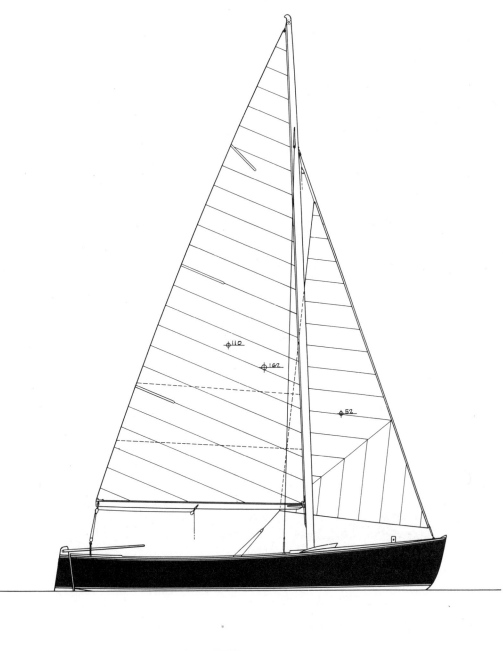

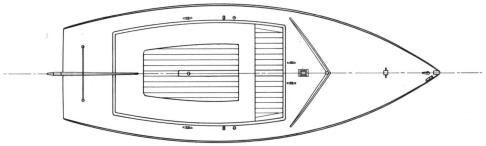

The well-known Rhodes 18, with her simple three-stay sloop rig and a somewhat unusual cockpit seating arrangement.

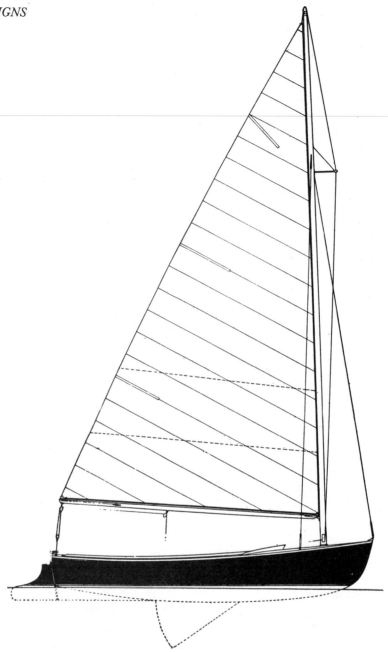

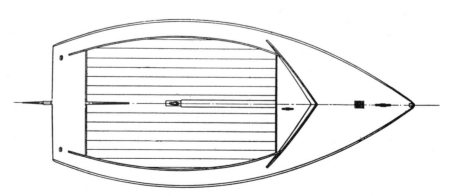

The 13½-foot Wood-Pussy is a fast racing catboat as well as a comfortable small daysailer. Notice the extra-wide cockpit and the unique way the halyard is led over the strut.

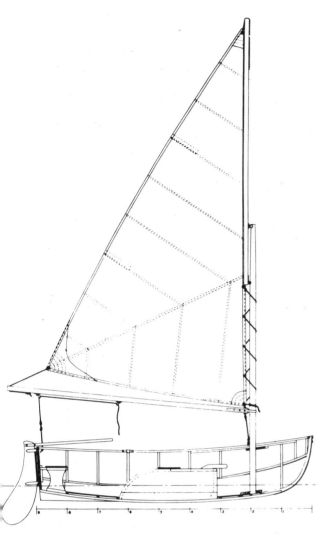

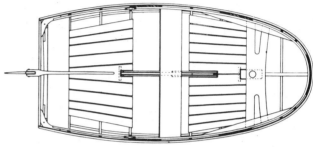

The Dyer Dhow is probably the most popular sailing tender for yachts. The design is usually credited to Bill Dyer, but Phil Rhodes had a hand in it. (Your New Boat *by the Editors of* Yachting)

The boats discussed so far in this chapter have been centerboarders, but Phil Rhodes also designed a number of small keelboats. One of the most attractive of these is a one-design class sloop called the Marlin. Designed for Bill Dyer in 1937 and built at his plant, The Anchorage, the Marlin has been described as "a baby six-meter in appearance and performance." The sloop measures 18 feet 1 inch by 12 feet 3 inches by 5 feet 3 inches by 3 feet 10 inches. Specifications called for white oak backbone and frames, 7/16-inch Philippine mahogany planking, and galvanized screw fastenings. Billed as a good, safe trainer for junior sailors, the Marlin carries about 430 pounds of iron ballast on her keel for sufficient stability, and she is fitted with air tanks that make her unsinkable.

The standard Marlin is rigged as a fractional marconi sloop with a conventional crosscut mainsail; the total sail area is an adequate 140 square feet. The standard rig has a boomed self-tending jib, which makes it ideal for singlehanding. An interesting option on the Marlin is a rig for predominantly breezy areas: it supports only 114 square feet of sail. This rig features a loose-footed, miter-cut main and a smaller foretriangle with an overlapping genoa. It would appear that the boat might have somewhat more weather helm with the heavy-air rig, since the mast has considerable rake and the jib stay is well abaft the stem head, but a tendency to round up in a strong puff is a good safety feature for an open-cockpit training boat.

Despite having a short waterline, which can cause a small boat to hobbyhorse, the Marlin was said to be exceptionally dry in a chop, and she proved a smart sailer in most conditions. The sloops were raced as a class at Harbor Springs, Michigan, and at several yacht clubs on the East Coast.

Also in 1937, Rhodes designed a number of small

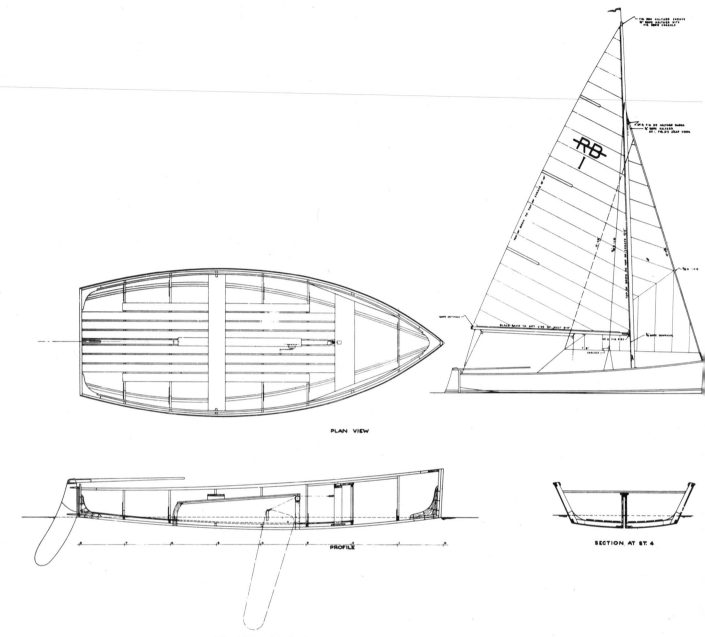

PLAN VIEW

PROFILE

SECTION AT ST. 4

The 14-foot Rhodes Bantam, an enlarged, sloop-rigged version of the Penguin.

sailers for the South Coast Boat Building Company of Newport Beach, California. Phil had a solid relationship with this company, which began when his old friend Weston Farmer, while working for South Coast, raved about Rhodes' talent to company head Walton Hubbard, Jr. As a result, Phil was commissioned by Hubbard to design not only the Rhodes 33 (Chapter 16) but also many other craft, including the small one-designs Eagle, Dolphin, Albatros [sic], and Falcon. Of these small fry, perhaps the most successful, at least in performance, was the Falcon, a round-bilged centerboard sloop measuring 16 feet 6 inches by 14 feet 9 inches by 5 feet 8 inches by 6 feet 6 inches (board down). All the South Coast boats designed by Rhodes are well balanced and sail well, but the Falcon proved stiffer and relatively faster. She has a small, easy-to-handle jib and a simple three-stay rig affording minimal windage and weight aloft.

A popular class of daysailer is the Rhodes 18, which was designed in 1938 for the Cape Cod Shipbuilding Company for use as a junior trainer by the

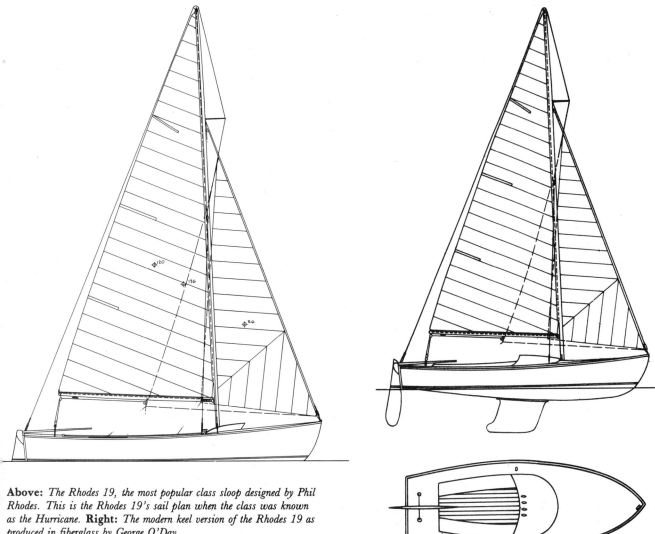

Above: *The Rhodes 19, the most popular class sloop designed by Phil Rhodes. This is the Rhodes 19's sail plan when the class was known as the Hurricane.* **Right:** *The modern keel version of the Rhodes 19 as produced in fiberglass by George O'Day.*

Stamford (Connecticut) Yacht Club. About a dozen boats were originally built for this club, and they were given bird names — *Bluebird, Blackbird,* etc. After this fleet became well established, the builder made the boat available as a stock one-design. She could be had as a keelboat or a centerboarder, but the latter was more popular. Her fractional sloop rig supports 162 square feet of sail, and she can carry a genoa jib and spinnaker. Her measurements are 18 feet by 16 feet by 6 feet 3 inches. The keel model draws 2 feet 8 inches, while the centerboarder draws 4 feet 7 inches.

Cape Cod Shipbuilding was one of the first plants to begin building plastic boats, and as early as 1948 Rhodes 18s were produced in fiberglass. For some reason, however, those models had about two inches more freeboard amidships, which created a less

graceful sheerline. (Some years later, I understand, the freeboard was lowered a bit.) At one time, the tiller was brought through a slot in the transom, which limited the amount the rudder could be turned, but this modification also was abandoned, and the tiller was re-established above the deck level.

Aluminum spars were introduced just before the changeover to fiberglass. They weighed about 12 pounds less than the wood spars, and I am told that they not only had a favorable effect on stability, but also improved the boat's pitching characteristics.

Almost 700 Rhodes 18s have been built to date, and they are still going strong in various parts of the United States. Bob Howard, who often has raced in this class, recently wrote me that some of the most active racing fleets are in western Long Island Sound (Larchmont area), Greenwich, Connecticut,

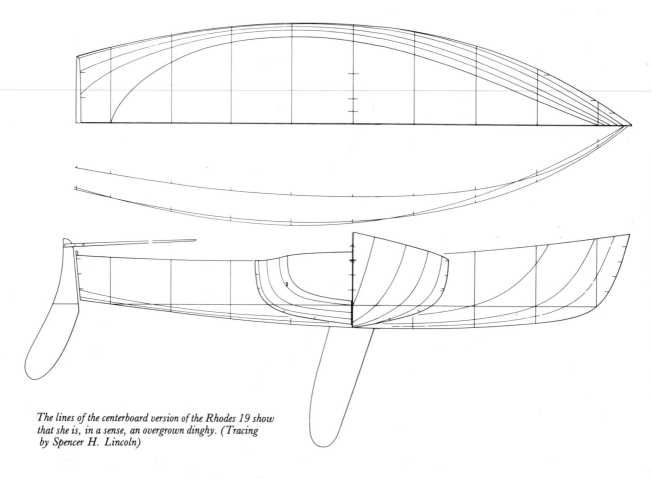

The lines of the centerboard version of the Rhodes 19 show that she is, in a sense, an overgrown dinghy. (Tracing by Spencer H. Lincoln)

Barnstable, Massachusetts, and Biddeford Pool, Maine. Bob made the following comments about the various models of Rhodes 18s: "From 1965 through 1967 I was racing various boats in the Greenwich fleet. We mixed up the boats, racing them all together. The fiberglass centerboard boats were lightest by 150 or 200 pounds, followed by wooden centerboarders and keel fiberglass boats. Results over the season were always close, although it was believed the keelers were slow; so I bought one, and found it a windward witch in light air and a boat that would fling itself downwind in any condition. Got second in the nationals with it."

One reason for the longevity of the class, aside from good all-around performance, is that the boats always have been well built. Bob says that his present Rhodes 18, a wood centerboarder, is now 33 years old and in good shape.

During the mid-1940s, there was a rash of new small boat classes by various designers, and one of Phil Rhodes' most interesting contributions was the Wood-Pussy. Although the sail symbol for this class depicts a cat with an arched back, a wood pussy is actually a skunk. Nevertheless, the name did not scare off many potential buyers, and the boat enjoyed great popularity. In 1947 it became a national class, with rigid one-design racing rules. Perhaps the most interesting aspect of this boat is that it is a cross between an old-fashioned beamy catboat and a sporty racing dinghy.

Designed for and built by Palmer Scott and Company of New Bedford, Massachusetts, the Wood-Pussy was originally carvel planked, but later she was made of fiberglass and also of molded plywood. With a beam of 6 feet for her length of 13½ feet, she is suitable for family sailing as well as racing. The beam also provides good stability and allows a big sail of 119 square feet, although the original sail was listed at only 100 square feet. An unusual feature of the cat rig is the main halyard that runs over a strut so that the halyard acts as a jumper stay to prevent excessive mast bend. Since the boat draws only about 7 inches with the board up (2½ feet with it down), she is ideal for beaching. The only drawback

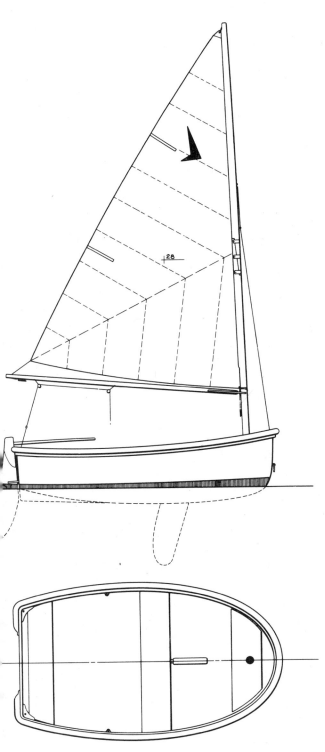

The 7-foot Seafarer dinghy is ideal as a sailing tender for small yachts.

to the shallow draft is that the large rudder is also shallow, which leads to some loss of control when the boat heels. But advertising literature stresses that this is a built-in safety device — a knockdown will automatically cause her to luff up into the wind to help prevent a capsize.

Mention should also be made of a round-bow, hard-chine yacht tender/sailing dinghy known as the Dyer Dhow, because, even though Bill Dyer is usually credited with the design, Phil Rhodes was a collaborator. In fact, one of Phil's designers, Charles Wittholz, drafted the plans. The original nine-foot model, designed during World War II, was intended for use as a lifeboat on Navy minesweepers and P.T. boats. Later the Dhow was produced in several sizes and used primarily as a yacht tender. It proved ideal for this service because of its versatility in affording good capacity, buoyancy, and performance when towed, rowed, or sailed. Furthermore, even the nine-foot model is light enough to be lifted aboard the mother vessel by two men. The nine-footer has a beam of 4 feet 5 inches, and it has a simple cat rig with a two-piece mast that supports 45 square feet of sail. The Dyer Dhow, now built in fiberglass, is still popular for class racing; as a tender, carried on the deck or cabin top of a yacht, it is nearly as prevalent as a gull.

Another of Phil's popular small boat designs, which came at the close of World War II, is the Rhodes Bantam. A hard-chine dinghy, measuring 14 feet by 5 feet 6 inches by 4 feet 2 inches, the Bantam could be considered a big sister of the Penguin. The main purpose of this design was to provide sporty racing, such as that enjoyed by the International 14 class, but at a cheaper price. Another requirement was sufficient room for adult comfort. As Phil Rhodes put it, "One of the nice aspects of the Bantam is that she is small enough for juniors and large enough for seniors, and one that is equally enjoyed by both."

Originally built of wood by Skaneateles Boats, Inc., in New York, Rhodes Bantams are now made of fiberglass. Plans have been ordered by builders throughout the United States, as well as in other countries, and the first international championship was held in New York in 1947.

The Bantam sports a fractional sloop rig of 125 square feet and carries a genoa and spinnaker. Interestingly enough, an early sail plan shows a Bantam with a jib-headed mainsail held out with a sprit, but the plan adopted for the standard 14-foot one-design has a conventional boom. An advantage of the sprit rig was that it allowed a permanent backstay to obviate the need for runners, but an obvious disadvantage was that the sprit cut into the sail on one tack. The modern rig with boom does away with the need for backstays by having adjustable shrouds set slightly abaft the mast.

Phil's most popular racing daysailer above the dinghy size is undoubtedly the Rhodes 19. This boat originated in 1945 when the Allied Aviation Corporation of Cockeysville, Maryland, which had been building aircraft of molded plywood, began laminating hull shells of a 19-foot Rhodes centerboarder then known as the Hurricane class. Palmer Scott and Company bought some of these unfinished hulls and added foredecks, cockpit shelters, and cast-iron keels. This keel version of the Hurricane became known as the Smyra when it was adopted as a class boat for the Southern Massachusetts Yacht Racing Association. A Smyra hull was used as the plug for the mold of a fiberglass model first produced by the Marscot Plastics Company. In the late 1950s, when the O'Day Corporation of Fall River, Massachusetts, took over production and sales, the boat's class name was changed to Rhodes 19. About 50 of these craft were sold in 1959, and the next year a Rhodes 19 class association was formed. Now there are nearly 3,000 boats, with fleets all over the United States.

Available in a centerboard as well as a fin-keel model, the centerboard version of the Rhodes 19 draws from 10 inches to 4 feet 11 inches (board down), while the keel boat draws 3 feet 3 inches. The hull measurements are 19 feet 2 inches by 17 feet 9 inches by 7 feet. A fractional sloop rig supports 175 square feet of sail. Although the foretriangle is small, a spherical-type spinnaker provides plenty of power on reaches and runs. The rigging is quite basic, with a permanent backstay to obviate the need for runners, and jumper stays to prevent excessive mast bend. Many of the hot-shot class racers prefer mid-boom sheets and travelers for easy control and to bend the boom, thereby flattening the main in fresh winds.

Rhodes 19s are very smart sailers, as evidenced by the fact that they have been chosen for the Mallory

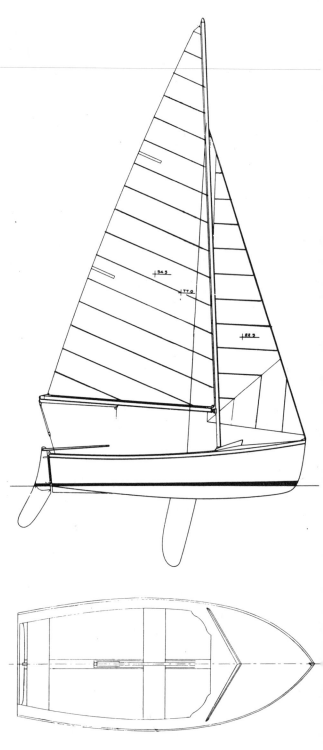

The 10-foot 10-inch sloop-rigged dinghy Robin has some uncommon features, including a roller-reefing main and a kickup rudder. The Robin not only has a foredeck and washboards but also narrow side decks to keep out water and to allow comfortable hiking.

nd Adams Cup series (the national championships
or men and women). The keel model especially
irives on heavy weather, and one of these boats
on her division in the fresh-wind One-of-a-Kind
egatta held on San Francisco Bay in 1967. She beat
uch speedsters as the International Tempest, 110,
nd 210 class boats.

A cabin version of the Rhodes 19 is known as the
Mariner (and later the Mariner 2 + 2). The latest
nodel can sleep four extremely intimate people in
vo quarter berths and a V-berth. This boat, which
as a large, self-draining cockpit, is available with a
enterboard and a kickup rudder that reduce draft to
bout 10 inches. It is self-righting with the board
own. A tabernacle allows the mast to be lowered or
uised very easily, a feature that makes the boat ideal
or trailering.

Not to be forgotten are some of the smallest boats
om the Rhodes board. They are the Robin and the
-foot Seafarer dinghy. The latter fills the need for
ue smallest-size sailing dinghy that can be carried
board a small cruising yacht. The 7-foot length
ften allows it to be carried on the cabin top of a
30-foot cruiser, yet the dinghy's 4-foot beam affords
a maximum load capacity of four persons in calm
water when the boat is used as a tender. The cat rig
carries a sail of only 28 square feet.

The Robin, designed in 1963, is about the smallest dinghy that can carry a sloop rig. In fact, there
are two mast positions so that the boat can be sailed
as either a sloop or a catboat. She measures 10 feet
10 inches overall, has a beam of 4 feet 8 inches, and
draws 6½ inches. Her sail area is 80 square feet as a
sloop, and she carries a spinnaker. Aside from her
rig, another unusual feature is the foredeck, which
helps keep spray out of the bilge when sailing in a
chop. Originally the boats were built of mahogany
plywood by the Evanson Boat Company of Riverside, New Jersey, but now they are made of fiberglass. They have always been available in kit form.

Apparently Phil Rhodes did not always insist on
substantial royalties for his popular small boats. If
he had, he might have made a moderate sum. It
seems that Phil was always more interested in turning out a good boat than he was in making a real
profit on them.

44

A Selection of Powerboats
The Evolution of a Youthful Interest

Even if Phil Rhodes' first love was for sailboats during most of his professional career, he kept his youthful interest in powerboats and turned out a great many of these craft. In fact, he designed close to 100 pleasure powerboats (including hydroplanes and runabouts), and a sampling of these follows.

Phil's early powerboat designs were mostly runabouts and hydroplanes, and it wasn't until the late Twenties that he steadily started getting commissions for power cruisers. One of the first of these was a stock 45-footer he designed for M.M. Davis & Sons of Solomons, Maryland, in August 1928. The design was marketed by M.M. Davis as the Davis 45, and at least two of these craft were built during the spring of 1930.

The Davis 45, measuring 45 feet by 44 feet 6 inches by 11 feet 6 inches by 3 feet 6 inches, was described in a rather elaborate advertising brochure, which featured an attractive watercolor of the cruiser on its cover. "Dignified simplicity," "smartness of line," "brutish power," and "ultramodern," was the evaluation of the boat in the promotional literature. The Davis people were careful to distinguish the Davis 45 from a run-of-the-mill pro-

duction boat. They referred to their boat as a "standardized product built with custom integrity by craftsmen . . . who have devoted their entire lives to the building of honest boats in this same Davis Shipyard where their grandfathers served before them . . . ." Today, she would probably be referred to as a semi-custom or limited production boat.

Her construction is first class, with all structural members being of white oak and her planking of Oregon fir. To ensure a strong, hefty hull, her specifications call for frames measuring 1⅝ inches by 2 inches on 10-inch centers and planking finished at 1¼ inches. Both of these members exceed the stock size found on many boats of the same size and type. Her deckhouse, trim, and joinerwork are entirely of Honduras mahogany and they are finished bright, as are her fir side decks and after decks. All fittings and hardware are of manganese bronze; the propeller is of the same material, while the shaft is Tobin bronze.

The primary consideration in the design of this boat was cruising comfort. Indeed, she has many of the sensible features found on powerboats of her day. Among these is a sizable shelter that protects

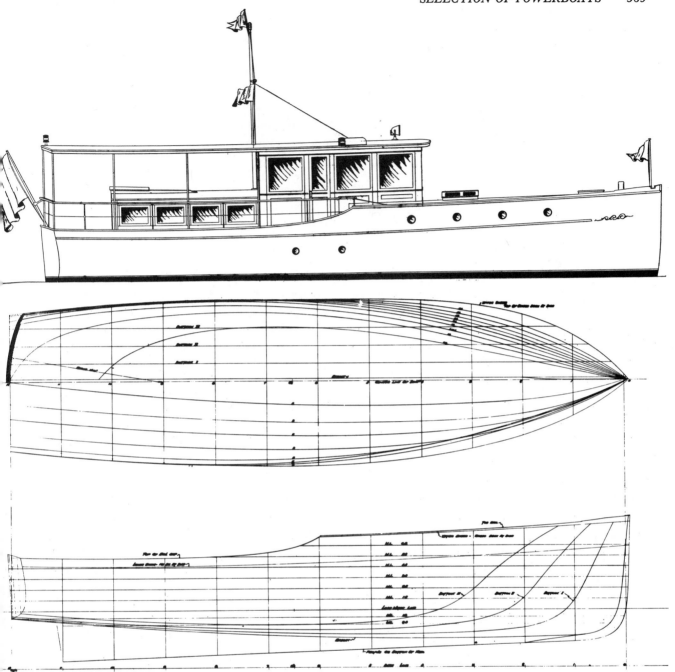

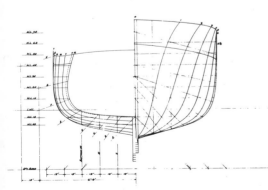

Top: *The Davis 45, an early stock power cruiser designed for M.M. Davis of Solomons, Maryland. Phil's love for drawing is indicated in his rendering of the flags.*

The Davis 45 lines show a displacement round-bottomed hull with a fairly sharp entrance but with good flare forward and a full, flattish stern with some tumblehome at the transom. (Plans photographed by Claire White Peterson. Courtesy of Mystic Seaport)

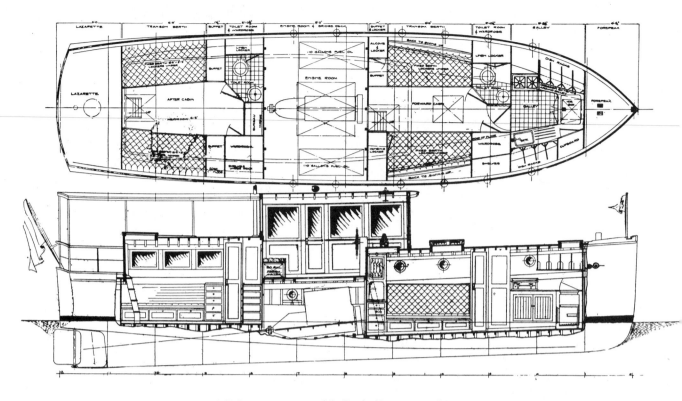

The divided stateroom/pilothouse arrangement of the Davis 45 seems to anticipate a layout pattern that Rhodes later used in many varied forms.

guests from the sun. (It is interesting that, despite the fact that the harmful effects of the sun have been "discovered" recently, modern powerboats provide so little shade on deck.) Also, there is a good location for a dinghy on the after cabin trunk, where it can be stowed upright without filling with rain water. The pilothouse affords complete protection, and it is elevated to allow good visibility and all possible room to service the engine underneath.

The layout provides privacy, with the after and forward cabins well separated. The owner's cabin aft is huge and has its own enclosed head, bureau, "colonial buffets," and large wardrobe. The forward cabin serves as a saloon, has an enclosed head, and can be used to sleep as many as four guests. The galley is up in the bow, forward of the head. An alternate layout shows the forward cabin sandwiched between an enclosed galley and a head and small fo'c's'le, with an extra head for a paid hand.

Power was supplied by a 150-horsepower Kermath gasoline engine; or, for $600 more, a 60-horsepower Cummins diesel could be installed. The Davis brochure claimed that the diesel could drive the boat at 10.5 m.p.h. at an operating cost of only 18 cents per hour. Although the horsepower of

the gasoline engine is more than double that of the diesel, it drives her only 2½ m.p.h. faster, which indicates that the Davis 45's displacement hull cannot be pushed very much faster than her theoretical hull speed. With her extremely long keel, single screw, and small rudder, the Davis 45 must turn rather slowly, but the helm itself should turn easily, for the rudder is balanced, and the large prop directly ahead of the rudder helps kick the stern around.

Like most cruisers of her day, the Davis 45 has a very square-shaped profile, with many right angles and vertical lines, as seen in her plumb ends, and her superstructure, windows, mast, and stanchions. Although her sheer might appear to be rather flat for a Rhodes design, the raised-deck configuration was the popular form of the time. Her styling (if that term could be considered appropriate) is basically functional, though, reflecting the era when considerations of mass market appeal did not strongly influence design.

This same classic, boxy appearance is also evident (at least in her superstructure and her plumb bow) in the tunnel-stern cabin launch or "day boat" shown in the accompanying plans.

Phil designed her in 1929 for a client who resided

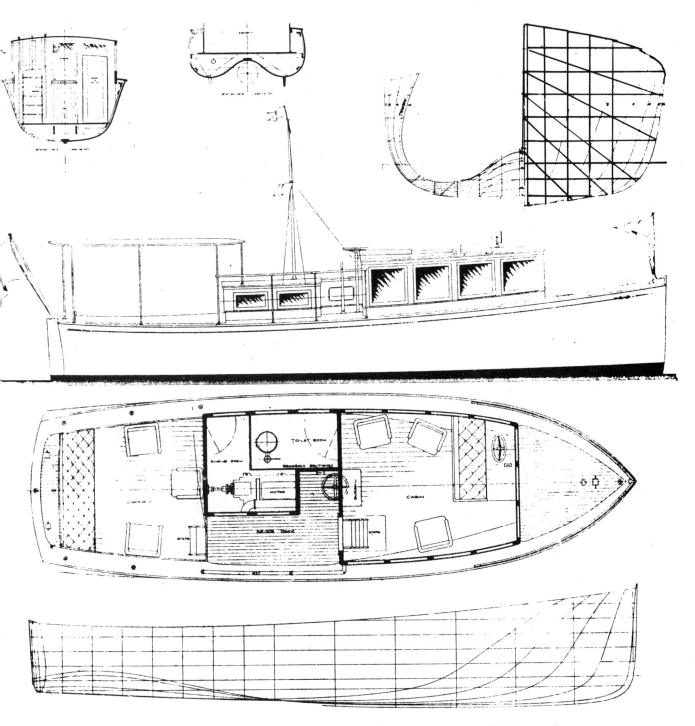

This early Rhodes 32-foot day boat used for ferry work has the same kind of bow as the Davis 45, but her stern is tunnel-shaped so that the propeller can be recessed for shoal-water operations. (The Rudder, *June 1930*)

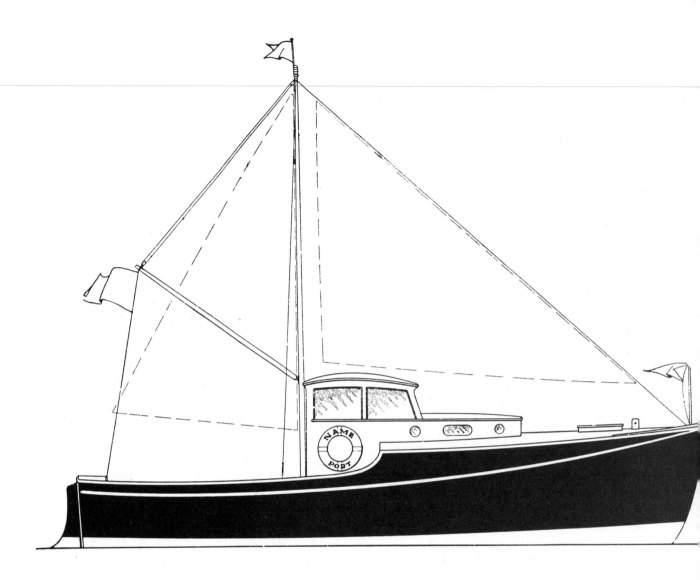

Above: Lady Jane, *a 27½-foot stock sportfisherman influenced by Maine coast lobsterboats.* **Below:** Lady Jane's *accommodations plan shows her large cockpit, tiny pilothouse, and cabin for two.* (Yachting)

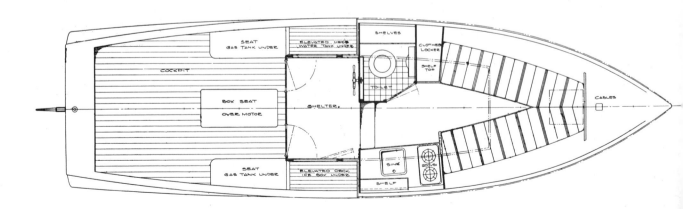

Lady Jane *underway. She appears to be a successful blend of yacht and workboat.* (Yachting)

on the lower eastern shore of the Chesapeake and intended to use her for commuting between an island estate and the Virginia mainland. Anyone familiar with this area knows that the water there is rather thin, and this is the reason for the tunnel-shaped stern: it reduces draft and protects the propeller. The boat is 32 feet long overall, and she has a beam of 9 feet 6 inches, yet she draws only 18 inches.

The shoal waters of the Chesapeake can get plenty choppy during stormy spells and even during the brief summer squalls, which are not unusual in the area; so the Rhodes launch has a fairly sharp bow (without sacrifice to necessary buoyancy) and generous flare to control the spray. The stern sections are quite buoyant to support the weight of passengers, who normally would be concentrated in the cockpit located all the way aft. Not shown on the sheer plan are two skegs aft to protect the propeller and rudders in the event of a grounding.

The forward cabin is arranged to house the passengers during inclement weather, but it could easily be equipped with berths and a galley if the boat were to be used for normal cruising. The asymmetrical deck plan allows passengers to board the docked boat from the starboard side and then to proceed aft or forward depending on the weather. The elevated bridgedeck in way of the rail and gate allows easy boarding. There are two steering positions, one on deck abaft the deckhouse and another below for times when the helmsman needs protection. The boat is powered by a 225-horsepower Kermath gasoline motor, which can drive the boat at 20 m.p.h. The head is cleverly worked in on the port

side of the engine, and this takes advantage of what would be wasted space. Part of the head partition can be removed to permit easier access to the engine's port side.

The boat's sheerline is graceful and she has a nicely crowned transom. The rear view of this broad tunnel stern might make a dignified observer hope that the boat will never be named *Fanny,* but when the vessel is afloat and loaded, the bottom of her transom is well submerged, and her stern appears to be quite normal.

An early powerboat with a great amount of character is a 27½-foot offshore fisherman that Phil designed in February 1934. The idea for this boat was conceived by William Dyer, who commissioned Rhodes to design an able sportfishing cruiser with the seakeeping ability and general appearance of a Maine coast lobsterboat. Dyer offered her as a stock model, and the first one was ordered by Richard A. Aldrich of Providence, Rhode Island, who named his boat *Lady Jane.* Built by Dyer's firm, The Anchorage, Inc., *Lady Jane* was framed with oak and planked with Philippine mahogany. Power was supplied by a Chrysler Ace engine, which could push her at better than 16 m.p.h. Her measurements are 27 feet 6 inches by 25 feet 4 inches by 7 feet 10 inches by 2 feet 6 inches.

Although this model has a raised deck forward, a prominent rub strake curves upward from stern to stem, giving the boat a bold sheerline. The stem has some rake and is mildly suggestive of a clipper bow, while the transom is canted slightly and supports a

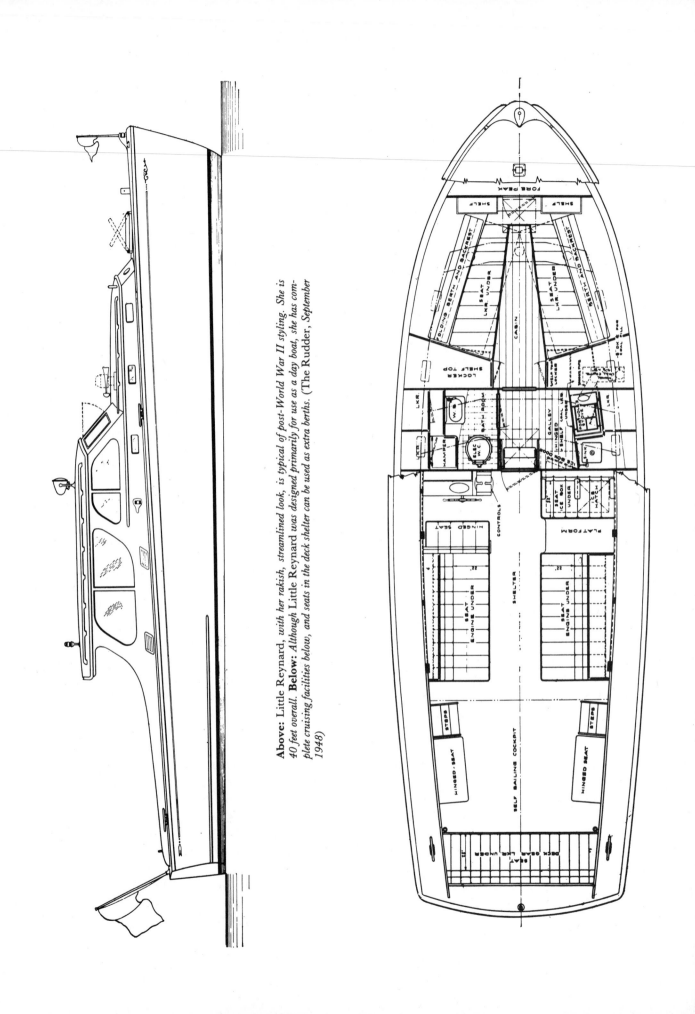

Above: Little Reynard, with her rakish, streamlined look, is typical of post-World War II styling. She is 40 feet overall. **Below:** Although Little Reynard was designed primarily for use as a day boat, she has complete cruising facilities below, and seats in the deck shelter can be used as extra berths. (The Rudder, September 1948)

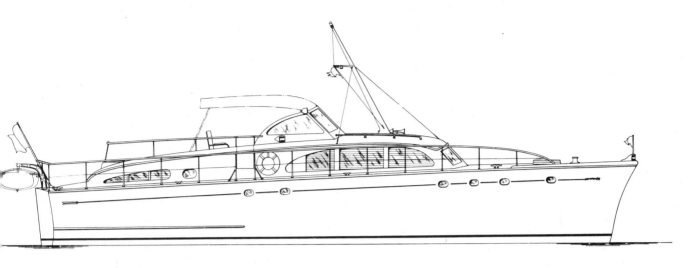

Above: Narada II, *the heavy-displacement, able, and comfortable 52 ½ -foot cruiser designed for Ambassador L. Corrin Strong.* **Below:** *Narada II's arrangement plan shows her aft galley, an unusual location in a yacht that carries a paid hand.*

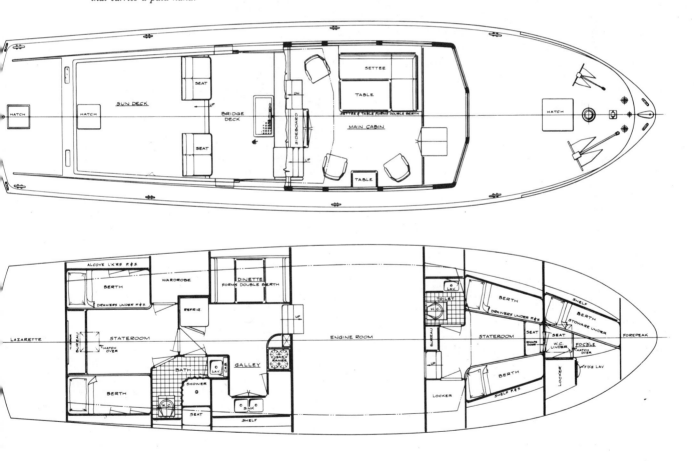

Narada II *was particularly handsome when she was finished bright. (Courtesy of Mystic Seaport)*

shapely outboard rudder. Unlike the boats previously discussed in this chapter, *Lady Jane* has a raked windshield and the top of the pilothouse is crowned in both the athwartships and fore-and-aft directions. Character is added by the derrick boom and short mast, which can support a sail area of 136 square feet in the form of a jib and loose-footed trysail.

The main purpose of these sails is to steady the boat in rough waters, but they can be used as auxiliary propulsion in the event of engine failure or to save fuel when the destination lies downwind. In a design profile that appeared in *Yachting* magazine, it was written that *Lady Jane* can heave-to beautifully under trysail alone. Apparently the trysail can hold her bow up to the wind despite the high bow and considerable windage forward, which indicates that the boat has a fairly prominent forefoot. The boom

can be used to lift a dinghy or any heavy gear into the large, self-bailing cockpit.

The "pilothouse" is little more than a small shelter for the helmsman, but it is a real wheelhouse in the sense that it affords complete protection, its after end being closable with doors. The plans show two swinging doors, but the *Yachting* analysis indicates that there is a sliding door. Down below are a galley, an enclosed head, a hanging locker, and two seven-foot berths. There is over six feet of headroom below and in the pilothouse, yet the superstructure is not so tall as to hurt the boat's appearance.

These fishermen proved quite popular; at least they were still selling in 1938. Evidently their greatest appeal was that they are exceedingly functional craft with a distinctly salty flavor.

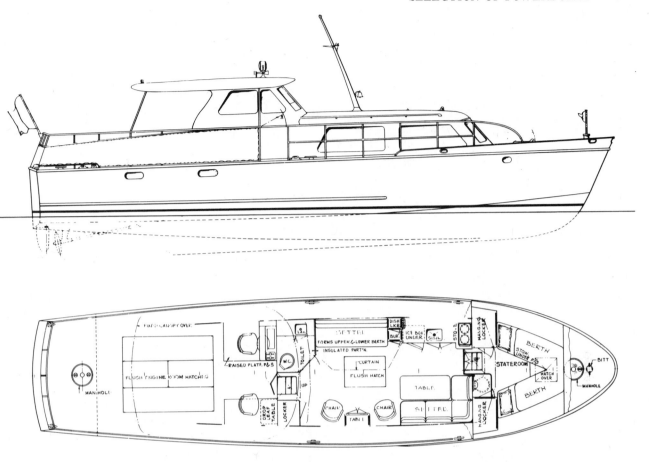

Phil Rhodes' own express cruiser, Touche Too, *was derived from the fast, oil-rig personnel launches. She is 52 feet 3 inches overall. Her layout is arranged more for day tripping than for cruising.*

A good example of a medium-sized, seakindly day cruiser with overnight accommodations is *Little Reynard,* which Rhodes designed for Thomas W. Lamont in 1946. She reflects the post-World War II styling, with more of a modern, somewhat streamlined look. The boat is not actually streamlined, obviously, for the after end of the shelter, especially when it is open, creates strong eddies. Although Phil Rhodes is best known for his beautiful concave sheerlines, the reverse sheer seems entirely appropriate on *Little Reynard.* It is quite moderate and gives her a sleek appearance.

This boat was superbly built of wood by the Henry Nevins yard at City Island, New York. Her dimensions are 40 feet by 38 feet by 12 feet 9 inches by 3 feet, and she is powered by two Gray Super-Six 330 engines. She is round bottomed, with little deadrise aft, and she has two small rudders, one abaft each propeller. Shortly after being built, she made a trip from Maine to Florida and back and was

described as being an excellent sea boat when she ventured offshore. Despite the fact that *Little Reynard* does not have a true planing hull, she can make 21 m.p.h. with the engines wide open.

Accommodations are minimal for a 40-footer, but she was intended primarily as a day boat, with a large, comfortable cockpit and ample deck space under the shelter. Nevertheless, there are two folding berths, an enclosed head, and a galley below. Also, the shelter seats over the engine boxes can be made into berths when necessary. Since *Little Reynard* was used Down East most of the time, she was fitted with a coal stove designed by Phil's friend "Porthole Pete" Chamberlain. Known as Porthole's Constant Cooker, it served *Little Reynard* as a cooking stove and as a heater for Maine's chilly weather. The icebox is under a seat opposite the helm, and it is available not only through a hatch under the seat, but also through a side door that opens into the galley.

Touche Too *at cruising speed. Her V-bottomed form and light weight allow easy planing. (Courtesy of Mystic Seaport)*

A larger yacht with a fairly similar, seakindly hull form but with a great deal more in the way of accommodations is *Narada II,* which was the replacement for the cutter of the same name described in Chapter 13. Designed for L. Corrin Strong while he was the U.S. ambassador to Norway, *Narada II* was beautifully built of the best woods by the Bjarne Aas yard at Fredrikstad, Norway, in 1955. She was intended for use on the Oslofjord as well as for later use in Maine and on the Chesapeake Bay. This meant that she had to be seaworthy and also a good gunkholer. Her measurements are 52 feet 6 inches by 49 feet 7 inches by 14 feet 6 inches by 3 feet 9 inches.

Her owner's desire for comfort and seakindliness over speed dictated a nonplaning hull with a round-bottomed form. Even so, her twin General Motors 6-71 diesels can push her up to 17 or 18 m.p.h. Her twin screws also make her very maneuverable. I had

the good fortune to take a few day trips on this boat, and they were most enjoyable. One particular excursion that sticks out in my mind was an interesting cruise in Maine from North Haven to Matinicus Rock, one of the wildest spots on the Atlantic seaboard. More than once on my trips aboard *Narada,* we experienced rough seas, but she always had an easy motion and was quite dry.

Her layout below is somewhat unusual in that the galley is aft, just forward of the owner's stateroom, rather than in the more customary location just abaft the paid hand's quarters in the fo'c's'le. The reason for this plan is that Mrs. Strong enjoyed cooking and did not expect the paid captain to work in the galley. At the same time, the arrangement allows wide separation between the two staterooms and thus affords maximum privacy. There are two dining areas, a small one opposite the galley and another, which also makes an attractive settee and a double berth conversion, in the sunken deckhouse. The heads are nicely arranged so that guests have a choice of using one forward or one aft, yet, with its two doors, the after head compartment can be made completely private for the owner.

On deck, the helmsman is protected by a wind and spray shield, and the plans show a removable helmsman's shelter, but I don't recall ever seeing the shelter rigged. There is a large comfortable sun deck farther aft, and stern davits can handle a good-sized dinghy.

After the war, Rhodes designed a number of launches for commercial use, particularly for servicing offshore oil installations. Most of them were ruggedly built of steel to enable them to withstand the rigors of commercial use. They were all designed with emphasis on good performance in rough water, dryness, and good stability, combined with simplicity of construction and resulting economy.

In 1957, Rhodes designed a fast 52-foot 3-inch launch for ferrying personnel between onshore facilities and drilling rigs offshore. Two versions were designed, one a steel 24-passenger model for ferrying oil rig crews, the second, an aluminum version with better accommodations for ferrying oil company executives. Rhodes adapted the latter version for his own personal use as an express cruiser. *Touche Too* (as she was named) was intended for occasional sportfishing and weekend cruising, and one important purpose was to follow yacht races on Long Island Sound and to observe the America's Cup trials and challenge races off Newport, Rhode Island. Phil was never a show-off, but when it seemed desirable to get somewhere in a hurry, he didn't mind demonstrating *Touche Too*'s fleetness, and he sometimes led the way home after the Cup races and other events.

Her hull measurements of 52 feet 3 inches by 49 feet 4 inches by 12 feet 8½ inches provide a large volume for ample accommodations, but *Touche Too* is arranged more for day tripping than for cruising with guests. In fact, there are only two permanent berths, those in the forward stateroom, although the settee in the deckhouse can be converted to upper and lower berths. The deckhouse, which Phil called a lounge, is long and well lighted with large win-

dows. It has three sitting areas with tables, with the forward one, opposite the galley, being used for dining. Although there is only one head compartment, located at the after end of the lounge, there is an additional hideaway head in the stateroom.

A permanent shelter protects the helmsman, and its top extends well aft to shade and protect the forward part of the after deck. The top also extends well beyond the windshield and shelter sides, which helps keep the sun out of the helmsman's eyes. Being on the same level, the bridge and after decks make an especially large lounging area. Weather cloths at the rails run all the way aft, but to improve the view and give a more sleek appearance, perhaps, they slope down to a lower level at the stern, where less spray protection is needed.

Touche Too's two General Motors 6-71 turbocharged aluminum-block diesel engines drive her at speeds of up to 35 m.p.h. and provide an easily sustained cruising speed of about 25 to 28 m.p.h. The V-bottomed form with hard chines allows quick planing, especially since the hull is quite light. Her aluminum hull, built by Paasch Marine Service of Erie, Pennsylvania, is ¼ inch thick on the bottom and ³⁄₁₆ inch on the sides. As with all Rhodes launches, the hull form utilizes developable curves, allowing the plating to take the shape of the hull without difficulty. Framing is longitudinal, and there are additional web frames and four watertight bulkheads. Like the hull, the superstructure is of aluminum, and it is insulated with fiberglass to absorb noise.

In 1962, Paasch built another aluminum Rhodes express cruiser. She was named *Grey Ghost* and was built for Vanderburgh Johnstone of Palm Beach, Florida. At 55 feet in length, she was similar in size to *Touche Too* but was not as fast and had more complete accommodations.

Grey Ghost and *Touche Too* have the same draft of 3 feet 6 inches, but *Grey Ghost* is a bit over one foot longer on the waterline. With a beam of 16 feet, however, the Johnstone powerboat is much wider. Her V-bottomed hull has moderately high chines with some dihedral carried far aft, and this gives the same effect as an outboard spray rail. This form has proven to be very effective in knocking down the bow wave. A pair of General Motors V8-71 diesels provide a top speed of 26 m.p.h. and a continuous

The first Grey Ghost, *a 55-foot aluminum express cruiser with more beam and more cruising amenities than* Touche Too.

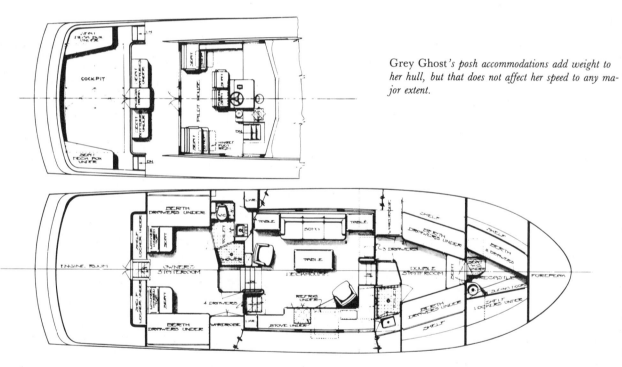

Grey Ghost*'s posh accommodations add weight to her hull, but that does not affect her speed to any major extent.*

Grey Ghost *demonstrating the effectiveness of her chines in flattening her bow wave.* (The Rudder, *March 1963*)

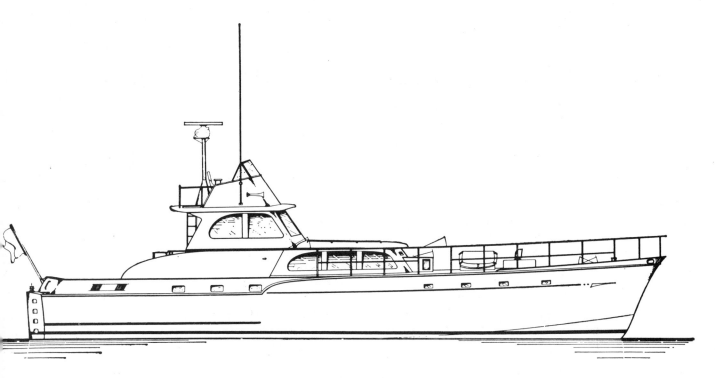

Above: *At 66 feet 8 inches,* Grey Ghost *(II) is essentially an enlarged version of the first* Grey Ghost.
Below: Grey Ghost *(II)'s larger size allows a forward galley and roomier deckhouse. (Yachting, September 1967)*

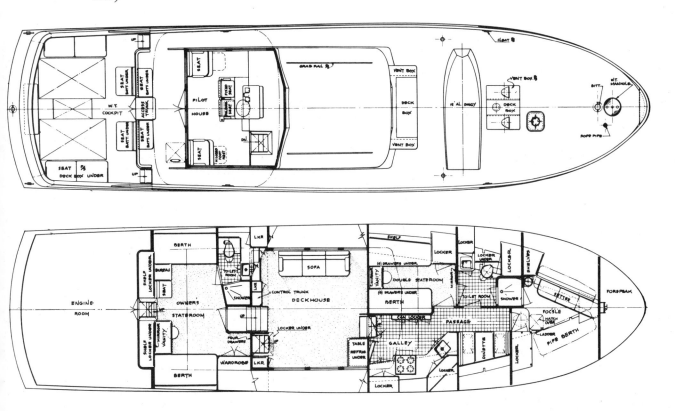

Grey Ghost (II) underway riding very level and with a low bow wave. Her long forebody gives her a sleek appearance. (Yachting, September 1967)

cruising speed of 21 m.p.h. even in choppy waters. Her fuel capacity of 600 gallons and water capacity of 250 gallons permit a respectable cruising range. Propeller shafts and rudders are Monel and stainless steel, respectively, and they are well insulated to guard against corrosion.

About the only compromise in the arrangement plan is that the galley is located in the deckhouse. This cabin is quite large, however, and there is ample area for lounging. Next forward is a full-width guest stateroom with enclosed head. The owner's stateroom aft is particularly roomy, and it has a large private head compartment with a shower stall. A third head for the crew's use is located in the fo'c's'le. The pilothouse might be used as a separate lounge, since it is completely enclosed and has comfortable seats with hinged foot rests. There is a large cockpit aft for those who like to be out in the open in fair weather. A boarding ladder, recessed into the transom, is provided for safety and convenience.

About two years after Grey Ghost was designed, Van Johnstone ordered a larger cruiser. This boat, named Grey Ghost (II), was also built of aluminum by Paasch. At 66 feet 8 inches by 16 feet 9 inches, she is basically a stretched-out version of the first Grey Ghost. The extra length allows her to have the galley forward of the deckhouse and allows room in the fo'c's'le for an additional paid hand. Otherwise, there are few differences, except that Grey Ghost (II) has a flying bridge and her guest stateroom does not extend across the full width of the boat. Of course, there is a lot more room on the foredeck of the larger boat, and a 13-foot tender can be carried there.

She is powered by twin General Motors V12-71 diesels, which give her a top speed of 24 knots and a sustained cruising speed of 20 to 21 knots. Her tanks carry 850 gallons of fuel and 300 gallons of water.

Phil's love for motorboats began when he was a child, and his design roots go back to his backyard creation named Dusty. In studying the forms and details of his later works, it is evident that even though his yachts became highly developed and meticulously refined, Phil never seemed to lose his boyhood enthusiasm and freshness of thought in powerboat design.

Conclusion

Phil Rhodes lived in an era of yachting history when a great many changes took place. Aside from the obvious technical advances in equipment, and new materials for rigging, sails, and hulls, there was a gradual change in certain philosophical aspects of yachting. In general, it could be said that during his lifetime the huge, luxurious yachts died away and smaller craft became available to more people; there was a steady decline in professional crews and more self-sufficiency among amateurs; racing and perhaps even cruising became more serious (but not necessarily less fun); and there developed a shift in the concept of what constitutes a seagoing boat.

On the latter subject, most yachtsmen during the first quarter of the 20th century felt that only a heavy, low-rigged yacht based on a workboat type, such as a pilot boat, a Redningsskoite, or a fisherman, was a fit boat for extensive blue-water sailing. Designer John G. Alden, for instance, with his *Malabar* series, did much to promote the modified Gloucester fishing schooner as a fast seagoing cruiser. But a radical if gradual change in thinking took place when the young upstart Olin Stephens proved the ability of leaner, lighter, and longer-

ended ocean racers with tall marconi rigs — boats such as *Dorade* and *Stormy Weather*.

It is difficult to pigeonhole Rhodes, because his designs are so varied, but in general his work in the field of seagoing sailing yachts seems to fall somewhere between Alden and Stephens. A Rhodes boat might be described as being a bit heavier, more comfortable, often more graceful, and not quite as racy as one by Stephens. On the other hand, a Rhodes boat may be thought of as being lighter, yachtier, more expensively built, and a better all-around performer than the kind of boat one associates with Alden. Of course, these are gross generalizations, and there are many individual exceptions.

Probably best known for his offshore center-boarders, Rhodes turned out this type in two general forms. First was the ocean racer, which evolved through *Ayesha* and *Alondra* to *Carina* and up to the size of *Escapade*. Mention should also be made of the distinctive ocean racers *Kirawan II (Hother)* and *Thunderhead*. Second was the heavily powered sailer bordering on the motorsailer. The latter form might be traced back to the landmark design *Tamaris*, and this concept developed such distinguished yachts as the Rhodes 77s, *Kamalii, Curlew III, Barlovento II,* and the 70-30 type, such as *Criterion.*

Rhodes was equally successful in producing non-centerboard designs, and a brief summary of his important and influential boats of this type would include *Tidal Wave, Maruffa, Narada, Kirawan, Arabella, Copperhead,* the Rhodes 27 class, the Bountys, *Altair, Caper,* and of course *Weatherly.* In the field of power yachts, it is important to mention large yachts such as *Pilgrim,* as well as *Touche Too,* the *Grey Ghost*s, and the *Virginia Reel*s, the latter being 30/70 motorsailers. Then there is Phil's work with small boats and one-designs, which produced such craft as the ubiquitous Penguin and Rhodes 19 classes.

These designs and others are monuments to the Rhodes genius, but it is not just his innate talent as a designer that makes these boats successful; it is also Phil's unusual sense of responsibility toward his clients. Above all, he wanted them to be safe, comfortable, and completely satisfied, and he worked untiringly to achieve that end.

Phil Rhodes contributed to both the science and the art of yacht design. As an engineer and architect he worked out some unique solutions to problems in building, powering, arranging, and equipping his boats. But he probably will be remembered best as an artist and purveyor of good taste. It is not always easy to put it in words, but most Rhodes designs can be identified by their grace and beauty. They seem aesthetically balanced, properly proportioned, and smoothly shaped, while their sheerlines are gracefully and distinctively curved.

It seems certain that Phil Rhodes will continue to influence the field of yacht design, for his boats are unusually functional, and above all, they are a pleasure to behold. There's no denying the man had an eye for a yacht.

Appendix

390 Philip L. Rhodes Yacht Designs

The following list of yachts is based on two Rhodes design indexes. The first was made before Phil joined Cox & Stevens, and this list is handwritten, often abbreviated, and there is a page or so missing. Some of the design numbers are out of order because some boats were assigned numbers in the index after they were designed. Some were not even assigned numbers. The second index, made after Phil joined Cox & Stevens, is mostly typewritten, and it is generally more orderly, but some information is missing or sketchy. The author has attempted to fill in the information whenever possible. These designs are for yachts only, and when numbers are omitted, they usually represent commercial craft. For the most part, utility and passenger launches, hydrofoil craft, yacht tenders, rowing boats, non-sailing dinghies, and outboard runabouts are not included in this list. The dates listed are for the design, not for the time when the yachts were built.

#? — 40' x 10' sloop-rigged motor cruiser *Jerry* for *Motor Boating* Ideal Cruiser series — Sept. 1917

#? — 20' x 5' motorboat *Hike You* for *Motor Boating*'s Ideal Runabout contest — Jan. 1918

#? — 30' x 24' x 9'8'' x 5' gaff-rigged keel yawl *Volante* for *Motor Boating* — July 1919

#? — 32' x 10' yawl-rigged motor cruiser *Tern* for Detroit yachtsman — May 1920

#2290 — 18' sailing dory for use at Port Huron, MI — Aug. 1921

#2390 — 24' x 20' x 7'9'' x 4'4'' aux. sloop *West Wind* for Julian Cendoya of Santiago, Cuba — 1921

#2270 — 22'6'' x 18'6'' x 6'6'' aux. dory for Robert S. Collyer of New York City — March 1922

#2400 — 36'1'' x 29'3'' x 11'1'' x 5'6'' schooner *Mary Jeanne II* for Julian Cendoya — 1922 (Chapter 1)

#? — 26' x 20'6'' x 8' x 4'6'' aux. sloop *Pinafore* — Jan. 1924

#? — 32' x 28' x 10' x 5'8'' gaff schooner for *Yachting* magazine — April 1924

#32 — 30' LOA cutter for W.E. Dickinson — 1924

#? — 33' x 6'4'' x 1'2'' passenger runabout *Miss Buckeye* for Henry Fink — 1925

#310 — 30'8'' x 23' x 8'11'' x 5'3'' aux. yawl for Julian Cendoya — Feb. 1925

#430— 28' motor cruiser for A.L. Brudi — Jan. 1926

#? — 36' x 31'6'' x 10'8'' x 4' aux. ketch *Cormorant* for Robert B. Noyes — 1926

#440 — 26' LOA double-ended gaff-rigged cutter *Caribe* for Julian Cendoya — July 1926 (Chapter 3)

#480 — 34' x 26' x 10' x 4'10'' aux. yawl *Seawitch* for Donald H. Sherwood — Dec. 1926 (Chapter 2)

#? — 9½' dinghy now built of fiberglass called ''Sea Hawk'' — 1926

#490 — 27'6'' x 23' x 9' x 4'9'' aux. cutter *West Wind* for Edward L. Palmer of Baltimore — 1927

#56 — 32'4'' x 31' x 11' x 5' double-ended ketch *Tidal Wave* for Samuel Wetherill — 1927 (Chapter 3)

#59 — 30' LWL double-ender for William E. Baker — July 1927

#60 — 45' x 42' x 11'3'' x 5' offshore cruiser and fisherman for Luis Puig — Aug. 1927 (Chapter 27)

#61 — 28' x 8'6'' x 2'6'' raised-deck cruiser *Nudot* built by Frank Grimes for A.L. Brudi — Aug. 1927

#630 — 18' x 5' stock runabout for Marine Supply Co., Camden, ME — 1927

#640 — 36' x 25' x 9'6'' x 5' cutter *Windward* for Aubrey E. King of Baltimore — 1927 (Chapter 4)

#650 — 7-meter version of *Tidal Wave* for Julian Wright, Paris — Sept. 1927

#660 — 20' x 6' sailing dory for Robert S. Carouj, CA — Nov. 1927

#690 — 40' x 32'1'' x 12' x 5'6'' cutter *Saki* built by M.M. Davis for W.E. Hill of New York City — Feb. 1928

#700 — 30' LWL bugeye for M.M. Davis — Feb. 1928

#720 — 35' x 8' 150 hp runabout built by Casey Baldwin for John F. Lash, Toronto — Feb. 1928

#740 — 105' x 80' x 22' x 12' gaff-rigged ketch — March 1928

#750 — 45' x 32' x 11' x 6'3" cutter for G.M. Buckley — March 1928 (not built)

#790 — 48' x 10' twin-screw commuter and day boat for Sidney Ollendorff, Jr. — March 1928

#770 — 31' x 25' x 10' x 6' cutter for L.M. Bailliere — April 1928 (not built)

#850 — 55' schooner for W.S. Galloway — May 1928

#880 — 40' stock motor cruiser for M.M. Davis & Son — Aug. 1928

#890 — 45' x 44'6'' x 11'6'' x 3'6'' stock cruiser for M.M. Davis & Son — Aug. 1928 (Chapter 44)

#910 — 26' x 6'6'' round-bottomed runabout for Down East Boat Corp. — Aug. 1928

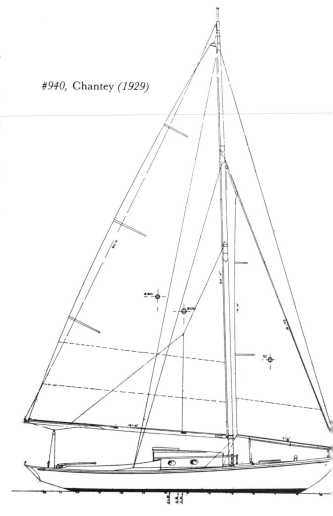

#940, Chantey *(1929)*

#920 — 47' x 34' x 12' x 6' schooner for William Edgar Baker   — Aug. 1928

#930 — 22' runabout for Skaneateles Boat Co. — Sept. 1928

#940 — 23' x 17'6'' x 7'3'' x 3'7'' centerboard sloop *Chantey* for H.H. Larkin — Sept. 1928 (Chapter 10)

#960 — 38' yawl for Clay Primrose of Baltimore — Oct. 1928 (not built)

#970 — 24'6'' x 15'6'' x 5'10'' x 4' knockabout, one-design for the Junior Yacht Racing Association — Oct. 1928 (not built)

#1000 — 24' x 6'6'' runabout for Peterborough Canoe Co. — Nov. 1928

#1010 — 60' x 13'3'' express cruiser for John T. Carroll — Dec. 1928

#1020 — 43' x 32' x 10'6'' ketch for J.M. Nelson, Jr. — Dec. 1928

#1060 — 55' x 45' x 16' x 4' bugeye yacht *Loretta* for Frank H. Reagan of Baltimore — 1929 (Chapter 5)

#750, Awa, built as Bangalore *(1930).*

#1070 — 50' x 12' cruiser for Herbert Brown — Feb. 1929

#1080 — 50' x 14' cruiser for Gilbert Wehr of Baltimore — Feb. 1929

#1110 — 65' x 51' x 18'6'' x 4'6'' centerboard schooner for Mr. Morse of Baltimore, built by M.M. Davis & Son — Feb. 1929

#2300 — 44'6'' x 9'4'' cruiser for H.C. Burr — Feb. 1929

#1120 — 36' x 27' x 10'9'' x 4'2'' aux. ketch for William Edgar Baker — Feb. 1929

#750 (development of previous #750) — 43' x 30' x 10'9" x 6'5" cutter *Awa* for G.M. Buckley (*Banga-*

lore under E.B. Lumbard won Chicago-Mackinac Race 1939 and 1940) — May 1929

#1210 — 72' twin-engine power cruiser for A.R. Chaloner — July 1929

#1230 — 182' x 171'3'' x 28'6'' x 11' seagoing diesel yacht — July 1929

#1240 — 18' outboard cruiser *Allegra* for *Mechanix Illustrated* magazine (Weston Farmer, editor) — Aug. 1929

#1250 — Oyster Bay One-Design — Aug. 1929

#1260 — 64' express powerboat for magazine article (Weston Farmer) — Aug. 1929

#1270 — 65' x 13' power cruiser for A.R. Chaloner — Aug. 1929

#1280 — 53' cruiser for A.F. Jenkins of Baltimore — Aug. 1929

#1290 — 65' cruiser for H.B. Noble — Sept. 1929

#1300 — 32' x 9'6'' x 18'' day boat for Cushman-Curtis — 1929 (Chapter 44)

#1310 — 60' x 13'6'' x 3'6'' express cruiser for Waddleton — Sept. 1929

#1320 — 32' x 20' x 7'6'' x 3'9'' centerboard aux. sloop for Gordon Taylor of Jamestown, NY — Sept. 1929

#1340 — 60' x 45' x 15' x 8' schooner for R.W. Smith — Oct. 1929

#1350 — 55' x 18' x 3' houseboat *Mother Goose* for Hobart Ford — Oct. 1929

#1360 — 32' x 20' x 7' x 4'10'' aux. sloop for H.C. Stockton, Birmingham, AL — Oct. 1929

#1380 — 35' x 22' x 8' x 3' centerboard sloop, ''Great South Bay One-Design'' — Nov. 1929

#1390 — 61'7'' x 46'10'' x 16' x 4'6'' bugeye ketch *Orithia* for Haliburton Fales of New York, built by M.M. Davis & Son — Dec. 1929 (Chapter 5)

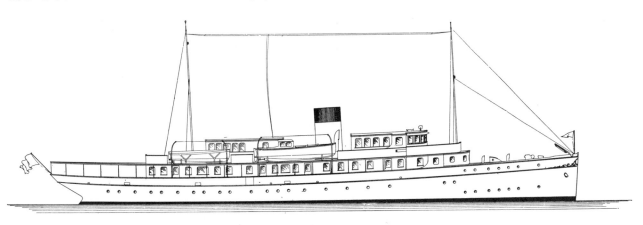

#1230, Seagoing Diesel Yacht (1929)

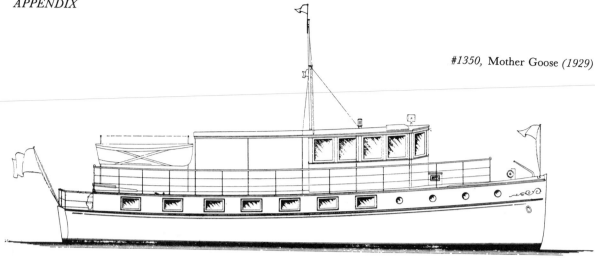

#1350, Mother Goose *(1929)*

#1400 — 15'6'' LWL sloop, "Great South Bay One-Design" — Dec. 1929

#1410 — 22' x 6'3'' V-bottomed runabout for Mrs. D.H. Sherwood — 1930 (not built)

#1430 — 48' x 37'6'' x 12'6'' x 7' cutter *Skal* for Hobart Ford and George V. Smith — Feb. 1930 (Chapter 6)

#1440 — 40' x 32'6'' x 11'3'' x 5' cutter like *Tidal Wave* for H.S. Sayres — April 1930 (Chapter 3)

#1450 — 43' x 32'6'' x 12' x 4' centerboard yawl for Morton Waddell of New York — April 1930

#1460 — 34' x 26' x 11' x 2'6'' centerboard yawl for John H. Bartlett, Jr. — April 1930

#1480 — 17' centerboard V-bottomed knockabout for Register — May 1930

#1500 — H.D. Bixley, "Suicide Class" (hydrofoil centerboard) — May 1930

#1510 — Cruiser for Liggett, Minneford Yacht Yard — June 1930

#1520 — 50' LWL cutter for Donald H. Sherwood — 1930 (not built)

#1540 — 30' LWL cutter for James H. Dunbar — June 1930

#1530 — 22' LOA outboard cruiser for Outboard Motors Corp. — July 1930

#1550 — 10' air-drive boat for publication *How to Build Twenty Boats* (Weston Farmer) — July 1930

#2280 — 24' x 5'8'' sailing dory for W. Pierson — July 1930

#1560 — Revised *Tidal Wave*, double-ended ketch *Queequeg* for B.M. Varney of Los Angeles — Sept. 1930 (Chapter 3)

#1570 — 45' LWL ketch for W.B. Henry — Sept. 1930

#1600 — 30'8'' x 27'1'' x 10'2'' x 5' double-ended ketch *Dog Star* (ex-*Tide Rip*) for William Edgar Baker — Oct. 1930 (Chapter 3)

#1580 — 39'11'' x 31' x 11' x 5' canoe-stern cutter *Narwhal* for H.S. Sayres — Nov. 1930 (Chapter 7)

#1620 — 43' x 32' x 12' x 6' ketch for McCoy — Nov. 1930

#1630 — 16' catamaran for L.N. Hampton — Nov. 1930

(another 16' catamaran was designed for same client — June 1931)

#1640 — 35'9'' x 25'5'' x 9'6'' x 5'6'' yawl for Bradford, built by M.M. Davis — Nov. 1930

#1650 — 36' power cruiser for Dr. Deane, built by Minneford Yacht Yard — Dec. 1930

#1660 — 30' x 22' x 9' x 2' centerboard sloop for E. Hayes — Dec. 1930

#1670 — 46' x 35' x 11'6'' x 6'6'' ketch for G.C. Newbury, built by M.M. Davis & Son — Jan. 1931

#1680 — 32' power cruiser for Robert Jordan — Feb. 1931

#1690 — 30'6'' x 9'2'' x 2'5'' cruiser for Frazier and Sebree, Inc. — Feb. 1931

#1700 — 34'11'' x 31' x 11' x 5' *Tidal Wave*-type double-ended ketch *Yojo* for William C. Thum, Pasadena, CA — March 1931 (Chapter 3)

#1700 (S[1]) — 36'5'' x 31' x 11' x 5' variation of *Yojo* named *Skaimsen* — 1960 (Chapter 3)

#1970, Auxiliary Schooner (1933)

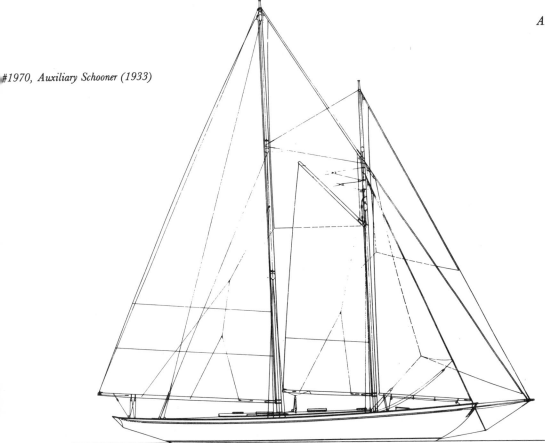

#1730 — *Tidal Wave*-type for John Wynn of Los Angeles — April 1931

#1740 — 55' LWL aux. schooner for Darlington — May 1931

#1780 — 56' twin-screw offshore cruiser for C.D. Jencks of Pawtucket, RI — Sept. 1931

#1790 — 39' x 32' x 11'6" x 3'9" canoe-stern centerboard ketch *Saona* (later *Lady Patty*) for R.B. Noyes — 1931 (Chapter 7)

#1800 — 64' x 45' x 16' x 5' centerboard ketch for Marine Construction Co. — Oct. 1931

#1710 — 32'8" x 25' x 10' x 5' cutter for Arthur B. Fels of Portland, ME — Nov. 1931

#1820 — 46' x 32' x 11'6" x 6' *Narwhal*-type for E.C. Read of Milwaukee — Dec. 1931

#2460 — 46' x 33'2½" x 11'8½" x 4'2½" aux. yawl *Ayesha* for John Hogan — 1932 (Chapter 8)

#1840 — 18' V-bottomed sloop (centerboard skipjack) for Jack Spurr — March 1932

#1850 — 25'4" x 22' x 7'6" x 4' sloop *Nixie* for P.L. Rhodes — March 1932 (Chapter 9)

#1870 — 24' x 18' x 7' x 4' aux. sloop *Mimi II* for Dr. R.P. Batchelor — June 1932 (Chapter 10)

#1880 — 32' LWL aux. ketch *Baby Narwhal* for H.S. Sayres — June 1932

#1900 — 30' x 27' x 10' x 4'6" raised-deck cutter for William Dyer — Aug. 1932

#1910 — 50' x 40' x 14' x 5' *Saona*-type centerboard aux. ketch for E.C. Read — Sept. 1932

#1920 — aux. ketch *Tidal Wave II* for Samuel Wetherill — Sept. 1932

#1930 — 35'8" x 23'4" x 7'3" x 4'10" one-design for Long Island Sound Yacht Racing Assn. — Oct. 1932 (not built)

#1940 — 26' x 8'3" x 2'3" V-bottomed day cruiser for *Mechanical Package* magazine (Weston Farmer, ed.) — Nov. 1932

#1970 — 60' x 43' x 13'8" x 8'6" aux. schooner for Carter — Feb. 1933

#1980 — 56' x 44' x 14'3" x 7' aux. schooner for Lloyd — Feb. 1933

#1990 — 60' LWL staysail schooner for Capt. J.M. Berman, built by M.M. Davis & Son — March 1933

#2000 — 18' centerboard sloop for Telander — March 1933

#2040 — 32' LWL ketch for R.A. Piel — May 1933

#2050 — 43' x 35' x 13' x 4'6" coaster-type schooner for R.A. Piel — May 1933

#2060 — 63'4" x 47' x 14'6" x 9' yawl for Cruising Club of America design contest — May 1933

#2090 — 13½' arc-bottomed sailing dinghy (forerunner of "Penguin") for E.B. Terry, Kobe, Japan — June 1933

#2100 — 11½' arc-bottomed sailing dinghy (prototype of "Penguin") for William Dyer — July 1933 (Chapter 43)

#2120 — 36'8" x 29'2" x 10' x 4' (634 sq. ft. sail area) *Saona*-type ketch for Galloway — July 1933

#2130 — 40' LWL cutter for Robert Roebling — Aug. 1933

#2140 — 67'6" x 50' x 16'6" x 5'6" centerboard yawl for D.H. Morris, Jr. — Sept. 1933

#2150 — 50' x 36' cutter/yawl for Larchmont Yacht Club — Sept. 1933

#2180 — 31' x 24' x 8'5" x 3'10½" sloop *Jingleshell* for Elihu Root, Jr. — Nov. 1933 (Chapter 15)

#2190 — 26' fisherman for William Dyer — Dec. 1933

#385 — 32' LWL fishing cruiser for A.A. La Fountain — 1933

#386 — 32' LWL *Narwhal*-type cutter for E.B. Terry — 1933

#2210 — 16'3" raised-deck one-design sloop for William Dyer — Feb. 1934

#2230 — 27'6" x 25'4" x 7'10" x 2'6" stock sportfisherman *Lady Jane* for William Dyer — Feb. 1934 (Chapter 44)

#2260 — 51'1" x 37'1" x 11'6" x 7'6" yawl for Donald Sherwood — March 1934 (not built)

#? — 32' LWL *Narwhal*-type ketch for Herman Offhouse — 1934

#387 — 10' LOA round-bottomed sailing dinghy (Class "D" Dyer Dink) for William Dyer — 1934 (Chapter 43)

#388 — 28'6" x 21' x 8' x 4'6" stock aux. sloop *Cubana*, Trident Class, for P.F. Combiths — 1934

#389 — 67'6" x 49'7" x 15'3" x 8'6" aux. yawl *Maruffa* for Henry B. Babson — 1934 (Chapter 11)

#390 — 30' x 21'8" x 7'9" x 4'6" aux. sloop *Trivet* for C.W. Moore, built by M.M. Davis — 1934

#396 — 32'9" x 27' x 10' x 4'10" stock aux. cutter for Minneford Yacht Yard — 1935 (Chapter 12)

#397 — 45'10" x 34' x 11'3" x 6'6" aux. cutter *Narada* for L. Corrin Strong — 1935 (Chapter 13)

#397[1] — aux. cutter *White Squall* for Donald H. Sherwood — 1949 (Chapter 12)

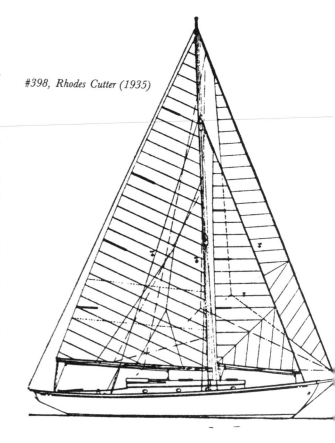

#398, *Rhodes Cutter (1935)*

#397[2] — aux. yawl *Pavana* for L. Corrin Strong — 1949 (Chapter 13)

#398 — 28' LWL aux. sloop for Elihu Root, Jr. — 1935 (forerunner of 37'3" x 28' x 9'10" x 4'11" aux. cutter, "Rhodes Cutter," for H.P. MacDonald of Gray Boats — 1937) (Chapter 15)

#399 — 53' x 38'9" x 12'6" x 7'6" aux. cutter *Kirawan* for Robert P. Baruch — 1935 (Chapter 14)

#400 — 22'1" LWL sloop for Elihu Root, Jr. — 1935

#401 — 65' x 63'9" x 15' x 4' diesel cruiser *Libra II* for Graham C. Thomson, built by Julius Petersen — 1935

#402 — 16'6" LOA wishbone-rigged centerboard sloop, Indian Harbor One-Design, built by William Dyer — 1935

#403 & #404 — 24' LWL *Jingleshell*-type sloops, *Vanette* and *Briny*, for B.H. Inness Brown and Newton G. Loud — 1935

#405 — 10' one-design sailing dinghy — Lane Tech Dinghy (said to be the Rainbow Class dinghy designed for use by Chicago underprivileged children) — 1935

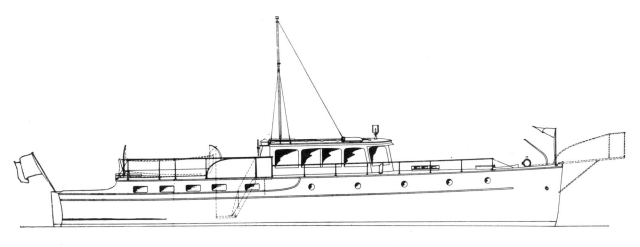

#401, Libra II (1935)

#406 — 45' x 35' x 11'6'' x 7'3'' aux. ketch *Mary Otis* for William D. Stephens (accompanied Samuel Eliot Morison on Columbus research expedition), built by Harvey Gamage — 1936

#407 — 45' x 32' x 11' x 6'3'' aux. yawl *Dryad* for James H. Dunbar of Cleveland (and later Gibson Island, MD), built by H.B. Nevins — 1936

#408 — 72' LWL steel diesel cruiser for Mellon — 1936

#409 — 19' x 16'4'' sailing double-ended Kusten-jolle skiff *Toddy* for Robert P. Baruch — 1936 (Chapter 19)

#410 — 57'6'' x 42'7'' x 14' x 6'3½'' centerboard yawl *Alondra* (later *Caribbee)* for Robert B. Noyes — 1936 (Chapter 8)

#411 — 45'10'' x 34' x 11'3'' x 6'6'' aux. yawl *Cherry Blossom* (near sister to *Narada)* for E.T. Rice — 1936 (Chapter 13)

#413 — 40'5'' x 30' x 10'7'' x 4'10'' sloop *Vanward* for B.H. Inness Brown — 1936

#406, Mary Otis (1936)

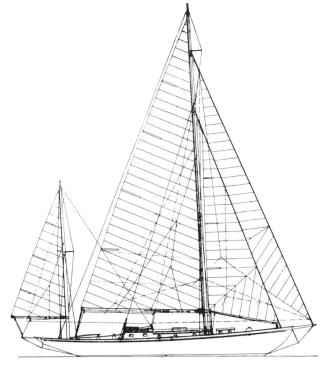

#407, Dryad (1936)

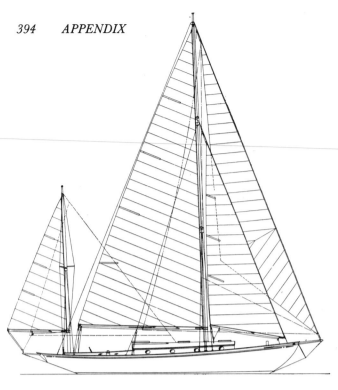

#414, Golden Eye *(1936)*

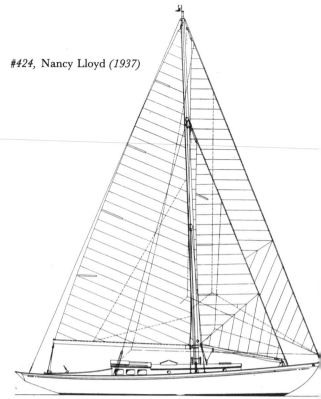

#424, Nancy Lloyd *(1937)*

#414 — 41'3'' x 30' x 11' x 6' aux. yawl *Golden Eye* for H.P. Wells, built by Minneford Yacht Yard, Inc. — 1936

#415 — 46'3'' x 35' x 11'9½'' x 5'5'' aux. ketch *Arabella* for Elihu Root, Jr. — 1936 (Chapter 15)

#416 — 34' x 23'4'' x 7'9'' x 5'3'' racing one-design sloop, ''Lake One-Design'' — Jan. 1937 (Chapter 16)

#417 — 70' diesel cruiser *Cajun* for John Legier — 1937

#418 — 45'1'' x 32'1'' x 11'2'' x 6' aux. yawl *Anitaw* for James Talcott, Jr. — 1937

#420 — 17' x 15' x 6' x 11'' centerboard sloop, ''Edgartown Rover Class,'' for F.T. Meyer — 1937 (Chapter 43)

#421 — 18'1'' x 12'3'' x 5'3'' x 3'10'' keel sloop, ''Marlin Class,'' for William Dyer — 1937 (Chapter 43)

#422 — 20'7'' LWL aux. centerboard ketch for Paul Burke — 1937

#423 — 81' x 65' x 20'3'' x 6' centerboard aux. ketch *Tamaris* for Ralph T. Friedmann — 1937 (Chapter 17)

#424 — 47' x 34' x 11'8'' x 4'6'' centerboard aux. cutter *Nancy Lloyd* for Dr. Austin Lamont, built by H.B. Nevins — 1937

#425 — 7'6'' x 3'11'' ''Mystic Pram'' dinghy for E.T. Rice — 1937

#427 — 72'6'' x 54' x 17' x 7'10'' aux. yawl *Escapade* for Henry Fownes — 1937 (Chapter 18)

#428 — 46'3'' x 37'6'' x 12'6'' x 4'9'' double-ended centerboard cutter *Kirawan II* (later *Hother*) for Robert P. Baruch — 1937 (Chapter 19)

#429 — 19' x 15'6'' x 6'2'' x 1'6½'' (x4') stock centerboard (or keel) sloop *Eagle* for Walton Hubbard, Jr., of South Coast Boat Building Co. — 1937 (Chapter 43)

#430 — 27'11'' LWL racing sloop for R.B. Noyes — 1937

#431 — 19'6'' x 15'5'' x 6' x 3' stock keel knockabout *Dolphin* for Walton Hubbard, Jr., of South Coast Boat Building Co. — 1937 (Chapter 43)

#432 — 32' LWL ''Mackinaw-type'' *Butcher Boy* for H.N. Barkansen — 1937

#433 — 14' LWL ''Marlin-type'' Arrowhead Class for Harris — 1937

#434 — 22'8'' x 15'9'' x 5'10'' x 3'10'' stock keel sloop *Albatros* for Walton Hubbard, Jr., of South Coast Boat Building Co. — 1937 (Chapter 43)

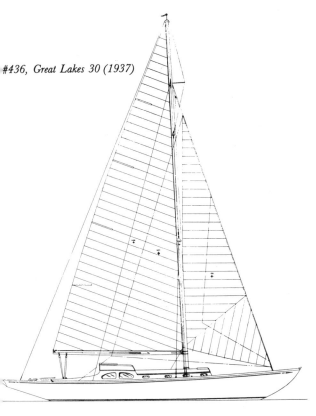

#436, Great Lakes 30 (1937)

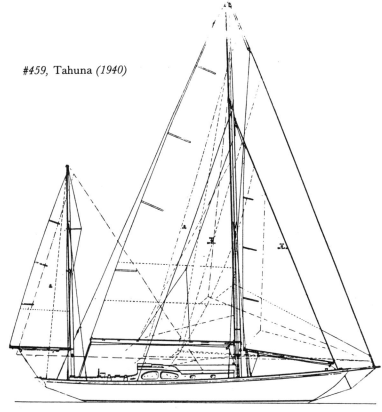

#459, Tahuna (1940)

#435 — 16'6'' x 14'9'' x 5'8'' x 6'6'' stock keel sloop *Falcon* for Walton Hubbard, Jr., of South Coast Boat Building Co. — 1937 (Chapter 43)

#436 — 42'10½'' x 29'4½'' x 9' x 6'2'' aux. sloop ''The Great Lakes 30'' (originally called ''Chicago One-Design'') for Henry Babson — 1937

#437 — 27'2'' x 22'1'' x 8'3'' x 4'2'' stock aux. sloop *Little Sister* for H.P. MacDonald — 1937 (Chapter 12)

#439 — 11'3'' Class A sailing dinghy for N.N. Hathaway — 1937

#440 — 13'6'' LOA stock centerboard catboat for Walton Hubbard, Jr., of South Coast Boat Building Co. — 1937

#441 — 33'8'' x 22'4'' x 6'10'' x 5' one-design sloop, ''Rhodes 33,'' for Walton Hubbard, Jr. — 1938 (Chapter 16)

#443 — 62' diesel cruiser for Donald Roebling — 1938

#444 — 47'8'' x 34' x 11'4'' x 6'10'' aux. sloop *Copperhead* for John T. Snite — 1938 (Chapter 20)

#445 — 26' LWL aux. cutter for J.A. Vorstelman — 1938

#446 — 39' x 28' x 9'8'' x 5'10'' aux. sloop *Surf Bird* for Morris Lloyd (and #446-L — *Gurkha II* for Gari Stroh) — 1938

#447 — 39'2'' x 27' x 9'8'' x 5'10'' aux. one-design sloop, ''Rhodes 27,'' for Fishers Island Y.C. — 1938 (Chapter 21)

#448 — 18' x 16' x 6'3'' x 2'8'' (keel model) ''Rhodes 18'' class sloop for Cape Cod Shipbuilding Co. — 1938 (Chapter 43)

#449 — 36' LWL aux. centerboard yawl for Hans Ahlstrom — 1938

#453 — 40' LOA offshore cruiser for the South Coast Boat Building Co. — 1938

#451 — 32' LOA stock cruiser for the South Coast Boat Building Co. — 1939

#452 — 38'9'' x 27'6'' x 9'8'' x 5'8'' aux. class sloop ''Bounty'' for Coleman Boat Co. — 1939 (Chapter 22)

#454 — 18' LOA fishing skiff for W.W. Swan — 1939

#456 — 28' LOA stock cruiser for the South Coast Boat Building Co. — 1940

#457 — 49'10'' x 35' x 11'10'' x 6'6'' aux. yawl *Phoebus* (later *Gallant)* for Harry Smith, built by Willis Reid & Sons — 1940

#459 — 44' x 31' x 10'11'' x 6'10'' aux. yawl *Tahuna* for Henry Babson and Joseph Moeller, built by Palmer Johnson — 1941 (Chapter 20)

#461 — 20' LWL sloop for Elihu Root, Jr. — 1941

#462 — 38'10" x 27' x 9'9" x 5'10" stock "New Weekender," aux. sloop for Donald B. Abbott, built by Palmer Scott & Co. — 1941

#463 — 46'4" x 34' x 11'5" x 6'6" aux. yawl *Carina* for James Rider, built by Herman Lund — 1941 (Chapter 28)

#464 — 33'9" LWL aux. sloop for F. Gordon Reid — 1941

#465 — 30' x 20'6" x 8' x 4'6" stock aux. sloop, "Visitor Class," for Donald B. Abbott, built by Palmer Scott & Co. — 1941

#468 — 23' LWL aux. sloop *Chelsie May* for Dr. Jures (later evolved into "Windward Class") — 1941

#469 — 11' LOA Class A dinghy for Skaneateles Boats — 1941

#471 — 70' LOA diesel express cruiser *Eldarette* for A.V. Davis — 1941

#c485 — 37'9" x 35'10" x 12' x 3'9" sportfisherman for Marine Basin Co. — 1943

#c490 — 20'6" x 18' x 7'6" x 3'8" sloop, "Dater Class," for Donald Abbott — April 1944 (Chapter 9)

#c491 — 13'6" x 6' x 2'6" one-design catboat "Wood-Pussy" for Palmer Scott & Co. — 1944 (Chapter 43)

#c492 — 27'6" x 22'6" x 8'6" x 4'6" sloop, "Caller Class," for Donald Abbott — Sept. 1944 (Chapter 9)

#c493 — 67' LWL aux. ketch *Corrine* for John Q. Adams — 1944

#c494 — 12' LWL sloop, "Trainer," for Donald B. Abbott — Oct. 1944

#c497 — New Rhodes 27 *Patricia* for A.P. Davis (10 built) — Dec. 1944 (Chapter 21)

#c498 — 56' x 38' x 13'6" x 5'6" aux. centerboard yawl for Wheeler Shipbuilding Corp. — 1945

#c499 — 52'4" x 38' x 13'3" x 6'6" aux. ketch *Merry Maiden* (sister to *Jane Dore III* for Hobart Ford) for H. Irving Pratt — 1945 (Chapter 23)

#c502 — 36' x 24' x 7'4" x 5' sloop, "Evergreen Class," built by Eden Shipyard — 1945 (Chapter 16)

#c505 — 8' molded dinghy (Corolite) for Donald B. Abbott, built by Columbia Rope Corp. — 1945

#c507 — 14' x 5'6" x 4'2" (board down) sloop-rigged dinghy, "Bantam Class," for Skaneateles Boats — 1945 (Chapter 43)

#519, Infanta *(1945)*

#c508 — 19'2" x 17'9" x 7' x 3'3" (keel model) class sloop, "Rhodes 19," for Allied Aviation — July 1945 (Chapter 43)

#c510 — 9' x 4' molded-plywood dinghy, "Bob Cat," for Allied Aviation for use by Mentor Harbor Y.C. — 1945

#c516 — 77'2" x 55' x 19' x 6'6" aux. ketch *Maaroufa* (first Rhodes 77) for Henry Babson — Oct. 1945 (Chapter 24)

#c518 — 35' x 23' x 7'2" x 5'2" "Eastern Interclub One-Design," for "Dupont, etc." — 1945 (Chapter 16)

#c519 — 47' x 32' x 11'8" x 6'8" aux. yawl *Infanta* for Houlder Hudgins, built by Kretzer Boat Works — 1945

#c523 — 27'6" LWL aux. sloop for H. Johnson — 1946

#c524 — 20' LWL aux. one-design sloop for F. Meyer — 1946

#c525 — 25' x 20' x 8' x 3'10" cruising sloop, "Idler Class," for Kargard Boat & Engine Co. — 1946

#c526 — 16' catboat for Donald B. Abbott — 1946

#c527 — 50'6" x 35' x 13' x 5' steel centerboard yawl *Steel Sylph,* built by Arthur Tickle Engineering Works — 1946

#c528 — 47'11" x 45' x 14'2" x 4' diesel cruiser *Loretta II,* built by Arthur Tickle Engineering Works — 1946

#c529 — 28' LOA power cruiser for Brooks — 1946

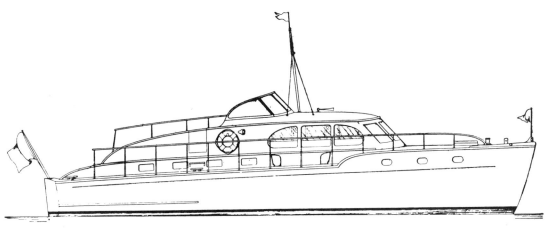

#528, Loretta II *(1946)*

#c530 — 12' sailing dinghy for Allied Aviation — 1946

#c531 — 42'9'' x 29' x 10' x 6'4'' aux. sloop *Marmetta* for E. Hayes, built by Blanchard Boat Co. — 1946

#c532 — 35' x 24' x 9' x 5'6'' aux., ''Rhodes 24,'' for L. James — 1946

#c533 — 10' LWL sailing dinghy for Haggerty Co. — 1946

#c534 — 54' cruiser for Burger — 1946

#c535 — 45' LWL steel ketch for Isaac Harter — 1946 (not built)

#c538— 37' LOA steel houseboat for Hall Kneen — 1946

#c539 — 16' LOA molded-plywood inboard runabout for Allied Aviation — 1946

#c542 — 67' LOA steel cruiser for Burger Boat Co. — 1946

#c543 — 40' x 38' x 12'9'' x 3' power cruiser *Little Reynard* for Thomas W. Lamont, built by Nevins — 1946 (Chapter 44)

#c544 — 85' LWL aux. schooner for Tucker — 1946 (not built)

#c545 — 23'6'' LWL stock aux. sloop, ''New Over-Nighter,'' for Donald B. Abbott — 1946

#c549 — 40' LOA fishing cruiser for Jack Burrus — 1947 (not built)

#c552 — 30'4'' x 24' x 8'10'' x 4'9'' aux. sloop, ''Truant Class,'' for Kargard, Fultz & Howe — 1947

#c555 — 42' LWL aux. for Clayton Ewing — 1947 (not built)

#c557 — 26' LOA cruising sloop for the Williams Boat Co. — 1947 (not built)

#c560 — 58' x 42' aux. centerboard ketch *Caribee* [sic] for Carleton Mitchell — Nov. 1947 (not built)

#c562 — 35'3'' x 33'2'' x 11' x 2'9'' day cruiser for V.Z. Reed, Jr., built by The Anchorage, Warren, RI — 1947

#c563 — 81'9'' x 58' x 19'10'' x 7' wood aux. ketch *Constellation* for McKay Products Corp., built by Purdy Boat Co. — 1948

#c569 — 62'3'' x 44'7'' x 14'10'' x 8'6'' aux. ketch *Alert* for K.K. Bechtel — 1948

#569, Alert *(1948)*

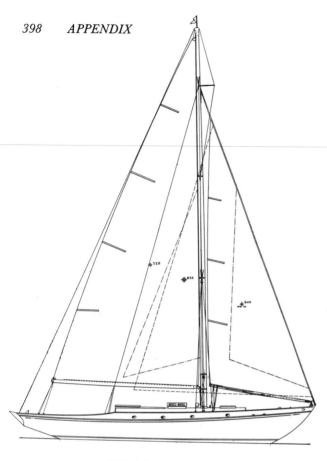

#586, Water Witch *(1949)*

#c574 — 35' x 23'6'' x 9' x 3'9'' aux. centerboard sloop for W.R. Jack — 1948

#c581 — 50'2'' x 37' x 12'9'' x 5'6'' aux. yawl *Xanadu* for Kilkenny Yachts, Inc. — 1949

#c584 — 46'6'' x 32' x 12'3'' x 5' steel aux. ketch *Shelmar,* built by Burger Boat Co. for Robert C. Wood — 1949

#c585 — 32'9'' x 26' x 10'3'' motorsailer for George Patterson — 1949 (not built)

#c586 — 43'6'' x 30' x 11'7'' x 4'6'' aux. centerboard sloop *Water Witch* for Harold F. Seymour, built by Martin Bros. — 1949

#c588 — 36'6'' x 25' x 10' x 4' aux. centerboard sloop, ''Whistler Class,'' for D. DesBarats. 14 boats built by Thomas Knutson Shipbuilding Corp. and others — 1949

#c590 — 30' sportfisherman for Standard Marine Equipment Co. — 1949

#c592 — 7'6'' fiberglass dinghy for South Coast Boat Building Co. — 1950

#c595 — 90'6'' x 77' x 20'10'' x 7'7'' steel ketch-rigged motorsailer *Vagabondia* for Dr. M.T. Mellon, built by Amsterdam Shipyard, Inc. — 1950

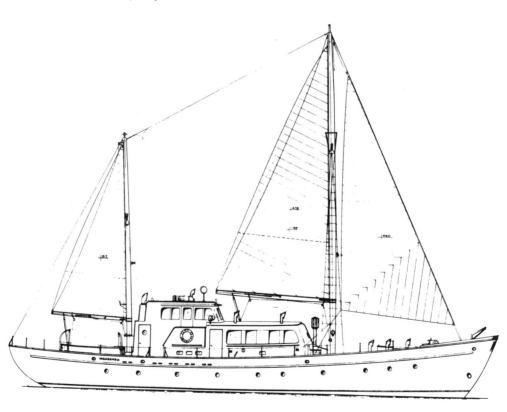

#595, Vagabondia *(1950)*

#599, Blue Water *(1950)*

#c599 — 52'4'' x 34'6'' x 12'6'' x 6'0'' aux. yawl *Blue Water* for Alexander W. White, built by Abeking & Rasmussen — 1950

#c600 — 50'4'' x 34'6'' x 12' x 7'11'' aux. yawl *Windfall II* for F.T. Nichols, built by Abeking & Rasmussen — 1950

#c601 — 54'6'' x 38' x 13'7'' x 6' aux. centerboard yawl *Ocean Queen V* for Raymond M. Demere — 1950

#c602 — 20' LWL aux. sloop for Mrs. C.F. Merritt — 1950

#c606 — 60' x 42' x 15'4'' x 5'6'' aux. centerboard yawl-rigged research vessel *Sonic 4* for L.C. Paslay, built by Burger Boat Co. — 1951

#c608 — 77' x 65' x 18'8'' x 5'9'' centerboard motorsailer *Criterion* for Charles H. Cuno — 1951 (Chapter 25)

#c610 — 79'2'' x 68' x 18'2'' x 6'6'' motorsailer *Dolphin* for H. Nelson Slater — 1951 (Chapter 26)

#c611 — 50'4'' x 34'6'' x 12'6'' x 6' centerboard aux. yawl for Jack Brown (sister to Francis Wetherill's *Jubilee)* — 1951

#c613 — 47'6'' LWL centerboard aux. ketch for Chester Meyer — 1951

#c612 — 83'10'' x 70' x 20'2'' x 6'1'' motorsailer *Sea Prince* for John Conroy — 1952 (Chapter 25)

#c614 — 47'6'' LWL steel aux. ketch for E.B. Benjamin — 1952

#c616 — 36' x 34' sportfisherman for F.S. Woodsmall — 1952

#c617 — 28' LOA cruiser for Welin Davit — 1952

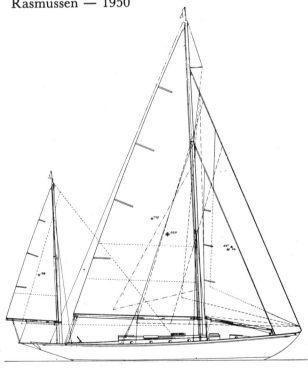

#601, Ocean Queen V *(1950)*

#606, Sonic 4 *(1951)*

#618, Olsching (1953)

#c618 — 45' x 32' x 11'9'' x 5' aux. centerboard cutter *Olsching* for Magnus Zeppelin (6 sisters built, including *Jane Dore IV* and *Nutmeg*) — 1953

#c620 — 36'3'' LWL steel aux. centerboard yawl *Kuling* (forerunner of *Carina* (II)) for Donald Scott, Jr. — 1954 (Chapter 28)

#c623 — 48'6'' x 35' x 11'9'' x 7' aux. cutter *Tasco II* for Thomas A. Short — 1954

#c625 — 52'6'' x 49'7'' x 14'6'' x 3'9'' diesel cruiser *Narada II* for L. Corrin Strong — 1954 (Chapter 44)

#c626 — 48' LOA diesel cruiser for Mohawk Metal Products — 1954

#c627 — 40' steel diesel fishing cruiser for Gulfport Shipping Co. — 1954

#c628 — 65' diesel cruiser for George F. Baker, Jr. — 1954

#c629 — 44' x 40' x 13'1'' x 4'6'' steel cruiser-fisherman motorsailer *Virginia Reel* for Arthur M. Stoner — 1954 (Chapter 27)

#c632 — 42'3'' x 29' x 10'6'' x 6' aux. class sloop *Altair* for Bradford Smith, Jr. — 1955 (Chapter 31)

#c633 — 42'3'' x 29' x 11'3'' x 4'7'' centerboard version of *Altair* named *Erewhon* for Albert W. Fribourg — 1955 (Chapter 31)

#c634 — 32' x 22' x 8'6'' x 4'6'' stock aux. sloop ''Temptress'' for Reisinger Marine Sales — 1955

#c635 — 53' x 36'3'' x 13' x 6' aux. centerboard yawl *Carina* (II) for Richard S. Nye — 1955 (Chapter 28)

#c636 — 36' x 24' x 9'3'' x 5'3'' aux. sloop ''Mariner'' for W.B. von Stumm (10 sisters built) — 1955

#c638 — 38' x 33' x 12' x 4'6'' motorsailer *Duchess III* for James W. La Marque, built by Chester Seacraft Industries — 1955

#c639 — 77' x 69'6'' x 18'7'' x 4'9'' offshore power cruiser with steadying sails, *Seafarer,* for H.P. Metcalf — 1955

#c640 — 88'3'' x 62'6'' x 20'11'' x 6' aux. ketch for George Storer — 1955 (not built)

#c642 — 90' x 75' x 21'6'' x 6' centerboard motorsailer *Bar-L-Rick* for Henry D. Belock — 1955 (Chapter 25)

#c641 — 99' x 94'6'' x 23' x 4' Thames-barge-type yacht with three-masted schooner rig *Rara Avis* for Paul L. Hammond — 1956 (Chapter 29)

#c649 — 35' LWL light alloy ketch for Dr. Austin Lamont — 1956

#c650 — 32' LOA V-bottomed centerboard sloop for James W. Crawford, Jr. — 1956

#c651 — 33' LWL gaff schooner for Walter Barnum — 1956 (not built)

#c653 — 60' x 42' x 15'5'' x 5'6'' aux. centerboard steel yawl *Cibola* for Wheeler Nazro (sister to *Sonic 4*) — 1956

#c654 — 64' x 47'6'' x 17'4'' x 5'6'' motorsailer *La Belle Sole* for H.M. Dancer (five sisters built) — 1956 (Chapter 30)

#c655 — 32' LWL centerboard cutter *Hi-Q-II* (similar to #c618) for E.R. Capita — 1956

#c658 — 40'10'' x 28' x 10'3'' x 5'9'' fiberglass aux. class sloop, ''Bounty II,'' for Coleman Boat & Plastics Co. — 1956 (Chapter 31)

#c659 — 32' LWL steel centerboard sloop *Masker* for Robert Way — 1956

#c661 — 56'3'' x 38' x 12' x 8' aux. sloop *Caper* for H. Irving Pratt — 1957 (Chapter 32)

#c663 — 97'7'' x 72'6'' x 23'7'' x 6'6'' centerboard aux. ketch *Curlew III* (later *Fandango)* for D.C. Ellwood — 1957 (Chapter 33)

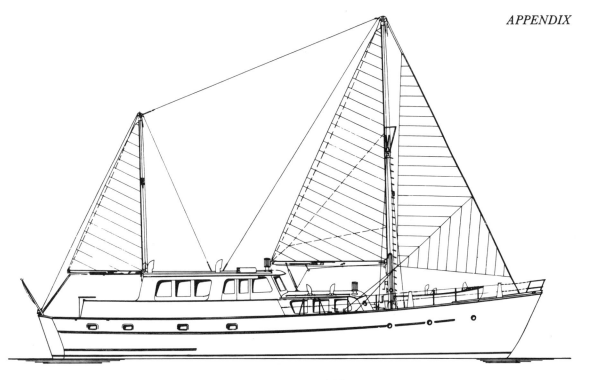

#639, Seafarer *(1955)*

#c666 — 38'6'' x 28'6'' x 9'10'' x 5'9'' aux. semi-fin-keel sloop *Firande* for Franklin M. Gates — 1957 (Chapter 34)

#c667 — 75'3'' x 54' x 18'2'' x 9' aux. ketch *Kamalii* for E.L. Doheny III — 1957 (Chapter 35)

#c668 — 40' x 31' x 11'6'' x 4' aux. centerboard cutter *Wunderbar* for George Hoffmann — 1957

#c669 — 39' offshore fishing boat *Ocean Fancy* for George P. Margulies — 1957

#c673 — 65' LWL welded-steel centerboard ketch for George B. Storer — 1957 (not built)

#c674 — 52'3'' x 49'4'' x 12'8½'' x 3'6'' diesel express cruiser *Touche Too* for Philip L. Rhodes — 1957 (Chapter 44)

#c676 — 69' x 46' x 11'10'' x 9' twelve-meter boat *Weatherly* for Henry D. Mercer Syndicate — 1957 (Chapter 36)

#c681 — 71'8'' x 50' x 18' x 5'6'' centerboard aux. ketch *Barlovento II* for Pierre S. DuPont III — 1958 (Chapter 37)

#c683 — 72'3'' x 50' x 16'3'' x 9'3'' ketch *Gael* for Robert Fievet — 1958

#c685 — 57'6'' x 52'6'' x 16'6'' x 4'5'' motorsailer *Dragger Lady* for William A. Parker, built by Gebr. Dolman — 1958

#c688 — 53'6'' x 36'3'' x 13' x 6' aux. yawl *Nina VI* for Dr. Franco Mazzucchelli — 1958

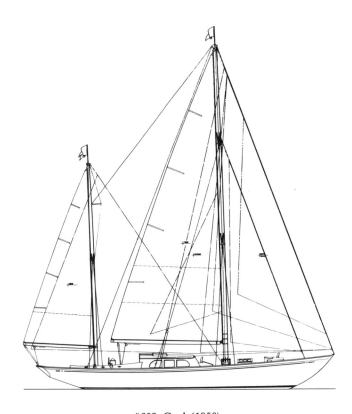

#683, Gael *(1958)*

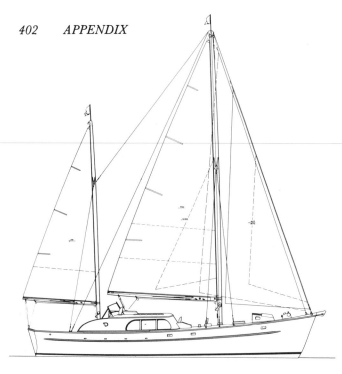

#685, Dragger Lady *(1958)*

#c700 — 32' x 22'1'' x 8'9'' x 4'9'' fiberglass aux. stock sloop, ''Chesapeake 32,'' for George B. Walton, Inc. — 1958 (Chapter 42)

#c698 — 47' offshore cruiser for Jarvis Jennings — 1959

#c701 — 45'3'' x 31' x 11'3'' x 6'6'' aux. sloop *Blue Water* (II) for Alexander M. White, built by Brigham's Shipyard — 1959

#c702 — 35' x 26'3'' x 10'6'' x 4'6'' stock plastic motorsailer, ''Bahama,'' for Brian Acworth (Seafarer Yachts) — 1959

#c703 — 105' x 95'5'' x 20' x 6' round-stern diesel cruiser *Ivara* for John Loudon — 1959

#c705 — 40' LWL centerboard ketch with clipper bow and great cabin for Rafael Obregon — 1959 (not built)

#c708 — 45' LWL aux. yawl for Frank P. Krieger — 1959

#c709 — 40' LWL offshore cruiser for Niccolo de Nora — 1959

#c710 — 28'6'' x 20' x 8' x 3'10'' fiberglass stock sloop, ''Ranger,'' for Seafarer Yachts — 1959 (Chapter 42)

#c711 — 99' x 75' x 25' x 6'9'' centerboard aux. ketch *Fei-Seen* for Robert D. Huntington — 1960 (Chapter 33)

#c712 — 70'5'' x 63'6'' x 19' x 5'1'' centerboard motorsailers *Sharelle* and *Kanaloa* for C.F. Devine and J.A. Qualey, Jr. — 1960

#c713 — 46'4'' x 34'6'' x 14'2'' x 4'6'' steel motorsailer *Bluejean* for W.A. Barrows — 1960

#c715 — plastic sloop for Robert H. Peirce — 1960

#c719 — 24' LOA fiberglass stock sloop, ''Meridian,'' for Seafarer Yachts, Inc. — 1961 (Chapter 42)

#c689 — 65'1'' x 59' x 17'2½'' x 5' sloop-rigged motorsailer *Virginia Reel* (II) for Arthur M. Stoner — 1958 (Chapter 27)

#c690 — 50'11'' x 36' x 13'3'' x 5' aux. centerboard ketch *Osprey* for Alfred Zantzinger, built by Henry Hinckley — 1958

#c691 — 29' LWL centerboard yawl for Olsen Marine Products — 1958

#c692 — 33' x 22'11'' x 10' x 3'6'' centerboard aux. fiberglass stock sloop, ''Swiftsure,'' for Brian Acworth of Seafarer Yachts — 1958 (Chapter 42)

#c693 — 21' LWL plastic sloop, ''Annapolis 30,'' for Olsen Marine Products (built to different dimensions and specifications) — 1958

#703, Ivara *(1959)*

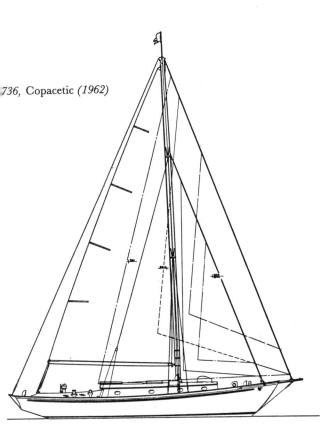

736, Copacetic (1962)

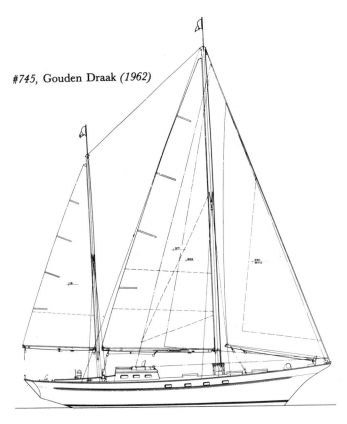

#745, Gouden Draak (1962)

#c720 — 48'9'' x 37' x 13' x 5'6'' centerboard aux. cutter *Thunderhead* for Paul Hoffmann (sister named *Kahili* built for Frank Zurn) — 1961 (Chapter 38)

#c721— 26' sportfisherman for Universal Ltd. — 1961

#c722 — 35' LOA sportfisherman for Universal Ltd. — 1961

#c723 — 7'1'' x 4' fiberglass sailing dinghy for Seafarer Yachts — 1961 (Chapter 43)

#c724 — 76' x 52'6'' x 17' x 9'6'' aux. ketch *Gael* (II) for Robert Fievet — 1961

#c727 — 42' stock power cruiser, ''Regency 42,'' for Stevenson International — 1962 (Chapter 30)

#c729 — 38'3'' x 31'3'' x 11'9'' x 4'9'' stock motorsailer, ''Vagabondia 38,'' for Stevenson International — 1962 (Chapter 30)

#c733 — 28' fiberglass cruiser for V. Gallart — 1962

#c735 — 55' x 50'8'' x 16' x 3'6'' express cruiser *Grey Ghost* (I) for Vanderburgh Johnstone — 1962 (Chapter 44)

#c736 — 37'6'' x 28' x 10'6'' x 5'6'' aux. sloop *Copacetic* for Harold S. Cherry (also *Faire Hope* for A.L. Aydelott) — 1962

#c738 — 40' LWL steel centerboard ketch *Skywave* (smaller version of *Barlovento II*) for Paul Bartlett — 1962

#c740 — 137' x 121'6'' x 23' x 7' seagoing diesel yacht *Chambel III* for M.P. Richier — 1962

#c742 — 29' centerboard aux. yawl for Frank Hoppe — 1962

#c744 — 60' x 42' x 16' x 4'11'' steel centerboard ketch *Rainbow* for Ellwood Peterson (also *Katrina-C* for R.E. Pflaumer) — 1962

#c745 — 46' x 32' x 12'10'' x 5' steel centerboard ketch *Gouden Draak* for Hugh W. Byfield (six of these boats built, one in ferrocement) — 1962

#c746 — 50' LWL wood aux. ketch *Tortuga* for Dr. Paolo Sozzani — 1962

#c748 — 37' LWL aux. cutter for Donald B. Dalziel (keel version of *Thunderhead*) — 1962

#c749 — 32'8'' x 22'4'' x 9'3'' x 4'6'' stock fiberglass aux. sloop, ''Vanguard,'' for Pearson Corp. — 1962 (Chapter 42)

#c750 — 140'8'' x 122'6'' x 26' x 7'6'' diesel yacht *Pilgrim* for General Robert W. Johnson — 1962 (Chapter 39)

#c752 — 60' self-propelled houseboat *Cajun Girl* for R.W. Ford — 1963

#c753 — 40'9'' x 28' x 10'9'' x 5'9'' stock fiberglass aux. sloop (or yawl), ''Rhodes Reliant,'' for Herbert Hayes (Cheoy Lee) — 1963 (Chapter 42)

#c739 — 10'10'' x 4'8'' x 6½'' sloop-rigged dinghy, ''Robin Class,'' for Evanson Boat Co. — 1963 (Chapter 43)

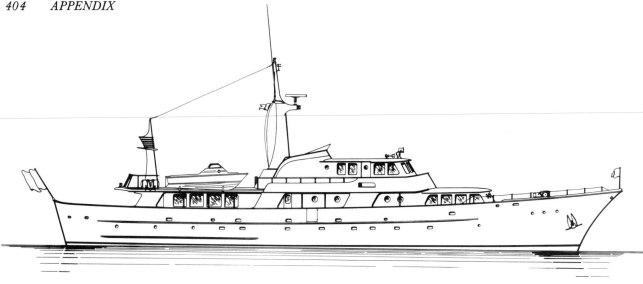

#807, Manu Kai *(1968)*

#c756 — 23'2'' x 17' x 7'6'' x 3'9'' stock fiberglass sloop, "Tempest," for O'Day Corp. — Aug. 1963 (Chapter 42)

#c757 — 16'6'' LWL fiberglass sloop for Glastron Boats, Inc. — 1963 (not built)

#c764 — 26'3'' x 19' x 8' x 4'3'' stock fiberglass sloop, "Outlaw," for Petty & McGregor (later O'Day Corp.) — 1963 (Chapter 42)

#c763 — 32' power cruiser for J.J. Gallart — 1964

#c767 — 66'8'' x 16'9'' x 4'7'' diesel express cruiser *Grey Ghost* (II) for Vanderburgh Johnstone — 1964 (Chapter 44)

#c768 — 45'2'' x 33'4'' x 12'8'' x 5'3'' stock cruising aux. ketch *Meltemi* for Martin Fenton (3 others built) — 1964 (Chapter 30)

#c770 — 119'6'' x 22'6'' x 5'6'' diesel yacht *A and Eagle* for Anheuser-Busch Corp. — 1964 (Chapter 39)

#c771 — 30' LOA high-speed powerboat for Kretzer Boat Works — 1965

#c772 — 37' LWL aux. ketch *Vamous* for Robert P. Koenig — 1965

#c777 — 28' LOA fiberglass sloop for South Coast Seacraft — 1965

#c778 — 57' LOA aluminum cruiser *Kilkerry* for William J. Williams — 1965

#c780 — 15' fiberglass sloop for Sears, Roebuck — 1965 (not built)

#c782 — 38' LWL steel centerboard sloop *Kamphana* for John C. West (three others built) — 1966

#c783 — 21'3'' LWL stock fiberglass sloop, "Venture 28," for A. Wayne Johner — 1966

#c784 — 50'2'' x 35' x 12'7'' x 7'1'' aux. yawl *Froya II* for Oivind Lorentzen, Jr. — 1966 (Chapter 40)

#c785 — 62'6'' LWL steel motorsailer *Cacique* for Laurance H. Armour, Jr. (one sister built) — 1966

#c786 — 38' LWL steel centerboard yawl *Kuenda* for Arturo Acevedo — 1966

#c792 — 41'3'' LOA motorsailer *Salmagal III* for Arthur B. Homer — 1966

#c793 — 122'10'' x 97'6'' x 28'6'' x 7' three-masted aux. yacht *Sea Star* for Laurance S. Rockefeller — 1966 (Chapter 41)

#c794 — 12' aluminum sailing dinghy, "Petrel," for Aluminum Co. of Canada — 1966

#c796 — aluminum *Meltemi*-type ketch *Branta* for Harvey Picker (one sister built) — 1967

#c799 — 52' *Virginia Reel*-type steel motorsailer *Saba II* for Leon Falk, Jr. — 1967

#c802 — 75'6'' LOA double-ended steel centerboard ketch for J.E. Ottaviano — 1967

#c801 — 44' LWL *La Belle Sole*-type motorsailer *Bonbelle* for Robert W. Paulin — 1968

#c804 — 21' fiberglass sloop, "Rhodes Continental," for General Boats — 1968

#c805 — *Curlew III*-type centerboard aux. ketch *Astral* for C.C. Vanderstar — 1968 (Chapter 33)

#c807 — 137'7'' x 124' x 24' x 6' diesel motor yacht *Manu Kai* for J.R. Krieger — 1968

#c808 — 52' aluminum power cruiser for Robert J. Silton — 1968

#c809 — 45' LOA aux. ketch for Mario della Valle — 1969 (not built)

#c810 — 76'9'' aluminum powerboat for Roger Triplett, Sr. — 1969 (not built)

#c815 — 170' LOA diesel yacht for Cannes Investment Co. — 1969

#c816 — 52' fiberglass *Virginia Reel*-type *Discoverer* for Marine Distributors, Inc. — 1969

#c817 — 90' offshore motor yacht for Lester Finkelstein — 1970 (not built)

#c818 — 97'7'' LOA modification of *Astral* for Donald Gillis — 1970

#c822 — ''Traveller 32,'' fiberglass version of *Dog Star* — 1970 (Chapter 3)

#c823 — 42' LWL laminated wood ketch for Donald B. Dalziel of Berkeley, CA, built by Lester Stone Yard — 1970

Sea Diamond, *formerly* Bar-L-Rick *(page 213), Rhodes design #c642. The model was built by Ned Freeman.*

Index

743005